King Jesus

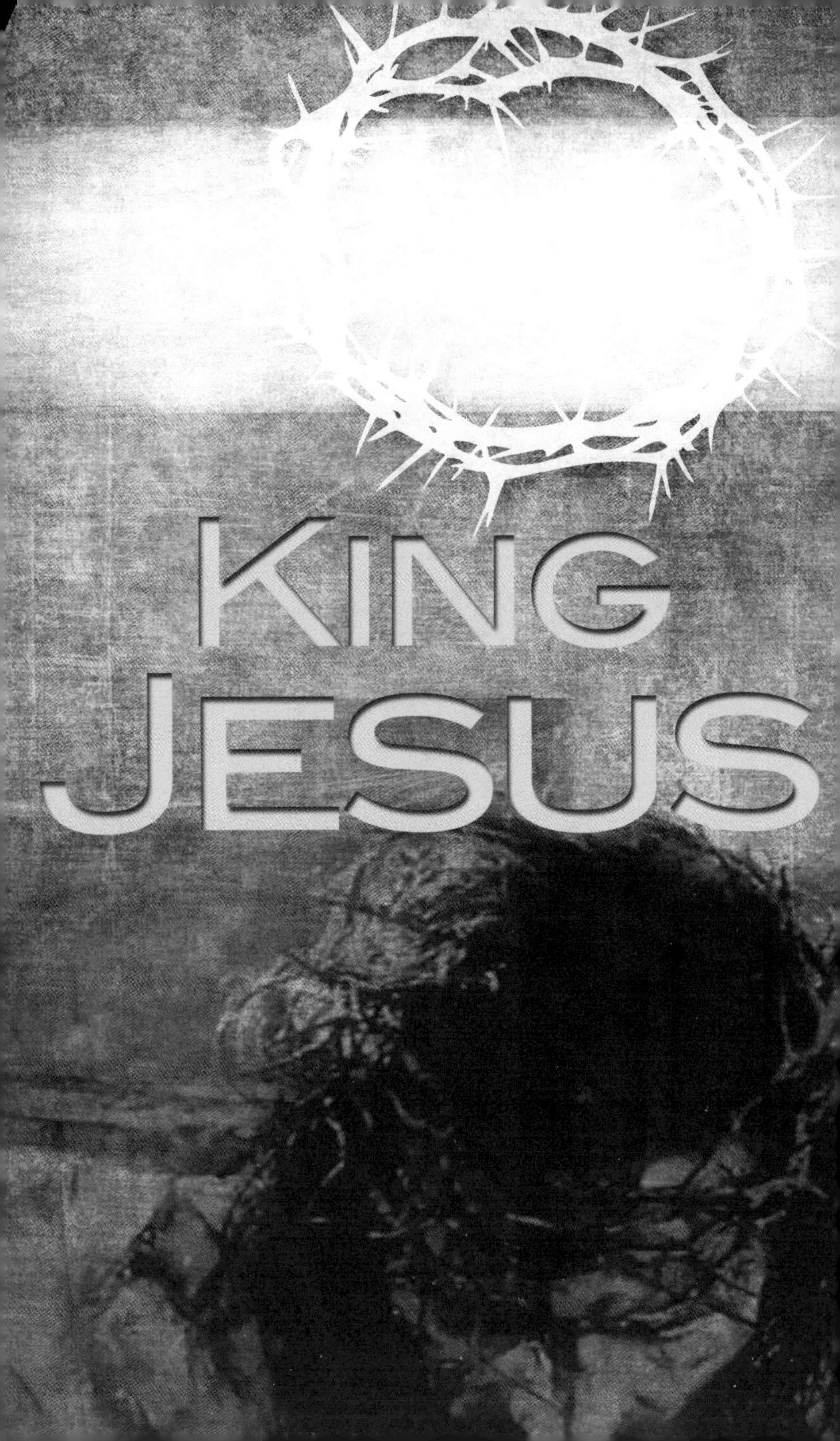
KING
JESUS

G. STEVE KINNARD

King Jesus

*A Survey of the Life, Ministry,
and
Teaching of Jesus the Messiah*

ILLUMINATION
PUBLISHERS

King Jesus: *A Survey of the Life, Ministry, and Teaching of Jesus the Messiah*

© 2013 by G. Steve Kinnard

Printed in the United States of America

ISBN: 978-1-939086-57-0

Book interior design: Toney C. Mulhollan
Cover design: Toney C. Mulhollan

About the author: Dr. G. Steve Kinnard has served the New York City Church of Christ as an evangelist and teacher for thirty years. He has written over a dozen books including *Like a Tree Planted by Streams of Water* and *The Way of the Heart*. He received his undergraduate degree at Freed-Hardeman College and his Master of Divinity with Languages from Southeastern Baptist Theological  Seminary. He completed his Doctor of Ministry degree at Drew University. He serves as adjunct professor of Bible at Lincoln Christian University. Steve and his wife, Leigh, live in Rockland County, New York.

 ILLUMINATION PUBLISHERS

www.ipibooks.com
6010 Pinecreek Ridge Court
Spring, Texas 77379-2513, USA

TABLE OF CONTENTS

Dedication

This will probably be the most important book I ever write. Therefore I dedicate this book to the most important person in my life: my wife, Leigh.

Without you:
Day darkens,
Laughter quells,
Love pines,
Joy abates.

With you:
Day brightens,
Laughter swells,
Love entwines,
Joy celebrates.

Thanks for wearing my ring for over thirty years and for gracing me with your ring.

GSK–CLK May 23, 1981

Chapter 1

Preface and Introductory Material

With great curiosity we search out the thoughts of man, and yet we neglect the thoughts of God. One word of the good news of the Gospel is more precious than all the other books in the world put together—it is the source of all truth.[1]

—Francis Fenelon, spiritual writer and mystic

This book, *King Jesus*, was written for me, and by writing it for me, I hope that it strikes a chord with you as well.

In December of 2008, I started thinking about writing a book on the life of Jesus—I felt compelled to write it. I believe it is the most important book that I have ever written. In our fellowship of churches, which we call the International church of Christ, dozens of books have been published, but very few of them have been about the Gospels or the life of Jesus.

We also have several "On to Maturity"-type courses, which have been written to help new converts grow in their faith. I've noticed that most of these courses are based on the Book of Acts or Romans, but rarely do they include a study of one of the Gospels. Why is this?

I feel like we have things backwards. We should start with Jesus. There must be a reason the New Testament begins with Matthew, Mark, Luke, and John. They weren't the first books written, nor were they the first books collected into a canon. But they do appear first in the New Testament. In fact, John might have been the last of the New Testament books to be written, but it is the fourth book in our New Testament canon. Again, there must be a reason for this. Why not a book on the life and teachings of Jesus the Messiah? Why not include a course on the life, teachings, and ministry of Jesus as a required class for our young Christians or fulltime staff trainees?[2]

This One's for Me

As I began writing this manuscript, I ran into a problem. I couldn't determine how I wanted to approach this work. During the same month in which I began this project, I read an article in *The New York Times* about legendary film actor/movie director Clint Eastwood. The reporter asked Mr. Eastwood about his role as a movie director (Mr. Eastwood has directed twenty-nine full-length movies). The reporter asked, "Whom do you make your movies for?" Mr. Eastwood answered in his characteristic matter-of-fact manner, "You're looking at him."[3] After reading this line, I knew how I needed to approach the book—this one is for me.

In this book, I take everything that I have learned from my fifty-five-plus years of life and forty-plus years of personal Bible study, biblical training, and discipleship and apply these lessons to writing a practical, meaningful, spiritual mosaic of the life, ministry, and teachings of Jesus the Messiah. The result is a study of the life of Jesus that is quite a bit less informational and quite a bit more spiritual than it would have been if I had written it just five years earlier.

Purpose
The purpose of this book is to give an overview of the life, ministry, and teachings of Jesus of Nazareth.

Approach
In this study of the life, ministry, and teachings of Jesus the Messiah, I use a three-pronged approach to the Gospels (think of a fork with three prongs).

- First, I read and compare the four Gospels side by side, building a mosaic of the life and teachings of Jesus the Messiah. I use as my text for this study *A Harmony of the Four Gospels, the New International Version (Second Edition)* by Orville E. Daniel.
- Second, as I read, I notice who Jesus says he is and how the gospel writers portray him. The outcome of this type of reading is to see Jesus as the King/Christ/Messiah of Israel. If you miss this point, then you need to reread the Gospels, because you've missed the point of each of the gospel writers. You also missed the gospel.
- Third, as I read, I place special emphasis on a spiritual reading of the text versus an informational reading. (More on that later.)

Clarification
Let's look a little closer at each prong of this three-pronged approach to the life and teachings of Jesus the Messiah.

First, when I was a teenager, someone gave me *A Harmony of the Four Gospels* by A.T. Robertson. This was the first time I had seen the four Gospels placed side by side. With this tool, I could easily compare the way the gospel writers wove the individual stories of Jesus' preaching, healing, and teaching into a larger story with a spiritual message concerning King

Jesus. Matthew could use the stories to emphasize to his predominately Jewish audience that Jesus was the Jewish Messiah—a Messiah unlike the one they had been anticipating. Luke could use the same stories to point out to a Gentile world that Jesus was the Lord (King) of the Universe who came to offer salvation to all humanity. The gospel writers used the same stories to tell a spiritual story about Jesus the King/Messiah/Christ/Lord.

Second, if you read N.T. Wright or Scot McKnight, then you are familiar with the idea that the Gospel writers portray Jesus as the King/Messiah/Christ/Lord of Israel. This story begins in the Hebrew Bible. The story of Jesus is so closely associated with the story of the Hebrew Bible that the two cannot be separated. The story of the kingdom, which was the main message of Jesus' teachings, begins in the Hebrew Bible. We can't divorce the story of Jesus from the Old Testament. It is the completion of the story that began with Adam and Eve, was carried on through Abraham, Moses, Israel, Samuel, and David. It was told and retold by the prophets. The message of the Gospels is that Jesus of Nazareth is the King/Messiah/Christ/Lord of Israel who was promised in the Old Testament. This point—which is the gospel—is made by each of the four gospel writers. To miss it is to miss the point of the Gospels and therefore to miss the gospel itself.

Third, in my late forties, I read a book by M. Robert Mulholland Jr., entitled *Shaped by the Word*. This book enlightened me to the fact that for most of my life I had been reading the Bible for information and not for spiritual insights. My default process in my approach to Bible study was informational Bible reading. I had been trained both in church and at school to read the Bible this way. Informational reading asks questions like:

- Who is the main character in the story?
- Who are the minor characters?
- What is the plot of the story?
- Is there a subplot?
- What figures of speech does the author use?
- How does the author use symbols in the story?
- What is the theme of the story?
- What type of literature is this—poetry, narrative, proverb, or history?
- Most important, if I'm tested on this material, what do I need to know to pass the test?

These are all legitimate questions; the use of informational reading in our study of a text is a perfectly fine way to start reading the Bible. But if you stop with informational reading, you never get to the most important question that Bible reading should invoke, which is:

> Dear God, as I read this passage of Scripture, what lesson do *you* want me to learn so that I can become more like Jesus?

This question is the difference between informational Bible reading and spiritual Bible reading.

I had to learn how to read the Bible spiritually, and this has revealed a new dimension to Bible study that feeds my soul, nurtures my spirit, and enriches my heart.

Two Images

Let me give a word of warning here through the use of two images. The first image is that of a well. Imagine that you are looking down a well into a pool of water. The well is dark and you can barely make out the image of someone in the water staring back at you. You stare and stare hoping that your eyes will adjust to the dark so that you can clearly see who is looking up from the water at you. As your eyes finally adjust, you realize that the water in the well is like a mirror, and the image you see at the bottom of the well is your own.

The second image is taken from Nathaniel Hawthorne's short story, "The Great Stone Face." In a village in New England, nature had carved an image of a man's face into the side of a mountain. The image contained what people considered to be perfect attributes of humility, compassion, strength, and love. The people from the village believed that one day a man with this image of the Great Stone Face would come to the village to bring prosperity to the village.

A young boy loved to stare up at the Great Stone Face. He would wake up in the morning looking at it. He would take time at school during recess to stare up at the face. He would watch the sun set over the face in the evening. Eventually, the boy grew up and left the village to go to college. After spending several years away from the village, the boy returned one day with a desire to look up into the countenance of the Great Stone Face. As he walked down the sidewalks of his hometown, people stared at the young man. He took their stares as a sign that they did not recognize him as one of their own. He made his way to the image of the Great Stone Face. What he saw surprised him. He realized that the image that stared down from the mountain was his own. He had meditated on the image of the face for so long that he had become that image.

How we focus to see Jesus is very important. Some look at Jesus while bringing their own preconceptions and misconceptions of him to the text. When this happens, it's like looking into the bottom of a well—we only see our own reflection looking back.

Or, we can come to Jesus without any preconceived ideas, asking him to reveal himself to us as he truly is and asking him to work on us and to shape us into his image. That is like the man who stared at the Great Stone Face so much that he became its image.

Study and Do

Ezra 7:10 reads, "For Ezra had set his heart to study the Law of the Lord, and to do it and to teach his statutes and rules in Israel (ESV)."

Notice the flow of this verse. Study and do, then teach decrees and laws. As we explore the life of King Jesus, let's study Jesus and do what he says. Study and action come before teaching and should be our launching point.

What is Joe-Disciple-Ordinary-Church-Member looking for in a book on Jesus? The very idea that brought us to Jesus in the first place: change. We want Jesus to help us change our lives. We want to become more like him. A meaningful study of the life and teachings of Jesus the King should end with a concrete decision to change one's life in a lasting way so that one might bring more glory to God by becoming more like Jesus. I pray that this study of the life of Jesus will help you make decisions to change your life to be more Christ-minded.

Why Study the Gospels?

Before you begin any task there is a simple three-letter word that forms a question that begs to be asked: *Why?* In this case, why study the life of Jesus? From a secular point of view, you might study Jesus of Nazareth because no single person in the history of humanity has changed the world more than he. From a religious point of view, Jesus is the founder of the Christian religion. From a spiritual point of view, Jesus came into the world to reveal God to humanity. Therefore, when we see Jesus, we see God. From the point of view of a disciple of Jesus, he is our Lord and our Savior.

The Gospels—Simple and Complex

The Gospels are both simple and complex. For centuries, millions of ordinary Christians with no technical training have heard or read them and been shaped and changed by them. On one level, their meaning is obvious: Jesus is the Light of the World, The Bread of Life, and the Son of God; we are to love one another as he loved us; we are to love the Lord our God with all our heart, soul, strength, and mind.

On the other hand, they are complex documents. They are written in an ancient language that most people today do not understand. They have a complex history. They combine pre-Easter memory with post-Easter testimony. They make allusions to the Jewish Bible and to the first-century world that are not always apparent to us. They combine memory and metaphor. But their complexity is not a deficiency or defect to be lamented. Rather, their complexity contributes to their richness.[4]

—Marcus Borg, scholar and author

The primary source of our study of the life, ministry, and teaching of Jesus the Messiah is the account given in the four Gospels. The Gospels are not standard biographies. Although they are concerned with giving historical facts about Jesus, their primary concern is to portray the theological message of Jesus to different audiences.

Matthew is the longest of the Gospels. It was written primarily to a Jewish audience and stresses that Jesus is the Messiah, the king.

Mark is the earliest of the Gospels and also the shortest, being a mere sixteen chapters in length. It was written primarily to a Gentile audience, and Mark stresses that discipleship to King Jesus comes only through following Jesus to the cross.

Luke was written to a predominately Gentile audience. Luke traces the genealogy of Jesus back to Adam and in doing so he connects Jesus with all of humanity. Luke underscores that Jesus, not Caesar, is Lord.

These first three Gospels present a very similar account of the life of Jesus and have been called the Synoptic Gospels. Synoptic means "common" or "similar."

John was written decades after the first three Gospels. John presents a very different view of Jesus. His Gospel includes a narrative account of Jesus' life and is more spiritual and theological.

Why Approach the Study in a Fourfold Way?

The strength of approaching the life and teachings of Jesus the Messiah through a harmony of the Gospels comes in being able to use a scripture-by-scripture approach, viewing the gospel events in parallel. You also get to understand portions of all of the Gospels.

The weakness comes in that you lose some of the thematic continuity of the individual Gospels. Each Gospel tells its own story. You could say that each Gospel gives a different version of the same gospel.

Historicity

Is the story true? People attack the historicity of the Gospels. Stephen Mitchell in his *The Gospel According to Jesus* quotes Thomas Jefferson (yes, that Thomas Jefferson of US history fame). Jefferson wrote:

> The whole history of these books, the Gospels, is so defective and doubtful that it seems vain to attempt minute inquiry into it and such tricks have been played with the text and with the other books relating to them that we have a right to entertain great doubt as to which parts are genuine.[5]

Mitchell goes on to sift through the Gospels in order to (in his words) sift "diamonds from dunghills." Mitchell wants to get to the original words of Jesus.

The Jesus Seminar is a group of forty to seventy scholars who discuss the historicity of the Gospels. Their work culminated in the publication of *The Five Gospels*, a work presenting the true sayings of Jesus based upon a vote by these scholars and semischolars. The vote was cast by colored beads. The colors signified:

> Black: No, not Jesus.
> Gray: Perhaps, maybe it's Jesus.
> Pink: Sounds like this could be Jesus.
> Red: Yep! This is Jesus.

Only twenty percent of the final published words of Jesus were pink or red. None of John was red or pink. It was all black except for three phrases in gray. This means that these scholars believe that John's Gospel does not contain any authentic word or words of Jesus.

What was in red? Words like, "Love your enemies," "Turn the other cheek," "Our Father." One scholar asked the committee an interesting question. He asked, "Why would anyone want to kill someone who only said these things?" It doesn't ring true that these were the only authentic words of Jesus in the Gospels.

The author C.S. Lewis demonstrated that if Jesus claimed to be Lord then he had to be one of three things: Either he truly was Lord, or he was a liar, or he was a raving lunatic.

People who want to attack Lewis do so by saying that Jesus never claimed to be Lord. They add a fourth "L" to the equation. "L" for "Legend." They say the early church elevated Jesus to become Lord. This would be the same as Siddhartha becoming Buddha or Mohammed becoming the Prophet Mohammed.

Are the Gospels legend or truth? Are they historical or not? If you studied at a secular university, your professors most likely taught that the Jesus of history is quite different from the Jesus of faith. Some say that it is impossible to reconstruct the historical Jesus, that what we have in the Gospel accounts is the Jesus of faith. In other words, they are saying that the Jesus of the Gospels is the Jesus of legend.

If you throw out the Gospels as being nonhistorical, then we have very few indisputable facts about the life of Jesus. We can say with confidence that Jesus did live. He lived in Judah and Galilee. He was a religious leader. He died an ignoble death. That's about all that we can say using sources outside the Gospels. (*See Appendix Two for some of these sources.*)

But, we also can say that something special happened after his death. Look at how Christianity grew after the death of Jesus. Without very many resources, the teachings of Jesus spread throughout the Mediterranean world in such a phenomenal way that within 270 years of his death, Christianity was the predominant religion in the area. This happened despite the fact that the authorities of the time (both Jewish and Roman) were trying to stamp out Christianity. The teaching of Jesus grew to the point that seven million people out of fifty million people in the Roman world wore the name Christian. They proudly wore this name in spite of the fact that whoever claimed to be a Christian might suffer loss of property, find himself in jail, be crucified, or be fed to lions. Secular historians cannot deny this fact.

Was Jesus only a great man with amazing ideas? Could this be the reason his disciples were willing to die? Or was it the resurrection?

Can We Trust the Gospels?

Yes, and here are a few reasons why the Gospels can be trusted.[6]

1. In the first-century world, knowledge was often passed from person to person. There was written history, but there was also oral history and oral tradition. Often, people trained their minds to remember stories, traditions, and quotes. Rabbinical training in the time of Jesus was mostly memory work. Students had to quote the rabbis. The disciples would have been able to memorize the words of Rabbi Jesus.

2. Rules of writing history did not allow for fabrication. The standard for historical stories of the time was that you could not add to the details of a story or fabricate a story. You could paraphrase, but you could not change the basic content of the story.

3. People kept written records. One rabbi said, "If your rabbi is teaching and you have no paper, write it on your sleeve." The average person had only seven garments. To destroy a garment by writing on it was expensive. What is the point of this saying? If you are a student, make sure you have something with you to record the words of your rabbi. His words are precious and must be remembered exactly as they are spoken.

4. Jesus spoke in memorable ways: parables, poems, and pithy sayings.

5. Memorable events emblazon themselves on our minds forever, and the life of Jesus was filled with memorable events.

6. There is evidence within the Bible. In 1 Corinthians 7:10–12 Paul says, "Not I, but the Lord."

    To the married I give this command (not I, but the Lord): A wife must not separate from her husband. But if she does, she must remain unmarried or else be reconciled to her husband. And a husband must not divorce his wife.

    To the rest I say this (I, not the Lord): If any brother has a wife who is not a believer and she is willing to live with him, he must not divorce her."

    When Paul says, "Not I, but the Lord," he is saying, "I'm quoting Jesus here." When he says, "I, not the Lord," he is saying, "This is me, Paul the apostle, saying this." Paul makes a distinction between his words and the words of Jesus. He could do this because the words of Jesus were treated with great respect by the early church and they were accurately transmitted from one disciple to the next.

7. Also, consider the phenomena of living witnesses. So many people could have ruined the veracity of the Gospels by just showing the falsity of it. There were over one million people living in Palestine at the time of Jesus. The Jewish and Roman authorities wanted to stop the Christian movement. All they had to do was show that the basic premise of Christianity was a lie, but they were unable to do this.

8. People who wrote the books gave their lives for it. People don't usually give their lives for something that they know is false.

9. Archaeological evidence confirms the Gospels. For example: Jacob's well is in Samaria (I've been there). The Synagogue in Capernaum where Jesus healed the demoniac has been discovered, and you can visit it today (as I have on several occasions). You can also visit the Pool of Siloam in Jerusalem (I've been there also). The places mentioned in the Gospels are real places. Archaeology confirms the accuracy of the Gospels.

10. Luke approached his Gospel with the mindset of a historian.

Yes, the Gospels can be trusted. The early disciples were careful to record the words of Jesus accurately. Therefore, trust their record.

The Nature of the Gospels

The Gospels are not strict biographies; they are testimonials. They are all written with a purpose in mind—to create faith in Jesus (Mark 1:1, Luke 1:1–4, John 20:31, Matthew 13:52, Matthew 28:18ff).

What Is a Gospel?

Here then we find the supreme mission of the Christian minister: It is to help men to fall in love with the character of Jesus. The Bible is an invaluable book chiefly because it contains a portrait of Jesus. The New Testament is immeasurably superior to the Old because in the New Testament we have the face of Jesus. The Holy of Holies of the New Testament is the Gospels because it is here we look directly into the eyes of Jesus. We often speak of the Gospel: What is it? Jesus![7]

—Charles Edward Jefferson, *Jesus the Same*

The word "gospel" (εὐαγγέλιον/*euangelion* in the Greek) means "good news, the report by the herald of a king." In the Ptolemaic period just before the birth of Jesus, εὐαγγέλιον/*euangelion*, the gospel, was proclaimed when a king was born and especially when he ascended the throne. Even earlier, εὐαγγέλιον/*euangelion* meant the fee paid to the messenger who brought reports of good news to a general in battle. The Christians adopted this term and applied it to King Jesus. They proclaimed εὐαγγέλιον/*euangelion* to announce his ascension to the throne of God.

The early Christians enriched the idea of εὐαγγέλιον/*euangelion* with the Jewish concept of the Living Word. For the Jew, the Word was never just a report or a story; it was always the living and active word of

God (Hebrews 4:12). The New Testament writers used the term "gospel" to mean the living Word of preaching Christ as King. The gospel writers were not journalists or historians recording an everyday story; they were believers heralding the birth and ascension of the King of the Universe. A gospel is not a biography in the sense that we use the word today. It is a tract designed to promote faith in Jesus, a man the writers knew to be like no other.

At the same time the gospel writers were keen to give an accurate account of Jesus. Luke makes this clear at the beginning of his Gospel, when he writes:

> Many have undertaken to draw up an account of the things that have been fulfilled among us, just as they were handed down to us by those who from the first were eyewitnesses and servants of the word. Therefore, since I myself have carefully investigated everything from the beginning, it seemed good also to me to write an orderly account for you, most excellent Theophilus, so that you may know the certainty of the things you have been taught.
>
> —Luke 1:1–4

The gospel writers were concerned that an orderly, historical account of Jesus' life be recorded so people could know who Jesus was. They circulated this account in the Gospels.

Some modern scholars express doubt about the historicity of the Gospels, comparing them to rabbinic *midrash* or commentary. D.A. Carson answers these criticisms by writing:

> We conclude that the evangelists, including Matthew, intended that their Gospels convey historical information. This does not mean they intended to write dispassionate, modern biographies. But advocacy does not necessarily affect truth telling: a Jewish writer on the Holocaust is not necessarily either more or less accurate because his family perished at Auschwitz. Nor is it proper in the study of any document professedly dealing with history to approach it with a neutral stance that demands proof of authenticity as well as proof on a lack of authenticity.[8]

The gospel writers were writing historical tracts that promoted the mission of Jesus. The Gospels were part memoirs, part theological treatises, part biography, part sermon, part doctrinal teaching, part profession of faith, part encouraging letter, and part homage to the Lord. Along with strict adherence to the truth, they were presentations of the good news that Jesus is the Messiah, the Son of God, and Immanuel, who came to save the world from sin.

Why Were the Gospels Recorded?

1. The early Christian community believed that Jesus was going to return quickly. As time passed and his Second Coming had not yet occurred, the need was felt to record the testimony of the ministry of Jesus. This historical record of Jesus' life and ministry kept the memory of Jesus alive as the eyewitnesses of Jesus passed away.

2. As more people became Christians (especially those outside of Palestine who were unfamiliar with the life of Jesus), there was a need to collect the stories of Jesus to educate the disciples.

3. Very early in the ministry of the church, false teaching about Jesus became commonplace. Gnostics, who denied that Jesus was God in the flesh, began circulating false teaching about Jesus. The Gospels were correctives to these false ideas.

4. As the early church grew, there was a need to provide material that could be used in worship services. The Gospels could be read in the worship of the early church as a means of encouragement.

How Do We Interpret the Gospels?

The Gospels are a different genre than the writings of Paul or the book of Revelation. When we read the Gospels, we should recognize the differences between the Gospels and the other books of the New Testament. Here are some guidelines for interpreting the Gospels.

1. Jesus spoke in Aramaic/Hebrew, but the Gospels were recorded in Greek. Since the Gospels were recorded in Greek, we are at best one step removed from the actual words of Jesus. We must attempt to go behind the Greek and understand the Jewish context of the life and ministry of Jesus. Since Matthew was written for a Jewish audience, he helps us grasp the Jewishness of the message of Jesus more than the other Gospels.

   It is also important that we do not divorce the Gospels from their Old Testament context. The story of Jesus is the fulfillment of the plan of God as promised to Adam and Eve and then to the nation of Israel. King Jesus is the Messiah of Israel. We must read the Gospel of Jesus within the context of Jesus fulfilling the promise of God in the Old Testament.

2. Look at the Gospels on two levels:
   • The historical concerns of who Jesus was and what he did
   • The retelling of the story of Jesus for the needs of the church

3. Understand the historical context of the Gospels and the time in which they were written.

4. Understand the forms that Jesus used in his teaching: proverbs, similes and metaphors, poetry, and irony.

5. When interpreting an individual pericope (an individual story):
   • Think horizontally: Consider how the story is used in the other Gospels.
   • Think vertically: Consider the historical context of the story.

A Two-Eyed Reading of the Gospels

N.T. Wright suggests a two-eyed reading of the Gospel accounts.[9] That's because the Gospels were written for two reasons. First, the gospel writers wrote the accounts to tell the story of Jesus. So as we read the Gospels, we can focus on the inspiring story of Jesus' life. Second, the gospel writers wrote with their first-century audience in mind. They told the story of Jesus for these readers. When we read the Gospels, we must also keep in mind the original audience to whom each Gospel was addressed.

How to Read the Gospels

N.T. Wright also suggests four ways to read the Gospels. I like these four helpful hints. What I like most about them is that with every point, Wright begins by stating, "Read the Gospels from cover to cover." If you want to understand the story of Jesus, you must begin by reading the story. The more you read the story, the more it becomes a part of you. Here are Wright's four points:

> First, read the Gospels from cover to cover, struggling to make more and more sense of exactly who Jesus was.[10]
>
> Second, read the Gospels from cover to cover, struggling with each book to see what each evangelist is saying as a whole.[11]
>
> Third, read the Gospels from cover to cover, struggling to ask another question. If this Jesus really did draw together the threads of the saving plan of the one true God; if on the cross, and in his resurrection, he really did deal with evil once and for all; if the people who read his story now, and make it their own, have the responsibility to implement his victory over evil in the world then how can people, today, retell the story so that the world gets the message?[12]
>
> But, fourth, read the Gospels from cover to cover, slowly, carefully and thoughtfully, wondering throughout: if I were in the crowd at that scene, what would Jesus say to me? ... In other words, put yourself into the story and see what happens.[13]

Rules for Reading

The Bible is not just any book. It is the word of God. Consider these scriptures:

> But as for you, continue in what you have learned and have become convinced of, because you know those from whom you learned it, and how from infancy you have known the holy Scriptures, which are able to make you wise for salvation through faith in Christ Jesus. All Scripture is God-breathed and is useful for teaching, rebuking, correcting and training in righteousness, so that the man of God may be thoroughly equipped for every good work.
>
> —2 Timothy 3:14–17

And we have the word of the prophets made more certain, and you will do well to pay attention to it, as to a light shining in a dark place, until the day dawns and the morning star rises in your hearts. Above all, you must understand that no prophecy of Scripture came about by the prophet's own interpretation. For prophecy never had its origin in the will of man, but men spoke from God as they were carried along by the Holy Spirit.

—2 Peter 1:19–21

How are we to read the Bible so that we can get the most out of our reading?[14]

1. Read the Bible daily.
2. Read the text repeatedly. G. Campbell Morgan, preacher and author, read the book he was going to focus on fifty times before he wrote or preached on it.
3. Read the Bible thoughtfully. Joshua 1:8 reads, *"Do not let this Book of the Law depart from your mouth; meditate on it day and night, so that you may be careful to do everything written in it. Then you will be prosperous and successful."*
4. Read it patiently. Don't quit. Keep at it.
5. Read it selectively. Ask:
   - Who? Who are the people, the characters?
   - What? What truths, events? What is the substance and context?
   - When? What day, what year, what king, what era, and what covenant?
   - Why? Why here? Why now? Why mention this?
   - Where? Where did this event take place?
   - Wherefore? What difference does it make?
6. Read prayfully.
7. Read reflectively.
8. Read purposefully. The Bible was written to equip us for every good work. It transforms our lives so that we can help others. Read with a desire to apply what you are reading to your life in order to help other people.
9. Read spiritually. Don't get so bogged down in the facts and details to the extent that you miss the message of the text. Ask, "God, what do you want me to learn from this reading?" Pray, "God, speak, for your servant is listening."

The Story of Jesus

I Love to Tell the Story

Text: Katherine Hankey, 1834–1911
Music: William G. Fischer, 1835–1912

I love to tell the story
of unseen things above,
of Jesus and his glory,
of Jesus and his love.

I love to tell the story,
because I know 'tis true;
it satisfies my longings
as nothing else can do.

Refrain:
I love to tell the story;
'twill be my theme in glory,
to tell the old, old story
of Jesus and his love.

I love to tell the story;
more wonderful it seems
than all the golden fancies
of all our golden dreams.
I love to tell the story,
it did so much for me;
and that is just the reason
I tell it now to thee.
Refrain

I love to tell the story;
'tis pleasant to repeat
what seems, each time I tell it,
more wonderfully sweet.
I love to tell the story,
for some have never heard
the message of salvation
from God's own holy word.
Refrain

I love to tell the story,
for those who know it best
seem hungering and thirsting
to hear it like the rest.
And when, in scenes of glory,
I sing the new, new song,
'twill be the old, old story
that I have loved so long.
Refrain

God created Adam and Eve and gave them stewardship over the Garden of Eden and every animal on the earth, but they rebelled against God.

They wanted to be like him and usurp his power, so God cast them out of the garden.

God established a covenant with Abraham, Isaac, and Jacob. During a famine, Jacob's family moved to Egypt. His descendants became great in number and Egypt made them slaves. They cried out for deliverance, and God raised up Moses who took them out of slavery. They journeyed to a land of promise where God renewed his covenant with them and made them into a nation named Israel. Israel asked for a king, so God gave them one. But the kings of Israel didn't govern the land the way that God wished his people to be governed, so God promised that he would raise up a king from the lineage of David who would govern his people justly. The nation rebelled against God's laws and he disciplined his nation through foreign invasion and then through captivity in a foreign land. But God never gave up on his people. He promised them a future king. The prophets spoke of this future king. Around 400 BC, prophecy ceased. Until...

Between 7–5 BC Jesus was born in Bethlehem. He grew up in a small, backwater village in Galilee named Nazareth. Some scholars say as few as ten families lived in this tiny village. Jesus spent most of his life in Galilee. He made yearly pilgrimages to Jerusalem, but he grew up as a Galilean.

The culture of Jesus' day was a Hellenistic-Jewish mixture. In first-century Jerusalem over half the inscriptions on the tombs were in Greek, not Aramaic or Hebrew. (This demonstrates how widespread the Greco-Roman influence was in Judea.) Jesus grew up speaking all three of these languages. Rome controlled Palestine but allowed local rulers to determine the day-to-day procedures within their governance.

Jesus lived only four miles, less than an hour's walk, from a major town in Galilee named Sepphoris. He learned the carpenter's trade from his adoptive father, Joseph. Since wood was scarce in Galilee, carpenters were also stonemasons. It is likely that Jesus accompanied Joseph to Sepphoris to find work repairing buildings that were destroyed when the Romans squelched a Jewish uprising in that city. Jesus would have gained firsthand knowledge of the animosity between the Jews and the Romans on those visits to Sepphoris. After Joseph died, Jesus supported his family through carpentry and stonemasonry.

When Jesus became thirty, a prophet arrived on the scene named John the Baptist. When John delivered God's prophetic word in the Judean wilderness, this broke 400 years of silence between God and his people. John's message was simple and straightforward: "Repent, for the kingdom of heaven is near." Many took this as a pronouncement of the end of the reign of Rome.

John was a wild man of the desert. He dressed in camel's hair garments and ate locusts and wild honey. Some believe John was an Essene, a member of the Qumran community beside the Dead Sea. John preached in the Judean wilderness outside of Jerusalem. He bade his audience to come to him. They did, by the hundreds. John was not a miracle worker. He immersed people in water for the forgiveness of sins. That's why he was known as John the Plunger or John the Immerser or John the Baptist. John was a preacher and a prophet. He had a message that burned on his heart, a message of the coming Messiah. People asked John, "Are you *The One?*" Without ego, he said, "No, not I." When Jesus showed up to listen to John, John pointed to Jesus and said, "There he is. He is *The One.*"

Herod Antipas, ruler of Galilee, executed John. John got into a squabble with Herodias, Herod Antipas' new wife, over the legality of their marriage (she had previously been married to Antipas' brother; therefore, under Jewish law her marriage to Antipas was illegal). John the Plunger wasn't concerned with political correctness. This cost him his head.

News of John's death reached Jesus and prompted him to begin his public ministry. As a miracle worker, Jesus drew multitudes of people, but he also preached and taught. He went from village to village and town to town preaching, teaching, and healing. His message was the same as John's: "Repent, for the kingdom of heaven is near." The people wondered if Jesus was going to drive the Romans out of Israel. Jesus had a different plan.

The bulk of Jesus' ministry centered around the Sea of Galilee, especially a three-city triangle of Capernaum, Bethsaida, and Corazin now known as the evangelical triangle. Capernaum served as Jesus' hometown during his ministry years.

Jesus broke social barriers. He met with tax collectors, sinners, the elite, and the downcasts. He touched lepers. He befriended prostitutes. In fact, he spoke with anyone who would give him an audience. Jesus didn't care if he stepped over class lines or if he offended someone's social mores. He cared about the need of the individual person more than the customs of society.

Jesus taught in a manner that was different from other rabbis, who quoted other rabbis for their authority. They would say, "Hillel said" or "Shammai said." But, Jesus said, "Truly, truly, I say to you (ESV)." Jesus' teaching sometimes contradicted the standard answers that people were accustomed to hearing. Jesus said, "You have heard it was said, but I say to you." People took note that Jesus taught differently from other rabbis. They noted that he taught with authority.

Not long into his ministry, some of the religious authorities began to take note of Jesus. They didn't like how the multitudes were drawn to him. They began to plot together how they might take care of this menace.

Jesus taught the crowds, but he only trained twelve to carry on his ministry after he was gone. On occasion, Jesus withdrew to teach these twelve specific lessons. He taught them in parables—memorable stories that were encoded with deep meaning. The parables held secrets that only the initiated could understand.

Jesus knew that the religious hierarchy planned on shutting down his ministry. He did his best to prepare his disciples for this event. At least three times he told them that he must die. But he added, "Don't lose heart, because three days after my death, I'm coming back." The disciples never really grasped what Jesus was trying to tell them, not until—the resurrection.

Jesus spent the last week before his death in and around the city of Jerusalem. He took his disciples to the Mount of Olives so they could get a panoramic view of the city. The view was spectacular. Jesus wept for Jerusalem.

In front of the Mount of Olives stood the magnificent temple complex, which covered thirty-five acres. The court was polished marble. The gold of the temple gleamed in the sunlight. The following day, Jesus shut the whole thing down. He spoke against the commercialism of the temple courts. He called it "a den of thieves." Jesus prophesied that the temple would be destroyed. Jesus' actions and words upset some of the religious elite. The professional clerics would later use Jesus' words concerning the temple against him.

During Jesus' last week in Jerusalem, the Jewish ruling body known as the Sanhedrin arrested Jesus. They tried him at night, which was illegal, but the Jewish authorities weren't going to fret over legalities. They had decided that for the good of the nation, this man who spoke against the temple must die.

The Jewish authorities handed Jesus over to the Romans for crucifixion. The Romans executed Jesus on a Friday. He died very quickly. It customarily took around three days for a victim of crucifixion to die. A public execution took time for a reason—the Romans wanted to make an example of the criminal. After Jesus was placed on the cross, death came within a few hours. When he died, the whole land went dark.

After his death, some of Jesus' followers placed his body in a borrowed tomb. Then, something amazing happened. The borrowed tomb became an empty tomb. Jesus started appearing to people around Jerusalem. He appeared to a few women, to some men, and then to a crowd of 500. The closest followers finally understood what Jesus meant when he told them that he would appear to them three days after his death. His appearing changed their lives. After a few weeks, Jesus left his followers again. Before he left, he commissioned them to go into the entire world and make disciples wherever they went. His followers embraced this commission. They went everywhere preaching the message of the cross and the resurrection. In a few short years, they turned the world upside down with his message.

End Notes

1. Francis Fenelon, *Christian Perfection: Devotional Reflections on the Christian Life* (Bethany House, 1976).

2. I don't mean to be offensive (that would be a terrible way to start a book), but I do mean to stir the waters a bit. I have a deep conviction on this point. I asked one teacher why he required a study of Paul's epistles in his staff-training curriculum and did not require a class on the life of Jesus or on any of the Gospels. He responded, "I believe we get enough Jesus through studying Paul." I wonder how Paul might respond to his statement.

3. I'm paraphrasing from the article. You can find it at: www.nytimes.com/2008/12/14/movies/14head.html?_r=1&scp=2&sq=clint%20eastwood&st=cse.

4. Marcus J. Borg, *Jesus: Uncovering the Life, Teachings, and Relevance of a Religious Revolutionary* (San Francisco: HarperSanFrancisco, 2006), 27.

5. As found in Stephen Mitchell's *The Gospel According to Jesus: A New Translation and Guide to His Essential Teachings for Believers and Unbelievers* (New York: Harper Perennial, 1993).

6. These points are taken from my notes on lectures by Dr. Dan Doriani. The class "The Life and Teachings of Jesus" can be found at www.worldwide-classroom.com. The website is produced by Covenant Theological Seminary. This is a very useful class, and I highly recommend it.

7. Charles Jefferson, *Jesus the Same*, Edited and Revised Edition (Woburn, MA: Discipleship Publications International, 1997).

8. D.A. Carson, *The Expositor's Bible Commentary with the New International Version* (Grand Rapids: Zondervan, 1995), 10–11.

9. Tom Wright, *The Original Jesus: The Life and Vision of a Revolutionary* (Grand Rapids: Eerdmans, 1996), 145.

10. Ibid.

11. Ibid., 146.

12. Ibid., 148.

13. Ibid., 149.

14. I borrowed some of this material from a video teaching series by Dr. Mark Bailey of Dallas Theological Seminary as found on iTunes U. Dr. Mark Bailey BE101–02–02 and Dr. Mark Bailey BE101–02–03.

Chapter 2

The Beginning of the Gospel of Jesus Christ

Tell Me the Old, Old Story[15]
Text: Katherine Hankey, 1886.
Music: W. Howard Doane. 1867.

Tell me the old, old story of unseen things above,
Of Jesus and His glory, of Jesus and His love.
Tell me the story simply, as to a little child,
For I am weak and weary, and helpless and defiled.

Refrain:
Tell me the old, old story; tell me the old, old story;
Tell me the old, old story of Jesus and His love.

Tell me the story slowly, that I may take it in,
That wonderful redemption, God's remedy for sin.
Tell me the story often, for I forget so soon;
The early dew of morning has passed away at noon.
Refrain

Tell me the story softly, with earnest tones and grave;
Remember I'm the sinner whom Jesus came to save.
Tell me the story always, if you would really be,
In any time of trouble, a comforter to me.
Refrain

Tell me the same old story when you have cause to fear
That this world's empty glory is costing me too dear.
Yes, and when that world's glory is dawning on my soul,
Tell me the old, old story: "Christ Jesus makes thee whole."
Refrain

Before we get to the birth/infancy narratives of Jesus, we must consider the prolegomena to the Gospels. Let's look at Luke's dedication in his Gospel and John's introduction to his Gospel.

The Dedication to Luke's Gospel—Luke 1:1–4

Many have undertaken to draw up an account of the things that have been fulfilled among us, just as they were handed down to us by those who from the first were eyewitnesses and servants of the word. Therefore, since I myself have carefully investigated everything from the beginning, it seemed good also to me to write an orderly account for you, most excellent Theophilus, so that you may know the certainty of the things you have been taught.

What do we learn from Luke's introduction about his approach to gospel writing?

1. Luke wasn't the first to try his hand at writing an account of the life of Jesus. In fact, many before him had attempted to record the story of Jesus. Most scholars believe that when Luke wrote his Gospel that he had, in hand, a copy of Mark's Gospel and an account of some of Jesus' sayings.

2. The gospel writers relied heavily on those who had been eyewitnesses of Jesus' ministry.

3. Luke carefully investigated the sources upon which he based his Gospel.

4. Luke was writing an orderly account. He had sifted through his sources, placed them in proper order, and then wrote his Gospel based upon his ordering of the sources.

5. Luke clearly stated his purpose for writing his Gospel. He wanted the reader to know for certain that his account was accurate and true.

According to Luke's introduction to his Gospel, he was writing a historical account of Jesus' life. It was history that was written to influence the reader toward a belief in Jesus; but nevertheless, it was history.

John's Prologue—John 1:1–14

In the beginning was the Word, and the Word was with God, and the Word was God. He was with God in the beginning.

Through him all things were made; without him nothing was made that has been made. In him was life, and that life was the light of men. The light shines in the darkness, but the darkness has not understood it.

There came a man who was sent from God; his name was John. He came as a witness to testify concerning that light, so that through him all men might believe. He himself was not the light; he came only as a witness to the light. The true light that gives light to every man was coming into the world.

He was in the world, and though the world was made through him, the world did not recognize him. He came to that which was his own, but his own did not receive him. Yet to all who received him, to those who believed in his name, he gave the right to become children of God—children born not of natural descent, nor of human decision or a husband's will, but born of God.

The Word became flesh and made his dwelling among us. We have seen his glory, the glory of the One and Only, who came from the Father, full of grace and truth.

Key Idea: A Light Breaks Through the Darkness

John speaks of Jesus as the light of the world. What does this mean? It must be an important image for John to begin his Gospel account with this idea. What can we learn from this image?

Notice that Jesus is the light. Any light that we might have in our lives is not generated on our own. We simply reflect Jesus' light in our lives—our light is indirect. Think of the sun and the moon. The moon doesn't generate light on its own; the sun is the source for the light of the moon. In the same way, Jesus is the source of light in our lives.

Since we reflect the light of Jesus, we need to ask, "How was Jesus a light to the world?" Let's look in the Gospel of John and see three functions of the light of Jesus as presented in John's Gospel.

1. The light of Jesus shows us who God is.

We all tend to have an image of God that is formed in our minds through our upbringing and our experience. We tend to see God in the image of our parents. If our father was a tyrant, then we see God as tyrannical. If our mother was overbearing and obsessive, then we tend to view God as an obsessive mom. Maybe we had a parent who kept offering love and then withdrawing love from us. If so, we have probably formed an image of a capricious God. If we have formed an image of God based on our experiences, this becomes our "gut-level" image of God.

Jesus came to free us from those images of God. He came to show us who God really is. He shows us that God cares enough to come into our world and live with us.

You can usually tell people who are good with children. They don't talk to the child as an adult speaking to another adult. Instead, they stoop down to the level of the child and talk eye to eye with the child. They don't use big, pretentious adult words, but they use the vocabulary of a child. They read children's books to the child and play children's games. This shows they are trying to meet the child on his or her turf.

Through Jesus, God shows us that he is willing to stoop down and meet us where we are. John 1:14 is one of the most important verses in the Bible. The Word (Jesus) became flesh. In Jesus, God comes knocking on your door. He moves into your neighborhood. He comes to show you who he is.

Jesus came into the world so that we might know God. We don't have to wonder or guess about the nature the God—Jesus reveals him to us. That is the point of the incarnation. (We will consider this more fully in the next chapter.)

2. The light of Jesus drives away darkness.

In John 3:19–21, Jesus says:

> *This is the verdict: Light has come into the world, but men loved darkness instead of light because their deeds were evil. Everyone who does evil hates the light, and will not come into the light for fear that his deeds will be exposed. But whoever lives by the truth comes into the light, so that it may be seen plainly that what he has done has been done through God.*

Light drives away darkness; therefore, Jesus drives away darkness. This is why we need a steady dose of Jesus in our lives—to keep the darkness away.

I'm originally from the South, where we have these giant cockroaches that come out at night. These bugs are big, nasty, and strong. They can cart away whole boxes of cereal and whole bags of sugar (I'm only barely exaggerating here).

Cockroaches are nocturnal. They love darkness and hate the light. When you turn on the light, they scurry for cover. They don't want to be exposed by the light, so it drives them away.

As light, Jesus drives darkness away. Jesus exposes deeds of darkness in our lives. Another way of saying this is to say that Jesus helps us deal with the sin problem in our lives. And we all have a sin problem. Romans 3:23 states, "For all have sinned and fall short of the glory of God." Isaiah 59:1–2 states that sin separates us from God:

> *Surely the arm of the LORD is not too short to save,*
> > *nor his ear too dull to hear.*
> *But your iniquities have separated*
> > *you from your God;*
> *your sins have hidden his face from you,*
> > *so that he will not hear.*

The sin problem is gigantic. How do we deal with it? We can't overcome sin by our own power, but Jesus can take care of it. This is what it means that Jesus can drive away darkness. He tells us to come into the light by living by the truth. In John 14:6, he says, "I am the way and the truth and the life." To embrace the truth is to embrace Jesus. Truth drives away lies, and light drives away darkness, so we need the truth and light of Jesus in our lives.

3. The light of Jesus serves as a guide for our lives.
  John 12:35–36 reads:

> *Then Jesus told them, "You are going to have the light just a little while longer. Walk while you have the light, before darkness overtakes you. The man who walks in the dark does not know where he is going. Put your trust in the light while you have it, so that you may become sons of light." When he had finished speaking, Jesus left and hid himself from them.*

The man who walks in the dark does not know where he is going. But with a little light, you can walk safely in darkness. Without light, darkness is filled with danger. With light, you can see whatever lies ahead. Jesus serves as a guide to help us make it through this dark world.

Think for a moment about the headlights on your car. With a beam of light that shines no more than twenty feet in front of your path, you can drive safely through the night. Have you ever tried driving at night without your lights? I've turned mine off at times just to see what it was like without them. Warning: Don't try that; it's not safe. But if you've tried it, then you know what I'm talking about. When your headlights are on, you can safely drive through the darkness of the night. These lights illuminate the path, just as Jesus illuminates the path before us.

In John 12:46, Jesus says, "I have come into the world as a light, so that no one who believes in me should stay in darkness." Jesus shows us how to get out of darkness. He is our guide, and we need a guide in this world. We live in a world filled with confusion. Couples are confused when it comes to marriage. They don't know how to have a satisfying marriage, as is shown in the high divorce rate in the United States. Parents are confused about how to raise their children. There are so many theories about childrearing that you can get dizzy trying to determine which approach is best. Many teens are confused by life, which is demonstrated by the alarming rate of teen suicides, teen pregnancies, and drug use among teens. Life is confusing and the world is a confusing place.

We live in an insecure time of economic confusion when jobs are scarce. Money doesn't go as far as it used to. Stocks have plummeted in value. Retirement funds have dried up. The government is stepping in to bail out failed businesses. If we put our trust in economic security, we are on very shaky ground.

Where do we put our trust? Jesus says, "Put your trust in the light." Too often we put our trust in things that don't come through for us. For example, some put their trust in relationships, money, education, careers, personal ingenuity, or intelligence. At times, these things come through; at other times, they are a big disappointment. Jesus is saying, "Put your trust in me. I'll guide you through the confusion."

John encourages us to put our trust in the light of Jesus. Like the headlights in the night, the light of Jesus will guide us through the darkness.

Conclusion

John uses this image of Jesus as light to open his Gospel. Remember—light doesn't originate in us. Jesus is the source of light. We reflect his light. The closer we are to Jesus, the stronger his light shines in our lives.

Reflection

Therefore what reward shall I give unto the Lord for all the benefits which He hath done unto me? In the first creation He gave me myself; but in His new creation He gave me Himself, and by that gift restored to me the self that I had lost. Created first and then restored, I owe Him myself twice over in return for myself. But what have I to offer Him for the gift of Himself? Could I multiply myself a thousand-fold and then give Him all, what would that be in comparison with God?[16]

—Saint Bernard of Clairvaux (1090/91–1153)

End Notes

15. Text by A. Katherine Hankey, 1866. The lyrics are similar to those of "I Love to Tell the Story." Both are drawn from Hankey's poem "The Old, Old Story." Music by W. Howard Doane, 1867. In the public domain.

16. Saint Bernard of Clairvaux, *On Loving God*, www.ccel.org/ccel/bernard/loving_god.txt. In the public domain.

Chapter 3

The Birth and Early Years of Jesus

All Hail the Power of Jesus' Name![17]
Text: Edward Perronet; alt. by John Rippon.
Music: Oliver Holden.

All hail the power of Jesus' name,
Let angels prostrate fall;
bring forth the royal diadem,
and crown him Lord of all.
Bring forth the royal diadem,
and crown him Lord of all.

Ye chosen seed of Israel's race,
ye ransomed from the fall,
hail him who saves you by his grace,
and crown him Lord of all.
Hail him who saves you by his grace,
and crown him Lord of all.

Sinners, whose love can ne'er forget
the wormwood and the gall,
go spread your trophies at his feet,
and crown him Lord of all.
Go spread your trophies at his feet,
and crown him Lord of all.

Let every kindred, every tribe
on this terrestrial ball,
to him all majesty ascribe,
and crown him Lord of all.
To him all majesty ascribe,
and crown him Lord of all.

Crown him, ye martyrs of your God,
who from his altar call;
extol the Stem of Jesse's Rod,
and crown him Lord of all.
Extol the Stem of Jesse's Rod,
and crown him Lord of all.

O that with yonder sacred throng
we at his feet may fall!
We'll join the everlasting song,
and crown him Lord of all.
We'll join the everlasting song,
and crown him Lord of all.

Key Idea: Jesus Is "Something Special"

When autumn arrives, my attention turns to football because I love it. My favorite football announcer is now retired. He was the great John Maddon (I'll speak of him in the past tense since he has retired from broadcasting, though he's not dead). He had an encyclopedic knowledge of the game. You could tell how much he loved the game by the way he spoke of it with a hallowed tone when referring to its traditions.

When John Madden discovered a new player that he felt would elevate the game, he anointed the player with praise. His voice went up in pitch, his breath quickened, and he said, "Now this kid! Now this kid is going to be something special! There is something special about this kid!" He'd then go on to explain the reasons why he felt like this rookie was going to be a special player. He would say, "He hits like a bulldozer," "He has a head for the game," "He's tough as nails," or "He's as quick as a bullet." This was John Madden's way of saying this player was the next great thing.

At the beginning of the Gospels, the gospel writers go to great lengths to say Jesus was something special. They say this through the genealogies. They say it through the pronouncement stories. They say it through the visitation stories of the shepherds and the Magi. They say it by quoting the prophets. They say it through the names and titles of Jesus: titles like Immanuel, Messiah/Christ, Jesus, Lord, and Savior. This was their way of anointing Jesus as the most special person to have ever been born. Let's look at some ways the Bible writers highlight the specialness of Jesus.

The Birth/Infancy Narratives

Children are known for speaking their minds. One of my favorite stories about a child speaking his mind goes like this:

Every night a mother placed her son in bed, she read him a bedtime story, and she said a prayer. Then, she left the room with the door slightly ajar allowing a ray of light to go from the hallway into the boy's room.

Every night the boy got up out of bed and pulled the door all the way open. "I need more light," he said to his Mom.

Mom answered, "Okay, just lie back down and go to sleep."

One night, as the child was asleep, the mother pulled the boy's door closed. The boy woke up a few minutes later and started screaming. The mother ran into the room and asked, "What's wrong?"

"You closed the door," the boy said with anger in his voice.

"Yes," said the Mom. "You are old enough to sleep with your door shut."

"But I'm scared," he protested.

In a loving, patient tone the mother replied, "Every night, before you go to sleep, we pray. When we pray, I always ask God to watch over you. Don't you know that God is here in this room watching over you?"

"Where?" asked the boy.

"He's right here in this room with you right now."

The boy said, "Where? I can't see him."

The mother responded, "You can't see him because he's a spirit. Since he is a spirit, he's invisible."

The boy thought for a minute and then said very matter-of-factly, "Mom! I don't need a God who is a spirit. I need a God who's got some skin on him."

And that, in a nutshell, is what the story of the incarnation is all about. The word "incarnation" means "to make flesh" or "the act of being made flesh." When Jesus came into the world, God took on some skin. Through the incarnation we are able to "see" God.

The birth/infancy narratives tell the story of the incarnation. They are more than just nice stories to read at Christmas; they declare that Jesus is something special. Robert H. Stein, in his *Jesus the Messiah*, writes:

> The essence of the Christmas story is not that Mary conceived as a virgin. Nor is the Christmas story a sentimental ode to motherhood. The essence of Christmas is that God's Son came into the world in human form and dwelt among us. It is the "fact" of the incarnation that is the key to Christmas, not the "how" by which this was brought about. It would be presumptuous to claim that the omnipotent God of all creation could not have brought about the incarnation in any other way.[18]

The birth/infancy narratives are found in Matthew 1:18–25 and in Luke 1:26–38, 46–56 and 2:1–38. The two gospel narratives differ in detail and in theme. Matthew was writing to a Jewish audience and wanted to emphasize that Jesus was the Messianic King. Luke was writing to a

Gentile audience and emphasized that Jesus was the Lord of the entire universe. Both spoke of this special child as being King Jesus.

We live with an unfortunate mistake in that according to our calendar Jesus was born before he was born. What? That's right; Jesus was born before he was born. Jesus was born in the days of Herod the Great, and Josephus tells us that Herod died in 4 BC. Therefore, Jesus had to be born before 4 BC. Of course we know that BC stands for "Before Christ." Therefore, Jesus was born before he was born.

Can we date it more accurately? Shepherds were present at his birth. They visited Jesus when he was a baby lying in a manger. The wise men came when he was a young child. Herod was still around when the Magi arrived in search of the Christ child because Herod asked the wise men when the star appeared. Therefore, Jesus was born at least a year or two before the death of Herod in 4 BC. Jesus might have been born in 6 or 7 BC. Therefore, Jesus was born six or seven years before he was born.

How about the day of Jesus' birth? The Greek Orthodox Church celebrates it on the 6th of January. The Western church celebrates it on the 25th of December. In pagan religion, the festival of the sun god was on the 25th of December. It is likely that Jesus was born in the spring of the year when the shepherds had their herds out in the field after the spring rains (perhaps in April). The 25th of December was picked as a way to lure the Christians away from the festival of the sun god.

We don't know exactly when Jesus was born; we don't know the exact day or the exact year, but we do know that there was a day and a year when an extraordinary child was born under extraordinary circumstances and that this child was the answer to ancient prophecy concerning the Messiah. This extraordinary child was King Jesus.

The Angel's Pronouncement: The Birth of Jesus Foretold—Luke 1:26–38

In the sixth month, God sent the angel Gabriel to Nazareth, a town in Galilee, to a virgin pledged to be married to a man named Joseph, a descendant of David. The virgin's name was Mary. The angel went to her and said, "Greetings, you who are highly favored! The Lord is with you."

Mary was greatly troubled at his words and wondered what kind of greeting this might be. But the angel said to her, "Do not be afraid, Mary, you have found favor with God. You will be with child and give birth to a son, and you are to give him the name Jesus. He will be great and will be called the Son of the Most High. The Lord God will give him the throne of his father David, and he will reign over the house of Jacob forever; his kingdom will never end."

"How will this be," Mary asked the angel, "since I am a virgin?"

The angel answered, "The Holy Spirit will come upon you, and the power of the

Most High will overshadow you. So the holy one to be born will be called the Son of God. Even Elizabeth your relative is going to have a child in her old age, and she who was said to be barren is in her sixth month. For nothing is impossible with God."

"I am the Lord's servant," Mary answered. "May it be to me as you have said." Then the angel left her.

Let's focus on the message delivered by the angel to Mary. Remember, an angel is a messenger—that is the meaning of the word "angel" (ἄγγελος/*angelos* in the Greek). The angel delivered God's message to Mary declaring in 1:37, "For nothing is impossible with God."

God is the God of possibility. If God can bend the laws of nature and cause a virgin birth, then he can do anything. Even Mary struggled with the idea of a virgin birth. She questioned the plausibility of the angel's pronouncement. The angel answered her question by letting Mary know that her relative Elizabeth was now with child, even though it was common knowledge that Elizabeth was barren. Then the angel declared, "Nothing is impossible with God."

You see, God is the God of possibility. Isn't it great to know that? We live in a world filled with negativity, uncertainty, skepticism, anxiety, doubt, mistrust, and worry—worry—worry. It seems that everything around us is unstable. From the hope for a better future for our kids to the security of our nation, it all seems to be tenuous and fragile. If we give in to fear, then we go to bed every night with nightmares and wake up every day with anxiety.

But our God is a God of hope, a God of possibility. Therefore, we should have hope in our lives. Of course, we might have to redefine some things. Success has often been measured by the size of your bank account, the type of car you drive, the square footage of your house, or the label inside the clothes you wear. Security has been measured by the size of your retirement account, the location of your winter home, and the realization that you have enough money stashed away to travel, golf, and eat at nice restaurants.

Perhaps the God of possibility is telling us that we should redefine success and security. Perhaps success should be defined by how happy you are in life, how many true friends you have, and how close you are to your spouse and your children. Perhaps security should be defined by how much you give back to others, how you benefit the lives of others, and how ready you are for eternity.

Through the birth of Jesus, the God of possibility is asking us to redefine what is really important to us in life.

The God of possibility is also telling us that it is okay to dream. We should let go of our negativity, our cynicism, and our fear of failure. He is saying to us, "Consider that with God, what seems impossible is possible."

In Matthew 17:20b Jesus says to his disciples, "I tell you the truth, if you have faith as small as a mustard seed, you can say to this mountain, 'Move from here to there' and it will move. Nothing will be impossible for you." The God of possibility wants us to be people who see that great things are possible.

Can God change your life? Of course he can. Can God change your character? Absolutely. Can God change your marriage? He can. Can God help you overcome sin in your life? He can help you overcome any addiction. God can help you succeed in life. See the possibilities with God.

But sometimes we fail to see the possibilities. We live our lives blinded by doubt and fear. Do you know how elephant trainers train elephants to keep them in captivity? Here is how one minister tells the story:

> In taming wild elephants in India, the natives first fasten them to large trees with huge chains. Then, these great beasts just out of the jungle pull and struggle and thrash about until exhausted. After this struggle with the chain has continued for a few days, however, the elephants give up. Then the trainers substitute ropes made of hemp for the chains, because they are more pliable and usable. These ropes of hemp are really merely ropes of straw and it is within the power of the elephant to snap them without undue effort. However, the elephant does not know. Because he does not believe that he can break away he goes the rest of his life bound by relatively weak ropes, the breaking of which is completely within his power. I am convinced that there are millions of people who could accomplish great things, if they only believed that they could. They are bound by ropes of doubt, which could be broken if only they had faith to break them.[19]

Don't let the chains of doubt keep you captive. God wants you to dream big dreams. The birth of Jesus announced that God is the God of possibility. Throw off the chains of doubt, worry, pessimism, cynicism, and negativity.

One verse that helps me see the possibilities is from Paul. He wrote in Philippians 4:13, "I can do everything through him who gives me strength." Paul focused on the possibilities.

Dream. Dream big. Dream about what type of person you want to become. Dream about what you want your legacy to be. Consider how you will give back to others. Dream of what you can be with God. And as you dream, think of that pronouncement made by an angel to Mary some 2,000 years ago: "For nothing is impossible with God."

The Pronouncement, Continued—Matthew 1:18–25

This is how the birth of Jesus Christ came about: His mother Mary was pledged to be married to Joseph, but before they came together, she was found to be with child through the Holy Spirit. Because Joseph her husband was a righteous man and did not want to expose her to public disgrace, he had in mind to divorce her quietly.

But after he had considered this, an angel of the Lord appeared to him in a dream and said, "Joseph son of David, do not be afraid to take Mary home as your wife, because what is conceived in her is from the Holy Spirit. She will give birth to a son, and you are to give him the name Jesus, because he will save his people from their sins."

All this took place to fulfill what the Lord had said through the prophet: "The virgin will be with child and will give birth to a son, and they will call him Immanuel"— which means "God with us."

When Joseph woke up, he did what the angel of the Lord had commanded him and took Mary home as his wife. But he had no union with her until she gave birth to a son. And he gave him the name Jesus.

Surprise![20] The Holy Spirit surprises Mary by placing the Savior in her womb. The angel surprises Joseph with the announcement that Mary is pregnant. Surprise! Surprise! Surprise!

Jesus the Messiah surprised people before he was born, during his life and ministry he surprised people, and he is still surprising people today. When you come to Jesus, expect surprises. He is unpredictable and cannot be put in a box. He will never become a cliché. He cannot be domesticated. Jesus always enters life in unexpected and surprising ways.

One such surprise came in the name given to Jesus through the prophets, the name Immanuel. Matthew records, "They will call him *Immanuel*—which means 'God with us.'" *The Renovaré Spiritual Formation Bible* makes this note concerning the name Immanuel:

> The Bible is all about human life "with God" and how God has made this "with-God" life possible and will bring it to pass. The name Immanuel, meaning "God is with us, " is the title given to the one and only Redeemer, because it refers to God's everlasting intent for human life—namely, that we should be in every aspect a dwelling place of God.[21]

The story of the Bible is the story of God revealing himself to humanity so that his people could experience the "with-God" life. How far would God go to provide us this "with-God" life? He went so far as to send Jesus into the world as Immanuel, "God with us." Surprise!

The ultimate "with-God" event in the Bible is the incarnation of Jesus. The name Immanuel reminds us that God will be "with us" personally through Jesus. Has this reality, the reality that God took on skin to be "with us" in the flesh, changed your life? How? Are you living the "with-God" life right now?

The Birth of Jesus the Messiah—Luke 2:1–7

In those days Caesar Augustus issued a decree that a census should be taken of the entire Roman world. (This was the first census that took place while Quirinius was governor of Syria.) And everyone went to his own town to register.

So Joseph also went up from the town of Nazareth in Galilee to Judea, to Bethlehem the town of David, because he belonged to the house and line of David. He went there to register with Mary, who was pledged to be married to him and was expecting a child. While they were there, the time came for the baby to be born, and she gave birth to her firstborn, a son. She wrapped him in cloths and placed him in a manger, because there was no room for them in the inn.

Mary the mother of Jesus learned in a firsthand way the desire of God to be with us. *The Renovaré Spiritual Formation Bible* makes note of Mary's unique perspective on Jesus as Immanuel:

Surely no one experienced Immanuel, "God with us," as did Mary, Jesus' mother. She who watched the Son of God expand her belly and shift his form inside her; who cradled in her arms a newly born, yet infinite, suckling babe; who taught a boy to walk and talk while sitting before him, her Teacher; who let go her grown offspring to see him embrace and die for a much larger family—this Mary lived as mama to God-made-flesh, while bowing in her heart to the King of kings and Lord of lords.[22]

Mary's willingness to bear Jesus in her womb is a great example of the spiritual discipline of submission. As Mary carried Jesus around in her physical body, all of us, as disciples, are to carry Jesus with us spiritually. What lessons can you learn from Mary about submission? What are the greatest challenges that you face when it comes to submission in your own life?

The Announcement: The Shepherds and Angels—Luke 2:8–20

And there were shepherds living out in the fields nearby, keeping watch over their flocks at night. An angel of the Lord appeared to them, and the glory of the Lord shone around them, and they were terrified. But the angel said to them, "Do not be afraid. I bring you good news of great joy that will be for all the people. Today in the town of David a Savior has been born to you; he is Christ the Lord. This will be a sign to you: You will find a baby wrapped in cloths and lying in a manger."

Suddenly a great company of the heavenly host appeared with the angel, praising God and saying,

"Glory to God in the highest,
and on earth peace to men on whom his favor rests."

When the angels had left them and gone into heaven, the shepherds said to one another, "Let's go to Bethlehem and see this thing that has happened, which the Lord has told us about."

So they hurried off and found Mary and Joseph, and the baby, who was lying in the manger. When they had seen him, they spread the word concerning what had been told them about this child, and all who heard it were amazed at what the shepherds said to them. But Mary treasured up all these things and pondered them in her heart. The shepherds returned, glorifying and praising God for all the things they had heard and seen, which were just as they had been told.

Let's consider the announcement to the shepherds and then take a quick look at the shepherds' response. The angel says to the shepherds, "Do not be afraid. I bring you good news of great joy that will be for all the people. Today in the town of David a Savior has been born to you; he is Christ the Lord."

First, who were these shepherds? For the most part, they represented the poor and the outcasts of their society. They were not the landed gentry or the religious hierarchy. They were not the political establishment. In a sense, they were just a bunch of nobodies. In another sense, they represented everyone who was in need of salvation. Robert H. Stein notes:

Shepherds were generally considered dishonest (b. Sanhedrin 25b). They were unclean according to the law. Their presence at the birth of Jesus was recorded by Luke to show his readers that the good news of the gospel is for the poor, for sinners, for outcasts, for people like these shepherds.[23]

I like Stein's comment. I would tack onto the end of it, "and the good news of the gospel is for people like you and me." God could have sent the angel to anyone: to Caesar in Rome, to Herod the Great in Caesarea by the Sea, to the High Priest in Jerusalem, or to the mayor of Bethlehem (if Bethlehem had a mayor). Instead, God sent the angel to lowly shepherds watching over their sheep in the fields outside of Bethlehem.

Second, what does the angel say to the shepherds? The angel says, "Do not be afraid." The first reaction of the shepherds to seeing the angel is terror. That's a natural reaction. It's night. The sheep are asleep. Then out pops an angel. If I had been one of those shepherds, I'd have been the first to run for the hills. The angel probably wouldn't have gotten to "Do not be afraid" before I was already gone. I'd have thrown my shepherd's staff at the angel and hightailed it out of there. I'd have found a new profession, something that didn't include being out in a field at night.

Fear is an emotion, so it hits us at times without warning. But God doesn't want us to be afraid. He especially doesn't want us to be frozen by fear.

The angel told the shepherds, "Do not be afraid." This pronouncement was made over and over in the Bible. Just earlier in Luke, the angel Gabriel told Mary, "Do not be afraid" (Luke 1:30). After the crucifixion of Jesus, several women went to visit the tomb of Jesus. An angel greeted them at the tomb and said, "Do not be afraid" (Matthew 28:5). Throughout his ministry, Jesus taught people not to fear. He tells his disciples not to fear men (Matthew 10:26). Before his crucifixion, Jesus tells the twelve, "Peace I leave with you; my peace I give you. I do not give to you as the world gives. Do not let your hearts be troubled and do not be afraid" (John 14:27). This was God's consistent message: "Do not be afraid."

God wants us to live confident lives. He wants us to be brave and courageous. If we trust in him, then he will equip us to be able to handle our fears and insecurities.

Also, the angel presented the gospel of great joy to the shepherds. God wants us to be joyful and happy. He gives us good news of great joy.

In John 15:10–11 Jesus says, "If you obey my commands, you will remain in my love, just as I have obeyed my Father's commands and remain in his love. I have told you this so that my joy may be in you and that your joy may be complete." Jesus wants us to experience complete joy in our lives. Not a fleeting, transient joy, which is here one moment and gone the next; but a lasting, unwavering joy that transcends the circumstances of life.

This doesn't mean that we will never be sad. Speaking of his death, Jesus said to his disciples, "So with you: Now is your time of grief, but I will see you again and you will rejoice, and no one will take away your joy" (John 16:22). There is a time to grieve. There is a time to be sad, but sadness need not permeate our lives. In Jesus, there is joy, a complete joy.

Joy comes from the knowledge of who Jesus is. The angel announces that Jesus is Savior, Christ/Messiah, and Lord. These are three big titles for one little baby in a manger.

> *Savior* means he came to save humanity.
> *Christ/Messiah* means he is the anointed one of God who came to fulfill all the prophecies of the Old Covenant.
> *Lord* means he is our master, our ruler, who can direct our lives and give us true joy and fulfillment in life.

Joy comes from knowing Jesus as Savior, Christ/Messiah, and Lord. This babe in a manger is King Jesus.

Third, what was the response of the shepherds? They responded in a couple of ways. They responded by going into Bethlehem to see the baby. The way I read the passage, the shepherds weren't actually commanded to find the baby. The angel suggested, "This will be a sign to you: You will find a baby wrapped in cloths and lying in a manger."

The shepherds discussed their next move. The text reads, "The shepherds said to one another, 'Let's go to Bethlehem and see this thing that has happened, which the Lord has told us about.'"

This took some effort on their part. It was night and they must have been tired. Instead of going into Bethlehem, they could have just gone to sleep. The fields around Bethlehem were hilly and full of stones. They could have said that the trip was too difficult at night. They could have procrastinated until morning. But once you procrastinate, it's easy to just say, "Oh, it's too late; the moment has passed."

They also had to think about transporting the sheep into Bethlehem. Wherever the shepherd goes, the sheep follow. They couldn't just leave the sheep out in the field unprotected.

How would the townsfolk react to a flock of sheep coming through town at night? How would the sheep react to being moved in the middle of the night? Angry sheep are not cute. The shepherds had multiple reasons not to go into Bethlehem, but they went to see what the angel had revealed to them.

They made the effort to see Jesus. Are you willing to make the effort to see him? When you have a question about Jesus, do you investigate the question or just let it drop? Do you take the time to read the Gospel accounts so that you can have firsthand knowledge of him?

It's good to go the extra mile. That's what the shepherds did. As far as we know, outside of Joseph and Mary, these shepherds were the first to see the baby Jesus. They could cling to that memory for the rest of their lives, but they only had that memory because they went the extra mile.

What extra effort do you need to make right now to find Jesus? Once you find him, everything changes.

Also, look at the response of the shepherds after they found Jesus. Verses 17 and 18 read, "When they had seen him, they spread the word concerning what had been told them about this child, and all who heard it were amazed at what the shepherds said to them." The angel did not command the shepherds to spread the word about what they had heard; the shepherds felt compelled to talk about what they had seen and heard. Why? Because when you learn something extraordinary (like the fact that a Savior, Messiah, and Lord had been born), you have to talk about it. There is no way to hold it in.

I don't know what they said. They might have sheepishly (pardon the pun) said, "You aren't going to believe what we've just seen." Or they might have shouted with conviction, "An angel told us about a baby who is our Savior, our Christ/Messiah, and our Lord." Whatever they said, they began to talk. Because if you saw what they saw and heard what they heard, wouldn't you have to talk about it as well? And I think that's the point. We *have* seen and heard what they saw and heard. Are we talking it up the way they talked it up?

A third response of the shepherds is found in verse 20, which reads, "The shepherds returned, glorifying and praising God for all the things they had heard and seen, which were just as they had been told." Simply put, when you hear and see the things the shepherds heard and saw, you can't help but praise God.

In conclusion, on a cloudless night in the fields outside of Bethlehem some 2,000+ years ago, shepherds saw and heard an angel announce the birth of a Savior, a Christ/Messiah, and a Lord. They went to see exactly what the angel revealed to them. After they saw Jesus, they went around telling everyone what they had seen and heard. When people heard their story, they were amazed. And today, 2,000 years later, people are still amazed to hear that a Savior, a Christ/Messiah, and a Lord has been born.

A Christmas Joke with a Moral

About three weeks prior to Christmas, two young boys were spending the night at their grandparents' house. At bedtime, the two boys knelt beside their beds to say their prayers. The younger boy noticed that his grandmother was standing just outside the bedroom door listening to them pray. When it was his turn to pray, he started praying at the top of his lungs. "I PRAY FOR A NEW BICYCLE...I PRAY FOR A NEW PLAYSTATION... I PRAY FOR A NEW FLAT SCREEN HIGH DEFINITION TELEVISION...I PRAY FOR A NEW IPOD..."

The older brother leaned over and nudged his younger brother and said, "Why are you shouting your prayers? God isn't hard of hearing." The little brother replied, "No, but Grandma is!"

MORAL: If you are praying to God, you can whisper. If you are praying to Grandma, yell.

The Presentation at the Temple, the Magi's Visit, the Flight to Egypt, and the Return to Nazareth—Luke 2:21–38, Matthew 2:1–23

If you follow a harmony of the Gospels, the next section moves between material in Luke to Matthew and back to Luke. First comes the circumcision of Jesus on the eighth day and then the presentation of the child at the temple during the purification ceremony of Mary (Luke 2:21–38). At the temple, two aged people noticed that there was something special about this child. Simeon's insight of the child came through guidance of the Holy Spirit. Anna's insight came through prayer and fasting. After seeing Jesus, both praised and worshipped God for allowing them to live to see the promise of salvation for all humanity, which would become a reality in Jesus.

Now we turn to material exclusive to Matthew's Gospel—the visit of the Magi, Herod's massacre of the infants, and the flight of the holy family to Egypt (Matthew 2:1–23). The Magi were wise men or astrologers from the East, who traveled to Bethlehem to worship, or pay homage, to Jesus. The word "homage" means "to pay respect to someone who is greater than you are, like a vassal paying respect to a lord." When we worship God, we show him that we respect his greatness. The Magi bowed before the child Jesus to demonstrate their respect. Bowing before God demonstrates respect for his majesty, and it serves as a reminder to remain humble before him. The Magi offered gifts to Jesus as a sign of worship, gifts that were expensive and highly symbolic: gold for kingship, frankincense for priesthood, and myrrh for his atoning death. Worship can include physical gifts like our tithes or it can include the gift of living a sacrificial life before the Lord.

In the Bible, God provided guidance through many different avenues. One avenue of guidance was through dreams. In this section, the Magi are warned in a dream not to return to Herod. Joseph, the earthly father of Jesus, receives instructions through dreams on three occasions in this passage. The first dream warned Joseph to leave Judea and take his family to Egypt in order to flee from Herod. The second dream instructed Joseph that Herod was now dead and thus it was safe to return to Judea. The third dream warned Joseph that he should not settle in Judea, so Joseph returned to Nazareth.

Jesus: The Early Years

The Growth of the Child Named Jesus—Luke 2:39–40

When Joseph and Mary had done everything required by the Law of the Lord, they returned to Galilee to their own town of Nazareth. And the child grew and became strong; he was filled with wisdom, and the grace of God was upon him.

Jesus at Twelve—Luke 2:41–51

Every year his parents went to Jerusalem for the Feast of the Passover. When he was twelve years old, they went up to the Feast, according to the custom. After the Feast was over, while his parents were returning home, the boy Jesus stayed behind in Jerusalem, but they were unaware of it. Thinking he was in their company, they traveled on for a day. Then they began looking for him among their relatives and friends. When they did not find him, they went back to Jerusalem to look for him. After three days they found him in the temple courts, sitting among the teachers, listening to them and asking them questions. Everyone who heard him was amazed at his understanding and his answers. When his parents saw him, they were astonished. His mother said to him, "Son, why have you treated us like this? Your father and I have been anxiously searching for you."

"Why were you searching for me?" he asked. "Didn't you know I had to be in my Father's house?" But they did not understand what he was saying to them.

Then he went down to Nazareth with them and was obedient to them. But his mother treasured all these things in her heart.

Luke is the only writer to include this story in his Gospel. No other story of Jesus as a young boy is found in the Gospels: These are missing years in his biography. Apocryphal stories do exist. There is a story of Jesus making sparrows out of clay and then causing them to fly away. There is also a story of Jesus killing a boy and then bringing him back to life. But these stories aren't found in the Gospels and they carry no historical weight.

What do we know of Jesus' childhood? We know that he grew up in Nazareth, a small village of only around 100 people. Only a dozen or so families lived there. Some scholars believe the word "Nazareth" is built on the Hebrew *netzer*, meaning "the sprig of a tree branch." They speculate that the people of the village were anticipating the arrival of the Messiah (the sprig from the branch of David) in Nazareth. If so, this was a town that was looking for the Messiah. But when the Messiah grows up in the midst of this village, the villagers miss him. They overlook Jesus. This foreshadows how throughout the Gospels the Jews will miss the fact that Jesus is King Jesus.

Nazareth was about a one-hour walk from Sepphoris, a Roman town in the area. It is easy to imagine Joseph taking young Jesus to Sepphoris on jobs when Jesus was a teenager. The word for carpenter can mean woodworker or stonemason. Based on the terrain around Nazareth, it is easier to believe that Joseph worked with stone rather than with wood. The land had abundant supplies of stone, but trees were scarce. Either medium provided Joseph great opportunities to teach Jesus lessons on life. Trips to Sepphoris would have given Jesus the opportunity to see the antipathy between the Jews and the Romans. Many of Jesus' future parables could have sprung from his time working with Joseph in Sepphoris.

Jesus' family made the yearly trip from Nazareth to Jerusalem for the Passover feast, a journey that took about a week's time. On the way back one year, Mary and Joseph lost track of Jesus. They thought he was with the rest of their family. Mary and Joseph have been criticized over the years for losing Jesus in Jerusalem, but it isn't hard to imagine them entrusting their twelve-year-old son to the care of other family members. In extended families, it would have been natural for relatives to look out for each other's children on this type of journey. Joseph asks Aunt Sara, "Isn't Jesus with you?" Aunt Sara says, "I thought he was with his cousins Samuel and Eli." Everyone begins to look for Jesus, but no one can find him. So Joseph and Mary return to Jerusalem.

They find Jesus at the temple sitting among the teachers asking and answering questions. These teachers were amazed at his knowledge. There doesn't have to be a supernatural element here. Jesus could have been a good student of the Word even at the age of twelve. We know through his ministry that Jesus had a thorough knowledge of the Hebrew Bible. For Jesus, it was natural to be in God's house talking about Scripture. His mother and Joseph didn't understand this. However, Mary treasured these thoughts in her heart.

The Continued Growth of Jesus—Luke 2:52

And Jesus grew in wisdom and stature, and in favor with God and men.

Jesus grew. Growth is a part of life. If a child grows, then his or her parents are happy. If the child doesn't grow, then the parents begin to worry. They might ask, "Is the child sick? Is he or she getting the proper nutrition? Are we doing something wrong?"

When my youngest brother Doug was a few months old, he stopped growing. He wasn't putting on any weight because he couldn't keep his food down. My mother took him to the doctor, and the doctor discovered a blockage that kept food from reaching his stomach. They operated on my brother and removed the blockage, and after that, he started growing. How did my mother notice that something was wrong? She couldn't see inside Doug's body to detect the blockage. She noticed he wasn't growing, so she induced that something was wrong.

Growth is a part of life. We want to better ourselves. We want to be able to look back at the end of a year and say, "These are areas where I've grown and improved this past year." That is an important key to growing. You have to be able to honestly evaluate whether you are changing, staying the same, or going backward.

In his Gospel, Luke notes four areas of growth for Jesus: (1) wisdom, (2) stature, (3) in favor with God, and (4) in favor with men.

In Stephen Covey's excellent book, *The 8th Habit: From Effectiveness to Greatness*, Mr. Covey mentions four areas of growth for every person: intellectual growth, physical growth, spiritual growth, and social/emotional growth.[24] Mr. Covey doesn't connect these four areas with the areas in which Jesus is noted to have grown as a child in Luke 2:40, but they do match up quite nicely. Take a look:

Wisdom = Intellectual Intelligence (IQ, Intellectual Quotient)
Stature = Physical Intelligence (PQ, Physical Quotient)
Favor with God = Spiritual Intelligence (SQ, Spiritual Quotient)
Favor with Men = Social/Emotional Intelligence (EQ, Emotional Quotient)

God is fully committed to our growth into solid, mature disciples of Jesus, but too often, we are haphazard about our own spiritual growth. It is hit or miss; we don't have a plan. We need to develop an individual plan for spiritual growth, and then we need to work the plan.

1. Wisdom, Intellectual Growth, IQ: "And Jesus grew in wisdom."

Intellectual growth is often associated with education, but true intellectual growth is more integrated with experience and life lessons than just hitting the books in schools.

Did Jesus go to school? If so, at what age did he begin school and when did he graduate? What subjects did he study? We simply do not have concrete answers to these questions. Scholarship is divided on how to answer them. Some scholars write that a village like Nazareth would have provided its children a structured school environment built around the synagogue. Other scholars believe these conjectured synagogue schools would have only provided education for the boys and not the girls. Unfortunately, the remains of a first-century synagogue have never been located in Nazareth, and scholars have only been able to locate four first-century synagogues in all of Galilee (in 2009, the fourth was discovered in Migdal).

Other scholars posit that the small villages of rural Galilee provided no formal education for their children. Most of the residents of Nazareth would never have learned how to read or write. But from my studies, it seems clear that children would have been taught how to read and write in their local villages.

We do know that Jesus knew how to read. He read from the Isaiah scroll. He memorized Scripture and had a vast knowledge of the Hebrew Bible. He knew enough about the Hebrew Bible at twelve to amaze temple scholars with his knowledge. At one point in his ministry, he knelt to write something in the dirt. Jesus must have learned to read and write as a boy. He seems to have been conversant in three languages: Greek, Hebrew, and Aramaic. As a rabbi, Jesus was expected to know the teachings of other learned rabbis. Most of this type of training was done through memorization, as written copies of rabbinic writings were sparse. Jesus had a great knowledge of both rabbinic and biblical sources, and he quoted from them in his ministry.

But the wisdom of Jesus wasn't just confined to scrolls and rabbinic traditions. Jesus studied life around him. Many of these life lessons can be found in his teachings, in both his one-line aphorisms and in his parables. Jesus made many references to nature: "Consider the lilies of the field," "the kingdom of heaven is like a mustard seed," and "four months more and then the harvest." Jesus used his knowledge of carpentry and construction in his teaching—for example, the parable of the wise and foolish builders. Jesus had a working knowledge of agriculture, referencing in his teaching the sowing of seed, the reaping of crops, and the time of the harvest season.

Jesus knew how the world around him worked. He understood taxation. He understood the military occupation of a country. He understood how the sacrificial system of the temple worked and how corrupt priests took advantage of the poor in that system. Where did Jesus learn these lessons? He paid attention to life around him. He learned from life's experiences.

How can we grow in wisdom? For most of us, we are afforded two avenues of education in today's world: academics in school and experience in life. Both are beneficial, and a well-rounded person walks down both avenues learning lessons along the way.

What are you doing to grow in wisdom? Are you quick to learn the lessons that life is teaching you? Are you able to integrate these lessons into your life choices? Are you a reader? Do you supplement your education through reading great books that stimulate the mind and sharpen your skills? Find time to focus on growing in wisdom.

2. Stature, Physical Growth, PQ: "...and stature."

Jesus grew physically. The Bible doesn't specifically mention Jesus' physical strength, but we can infer from different passages that Jesus was physically fit. For example, plying the carpenter's trade must have facilitated his physical growth. On several occasions, Jesus walked from Galilee to Jerusalem, a five-day journey by foot. He expelled ruffians from the temple court with only a whip. He endured the agony of a Roman scourging (the forty lashes minus one). This was a punishment that often killed men. After being beaten almost to death by the Romans, Jesus carried his own cross through the hilly, stony streets of Jerusalem. The picture we get from reading the Gospels is of a Jesus who was physically fit.

We should ask ourselves how we are doing in our physical growth. Are we taking care of our physical bodies? Our bodies are a gift from God. Paul refers to our bodies as the temple of God and the house of God's Spirit, writing, "Do you not know that your body is a temple of the Holy Spirit, who is in you, whom you have received from God? You are not your own; you were bought at a price. Therefore honor God with your body." (1 Corinthians 6:19–20). Since we are the sacred temple of God, we need to take care of ourselves. We need proper sleep, nutrition, and exercise.

What are your goals in the area of physical growth? What do you need to change to take better care of your physical body? Do you have goals to improve your nutrition? What are your exercise goals?

We are busy people, but we need to find time to focus on physical fitness. When we take care of our physical bodies, we are able to accomplish more for God.

3. Favor with God, Spiritual Growth, SQ: "...and in favor with God."

We live in a secular society that places very little value on spiritual growth. Therefore, when human growth and development are discussed, spiritual growth rarely enters into the discussion. But it should be a vital part of the discussion. We are spiritual creatures, and whether we want to admit it or not, all of us have a soul. This distinguishes us from the animal kingdom. Since we are spiritual beings, we need to nourish our spiritual natures.

Jesus nourished his spiritual nature: He grew in favor with God. He spent time focused on being close and staying close to God. He knew the Hebrew Scriptures and memorized Scripture. He took part in the Jewish feasts and holy days and honored God by making pilgrimages to the temple in Jerusalem. At times, he escaped from ministering to the crowds in order to have personal, dedicated time in order to draw close to God.

Jesus was a man of prayer. He slipped away from the disciples in order to be alone in prayer. He taught his disciples how to pray. He prayed before he made big decisions. He valued his time with the Father, waking up early in the morning, before sunrise, to be alone with his Father. This is who Jesus was.

Our spiritual growth deserves our attention. We need to stay in the Word and in prayer in order to grow spiritually. We need to take time to be alone with God.

Many of us received spiritual training when we were young disciples. We had people in our lives studying the Bible with us, praying with us, and asking us about our struggles. They gave us guidance and advice. My question is: What type of spiritual training are you getting right now?

How are you doing in this area of growth? What are your personal goals for spiritual growth? Let's make sure that we give attention to this vital part of our growth as disciples.

4. Favor with Man, Social/Emotional, EQ: "...and [in favor with] men."

Jesus was a social person who enjoyed the company of people. He conversed with strangers and enjoyed meals with people. He knew when to laugh and when to cry. He celebrated the joy of wedding feasts and grieved with loved ones at funerals. He had a circle of friends that walked with him throughout his ministry. Within that circle, there was an even closer group of friends with whom Jesus shared his more intimate moments.

Jesus could talk to the power brokers, the landed gentry, and the authority figures as easily as he could relate to the poor, the slaves, and the disenfranchised of society. He was relatable. He knew the social mores of his society (though he often disregarded these boundaries when they stood in the way of helping people).

Recent studies have shown the importance of social/emotional development in a person's ability to succeed in life. In Daniel Goleman's research, he has concluded that emotional intelligence (EQ) is just as important as intellectual intelligence (IQ) for becoming a successful person.[25] In fact, Harvard's Howard Gardner notes that IQ alone only predicts about six to ten percent of success in a career.[26] The rest of career success comes from other elements like hard work, fortunate circumstances, and social networking.

How are you doing in the area of social/emotional growth? Do you make time to be with people? Who are your closest friends? Do share your thoughts and feelings with these friends? Let's make sure we are growing emotionally and socially.

Summary

Notice how Jesus grew. Do you have a plan for growth in each of these areas? An oft-quoted leadership maxim goes, "To know and not to do is not to know." If you know that you should grow in these areas, you need to do something about it. For example, to grow in wisdom (IQ), go back to school for more education or get more on-the-job education, read books, and learn the lessons that life is teaching you. To grow in stature (PQ), exercise, join a gym, or train for a race. To grow in social/emotional intelligence (EQ), develop close friendships, get professional counseling, or read some books on social/emotional growth. To grow in spirit (SQ), read the Bible, get involved in church, or join a Bible study group.

The pathway to growth will be different for everyone. Find your pathway and walk it until you grow. Take time to evaluate how you are doing with your own growth in the areas mentioned above. Our ultimate goal as disciples of Jesus is to become more like him. If Jesus grew in wisdom, stature, and in favor in with God and men, then we should be growing in those areas as well.

End Notes

17. Text by Edward Perronet; alt. by John Rippon. Music by Oliver Holden. 1780. In the public domain.

18. Robert H. Stein, *Jesus the Messiah: A Survey of the Life of Christ* (Downers Grove, IL: InterVarsity, 1996), 79.

19. "Possibilities of Change," a sermon delivered by Batsell Barrett Baxter on January 1, 1967 at the Hillsboro Church of Christ, Nashville, Tennessee, and heard over radio station WLAC at 8:05 PM. Found on the Internet at www.stillvoices.org/sermons/baxter/010167.pdf.

20. Some authors use the exclamation point almost as much as they use the period. Not me. I learned early on that the overuse of the exclamation point devalues it. Therefore, I only use it when I intend for it to mean something great is happening. Like here. Surprise!

21. *The Renovaré Spiritual Formation Bible* (San Francisco: Harper San Francisco, 2005), 2292.

22. Ibid., 1885.

23. Stein, 75.

24. You can find a nice discussion of each of the areas of intelligence in Stephen R. Covey's wonderful book, *The 8th Habit: From Effectiveness to Greatness* (New York: Free Press, 2004).

25. Daniel Goleman, *Emotional Intelligence* (New York: Bantam Books, 2005).

26. See www.danielgoleman.info/blog/.

The Preparation of Jesus
for Public Ministry

At thirty, God prepared Jesus to begin his public ministry. This preparation came through three major events in the life of Jesus: the ministry of John the Immerser, Jesus' baptism, and Jesus' temptation.

John the Immerser—Matt. 3:1–12, Mark 1:1–8, Luke 3:1–18

For most Jews, the time preceding the appearance of John the Baptist was marked by the absence of God's prophets and his Spirit. Now once again a prophet was present in Israel. And he spoke of the coming Spirit. In light of all this it is not surprising that his appearance created great excitement. Was this man the returning Elijah? Was God visiting his people? Was the messianic age about to begin? Were those present living in the 'last days'?[27]

—Robert H. Stein, New Testament Scholar

God prepared the way for Jesus through the birth of John the Baptist. Enter Zechariah and Elizabeth, John's dad and mom. Zechariah means "Yahweh remembers." Elizabeth means "the covenant of God." Twice a day, Zechariah went into the Holy Place to put incense on the altar of incense, which represented the worship of the people to Yahweh. The priest would have this opportunity only once in his life; therefore, it was seen as a great honor. While performing this duty Zechariah received word from an angel that his wife would have a son, and they must name him John, meaning, "the grace of God."

Zechariah was told that John would serve as a Nazarite prophet who would prepare people for the Messiah. Zechariah asked for a confirming sign. The angel Gabriel told Zechariah that he would be unable to speak until John's birth.

After 400 years of silence, the voice of prophecy was heard once again through the ministry of John the Immerser. Even though John was the son of a priest and could have become a priest, he chose another course. He lived in the desert and not the city. John dressed differently from the priests, wearing a camelhair garment instead of priestly linen. He ate an organic diet of locusts and wild honey. He didn't go into the cities; he stayed in the Judean wilderness and bade the people to come to him. And they came. They came not to see how he dressed or what he ate, but to hear his message of repentance, a straightforward and direct message. He saw himself as a forerunner of the Christ, one who was sent to prepare the way for the Messiah.

John was a prophet like the great Old Testament prophets. He came preaching the prophetic word. His message sounded the trumpet call that the kingdom of God was at hand. Matthew introduces the ministry of John with these words, "In those days John the Baptist came, preaching in the Desert of Judea and saying, 'Repent, for the kingdom of heaven is near'" (Matthew 3:1–2).

John's message also contained the theme of repentance. His baptism was a baptism of repentance for the forgiveness of sins (Mark 1:2–3). For John, repentance had to be accompanied by deeds (Matthew 3:7–9, Luke 3:7–8). Marcus J. Borg, in his book entitled *Jesus*, writes about John's repentance, noting:

> Repentance had two related meanings in ancient Judaism. It was associated with return from exile; to repent is to return, to follow 'the way of the Lord' that leads from exile to the promised land. The Greek roots of the word suggest an additional meaning; to repent is to 'go beyond the mind that you have'—to go beyond conventional understanding of what life with God is about.[28]

John immersed people for the forgiveness of sins. The Jews practiced immersion as a ceremonial cleansing, but John's immersion was different in quantity and quality. The Jews immersed over and over; John plunged people under the water once and only once. The Jews immersed for ceremonial cleansing; John dunked people so that their sins might be forgiven. Vincent Taylor in his *The Life and Ministry of Jesus* describes John's baptism in these terms:

> John's action in using the rite of baptism is fully in agreement with the importance attached by the Jews to lustrations, but it differed from these in that, like proselyte baptism, it was administered once for all. It was a symbol, and yet more than a symbol, if, like the Old Testament prophets, John believed that symbolic actions were effective. How far he shared these beliefs we do not know, but the positive notes in his preaching show that in his view the essential condition in securing eschatological salvation was a radical and complete change of mind toward God.[29]

John wasn't interested in ritual purification. He wanted a changed heart. He was looking for true repentance. Those who showed true repentance in their lives were candidates for his baptism.

Jesus' Baptism—Matthew 3:13–17, cf. Mark 1:9–11, Luke 3:21–22

Then Jesus came from Galilee to the Jordan to be baptized by John. But John tried to deter him, saying, "I need to be baptized by you, and do you come to me?"

Jesus replied, "Let it be so now; it is proper for us to do this to fulfill all righteousness." Then John consented.

As soon as Jesus was baptized, he went up out of the water. At that moment heaven was opened, and he saw the Spirit of God descending like a dove and lighting on him. And a voice from heaven said, "This is my Son, whom I love; with him I am well pleased."

Why did Jesus go to John for immersion? John wondered the same thing, so he asked Jesus, "I need to be baptized by you, and do you come to me?"

John's baptism was a baptism of repentance for the forgiveness of sins. Jesus didn't need to have his sins forgiven, because he was without sin. Why then did Jesus go to John for immersion? Jesus asked John to baptism him in order "to fulfill all righteousness." A simple way to translate "righteousness" is "to do the right thing." The word is much bigger and has many more nuances than this simple definition, but this definition works in this instance. Jesus was baptized "in order to do the right thing." It was a matter of righteousness for him.

Jesus practiced the spiritual discipline of submission. He didn't need the baptism of John, but he knew that John was God's prophet. Jesus knew that John's movement was God's movement, and he wanted to be identified with John and his movement. Therefore, Jesus practiced submission and as an act of righteousness was immersed by John.

The immersion of Jesus was no ordinary immersion. That's because the person being immersed was no ordinary person. At the baptism of Jesus, God puts his stamp of approval on Jesus and transfers the prophetic mantel from John to Jesus.

The word "Christ," Χριστός/*Christos* in the Greek, means "to anoint." Another way of translating it is Messiah. The Messiah was the long-awaited king. When a king began his reign, he was anointed. For those with eyes of faith, they were able to interpret the baptism of Jesus as the anointing of the King.

Three events occurred that demonstrated that God was anointing Jesus. Matthew describes the first event in this way: "As soon as Jesus was baptized, he went up out of the water. At that moment heaven was opened." The opening of heaven signified that God approved of Jesus. There was no separation between God and Jesus. God opened heaven to demonstrate his approval of Jesus.

Second, Matthew added, "He [John] saw the Spirit of God descending like a dove and lighting on him." This symbolized the anointing of Jesus. Jesus was not anointed with oil by human hand. Heaven opened and the Spirit of God descended like a dove and lighted upon him. There was no anointing oil because the Spirit of God served as the anointing oil. This was an anointing unlike any other, the anointing of God's Messiah, the King.

Third, just to make sure that the events could not be misinterpreted, a voice from heaven declared, "This is my Son, whom I love; with him I am well pleased." Another way of translating this is, "This is my beloved one. I approve of him." God was putting his stamp of approval, and thus his stamp of authority, on Jesus.

Jesus submitted to God in baptism, and God anointed Jesus as his Messiah. This was an important preparatory step for Jesus as he began his ministry. In a sense, it served as his prophetic call. But Jesus was to be a prophet like no other—he was not only a prophet; he was God's son. He was not just a king; he was God's Anointed, the Christ, the Messiah.

Jesus' Temptation—Matthew 4:1–11, cf. Mark 1:12–13, Luke 4:1–13

> Then Jesus was led by the Spirit into the desert to be tempted by the devil. After fasting forty days and forty nights, he was hungry. The tempter came to him and said, "If you are the Son of God, tell these stones to become bread."
>
> Jesus answered, "It is written: 'Man does not live on bread alone, but on every word that comes from the mouth of God.'"
>
> Then the devil took him to the holy city and had him stand on the highest point of the temple. "If you are the Son of God," he said, "throw yourself down. For it is written:
>
> "'He will command his angels concerning you,
>   and they will lift you up in their hands,
> so that you will not strike your foot against a stone.'"
>
> Jesus answered him, "It is also written: 'Do not put the Lord your God to the test.'"
>
> Again, the devil took him to a very high mountain and showed him all the kingdoms of the world and their splendor. "All this I will give you," he said, "If you will bow down and worship me."
>
> Jesus said to him, "Away from me, Satan! For it is written: 'Worship the Lord your God, and serve him only.'"
>
> Then the devil left him, and angels came and attended him.

The baptism of Jesus and the temptation of Jesus are closely connected in the Gospels. From a spiritual perspective, the highs of our spiritual lives are often immediately followed by times of trials, testing, and temptation. This story of Jesus, in which he goes from the ecstasy of his baptismal experience to the agony of the wilderness event, has been played out time and again in the lives of individual disciples. The story sounds an alarm for all new converts to get ready for upcoming battles.

The temptation of Jesus was part of the preparatory work of the Spirit, who prepared Jesus for ministry. The Spirit led Jesus into the wilderness to be tempted by Satan. In the wilderness, Jesus experienced a time of solitude with God. In the Bible, the wilderness often stood as a place where God worked on people's hearts. After the exodus, God purified the hearts of the Hebrews through forty years of wandering in the wilderness. In the first century, people went into the wilderness to listen to John the Baptist. In the wilderness, they met a prophet who demanded fruit of repentance from them.

After being led into the wilderness, Jesus fasted for forty days. Strictly speaking, fasting means to go voluntarily without food for the purpose of centering one's focus on God.

In this story, God tested Jesus while Satan tempted Jesus. To speak properly, we are tested by God and tempted by Satan. Jesus understood things this way. We submit to God's testing and endure Satan's tempting. Sometimes it is difficult to discern between the two, but when, with eyes of faith, we discern that God is testing us, then, like Jesus, we practice submission and obedience to his testing. Through testing, God shapes us into the people he wants us to be. Jesus submitted to God's testing. He followed God's path to glory, the path which for Jesus began in a wilderness and ended on a cross.

There is a difference between being tempted by sin and giving in to sin and thus sinning. We need to understand that difference. Sometimes, we beat ourselves up over being tempted, but we cannot control temptation. We can, with God's help, control giving in to sin. We often have to face temptation, but we do not have to sin. Satan tempted Jesus in the wilderness, but Jesus did not sin. He did not give in to temptation.

In the first temptation Satan said, "If you are the Son of God, tell these stones to become bread." Jesus had fasted for forty days. He must have been terribly hungry. There would have been nothing wrong with him changing stones to bread. The temptation was stated with a conditional clause, "If you are the Son of God." This could also be translated, "Since you are the Son of God." Satan was saying, "You have the power to turn these stones to bread. Use your power for your own comfort. Use your power to ease the pain of your hunger."

But Jesus said, No. The Spirit led Jesus into the wilderness, and Jesus accepted the hunger pain caused by his fast. Now wasn't the time to eat. So he said to Satan, "Man does not live on bread alone, but on every word that proceeds from the mouth of God." In other words, "I have bread that you do not know. I will be sustained by God's word."

Jesus set us an example of how we can resist Satan's temptation—by having the Scriptures on our hearts. Memorization places the word of God in our hearts so that we can keep sin out of our lives.

The second temptation[30] concerned testing God. Satan took Jesus to the pinnacle of the temple and dared him to jump. Satan was saying, "If you jump, God will catch you." Jesus quoted Deuteronomy 6:16. It was a reference to what happened at Massah in Exodus 17. Here the Hebrews tested God by asking, "Why did you bring us up out of Egypt to…die of thirst?" They asked, "Is the Lord among us or not?" They demanded that God perform a miracle for them at their beckoning. God would not do that. Neither would Jesus. His answer to Satan was, "No. I will not test God like the Hebrews did."

In the third temptation, Satan tempted Jesus with, "All the kingdoms of the world…I will give you…if you will bow down and worship me." Jesus again quoted Scripture, "Worship the Lord your God, and serve him only." Jesus was not enticed by the kingdoms of this world. He had a power that Satan couldn't understand. Jesus was already King of a spiritual kingdom. This theme—the kingdom—was a major theme in his ministry. (We will consider this theme in the next section.)

In conclusion, Satan tempted Jesus three times, and each time Jesus answered Satan by quoting a scripture. Jesus was victorious over Satan. In his victory, Jesus set us an example of how to overcome Satan by the use of Scripture. He also validated the anointing he received at his baptism and proved that he was God's Son. *The Preacher's Commentary Series* notes, "The temptation of Christ and His victory authenticates His Person for our faith, assures our freedom in relation to the tempter, and affirms God's acceptance of His atoning work, for He did not die on the Cross for His own sins but for ours."[31]

Luke adds that Satan departed, "until an opportune time" (Luke 4:13). That's how it is with Satan; he is always looking for an opportune time to tempt us. That's why we always need to be on our guard against him.

The Kingdom of God

Before we begin this discussion, I want you to take a moment and list some of the major themes in the teaching and ministry of Jesus of Nazareth. Now take a look at your list. Of all these themes, which is the most prominent theme in Jesus' ministry? I would posit that the most prominent theme in the teaching ministry of Jesus is the theme of the kingdom of God.

Also, let me ask, "Why do we read the Bible?" When we read the Bible, we read on different levels:

1. The Truth Level

We read to learn God's revealed truth. We believe in a transcendent God who breaks into human history to reveal his truth to us. It is our task to discern the deep truths of God's word. 2 Timothy 2:15 reads, "Do your best to present yourself to God as one approved, a workman who does not need to be ashamed and who correctly handles the word of truth." 2 Timothy 3:15 states, "...and how from infancy you have known the holy Scriptures, which are able to make you wise for salvation through faith in Christ Jesus."

2. The Practical Level

A. We read for inspiration so that we might change our lives. The Bible is a practical book that equips us to live godly lives in Christ Jesus. 2 Timothy 3:16 notes: "All Scripture is God-breathed and is useful for teaching, rebuking, correcting and training in righteousness, so that the man of God may be thoroughly equipped for every good work."

B. We read to help others. We believe we need to teach others to obey everything that we have been commanded. Matthew 28:18–20 states:

> *Then Jesus came to them and said, "All authority in heaven and on earth has been given to me. Therefore go and make disciples of all nations, baptizing them in the name of the Father and of the Son and of the Holy Spirit, and teaching them to obey everything I have commanded you. And surely I am with you always, to the very end of the age."*

So in conclusion, we have a twofold challenge:

1. To carefully handle the word of truth, and
2. To make the word practical.

Unfortunately, one can often offset the other. One of these positions can be at odds with the other.

For example, we can teach the Bible on one level hoping to make it practical, relevant, real, and simple; but we should not do this at the price of forfeiting biblical truth. This happens when we teach simplistic formulas. For example:

*   Kingdom = Church = Kingdom
*   Disciple = Christian = Saved

Neither of these formulas is 100 percent accurate. They have been taught in an effort to simplify Scripture and make the Bible relevant. We have to be careful that we don't sacrifice the truth of the Bible for practicality. At the same time, we have to be careful not to sacrifice the practical, relevant nature of the Bible when we teach the deep truths of God's word. Jesus was both truthful and relevant. He was deep and practical. Jesus could baffle religious scholars and inspire uneducated sinners. He is our model here.

Jesus Launches His Ministry—Matthew 4:12–17, cf. Mark 1:14–15, Luke 4:14–15

When Jesus heard that John had been put in prison, he returned to Galilee. Leaving Nazareth, he went and lived in Capernaum, which was by the lake in the area of Zebulun and Naphtali—to fulfill what was said through the prophet Isaiah:

"Land of Zebulun and land of Naphtali,
the way to the sea, along the Jordan,
Galilee of the Gentiles—
the people living in darkness
have seen a great light;
on those living in the land of the shadow of death
a light has dawned."

From that time on Jesus began to preach, "Repent, for the kingdom of heaven is near."

The first proclamation of Jesus to the world had to do with the kingdom of God (Mark 1:14–15; Matthew 4:23, 9:35; Luke 4:14–15). He repeated the message of John the Baptist, "Repent, for the kingdom of heaven is near," and then went from town to village preaching "the good news of the kingdom." The kingdom was the central theme of Jesus' ministry. He spoke of the kingdom on over 100 separate occasions in the Gospels. He uses the word "kingdom" over 125 times. If you had to narrow the entire teaching ministry of Jesus down to one concept, a good choice would be—the kingdom of God.

The message of Jesus after his resurrection was the kingdom of God. Acts 1:3 states, "After his suffering, he showed himself to these men and gave many convincing proofs that he was alive. He appeared to them over a period of forty days and spoke about the kingdom of God." The theme of the kingdom of God serves as bookends for the ministry of Jesus. I say this to say: One of the most important themes (if not the most important theme in the ministry of Jesus) is the kingdom of God.

Jesus used the word "kingdom" in four distinct ways: the kingdom, the kingdom of God, the kingdom of heaven, and the kingdom of the Father. Some might think the phrase "kingdom of heaven" is the same as the heavenly realms, but that's not the case. "Kingdom of heaven" is found only in Matthew's Gospel. Matthew uses the phrase because he was writing to a predominately Jewish audience that was familiar with the phrase. Jews were very careful to use the word "G–d"[32] sparingly so as to make sure they did not use his name in vain. They would find words to substitute for "G–d." Therefore, Matthew substituted kingdom of heaven for kingdom of God, but the terms are used interchangeably.[33]

The word "kingdom" (βασιλεία/*basileia*) means the active/dynamic reign and rule of God. The kingdom of God is a dynamic concept in the Bible. It is not static. Ideas concerning the kingdom change throughout the Scripture. The kingdom of God is like a multifaceted diamond. When you look at the diamond from different angles you see different aspects of its beauty and character.

The kingdom of God is multidimensional. The kingdom of God spans above, beyond, and across our space-time continuum. Every now and then it breaks into where we live. The concept of the kingdom of God cannot be equated to one single idea or a single realm or place. Again, the kingdom of God is a dynamic concept. Dr. John Oakes writes:

> It is difficult to give a simple but accurate definition of the kingdom of God, as described in the Bible. Some would say that the kingdom of God is the church of Jesus Christ on the earth. Others would say that the kingdom of God is heaven. In truth, God's kingdom expresses itself in different ways at different times. In broadest terms, the kingdom of God is anyone or anywhere over which God rules.[34]

To keep it simple, think of God's kingdom as the rule and reign of God.

I like to think of the active/dynamic kingdom of God as presenting itself in the Scripture in five different manifestations. I want to emphasize that I am simplifying the manifestations of the kingdom when I mention only five. You could speak of at least four manifestations of the kingdom in just the Old Testament alone.[35]

Five Manifestations of the Kingdom as Presented in the Bible

I. The Universal/Eternal Kingdom of God
God reigns over the universe for eternity. Every other manifestation of the kingdom of God falls under this giant canopy. Daniel declared in Daniel 4:2–4a:

It is my pleasure to tell you about the miraculous signs and wonders that the Most High God has performed for me.

> *How great are his signs,*
> *how mighty his wonders!*
> *His kingdom is an eternal kingdom;*
> *his dominion endures from generation to generation.*

Psalm 103:19 reads, "The Lord has established his throne in heaven, and his kingdom rules over all."

II. The Covenantal People of God as the Kingdom of God in the Old Testament

As soon as God began the creation process, his kingdom broke into the world because God ruled over the creation of the world. When God spoke, creation happened. As soon as God created humanity, his covenantal kingdom broke into human history. God established a covenant with Adam and Eve, but they soon broke covenant. God established a covenantal rule with the Patriarchs. He transformed this covenant relationship into a covenantal people, the Hebrew people. He transformed this people into the covenantal kingdom of Israel. The kingdom of God in the Old Testament is multifaceted.

In a special sense, God ruled as sovereign King over his covenantal people. They were the special possession of God. He stated his dream for his people in Exodus 19:3–6:

> *Then Moses went up to God, and the LORD called to him from the mountain and said, "This is what you are to say to the house of Jacob and what you are to tell the people of Israel: 'You yourselves have seen what I did to Egypt, and how I carried you on eagles' wings and brought you to myself. Now if you obey me fully and keep my covenant, then out of all nations you will be my treasured possession. Although the whole earth is mine, you will be for me a kingdom of priests and a holy nation.' These are the words you are to speak to the Israelites."*

III. The Kingdom of God in the Person and Work of Jesus Christ

When Jesus began his ministry, the kingdom of God broke into the world through the person and work of Jesus.

In Matthew 12:28 Jesus said, "But if I drive out demons by the Spirit of God, then the kingdom of God has come upon you." The word for "has come" is Ἔφθασεν/*ephthasen*, and it the *aorist* active indicative of φθάνω/*phthanō*, which can be translated as "has come, came, has arrived, or arrived." This reads a little differently in Luke 11:20: "But if I drive out demons by the finger of God, then the kingdom of God has come to you." First, notice the word "then." This is the word, ἄρα/*ara*, which demonstrates a conclusion based on the condition. It can also be translated as "no doubt." Notice the aorist active indicative of the verb φθάνω/ *phthanō* used here as meaning "has come." Another way of translating Luke 11:20 is: "If I by means of the finger of God cast out demons, then let there be no doubt the kingdom of God has arrived upon you." In this passage, the coming of the kingdom is not viewed as a future event. The kingdom came in the person, ministry, and work of Jesus.

IV. The Community of God's People as the Kingdom of God in the Church

The ministry and work of Jesus is carried on through his church after his ascension. The church is his body. Therefore, the person and work of Jesus continue on in the second incarnation of Jesus—his church. The rule and reign of God, which began in the ministry of Jesus, is now manifested through his community, the church. Paul writes in Colossians 1:13–14, "For he has rescued us from the dominion of darkness and brought us into the kingdom of the Son he loves, in whom we have redemption, the forgiveness of sins." We are presently in the kingdom of his Son as manifest in the church. But let's be careful not to say, "The kingdom equals the church." The church is a part of God's kingdom, but the kingdom is larger than the church.

Consider this analogy: Paul writes in 1 Corinthians 10:11, "These things happened to them as examples and were written down as warnings for us, on whom the fulfillment of the ages has come." In other words, these things typologically were happening to them, but were written for our admonition for whom the ends of the ages have already come. Paul uses the perfect tense here: "have come and already are here." The end of the ages has arrived, but we are still waiting for the final manifestation of the end of times to come. In the same way, we are living in the kingdom, but we await another unveiling of God's kingdom to come at the end of time.

V. The Eschatological Kingdom of God at the End of Time

At the end of time (also known as the *parousia* or the second coming of Jesus) God will destroy the world thus ending the manifestations of his kingdom on the earth. All manifestations of his kingdom will be enveloped into the universal/eternal kingdom of God. At the Last Supper Jesus says that he "will not drink again of the fruit of the vine until the kingdom of God comes" (Luke 22:18, Mark 14:25). This seems to be a reference to the kingdom after judgment because Jesus goes on to say, "I assign you, as my Father assigned to me, a kingdom, that you may eat and drink at my table in my kingdom and sit on thrones judging the twelve tribes of Israel" (Luke 22:29–30 ESV). Thus the kingdom of God will have come full circle—from God in heaven down to the earth, and then from earth back to God in heaven as God reigns eternally over the universe. But this isn't entirely accurate, because when the kingdom of God was manifest on earth in various ways, the kingdom of God always existed in heaven with God and the heavenly host. This is the giant canopy that I mentioned earlier that extends beyond the earth and beyond time and in which God is always King over his kingdom.

Manifestations of the Kingdom of God

The Kingdom of God Eternal (God Reigns in the Heavenly Realms)

God Reigns in Covenant	God Reigns Through Jesus	God Reigns Through the Church
Old Testament	The Gospels	Acts–The *Parousia*

The Eschatological Kingdom of God (God Reigns in the Heavenly Realms)

Now here is the kicker—at times, a single scripture can present the kingdom of God in various manifestations. For example, take Joel 2:1–32. If Peter had not used Joel 2:28–32 in his sermon in Acts 2, then we would have no reason to apply this passage to the church. In context, it fits better with either the restoration of the kingdom to Israel or the future eschatological kingdom of God.

Many passages have eschatological language that could be applied to the present kingdom of God or to the future kingdom of God. In these passages, you have to make a choice of how you are going to interpret the use of "kingdom." You have terms like "The Day of the Lord," "the end of days," "the *parousia*," or "on that day," which might directly or indirectly refer to some manifestation of the kingdom of God. The apocalyptical passages in the synoptic Gospels (Matthew 24, Mark 13, and Luke 21) are a good example of this.

Consider the words in Jesus in Luke 21:25–33:

"There will be signs in the sun, moon and stars. On the earth, nations will be in anguish and perplexity at the roaring and tossing of the sea. Men will faint from terror, apprehensive of what is coming on the world, for the heavenly bodies will be shaken. At that time they will see the Son of Man coming in a cloud with power and great glory. When these things begin to take place, stand up and lift up your heads, because your redemption is drawing near."

He told them this parable: "Look at the fig tree and all the trees. When they sprout leaves, you can see for yourselves and know that summer is near. Even so, when you see these things happening, you know that the kingdom of God is near.

"I tell you the truth, this generation will certainly not pass away until all these things have happened. Heaven and earth will pass away, but my words will never pass away."

This passage speaks about the kingdom being near, but we've already seen that the kingdom was manifest in the ministry of Jesus. Therefore, this verse must be speaking of a different manifestation of the kingdom being near. When we read "kingdom" in the text, we have to be careful to ascertain which manifestation of "kingdom" the author means.

In the USA we don't use the word "kingdom" that much. The United States is a republic, not a kingdom. We have elected officials, not a king; but across history, more people have lived in kingdoms than republics. There are huge differences between republics and kingdoms. In republics, generally, the citizens of the nation have an opportunity to draft the rules of their land. In a kingdom, generally, the citizens of the kingdom have little to no say in forming their law. The king is sovereign; he sets the law and enforces it. The citizens are subject to the rules of the king.

The Jews of the first century knew what it meant to live in a kingdom. A millennium before the birth of Jesus, a fledgling Jewish nation asked God for a king. God gave them Saul, David, and Solomon. Then the United Kingdom divided into two kingdoms—Samaria in the North and Judah in the South. In 722 BC the Assyrians marched into Samaria and took the nation captive, thus ending the Northern Kingdom. Judah survived this onslaught only to watch the Babylonians march into Jerusalem and destroy the temple in 586 BC. From that point on, the Babylonians, the Persians, the Greeks, and the Romans ruled consecutively over the Southern Kingdom of Judah as a vassal kingdom.

Therefore, the average Jew living in the first century had firsthand knowledge of what it meant to live in a kingdom. The Jews dreamed of reviving the glory of the Kingdom of Israel in a unified kingdom like in the days of David and Solomon. They longed for a Davidic king, a Messiah, who would rule with a mighty sword, vanquishing the Romans from the land and reestablishing the glory of Jerusalem as the capital of the world. In first-century Judea, this was the popular Jewish expectation of the Messiah.

When people heard Jesus speak of the kingdom of God, they grew excited and wanted to know about this kingdom. They hoped that it would be the answer to their prayers. But Jesus' teaching of God's kingdom was radically different from the expectations of the people. He taught about a spiritual kingdom that offered healing to the sick, sight for the blind, hearing to the deaf, and salvation to the lost.

The words "kingdom of God" never appear in the Old Testament. The idea existed there, but the phrase was new with John the Baptist and Jesus. Ancient Israel worshipped God as King. Psalm 103:19 reads, "The Lord has established his throne in heaven, and his kingdom rules over all."

This is in a category of Psalms known as enthronement Psalms. They speak of God reigning as King. An example of this type of Psalm is Psalm 97.

> The LORD reigns, let the earth be glad;
>> let the distant shores rejoice.
>
> Clouds and thick darkness surround him;
>> righteousness and justice are the foundation of his throne.
> Fire goes before him
>> and consumes his foes on every side.
> His lightning lights up the world;
>> the earth sees and trembles.
> The mountains melt like wax before the LORD,
>> before the Lord of all the earth.
> The heavens proclaim his righteousness,
>> and all the peoples see his glory.
>
> All who worship images are put to shame,
>> those who boast in idols—
>> worship him, all you gods!
>
> Zion hears and rejoices
>> and the villages of Judah are glad
>> because of your judgments, O LORD.
> For you, O LORD, are the Most High over all the earth;
>> you are exalted far above all gods.
>
> Let those who love the LORD hate evil,

> *for he guards the lives of his faithful ones*
> *and delivers them from the hand of the wicked.*
> *Light is shed upon the righteous*
> *and joy on the upright in heart.*
> *Rejoice in the LORD, you who are righteous,*
> *and praise his holy name.*

In a special sense, God ruled as sovereign King over the nation of Israel. This nation was his special possession. As mentioned earlier, God stated his dream for his people in Exodus 19:3–6:

> *Then Moses went up to God, and the LORD called to him from the mountain and said, "This is what you are to say to the house of Jacob and what you are to tell the people of Israel: 'You yourselves have seen what I did to Egypt, and how I carried you on eagles' wings and brought you to myself. Now if you obey me fully and keep my covenant, then out of all nations you will be my treasured possession. Although the whole earth is mine, you will be for me a kingdom of priests and a holy nation.' These are the words you are to speak to the Israelites."*

The same idea occurred when Gideon was asked to be king in Judges 8:22–23. The text reads, "The Israelites said to Gideon, 'Rule over us—you, your son and your grandson—because you have saved us out of the hand of Midian.' But Gideon told them, 'I will not rule over you, nor will my son rule over you. The Lord will rule over you.'"

Even when Israel chose an earthly king like Saul or David, the king was viewed as "the Lord's anointed," who drew his authority from God's sovereignty. As Israel rebelled against the sovereign rule of God, God disciplined his people. He allowed foreign empires to defeat them in battle. During these times when Israel had suffered defeat or had no king, the people began to look forward to a time when God would deliver them from their enemies and establish their nation under a king who would lead them to a time of prosperity and peace (Isaiah 11, Ezekiel 37).

Ultimately, God planned to change the nature of his kingdom on earth. Daniel 2:44 records, "In the time of those kings, the God of heaven will set up a kingdom that will never be destroyed, nor will it be left to another people. It will crush all those kingdoms and bring them to an end, but it will itself endure forever." This idea of an eternal kingdom took hold in the minds of many of the first-century Jews living in Judea, and they began to long for God to establish his eternal kingdom in their lifetime.

This is also evident in Jeremiah 29:10–14, which reads:

> *This is what the LORD says: "When seventy years are completed for Babylon, I will come to you and fulfill my gracious promise to bring you back to this place. For I know the*

plans I have for you," declares the LORD, "plans to prosper you and not to harm you, plans to give you hope and a future. Then you will call upon me and come and pray to me, and I will listen to you. You will seek me and find me when you seek me with all your heart. I will be found by you," declares the LORD, "and will bring you back from captivity. I will gather you from all the nations and places where I have banished you," declares the LORD, "and will bring you back to the place from which I carried you into exile."

Many of the Jews began to look for a king who would sweep into Jerusalem and cast out their enemies. They wanted a military king who would restore the glory of the Davidic kingdom. They wanted a kingdom like the kingdoms of this world, but they wanted their kingdom to be superior in might, prosperity, and territory to the other kingdoms. They failed to realize that God had a different type of kingdom in mind because this new kingdom would come with a new covenant. Jeremiah wrote about this new covenant in Jeremiah 31:31–33:

> *"The time is coming," declares the LORD,*
> *"when I will make a new covenant*
> *with the house of Israel*
> *and with the house of Judah.*
> *It will not be like the covenant*
> *I made with their forefathers*
> *when I took them by the hand*
> *to lead them out of Egypt,*
> *because they broke my covenant,*
> *though I was a husband to them,"*
> *declares the LORD.*
> *"This is the covenant I will make with the house of Israel*
> *after that time," declares the LORD.*
> *"I will put my law in their minds*
> *and write it on their hearts.*
> *I will be their God,*
> *and they will be my people."*

What did the audience of John the Baptist and Jesus think when they heard the phrase "kingdom of God"? They injected their own hopes and wishes for a renewed Davidic kingdom into the phrase. Luke 19:11 states, "While they were listening to this, [Jesus] went on to tell them a parable, because he was near Jerusalem and the people thought that the kingdom of God was going to appear at once." His disciples were confused. They had missed the evidence of the kingdom all around them in the person and work of Jesus. They misunderstood Jesus' teaching on the kingdom.

After his resurrection from the dead, his disciples asked Jesus, "Lord, are you at this time going to restore the kingdom to Israel?" (Acts 1:6). Even Jesus' closest disciples misunderstood his teaching on the kingdom. They infused nationalistic fervor into the teaching. First-century Jews were looking for a Messiah who was going to expel the Romans out of their land and reestablish the glory of the Davidic/Solomonic Kingdom of Israel. When Jesus was arrested, he fought against this notion, saying in John 18:36–37:

> *"My kingdom is not from this world. If my kingdom were from this world, my followers would be fighting to keep me from being handed over to the Jews. But as it is, my kingdom is not from here." Pilate asked him, "So you are a king?" Jesus answered, "You say that I am a king. For this I was born, and for this I came into the world, to testify to the truth."*
>
> —NRSV

Jesus clearly says, "My kingdom is not from this world...my kingdom is not from here." Unfortunately, his disciples failed to comprehend this. They were caught up in the post-exilic hope for an earthly manifestation of the kingdom of God.

Much of the debate between Jesus and his contemporaries occurred over differing expectations concerning the kingdom of God. N. T. Wright notes:

> The time of restoration was at hand, and people of all sorts were summoned to share and enjoy it; but Israel was warned that her present ways of going about advancing the kingdom were thoroughly counter-productive, and would result in a great national disaster. Jesus was therefore summoning his hearers to be Israel in a new way, to take up their proper roles in the unfolding drama; and he assured them that, if they followed him in this way, they would be vindicated when the great day came. In the course of all this, he was launching the decisive battle with the real satanic enemy—a different battle, and a different enemy, from those Israel had envisaged.[36]

Thus we see the conflict between Jesus and the religious leaders of his day. They misunderstood each other. Jesus' own disciples misunderstood what Jesus meant by kingdom. Lest we judge them too harshly, we should admit that misunderstandings concerning Jesus' teaching on the kingdom of God persist today.

Misunderstanding the Kingdom Today

A. Liberal scholars have misunderstood the concept of kingdom of God. Here are several ways that scholars have wrongly defined the kingdom of God:

1. The Non-Eschatological School

This is the old liberal school that held sway in theological circles until the early part of the twentieth century. The word "eschaton" means "last things," so eschatology is the study of last things or the study of the end of time. The non-eschatological school says that few or none of the teachings of Jesus were about the end of time. These scholars see Jesus as a moral teacher. The kingdom of God represents the reign of God in the individual soul as the individual is transformed into God's image. A favorite verse for these scholars is Luke 17:20–21, which reads, "Once, having been asked by the Pharisees when the kingdom of God would come, Jesus replied, 'The kingdom of God does not come with your careful observation, nor will people say, "Here it is" or "There it is" because the kingdom of God is within you.'"

2. The Imminent Eschatological School

These scholars say that Jesus was consumed with eschatology. They see eschatological references in almost everything Jesus said. They believe that Jesus saw himself as king of the eschatological kingdom. He spoke about the kingdom coming in the apostles' lifetime/in their generation (Mark 13:30).

But, these scholars add, "Jesus was wrong!" They believe that Jesus miscalculated, that he got his followers excited for nothing, and his misguided teachings led to his crucifixion. They believe that Jesus' disciples continued to cling to his teachings after his death, still longing for the kingdom that did not come during his lifetime.

3. The Kingdom as Present Reality School

These scholars see Jesus as presenting a view of the kingdom as present reality in his personal presence; that is, the kingdom of God was the same as the presence of Jesus. For them, the message of Jesus was: "Embrace the kingdom; I am the kingdom." Jesus healed the sick, raised the dead, and fed the hungry; and all of this was a sign that the kingdom was present in the teaching and work of Jesus. In Matthew 12:28, Jesus says, "But if I drive out demons by the Spirit of God, then the kingdom of God has come upon you." These scholars say that the kingdom of God arrived through the person and work of Jesus. C. H. Dodd, a New Testament scholar, translates Mark 1:15 as, "The kingdom of God has come."[37] These scholars equate the whole of the kingdom with this one aspect of the kingdom. No need to speak of a future kingdom; the kingdom of God equaled the person and work of Jesus the Messiah. For them, that's the end of the issue.

B. Many conservative scholars have also misunderstood the kingdom. For example:

1. The Kingdom = The Church = The Kingdom School

In this school of thought, the New Testament writers present the kingdom and the church as synonymous. Therefore, every time you see the word "kingdom," you can substitute the word church. For example, in Matthew 6:33 Jesus says, "Seek first his kingdom and his righteousness, and all these things will be given to you as well." If kingdom=church=kingdom, then seeking the kingdom first is the same as seeking the church first. But is this what Jesus meant when he said, "Seek first his kingdom"?

2. The Kingdom Come School

Like some liberal scholars, some conservative scholars say that when Jesus preached he was consumed with eschatological thoughts. He planned on launching his kingdom into the world through his personal ministry, but the world wasn't ready for his kingdom. Therefore, he established his church as a nice compromise for a people who weren't ready. They believe that the kingdom will come after several apocalyptic events, including the rapture, Armageddon, and the tribulation of the church and that after these events, Jesus will establish his kingdom on this earth as a new millennial kingdom.

C. But there is a more biblical view of the kingdom that should be considered: The Kingdom as Paradox School. This view sees the kingdom as a multifaceted diamond that contains many levels of distinction and glory. This school of thought understands that the Scriptures speak of a present reality of the kingdom in the ministry of Jesus and in the continued ministry of Jesus through the church, but it also understands the kingdom as a future eternal kingdom of God that is waiting to break into our present reality.

Scholars in this school acknowledge that Jesus is King; therefore, the kingdom did arrive in the person and ministry of Jesus. But, they add, there is more that can be said about the kingdom. They see various paradoxical teachings about the kingdom throughout the Bible and in the teaching of Jesus. They say, "The kingdom is a paradox: Already, not yet." The Kingdom has arrived through the person and work of Jesus, but there awaits a more glorious kingdom for Jesus' followers. In the future kingdom, we will have resurrection bodies. In the future kingdom, we will live with God forever in heavenly bliss.

There is a multidimensional view of the kingdom in the ministry of Jesus. Consider these three aspects of the "coming of the kingdom" in Jesus' ministry:

1. The kingdom has come in the person and ministry of Jesus: Present kingdom.

John Bright in his book, *The Kingdom of God*, speaks of the continuity between the Old Testament and New Testament, but he also notes that there is a distinct difference between the manner in which the Old Testament speaks of the kingdom of God versus the way the New Testament presents this theme. He writes:

> To the Old Testament the fruition and victory of God's Kingdom was always a future, indeed an eschatological thing, and must always be spoken of in the future tense: "Behold, the days are coming"; "It shall come to pass in those days." But in the New Testament we encounter a change: the tense is a resounding present indicative—the Kingdom is *here!* And that is a very "new thing" indeed: *it is gospel*—the good news that God has acted! How real, how utterly central, was the present fact of the Kingdom to all the New Testament writers, …Nowhere is it better put than in the words of Jesus with which Mark begins the story of his ministry, and which sums up, perhaps better than anything else, the very essence of his teaching: "The time is fulfilled, and the kingdom of God is at hand; repent, and believe in the gospel" (Mark 1:15). What all the ages have desired to see now is here—in this Jesus (Luke 10:23–24). In him has the old order ended and a new order begun.[38]

Although the kingdom was yet to come, the kingdom was present in the person of Jesus; and thus the kingdom could be spoken of as having arrived in the person, work, and ministry of Jesus. (Already, not yet.) Yes, the kingdom was a present reality in the life of Jesus. He did say, "But if I drive out demons…, then the kingdom of God has come upon you." The exorcism of demons demonstrates that Jesus is more powerful than Satan and that Jesus was overthrowing the work of Satan (Matthew 12:29). Jesus speaks of this in terms of his kingdom being at war with Satan's kingdom. In Mark 3:24–27, he says:

> If a kingdom is divided against itself, that kingdom cannot stand. If a house is divided against itself, that house cannot stand. And if Satan opposes himself and is divided, he cannot stand; his end has come. In fact, no one can enter a strong man's house and carry off his possessions unless he first ties up the strong man. Then he can rob his house (cf. Matthew 12:25–26, Luke 11:17–18).

The Jews expected the overthrow of Satan to come at the end of time, but this was a present reality in the ministry of Jesus. John Bright records, "In the mighty works of Jesus, the power of the Kingdom has broken into the world; Satan has met his match (Luke 10:18, Mark 3:27); the cosmic end-struggle has begun."[39] Jesus empowers his immediate followers to offer the kingdom to those with willing hearts. Luke 9:1–2 reads, "When Jesus had called the Twelve together, he gave them power and authority to drive out all demons and to cure diseases, and he sent them out to preach the kingdom of God and to heal the sick."

The kingdom arrived in the person of Jesus. When the Pharisees asked when the kingdom of God would come, Jesus answered, "In fact, the kingdom of God is among you" (Luke 17:20).[40] The kingdom was in their midst in the person, teaching, and work of Jesus the Messiah. The Pharisees failed to perceive this; therefore, they missed their opportunity to enter the kingdom.

Others, some who were tax collectors and prostitutes, saw who Jesus was and entered the kingdom. In Matthew 21:31–32 Jesus says to the Pharisees:

> I tell you the truth, the tax collectors and the prostitutes are entering the kingdom of God ahead of you. For John came to you to show you the way of righteousness, and you did not believe him, but the tax collectors and the prostitutes did. And even after you saw this, you did not repent and believe him.

John's message of repentance and his preaching of righteousness foreshadowed the coming of the kingdom in Jesus.

Some understood that Jesus was the Messianic King, and they followed him as loyal disciples. Jesus offered his kingdom to those who made a decision to follow him. In Luke 12:32 Jesus says to his followers, "Do not be afraid, little flock, for your Father has been pleased to give you the kingdom" (present tense). Jesus tells his closest followers, "The knowledge of the secrets of the kingdom of heaven has been given to you, but not to them" (Matthew 13:11, cf. Mark 4:11, Luke 8:10). There are many mysteries of the kingdom, but Jesus gives his disciples the ability to discern its mysteries and know its secrets. This ability has already been given to the disciples as long as they follow the teachings of Jesus and allow the word of God to grow in their hearts.

Since the followers of Jesus participated in his kingdom, this set them apart from John the Baptist and his followers. Jesus makes this contrast saying, "I tell you the truth: Among those born of women there has not risen anyone greater than John the Baptist; yet he who is least in the kingdom of heaven is greater than he" (Matthew 11:11, cf. Luke 7:28). Notice Jesus uses the present tense in making this contrast. He goes on to say, "From the days of John the Baptist until now the kingdom of heaven has suffered violence, and the violent take it by force" (Matthew 11:12 ESV). The present kingdom is being violently assaulted by men of violence who attempt to take it by force. In a similar statement Jesus states, "The Law and the Prophets were proclaimed until John. Since that time, the good news of the kingdom of God is being preached, and everyone is forcing his way into it" (Luke 16:16). Again, Jesus uses the present tense to mark a distinction between John's ministry of the law and prophets and his ministry of preaching the good news of the kingdom.

Since the kingdom came with Jesus, he was able to offer salvation to people. For example, in Luke 19:9, Jesus says to the household of Zacchaeus, "Today salvation has come to this house, because this man, too, is a son of Abraham." People could embrace the kingdom through Jesus. The first beatitude reads, "Blessed are the poor in spirit, for theirs is the kingdom of heaven" (Matthew 5:3). Note that Jesus uses the present tense, "theirs is the kingdom of heaven." Present tense because Jesus taught the kingdom was a present reality. If the kingdom was not present, then why did Jesus urge his followers to "seek first the kingdom of God and his righteousness" (Matthew 6:33 ESV)?[41] We also see that as long as the king was present, there was no need for the friends of the bridegroom to fast (Mark 2:19). The kingdom was present in the life, ministry, work, and person of Jesus the Messiah.

2. The kingdom would come in the near future: Imminent kingdom.

At the beginning of Jesus' ministry, he declares, "The kingdom of God is at hand" (Mark 1:15 ESV). The kingdom of God is at hand (ἤγγικεν ἡ βασιλεία τοῦ θεοῦ/*engiken he basileia tou theou*) has also been translated as "the kingdom of God is near," and "the kingdom of God is rapidly approaching" (Matthew 3:2, 4:17). In Luke 10:9–11, Jesus tells his disciples:

> *"Heal the sick who are there and tell them, 'The kingdom of God is near you.' But when you enter a town and are not welcomed, go into its streets and say, 'Even the dust of your town that sticks to our feet we wipe off against you. Yet be sure of this: The kingdom of God is near.'"*

The Contemporary English Version translates this a little differently. The CEV states:

> *"Heal their sick and say, 'God's kingdom will soon be here!'*

> *"But if the people of a town refuse to welcome you, go out into the street and say, 'We are shaking the dust from our feet as a warning to you. And you can be sure that God's kingdom will soon be here!'"*

This is to say that the kingdom will appear in the near future. It is not yet. It is just around the corner.

Perhaps the most striking reference to the imminent arrival of the kingdom is found in Mark 9:1, where Jesus says, "I tell you the truth, some who are standing here will not taste death before they see the kingdom of God come with power" (cf. Matthew 16:28, Luke 9:27). The mother of James and John comes to Jesus with this request, "Command that in Your kingdom these two sons of mine may sit one on Your right and one on Your left" (Matthew 20:21 NASB, cf. Mark 10:37).[42] And of course, at the end of the gospels we must remember that Joseph of Arimathea and Jesus' disciples were still waiting for the kingdom to come (Mark 15:43). Also, we cannot forget how Jesus closely associated his kingdom with his church in Matthew 16:18–19.

The imminent nature of the kingdom can be seen in many of the parables of Jesus. When the fig tree puts forth leaf, you can be assured that summer is near (Matthew 24:32ff, Mark 13:28ff, Luke 21:29ff). This is an allusion to the nearness of the kingdom.

In Acts, Jesus' disciples taught about the kingdom of God. Acts 8:12 describes the ministry of Phillip with these words, "But when they believed Philip as he preached the good news of the kingdom of God and the name of Jesus Christ, they were baptized, both men and women."

Paul's ministry included teaching on the kingdom. He addressed the kingdom as a present reality. On Paul and Barnabas' return visit to various cities at the close of their first missionary journey, they went, "strengthening the disciples and encouraging them to remain true to the faith. 'We must go through many hardships to enter the kingdom of God,' they said" (Acts 14:22). Luke describes Paul's journey to Ephesus in Acts 19:8 this way: "Paul entered the synagogue and spoke boldly there for three months, arguing persuasively about the kingdom of God." Paul spoke to the elders in Ephesus, saying, "Now I know that none of you among whom I have gone about preaching the kingdom will ever see me again." When Paul was under house arrest in Rome, Luke wrote in Acts 28:23:

> They [the leaders of the Jews] arranged to meet Paul on a certain day, and came in even larger numbers to the place where he was staying. From morning till evening he explained and declared to them the kingdom of God and tried to convince them about Jesus from the Law of Moses and from the Prophets.

Paul's message was a message of the kingdom and of Jesus. Acts 28:31 notes, "Boldly and without hindrance he preached the kingdom of God and taught about the Lord Jesus Christ."

Paul wrote to the disciples in Colossae informing them that they were a part of God's kingdom. Colossians 1:10–14 reads:

> And we pray this in order that you may live a life worthy of the Lord and may please him in every way: bearing fruit in every good work, growing in the knowledge of God, being strengthened with all power according to his glorious might so that you may have great endurance and patience, and joyfully giving thanks to the Father, who has qualified you to share in the inheritance of the saints in the kingdom of light. For he has rescued us from the dominion of darkness and brought us into the kingdom of the Son he loves, in whom we have redemption, the forgiveness of sins.

The kingdom came in the person and work of Jesus the King. It also came in the church that Jesus built, but the church is not the final facet of God's kingdom. There is something more glorious to come when Jesus returns. As we live in the church, we live in the tension of being in God's kingdom while we are in a world that abhors the kingdom. As much as we love the kingdom in the here and now, we can't be totally comfortable in this world. We know that something better is around the corner. John Bright writes about this tension, noting:

> For the New Testament church is the people of the Kingdom of God. And that Kingdom is even yet 'at hand,' intruding into the earthly order. We can enter that Kingdom, can obey its bidding, can witness to its power, can pray for its victory, can (God help us!) steel ourselves to suffer for it. But we cannot escape its tension. For it is a Kingdom that we can neither create nor abandon—and remain the Church. It is ours, therefore, to find again, now in this time, the New Testament tension. Perhaps if we do so, we may be approved as good and faithful servants.[43]

Allow me to conclude this section with two quotes. F. F. Bruce writes:

> The Church cannot be identified with the Kingdom absolutely; but it is natural to think of the divine sovereignty in association with the sphere in which it is exercised, and at the present time the sphere in which submission to that sovereignty is most clearly seen (or ought to be) is the Christian Church.[44]

Howard Marshall writes:

> The Church is not to be identified as the Kingdom (a dangerous step taken in the middle ages that still survives in some areas!) but is the community created by the kingly rule of God. The Kingdom has come, yet not in its fullness, but what we have is the real thing and not a substitute.[45]

We shall now move on to look at the last and most glorious revelation of God's kingdom.

3. The kingdom is to come in the eschatological "Return of the King": Eschatological kingdom.

The kingdom, though present and though imminent, is still to come at the *eschaton* (the end of time). There will be a final judgment (Matthew 25:31ff). At the judgment, the sheep will be separated from the goats. The sheep will inherit the kingdom prepared since the beginning of the world. The goats will face eternal destruction. Jesus warned his followers that how they lived life in the here and now would effect where they would spend eternity.

Jesus offered his kingdom first to the Jews. Unfortunately, many of the Jews failed to recognize the presence of the kingdom in Jesus. Therefore Jesus said, "Many will come from east and west and recline at table with Abraham, Isaac, and Jacob in the kingdom of heaven, while the sons of the kingdom will be thrown into the outer darkness" (Matthew 8:11–12a, cf. Luke 13:28). Jesus reiterated this thought in the parable of the marriage feast in Matthew 22.

In the present reality we can experience the kingdom in Jesus and his church, but this present reality isn't all there is. Although this reality can be good—it's good to be a disciple of Jesus—it isn't *always* good. There's coming a time, in the sweet by and by, when it will all be good. In the future kingdom there will be no sorrows, no tears, no hunger, no pain, and no mortal bodies. The mortal will take on immortality; that's the future glory of God's kingdom. Thus we have the paradox of the kingdom: Already, not yet.

In the meantime, as we await the future, glorious kingdom of God, we live in tension between the two kingdoms—the present kingdom of the church and the future eternal kingdom with God in heaven. In this reality, we are confident but not overconfident. We have to keep watch, stay vigilant, and remain sober. Jesus might come today. When he comes, he will come unannounced as a thief in the night; therefore, we live in anticipation of the future kingdom, keeping watch so that it will not take us by surprise. Again, this is the paradox of the kingdom—already, not yet. We already enjoy the rich blessings of God's kingdom, but we have not yet experienced all that the future eternal kingdom will be.

There were times in the ministry of Jesus where he referenced the distant future kingdom that would come at the end. At the Last Supper Jesus said that he would not "drink again of the fruit of the vine until the kingdom of God comes" (Luke 22:18, Mark 14:25). This seems to be a reference to the kingdom after judgment because Jesus goes on to say, "I assign to you, as my Father assigned to me, a kingdom, that you may eat and drink at my table in my kingdom and sit on thrones judging the twelve tribes of Israel" (Luke 22:29–30 ESV).

Paul makes this note concerning the end of time: "Then comes the end, when [Christ] delivers the kingdom to God the Father after destroying every rule and every authority and power" (1 Corinthians 15:24 ESV). Of this future manifestation of God's kingdom, Paul also notes, "Flesh and blood cannot inherit the kingdom of God, nor does the perishable inherit the imperishable" (1 Corinthians 15:50).

In thinking of the kingdom, it is good to keep in mind its "already, but not yet" aspect. Bertold Klappert in *The New International Dictionary of New Testament Theology* summaries these thoughts, saying:

Jesus, therefore, preached the kingdom of God neither solely as a present reality nor exclusively as a future event. Rather, he was aware that the future rule of God was present in his actions and in his person. He spoke, therefore, of the future kingdom, which would suddenly dawn, as already realizing itself in the present.[46]

One concluding point—if we think of Jesus as the Messianic King and the kingdom being present in his life and work, then we can also speak of the kingdom of God as presented throughout the Gospels in four ways:

Past—as God reigned as King over Israel and his covenant people
Present—in the life and ministry of Jesus the Messianic King
Near Future—in the coming church of King Jesus
Distant Future—in the eschatological kingdom of God

The Lord's Prayer

In the Lord's Prayer, we see these words, "Your kingdom come, your will be done on earth as it is in heaven" (Matthew 6:10, Luke 11:2). Not many verses after this statement, Jesus directed his followers to seek the kingdom first (Matthew 6:33). How do you pray for the kingdom to come and also seek the kingdom first? That's the paradox of the kingdom. It is already, but not yet.

The kingdom is multifaceted. To seek Jesus is to seek his kingdom. But that's not all there is to the kingdom. The kingdom is manifest in the workings of the church in the world, but that's not the end of the story. A more glorious kingdom will come when the triumphant King returns with his angels at the end of time—the future eschatological kingdom.

Kingdom Hearts

Since the kingdom implies the rule and reign of God in the heart of each disciple, it behooves anyone who understands the majesty and might of God's kingdom to give his or her full heart to advancing the kingdom of God. This means both living a kingdom lifestyle and sharing that lifestyle with others. If you really understand the glorious benefits of being a citizen of God's kingdom, then you will naturally want to share the kingdom with other people.

What is a kingdom heart? What is the kingdom lifestyle? Let's look at a multitude of verses from Jesus in the Gospels to answer those questions.

The kingdom is a gift from God (Luke 12:32). Therefore, you have to receive the kingdom like a child (Mark 10:15). You must experience a spiritual rebirth to enter the kingdom (John 3:3). To enter the kingdom, you need poverty of spirit (Matthew 5:3, Luke 6:20).

You have to be careful how you enter the kingdom (Matthew 5:20). You must seek the rule of God first in your life (Matthew 6:33, Luke 12:31).

You must estimate the cost of entering the kingdom (Luke 14:28–32). In fact, you must be prepared to give up everything to enter the kingdom. Perhaps this is why it will be difficult for the rich to enter the kingdom (Matthew 19:24ff, Mark 10:23ff, Luke 18:25). The cost will be different for everyone. The cost might include familial relationships (Matthew 19:29, Mark 10:29, Luke18:29).

Entering the kingdom includes obeying the word of Jesus (Matthew 7:24–27). There are many ethical demands on those who enter God's kingdom (Matthew 5–7). You must be prepared to love your enemies. When someone does evil to you, you must not retaliate. You must take up your cross and crucify self on it daily (Matthew 10:38, Luke 14:27, Mark 8:34). And once you have decided to enter the kingdom, you cannot look back (Luke 9:62). Once you enter, prepare to be hated (Mark 13:13, Mathew 10:22), and prepare to be persecuted (Luke 6:22, Matthew 5:10–11).

After you enter the kingdom, you realize that whatever it cost you to enter, the joy of being in the kingdom was more than worth the entrance cost (Matthew 13:44–46: the hidden treasure and the pearl of great price).

After you have tasted the gifts of the kingdom, you must share what you have learned with others. You are now part of a mission—a mission to take the good news of the kingdom to the entire world (Matthew 28:19–20, Mark 16:15–16, Luke 24:47).

Ramifications

1. A study of the kingdom demonstrates how we need to carefully handle the word of truth. As noted at the beginning of this section, we read the Bible on different levels. We read the Bible searching for the truth of Scripture, and we read the Bible for practical guidance on how to live a godly life. We must not sacrifice truth for practical guidance; nor are we to abandon the practical guidance of Scripture when we delve the depths of God's truth.

As we attempt to simplify Scripture so that it can be taught and understood, we can't overlook the complexity and the grandeur of Scripture. The Bible should be treated with dignity, which means we must not change the teachings of the Bible in an attempt to make these teachings more easily understood. We must be careful here.

People need to appreciate the fact that the kingdom is huge, magnificent, glorious, stupendous, fantastic, surprising, and stunning. A full understanding of the kingdom of God cannot be communicated or grasped in a short Bible study. In many ways the kingdom is unfathomable. It is beyond our comprehension and glorious beyond words. We struggle to understand and appreciate all its subtleties and all its nuances. At the end of the day, we acknowledge that we are a part of something that is beyond our full comprehension, but this is no cause for panic or anxiety. Instead, we appreciate the fact that we are a part of something that is bigger than our lives, bigger than our minds, and bigger than our world. We are a part of God's eternal kingdom.

2. The study of the kingdom teaches us that the church is one manifestation of the kingdom of God, but we should not equate the church with the kingdom—this is too limiting. I don't say this to belittle the church. The church is one of the best things going in this world, but to be accurate, we must acknowledge that the kingdom is bigger than the church. We are not just a part of the church, we are also a part of God's eternal kingdom. As such, the church should be filled with kingdom-minded people.

Is it wrong to say, "I love the kingdom," and by that statement mean, "I love the church?" I wouldn't call it wrong; it's just not entirely accurate. If we understand that the church is a manifestation of God's glorious kingdom, then it is acceptable to say, "I love the kingdom," meaning the church as a part of God's kingdom.

I personally don't think we should become too picky here and correct our brothers and sisters every time we feel like they have used the term "kingdom" in an imprecise manner. These are kingdom-minded disciples who love the church and love God's kingdom. Let's show them some "kingdom" grace.

3. When we understand the kingdom properly, we get to take back the Lord's Prayer.

When I was growing up in the church of Christ in Middle Tennessee, I was taught that I could not pray the Lord's Prayer unless I changed "Your kingdom come, your will be done" to "Your kingdom has come, your will is being done." That's because we believed that the church and the kingdom were the same; therefore, the kingdom had already come in the form of the church.

When we understand that the kingdom is larger than the church, it enables us to continue to pray the Lord's Prayer as Jesus prayed it. When we pray, "Your kingdom come," we are praying for God's rule to come into our lives and into our world. We also note that the verbs in the Lord's Prayer are in the imperative. We are begging, pleading, beseeching, and imploring God to make this happen:

> *Our Father who is in the heavenly realms,*
> *Let your name be hallowed.*
> *Please, we implore you, let your rule and reign come.*
> *Please, we beg you, allow your will to be done*
> *as in heaven so on the earth.*
> *We beseech you to give us this day our daily bread.*

Please, forgive us our debts as we have forgiven our debtors,
And, we beg you, do not lead into temptation,
but deliver us from the evil one.

4. When we understand the kingdom properly, it makes Matthew 6:33 even more meaningful. To seek the kingdom of God first in your life means to seek the rule and reign of God in your life. This is much larger than seeking the church first. We need to realize that we are not just members of a church—we are citizens of God's eternal kingdom. We are engaged in a battle that is much bigger than our lives here on the earth.

5. A proper understanding of the kingdom teaches us that we share in the future greatness of the kingdom now. F. F. Bruce writes:

In the apostolic preaching both present and future aspects of the Kingdom had a place. According to the apostles' teaching, Christians have already been transferred from the dominion of darkness into the Kingdom of Christ (Col. 1:13) and receive "a Kingdom that cannot be shaken" (Heb. 12:28); yet they are heirs of a future Kingdom (Jas. 2:5 etc.), for which they work together (Col. 4:11), and their present suffering for it makes them worthy of it when it comes (2 Thess. 1:5; cf. Rom. 8:17; 2 Tim. 2:12).[47]

6. By embracing all the kingdom scriptures, we have an even more challenging and exciting call to discipleship. When we embrace all the scriptures about the kingdom, the call of what it means to be a part of God's kingdom is much greater than just being a church member.

It is interesting to me that in our kingdom study in our movement of churches we chose to use Matthew's accounting of "seek first the kingdom" instead of Luke's account. Look at Luke's rendering of the saying in Luke 12:29–34:

And do not set your heart on what you will eat or drink; do not worry about it. For the pagan world runs after all such things, and your Father knows that you need them. But seek his kingdom, and these things will be given to you as well.
Do not be afraid, little flock, for your Father has been pleased to give you the kingdom. Sell your possessions and give to the poor. Provide purses for yourselves that will not wear out, a treasure in heaven that will not be exhausted, where no thief comes near and no moth destroys. For where your treasure is, there your heart will be also.

This is a very challenging passage. Jesus teaches that to seek his kingdom and to be in his kingdom means that we help the poor. I've not seen this passage used in our kingdom study. In fact, there are many verses that aren't in our kingdom study. That's because, let's face it, our kingdom study was developed to get people committed to coming to the church services and not to see the grandeur, the majesty, the splendor, the magnificence, the glory, and the brilliance of God's eternal kingdom. By embracing all the kingdom scriptures, we have a more dynamic and challenging view of the kingdom.

Conclusion

Why spend so many pages discussing the kingdom? Because the predominant theme in the teaching and ministry of Jesus is the kingdom of God (kingdom of heaven). The kingdom of God is the rule and reign of God. When you think of God's kingdom, think of God's rule over your life.

The kingdom of God stands eternal outside the realm of human history, where God reigns as Sovereign over the entire universe. At times, the kingdom of God breaks into human history in various manifestations. One such manifestation was the kingdom of God as seen in the person and work of Jesus the King.

When we make Jesus the king of our lives, then we become citizens of his kingdom. To do this, we must put Jesus and his kingdom above everything else in our lives. Dallas Willard writes, "The person who does not seek the kingdom first does not seek it at all, regardless of how worthy the idolatry that he or she has substituted for it."[48]

As we will see in the chapters to follow, Jesus' call of discipleship is the call to make Jesus the King of our lives and to put his kingdom first in our lives. This is a noble call that requires great sacrifice. It is a call that gives each of us a new purpose, namely, as citizens of the kingdom to live lives worthy of the King.

End Notes

27. Stein, 95.

28. Borg, *Jesus: Uncovering the Life, Teachings, and Relevance of a Religious Revolutionary*, 118.

29. Vincent Taylor, *The Life and Ministry of Jesus* (New York: Abingdon Press, 1955), 57.

30. The second and third temptations are inverted in Matthew's and Luke's accounts.

31. M. S. Augsburger and L. J. Ogilvie, *The Preacher's Commentary Series*, vol. 24, *Matthew* (Nashville, Tennessee: Thomas Nelson, 1982), 18.

32. The Jews often spelled the word "G–d" without the vowel as a sign of respect and as an assurance that the name of G–d would not be used in vain.

33. There are times in Matthew where the phrase "kingdom of God" does refer to the heavenly realms; therefore, it is important to look at each use of this phrase individually and in context to detect its true meaning.

34. Found on Dr. Oakes' website, evidenceforchristianity.org, at: www.evidenceforchristianity.org/index.php?option=com_custom_content&task=view&id=3686.

35. These four OT manifestations of the kingdom are (1) the kingdom of God as God rules over creation, (2) the kingdom of God in the covenantal relationship with the Patriarchs, (3) the kingdom of God in the covenant on Sinai, and (4) the kingdom of God through the Kingdom of Israel.

36. N. T. Wright, *Christian Origins and the Question of God, vol. 2, Jesus and the Victory of God* (Minneapolis: Fortress Press, 1996), 201.

37. C. H. Dodd, *The Parables of the Kingdom* (New York: Charles Scribner's Sons, 1961), 44.

38. John Bright, *The Kingdom of God* (Nashville: Abingdon Press, 1953), p.197.

39. Bright, 218.

40. Also translated "in your midst" and "within you." But the best way to translate this verse is "among you."

41. To be fair, within the Sermon on the Mount, Jesus, at times, refers to the kingdom in the future tense. Concerning obeying the Law, Jesus says:

> *"Whoever relaxes one of the least of these commandments and teaches others to do the same will be called least in the kingdom of heaven, but whoever does them and teaches them will be called great in the kingdom of heaven. For I tell you, unless your righteousness exceeds that of the scribes and Pharisees, you will never enter the kingdom of heaven"* (Matthew 5:19–20 ESV).

Toward the end of the sermon, Jesus notes, "Not everyone who says to me, 'Lord, Lord,' will enter the kingdom of heaven, but only he who does the will of my Father who is in heaven." But Jesus is setting up a conditional statement. He's saying, "If you obey God's will, you shall enter the kingdom." He's not saying the kingdom is far in the future. He's saying that if you don't meet certain conditions, then you will never be a part of God's kingdom in the present or in the future.

42. Some would reference Luke 19:11 as evidence that the kingdom did not come in the person of Jesus, but that the kingdom was still being anticipated by the followers of Jesus. The verse reads, "While they were listening to this, he went on to tell them a parable, because he was near Jerusalem and the people thought that the kingdom of God was going to appear at once." The verse is not saying that the thinking of the followers was right. In this context, the followers might have had a false expectation of the coming of the kingdom. They might have anticipated that Jesus was heading into Jerusalem to expel the Romans from the land and restore greatness to Israel as a nation. Jesus doesn't speak directly to their thoughts concerning the kingdom. Instead he gives the parable of the ten minas.

43. Bright, 242–243.

44. F.F. Bruce, "The Kingdom Of God: A Biblical Survey," in *Evangelical Quarterly* 15, 1943, 263–68.

45. I. Howard Marshall, "The Kingdom of God in the Teaching of Jesus," in *The Bible in Transmission*, Winter 2008, Bible Society UK, 3.

46. Bertold Klappert in "King" in *The New International Dictionary of New Testament Theology, vol. 2* (Grand Rapids: Zondervan, 1967), 384.

47. F.F. Bruce, "The Kingdom of God: A Biblical Survey," in *Evangelical Quarterly 15*, 1943, 267.

48. I can't remember where I found this quote from Dallas Willard. I've read all of his books, as he is one of my favorite authors. His trilogy *The Spirit of the Disciplines, Renovation of the Heart*, and *The Divine Conspiracy* changed my life. Somewhere within one of his books, you will find this excellent quote and many other quotes that are just as challenging and inspiring.

Chapter 5

Jesus Launches His Public Ministry in Galilee, Judea, and Samaria: The Message and Mission of Jesus the Messiah

The pre-Easter Jesus was:

A Jewish mystic. . . . God was an experiential reality for Jesus, and his experience of the sacred is the most persuasive explanation of what else he became.

A healer and exorcist. His activity must have been remarkable; more healing and exorcism stories are told about him than about any other figure in the Jewish tradition.

A wisdom teacher. Jesus used the classic forms of wisdom (parables and aphorisms) and taught the classic subject matter of wisdom: what God is like, what life is like, and 'the way.'

A prophet. Like the canonical Jewish prophets, he was a radical critic of the domination system in the name of God and God's passion for justice. Perhaps more than anything else, this led to his execution.

A movement initiator. Even thought Jesus' mission was brief, a movement came into existence around him during his lifetime. Small and embryonic, including both followers and sympathizers, it embodied his vision of the character and passion of God.[49]

—Marcus J. Borg, Jesus Scholar

The Public Ministry of Jesus

A look at the beginning of Jesus' ministry from the Gospel of Matthew should help us see the nature of his ministry.

The Ministry of Jesus Changed People's Lives— Matthew 4:12–17, cf. Mark 1:14–15

When Jesus heard that John had been arrested, he returned to Galilee. He left Nazareth and made his home in Capernaum by the Sea in the region of Zebulun and Naphtali, in order that the word of the prophet Isaiah might be fulfilled:

Land of Zebulon and land of Naphtali
by the way of the sea, across the Jordon,

Galilee of the nations—
The people who live in darkness
Have seen a great light;
And on those living in the land and shadow of death,
A light has dawned.

From that time Jesus began to preach, saying, "Repent, for the kingdom of heaven is fast approaching."[50]

Jesus begins his ministry in the northwestern corner of the Sea of Galilee between the towns of Capernaum, Bethsaida, and Corazin. This has been called the "evangelical triangle," because the bulk of Jesus' ministry in Galilee occurred between these three towns. Capernaum became the home base of Jesus' ministry. It was a small, humble fishing village of some 1,000 residents located on the Sea of Galilee in the territory of Herod Antipas.

The message of Jesus' ministry was the same as that of John: "Repent (change), for the kingdom of heaven is near (at hand, fast approaching)." The dawn of the kingdom had arrived. As King, Jesus was ushering God's kingdom into the world. These were exciting times.

Jesus led a ministry of repentance. The word "repentance" (μετάνοια/ *metanoia*) means "change." Jesus' ministry was all about changing lives— everywhere he went lives were changed. He pleaded with people to give up sin. He taught them to embrace righteous living. He gave the Samaritan woman living water. He told the woman caught in adultery to go and sin no more. He healed the sick, cleansed the lepers, and caused the deaf to hear and the blind to see. He challenged Zaccheus to stop stealing and to make it right with everyone he had wronged. He came to offer people life and life to the full (John 10:10).

When we embrace the ministry of Jesus, we embrace helping people change their lives. This is what the church should be about. We help marriages heal. We help addicts overcome their addictions. We help people who are in debt to get out of debt. We are there for people when their children are in the hospital. We notice when people aren't at church, and we give them a call or stop by and see them to let them know we care. We throw our arms around people with severe psychological disorders knowing that we don't have the expertise to treat their illness, but we can be there for them in their times of greatest need. We comfort the dying, strengthen the weak, encourage the timid, help the faint of heart, have patience with knuckleheads, challenge the hard-hearted, and show love to everyone. This is the ministry of Jesus—it is about helping people. This is what the church embraces—the loving, compassionate, people-focused ministry of Jesus.

And this is what people want to see in the church: They want to see Jesus there. They want to see that the church has the heart of God. And what is the heart of God? Henri J.M. Nouwen writes about this in his excellent book on Christian leadership entitled *In the Name of the Father.* He writes:

> In our world of loneliness and despair, there is an enormous need for men and women who know the heart of God, a heart that forgives, cares, reaches out and wants to heal. In that heart there is no suspicion, no vindictiveness, no resentment, and not a tinge of hatred. It is a heart that wants only to give love and receive love in response. It is a heart that suffers immensely because it sees the magnitude of human pain and the great resistance to trusting the heart of God who wants to offer consolation and hope."[51]

The heart of God is a healing heart, a compassion heart, a forgiving heart. You see it in the ministry of Jesus who loved people unconditionally. It should be evident in the church today.

Another way of putting this is that we must love people. The ministry of Jesus was all about loving God and loving people. Dale E. Galloway in his book *20/20 Vision* writes, "Make love your number one aim and you will be right on target."[52] He also relates the following story:

> On a cold, windy Sunday morning in Chicago with the chill factor 15 below zero, a little orphan boy, Ralph, walked four miles to church. His friend, Mr. Kennedy, greeted him as he came in the door, "Glad to see you, Ralph; sure is cold out there today."
>
> With a smile Ralph said, "I sure did get cold walking this morning."
>
> Surprised, the older man inquired, "You mean, Ralph, that you walked in this cold wind to church this morning?"
>
> Ralph replied, "Yep, I didn't have money for bus fare."
>
> "Well, how far did you walk, Ralph?"
>
> "I walked four miles."
>
> Mr. Kennedy asked Ralph, "How many churches did you pass along the way walking your four miles?"
>
> Ralph thought for a moment. "I passed twenty-two churches."
>
> Impressed, Mr. Kennedy said, "Ralph why did you pass twenty-two churches to come to this church on this cold morning?"
>
> Ralph smiled a big Jimmy Carter smile and said, "Because I've discovered that here they love a fella like me."
>
> Young or old, people will inconvenience themselves and go many miles to attend a church where they find love. It's not the size or the site that makes a church great, but it is the spirit of love.[53]

Jesus was the spirit of love. He had a sense of urgency as he changed people's lives. He went from village to village and town to town in a hurry. He wasn't in such a hurry that he didn't stop to meet the individual needs of people, but he *was* in a hurry. He knew that he had much to do and a short time in which to do it.

All of this might seem a bit overwhelming, and it is overwhelming, but notice that Jesus did not try to do everything by himself. He chose a team of leaders to embrace the ministry with him. We see this in the next section of Matthew.

The Ministry of Jesus Was a Team Ministry— Matthew 4:18–22, cf. Mark 1:16–20

Walking by the Sea of Galilee, he saw two brothers, Simon called Peter and his brother Andrew. They were casting nets into the sea, for they were fishermen. He said to them, "Come, follow me, and I will make you fishers of men." Immediately, they left their nets and followed him.

Going on from there, he saw two other brothers, James the son of Zebedee and John his brother. They were in a boat with Zebedee their father, preparing their nets. He called them. Immediately, they left the boat and their father and followed him.[54]

Jesus called his first disciples, Peter and Andrew, while they were fishing on the Sea of Galilee. He gave them a new vocation—instead of being fishermen, they were to be fishers of men. The immediacy of their response demonstrates three facts. First, they must have had prior knowledge of Jesus. Why would they drop everything and follow Jesus unless they knew who he was? They could have been some of the disciples of John who were mentioned in Matthew 3. Second, the call to discipleship deserved an urgent, immediate response. When Jesus calls, we must quickly respond to his call. Third, the call also required a sacrifice. Peter and John left their nets and their livelihood to follow Jesus. James and John left their father and their family business to follow him. Jesus does not expect everyone to abandon his or her family to follow him or to leave his or her family business to be his disciple. However, if family or work become a stumbling block to discipleship, then following Jesus must be our priority.

"Come, follow me" is the call of a rabbi to his disciples. The disciples were to stay in constant contact with their rabbi and learn everything he had to teach them. They were to listen carefully and were often expected to remember the rabbi's exact words. The followers of Jesus were urged to do more than just listen and learn; they were to take an active part in his ministry. They were to be fishers of men.

The second set of brothers Jesus called was James and John, the sons of Zebedee. Jesus would change their name to the Sons of Thunder. They were mending their nets, either getting ready to go fishing or coming in from a night of fishing. In other words, they were at work. They were in business with their father, Zebedee, but Jesus called them to a new work—to go into business with his Father. James and John left their nets, their father, and their business to follow Rabbi Jesus. They were now to be fishers of men and would be a part of the team ministry of Jesus.

Later Jesus would send these men out two by two to minister to the Jews of Galilee. Gene Mims in his book, *The Kingdom-Focused Church,* writes about the team ministry, saying, "Ministry teams appear throughout the entire Bible. From the moment Jesus sent the Twelve on their first assignment to the ministry of Paul and Silas, the Bible teaches that Christians are to join forces to proclaim the good news."[55] The church today should follow the example of Jesus and build ministry teams.

In their insightful book, *Lead Like Jesus*, Ken Blanchard and Phil Hodges zero in on the importance of team leadership. They write about the team leadership of Jesus, noting:

> Once again, we look to Jesus as a model for team leadership. After Jesus spent time personally teaching and modeling the type of leadership He wanted them to adopt (Mark 6), he sent out His disciples to minister in teams of two. In doing so, Jesus empowered them to act on His behalf to support one another in accomplishing the work they had been trained to do.[56]

If anyone could have led out front all by himself, without the need of any compatriots or fellow workers, it was Jesus. The fact that he chose to model team leadership in his ministry underscores the importance of the concept. A leadership maxim states, "None of us is as smart as all of us." You could also add, "None of us is as strong as all of us," or "None of us is as loving as all of us," or "None of us is as effective as all of us." The church should embrace the team leadership model of Jesus, and ministry leaders in the church should also embrace this model.

The Ministry of Jesus Focused on Three Actions: Teaching, Preaching, and Healing—Matthew 4:23–25, cf. Mark 1:39

> And he went into the whole region of Galilee, teaching in their synagogues and preaching the good news of the kingdom and healing every disease and every sickness of the people. And reports of him spread into all of Syria, and they brought to him all who were sick with various diseases and suffering severe pain, and demoniacs, epileptics and paralytics, and he healed them. Large crowds followed him from Galilee and the Decapolis (the ten cities), Jerusalem, Judea and across the Jordan.[57]

Matthew defines Jesus' ministry with three participles—teaching, preaching, and healing. R.T. France, a NT scholar, writes:

> Jesus' ministry is summarized under three headings: teaching in their synagogues (i.e. biblical exposition, as in Lk. 4:16ff), preaching the gospel of the kingdom (i.e. public proclamation, as in 4:17), and healing, in which the power of the kingdom of heaven was actually brought into operation (cf. 12:28); John had preached the same message, but in Jesus' ministry what for John was future became present.[58]

Today our ministry should have the same elements as the ministry of Jesus. Are we teaching the precepts of the Bible, preaching the good news of the kingdom, and healing the hurt in people's lives through God's power?

The Inauguration of the Ministry of Jesus the Messiah— Luke 4:14–30

> *14–15 Jesus returned to Galilee in the power of the Spirit, and news about him spread through the whole countryside. He taught in their synagogues, and everyone praised him.*

Jesus returns to Galilee in the power of the Spirit. This is presumably different than when he left Galilee to be baptized by John in the Jordan. He returns to Galilee as a teacher. He is no longer the carpenter from Nazareth. His ministry has begun. People respond favorably to his message, but the favor of the people ends when he reaches his hometown of Nazareth.

> *16 He went to Nazareth, where he had been brought up, and on the Sabbath day he went into the synagogue, as was his custom. And he stood up to read.*

As we have seen, Nazareth was a backwater village of around one hundred people. Some scholars say that it was made up of a sectarian cult who believed they were the *netzer,* the bud of the plant of King David. In other words, these *Netzerene* believed that the Messiah would come from their number.

It was Jesus' custom to go to the synagogue on the Sabbath. When it came time for the reading of Scripture, the ruler of the local synagogue normally asked a worthy person to read from the Scriptures and to make a comment on the reading. Since Jesus had been teaching in towns around Nazareth, it makes sense that the synagogue official asked him to read from the Scriptures.

17–19 The scroll of the prophet Isaiah was handed to him. Unrolling it, he found the place where it is written:

"The Spirit of the Lord is on me,
because he has anointed me
to preach good news to the poor.
He has sent me to proclaim freedom for the prisoners
and recovery of sight for the blind,
to release the oppressed,
to proclaim the year of the Lord's favor."

Jesus chose this passage, Isaiah 61:1–2a. Take note of the fact that Jesus' reading is different from the text as found Isaiah. Jesus seemed to edit parts of the text. Also, Jesus ends the reading rather abruptly. Compare Isaiah 61:1–7:

The Spirit of the Sovereign LORD is on me,
because the LORD has anointed me
to preach good news to the poor.
He has sent me to bind up the brokenhearted,
to proclaim freedom for the captives
and release from darkness for the prisoners,
to proclaim the year of the LORD's favor
and the day of vengeance of our God,
to comfort all who mourn,
and provide for those who grieve in Zion—
to bestow on them a crown of beauty
instead of ashes,
the oil of gladness
instead of mourning,
and a garment of praise
instead of a spirit of despair.
They will be called oaks of righteousness,
a planting of the LORD
for the display of his splendor.

They will rebuild the ancient ruins
and restore the places long devastated;
they will renew the ruined cities
that have been devastated for generations.
Aliens will shepherd your flocks;
foreigners will work your fields and vineyards.

And you will be called priests of the LORD,
    you will be named ministers of our God.
You will feed on the wealth of nations,
    and in their riches you will boast.

Instead of their shame
    my people will receive a double portion,
and instead of disgrace
    they will rejoice in their inheritance;
and so they will inherit a double portion in their land,
    and everlasting joy will be theirs.

This text in Isaiah depicts a future day in which Galilee of the Gentiles would once again become Galilee of the Jews. The year of the Lord's favor is depicted as a year in which the Jews would take back their land, make slaves of the Gentiles who were occupying their territory, and change the lot of the Jews in Galilee forever. Remember that Jesus is in a settlers' village. The settlers know this prophecy; they have settled here to help reestablish the greatness of Judaism in Galilee. They are looking forward to a day in which God would change their situation and put the Jewish people back in control of Galilee and Judea.

Jesus doesn't read the whole prophecy. He stops short of declaring "the day of vengeance of our God." Did Jesus or did Luke edit the text? Most scholars say that Luke or the early church edited it to fit Jesus' agenda. But Kenneth Bailey takes a different approach, writing:

The Mishnah is the earliest collection of the sayings of the Jewish rabbis and was compiled by Judah the prince in about the year A.D. 200. It contains reflections and regulations set down by the rabbis from around 100 B.C. (and before) up to the time of the book's compilation. In it there are rules about the reading of the Scriptures in the synagogue. The reader was obliged to read the Torah as it was written. But if the reading was from the book of the Prophets, one was allowed to 'leave out verses in the Prophets.' How much could the reader skip? The Mishnah stipulates that the reader could omit 'Only so much that he leaves no time for the interpreter to make a pause.' The reading was in Hebrew. But most of the people only understood Aramaic. So when Scripture was read, a translator stood beside the reader and translated verse by verse into Aramaic for the benefit of non-Hebrew speaking listeners. As regards skipping back and forth, the idea was that the reader could read a verse for the translator to translate. While the translator was so engaged, the reader could turn to a verse somewhere else in the same book as long as it wasn't too far away. ... What is clear is that the editing found in Luke 4:17–19 is within the framework of these rules. It is possible, therefore, to see Jesus as the editor and to affirm that it is Jesus' agenda which Luke records.[59]

Jesus edits the text to suit his purpose. He turned this concept of "the year of the Lord's favor" on its ear. His kingdom would not be a militaristic or political kingdom. Instead, Jesus declares,

"The Spirit of the Lord is on me,
because he has anointed me
to preach good news to the poor.
He has sent me to proclaim freedom for the prisoners
and recovery of sight for the blind,
to release the oppressed,
to proclaim the year of the Lord's favor."

Jesus' ministry was a ministry of preaching good news (εὐαγγελίζω/*euangelizo*) to the poor. He proclaimed freedom (κηρύσσω/*kerysso*) for the prisoners and recovery of sight for the blind. His ministry was a ministry of compassion for the oppressed, whom he desired to release from their oppression. These are the actions that were to accompany "the year of the Lord's favor" (as seen in Isaiah).

What does this say to us today? To me, the key idea that is expressed here is compassion. Jesus came to help those who are hurting. He specifically mentions the poor, the prisoners, the blind, and the oppressed, but these aren't just images of people who are down on their luck, hurting, troubled, and in need of aid. These images also portray people who are meek and teachable. Because these people understand darkness, they are ready to accept the light of Jesus. These people need physical aid, but they also need spiritual aid. εὐαγγελίζω/*Euangelizo* and κηρύσσω/*kerysso* are associated with preaching the message of salvation to people. To help people physically without helping them spiritually is like putting a small bandage on a mortal wound. Christian aid should be accompanied with the good news of the gospel of Jesus.

20–21 Then he rolled up the scroll, gave it back to the attendant and sat down. The eyes of everyone in the synagogue were fastened on him, and he began by saying to them, "Today this scripture is fulfilled in your hearing."

The Scripture was read standing, and comments on the Scripture were delivered while seated. Jesus sat down. Everyone's eyes were fixed on him. Then he uttered this bold statement, "Today this scripture is fulfilled in your hearing." Wow! That must have raised some eyebrows.

22 All spoke well of him and were amazed at the gracious words that came from his lips. "Isn't this Joseph's son?" they asked.

The NIV translates this opening phrase with a positive slant, "All spoke well of him." The phrase literally says, "All testified concerning him." It can be taken as positive, negative, or neutral. The Contemporary English Version gives a neutral rendering, "All the people started talking about Jesus and were amazed at the wonderful things he said. They kept on asking, 'Isn't he Joseph's son?'" The New King James Version takes the same approach, "So all bore witness to Him, and marveled at the gracious words which proceeded out of His mouth. And they said, 'Is this not Joseph's son?'"

Some scholars believe that this should be translated as a negative reaction to Jesus because of the way he cut off the reading in Isaiah. They also believe that the synagogue audience would not have reacted well to his statement, "Today this scripture is fulfilled in your hearing." In this case, the question that is repeated by the crowd, "Isn't this Joseph's son?" should be understood as a statement of derision toward Jesus. This interpretation makes the next comment of Jesus more understandable.

> *23–27 Jesus said to them, "Surely you will quote this proverb to me: 'Physician, heal yourself! Do here in your hometown what we have heard that you did in Capernaum.' "*
>
> *"I tell you the truth," he continued, "no prophet is accepted in his hometown. I assure you that there were many widows in Israel in Elijah's time, when the sky was shut for three and a half years and there was a severe famine throughout the land. Yet Elijah was not sent to any of them, but to a widow in Zarephath in the region of Sidon. And there were many in Israel with leprosy in the time of Elisha the prophet, yet not one of them was cleansed—only Naaman the Syrian."*

Jesus takes the statement of his townspeople and kinfolk negatively. He says, "No prophet is accepted in his hometown."

But Jesus doesn't try to win the village to his side with flattery. Instead, he challenges them by selecting two Gentiles as examples of authentic faith. The widow of Zarephath gave up the last of her grain to feed Elijah the prophet. This was a selfless act of faith from a foreigner. Naaman the Syrian commander obeyed Elisha and dipped in the Jordan seven times and was cleansed of his leprosy. By mentioning these two Gentiles, these two foreigners, Jesus is saying that this widow and this Syrian commander were more likely to see the prophetic and messianic nature of Jesus' ministry than were the inhabitants of his own hometown. Kenneth Bailey writes:

To the congregation in the synagogue Jesus was saying:

"If you want to receive the benefits of the new golden age of the Messiah, you must imitate the faith of these Gentiles. I am not asking you merely to tolerate or to accept them. You must see such Gentiles as your spiritual superiors and acknowledge that they can instruct you in the nature of authentic faith. The benefits of the 'acceptable year of the Lord,' which I have come to inaugurate, are available to such people."[60]

If Bailey is correct (and I believe he is) then Jesus is directly challenging the people of his hometown to accept him as the Messiah. But Jesus' messianic program was going to be very different from the one they had been anticipating.

28–30 All the people in the synagogue were furious when they heard this. They got up, drove him out of the town, and took him to the brow of the hill on which the town was built, in order to throw him down the cliff. But he walked right through the crowd and went on his way.

What is the reaction of the people to Jesus' comments? They want to throw him over the cliff. This is the preamble to a traditional stoning. The accused would be thrown over the cliff and then people would hurl rocks down upon the victim until he was dead.

The town sees Jesus as guilty of blasphemy. What was the punishment for blasphemy? Stoning. They move in to execute him, but Jesus does some type of Obi-Wan-Kenobi Jedi mind-trick on them and he escapes through the crowd. I'm just kidding about Obi-Wan-Kenobi. This is no Jedi mind-trick. Jesus was confident, and when you are confident, people often wilt when you stand up to them.

The Mission of Jesus on the Earth

I love the old hymn, "Because He Loved Me So." It goes:

Why did my Savior come to earth,
And to the humble go?
Why did he choose a lowly birth?
Because he loved me so.[61]

This question: "Why did my Savior come to earth?" gets at the heart of the purpose of Jesus' ministry.

Often our answer to this question is too simplistic. We say Jesus came to save sinners or to seek and to save that which was lost. That was part of his mission, but it wasn't his whole mission. When you search the Gospels and ask, "Why did Jesus come to earth?" many answers appear in the text.

One way to answer this question is to look at the times in the Gospels when Jesus said, "I have come..." I give a sample of these statements as found in Mark's Gospel and John's Gospel. I list ten "I have come" statements. There are others. Also, at times Jesus said, "I was sent to ____." These verses also state Jesus' mission or purpose. You might want to look up all these references on your own. It is an interesting study as these statements answer the question: "Why did my Savior come to earth?" and teach about the purpose of Jesus' ministry.

The "I Have Come" Statements of Jesus

1. I have come to preach (Mark 1:38–39).
2. I have come to call sinners (Mark 2:17, Luke 5:32).
3. I have come to serve (Mark 10:45, Matthew 20:28).
4. I have come to give my life as a ransom (Mark 10:45, Matthew 20:28).
5. I have come to do God's will, i.e., to keep the saved, saved (John 6:38).
6. I have come for judgment (John 9:39).
7. I have come to give abundant life (John 10:10 ESV).
8. I came to be a light to lead people to God (John 12:46).
9. I have not come to judge the world, but to save it (John 12:47).
10. I have come to testify to the truth (John 18:37).

A Closer Examination of the "I Have Come" Statements of Jesus

1. Jesus Came to Preach—Mark 1:35–39

> *Very early in the morning, while it was still dark, Jesus got up, left the house and went off to a solitary place, where he prayed. Simon and his companions went to look for him, and when they found him, they exclaimed: "Everyone is looking for you!"*
>
> *Jesus replied, "Let us go somewhere else—to the nearby villages—so I can preach there also. That is why I have come." So he traveled throughout Galilee, preaching in their synagogues and driving out demons.*

Jesus came to preach, but notice how Jesus began his day of preaching: by connecting with the Father. He went off by himself to a solitary place and prayed. This seemed to be his daily habit. He took time to connect with the Father before embracing the arduous task of ministry.

A friend told me a story of a Native American grandfather's conversation with his grandson. It went like this:

> Grandson: Grandfather, I seem to always have a conflict inside my mind. I want to do what is right, but I find myself choosing to do what is wrong. Why is that?
>
> Grandfather: Son, all of us are born with two wolves inside our bodies. We each have a good wolf and a bad wolf. They fight against each other for supremacy.
>
> Grandson: Which wolf will win?

Grandfather: The wolf that you feed will win.

Jesus took time to feed the good wolf. If we take time every day to feed the good wolf through Bible study, prayer, mediation, and fellowship, then the good wolf will win. We will become spiritual people. After all, we are our daily habits.

Before Jesus preached, he set his mind about his mission. After he set his mind, he ministered to people.

Why did Jesus come to the earth? To preach. What does this mean? The word, "κηρύσσω/*karusso*/preach" means "to announce the message of the King." Jesus went from village to village announcing the arrival of God's kingdom.

I think one of the easiest ways to share the good news of God's kingdom with people is simply to say to them, "Come and see what I have found." This is what Philip does in John 1:43–46. Notice:

> The next day Jesus decided to leave for Galilee. Finding Philip, he said to him, "Follow me."
>
> Philip, like Andrew and Peter, was from the town of Bethsaida. Philip found Nathanael and told him, "We have found the one Moses wrote about in the Law, and about whom the prophets also wrote—Jesus of Nazareth, the son of Joseph."
>
> "Nazareth! Can anything good come from there?" Nathanael asked. "Come and see," said Philip.

Philip doesn't try to answer Nathanael's prejudicial question. He doesn't try to point out from the Hebrew Scriptures that the Messiah is to come from Nazareth. He simply says, "Come and see."

How do you share good news with people? Simply say, "Come and see." Be real. Be authentic. Let the Holy Spirit do his work on people's hearts.

2. Jesus Came to Call Sinners—Mark 2:15–17

> While Jesus was having dinner at Levi's house, many tax collectors and "sinners" were eating with him and his disciples, for there were many who followed him. When the teachers of the law who were Pharisees saw him eating with the "sinners" and tax collectors, they asked his disciples: "Why does he eat with tax collectors and 'sinners'?"
>
> On hearing this, Jesus said to them, "It is not the healthy who need a doctor, but the sick. I have not come to call the righteous, but sinners."

Why did Jesus come to the earth? He says, "I have come to call not the righteous, but sinners." Where could you find Jesus? Eating with sinners. He was comfortable doing so. A big part of the mission of Jesus centered on reaching out to the lost. He came to be with sinners, and this was reflected in his schedule and his day-to-day activities.

Allow me to ask some questions: Does your schedule reflect the desire to call sinners to repentance? How much time do you spend with sinners versus the time you spend with Christians? You might say, "Come to my house and you'll see because my house is full of sinners." But I'm talking about time that you actually control. Are you reaching out to non-Christians? Are you studying the Bible with people? Are you getting people to church and to Bible talk? These are ways that we can reach out to sinners.

3. Jesus Came to Serve—Mark 10:43–45

> Not so with you. Instead, whoever wants to become great among you must be your servant, and whoever wants to be first must be slave of all. For even the Son of Man did not come to be served, but to serve, and to give his life as a ransom for many."

Jesus was a king unlike any other, a king who came to serve. You see this throughout his ministry. He healed the sick, raised the dead, and caused the deaf to hear and the blind to see. That's who Jesus was. Rodney Cooper writes:

> In this verse, Jesus delivered the stunning summary of all his teaching on servanthood in the Gospel of Mark. He gave the disciples the supreme example of servanthood: himself. And they had seen him serve. They had seen him touch the unclean. They had seen him heal the multitudes. They had seen him feed thousands. Before it was over, they would see him wash the grime from their feet. They had seen the only one who truly deserved to be called "Lord" place himself in humble service to others.[62]

Jesus set us an example in the way he served. James R. Edwards writes, "What Jesus teaches about service and self-sacrifice is not simply a principle of the kingdom of God but a pattern of his own life that is authoritative for and transferable to disciples."[63]

How are you serving? There are needs everywhere. Serve children. Serve the poor. Serve the homeless. Serve the sick. Serve the community. Serve the church. Serve Jesus.

4. Jesus Came to Give His Life as a Ransom—Mark 10:45

> For even the Son of Man did not come to be served, but to serve, and to give his life as a ransom for many.

Jesus gave his life as a ransom. The word for ransom is λύτρον/ *lytron*. It is a price given to free someone from bondage or servitude. J.

R. Edwards writes, "In the language of the day, ransom referred to bail paid for prisoners of war and slaves, or release from jail. Both the Hebrew *kippur* and Greek *lytron* behind 'ransom' mean 'to cover over,' 'atone for,' or 'expiate.'"[64]

We are all captive to sin and death. We could not pay the price for freedom on our own, but Jesus pays the price for us with his own life. He gave his life so that we might live; he is our substitutionary atonement.

This is an aspect of the mission and ministry of Jesus that we cannot imitate. Only Jesus could give his life as a ransom for those imprisoned by sin. He was the perfect sacrifice.

We can serve like Jesus served, but we cannot die like Jesus died. He is the only one who could die for the sins of humanity, the only sacrifice worthy of atonement. The way he died and the purpose for which he died separate Jesus from the rest of humanity.

5. Jesus Came to Do God's Will, i.e., to Keep the Saved, Saved—John 6:38–40

> For I have come down from heaven not to do my will but to do the will of him who sent me. And this is the will of him who sent me, that I shall lose none of all that he has given me, but raise them up at the last day. For my Father's will is that everyone who looks to the Son and believes in him shall have eternal life, and I will raise him up at the last day.

Jesus clearly states, "I have come to do [God's] will." He then goes on to state what the will of God is: Not to lose any of his disciples, but to raise them up at the last day. He came to get his disciples to heaven.

Jesus lets us know that the journey of discipleship does not end at baptism. The goal is not just to baptize people, but also to get them to heaven. Baptism is the beginning of the journey. The goal, the destination, is heaven.

Jesus did not want to lose anyone. He felt protective of his people. This should be our mission as well—not to lose anyone.

We have to take care of each other. Some might need more care than others. There are all kinds of people in the fellowship: There are the strong and the weak. There are the impulsive and the logical. There are the overbearing and the oversensitive. There are positive people and negative people. There are extroverts and introverts. We need to help each other make it to heaven.

If you know someone who is struggling, discouraged, weak, faithless, uncommitted, or just plain lost—reach out to him or her. Bring them back into the fold. Strengthen them. Remember the shepherd from Luke 15 who left the ninety-nine sheep that were safe to search for the one that was lost. He searched until he found that one. When he found that lost one, he hoisted it upon his shoulders and carried it to safety. Be that shepherd.

6. Jesus Came for Judgment—John 9:39–41

> Jesus said, 'For judgment I have come into this world, so that the
> blind will see and those who see will become blind.'
>   Some Pharisees who were with him heard him say this and
> asked, "What? Are we blind too?"
>   Jesus said, "If you were blind, you would not be guilty of
> sin; but now that you claim you can see, your guilt remains.

In John 12:47, Jesus said, "For I did not come to judge the world, but
to save it." Yet here Jesus says, "For judgment I have come into the world."
Is this a contradiction? No. You have to consider the context of the passage. In chapter 12, Jesus is declaring that the purpose of his mission (and
also his death on the cross) was to save the world and not to judge or condemn it. In chapter 9, Jesus says that to reject him is to bring judgment.
This is what the Pharisees have done. Because they do not see Jesus as the
Messiah, they are blind, whereas some who are literally blind (like blind
Bartimaeus) see Jesus as the Messiah (the blind will see).

Jesus didn't come to judge the world, but to save it; but the presence of Jesus in the world means that some people will bring judgment
on themselves because of their spiritual blindness, namely, their lack of
faith. D. A. Carson writes:

> Jesus' point in 9:39 is not that the very purpose of his coming was to condemn, nor
> even simply to divide the human race. He came to save, not condemn (12:47). But
> saving some entails condemning others. In that derivative sense, Jesus has indeed
> come for judgment. This is the paradox of the revelation, that in order to bring grace
> it must also give offence, and so can turn to judgment.[65]

7. Jesus Came to Give Abundant Life—John 10:10

> The thief comes only to steal and kill and destroy; I have come that they may have life,
> and have it to the full.

The thief has no regard for others. Jesus is portraying the Jewish religious leaders as thieves. Jesus is not like them. He has great regard for
other people. Jesus came so that people might have life and have it to the
full (περισσὸν/*perisson*). Jesus is about abundant life. He wants everyone
to enjoy a life well lived. This doesn't mean that life is without struggles.
It's not prosperity theology; it is life with meaning and eternal purpose.
   D. A. Carson writes:

> Within the metaphorical world, life…to the full suggests fat, contented, flourishing
> sheep, not terrorized by brigands; outside the narrative world, it means that the life

Jesus' true disciples enjoy is not to be construed as more time to fill (merely "everlast-ing" life), but life at its scarcely imagined best, life to be lived.[66]

Jesus came into this world to offer us "life to be lived." Are you experiencing the full life that Jesus has to offer?

8. Jesus Came to Be a Light to Lead People to God—John 12:46

> *"I have come into the world as a light, so that no one who believes in me should stay in darkness."*

Jesus came into the world as light. What is the quality of light? It expels darkness, shining in the dark so that we might see. It beckons us to come out of the darkness. This is the nature of Jesus: He bids us to leave the darkness and to walk in his light.

9. Jesus Came the Save the World—John 12:47

> *"As for the person who hears my words but does not keep them, I do not judge him. For I did not come to judge the world, but to save it."*

William Hendriksen writes, "The main purpose of Christ's first coming was not to bring condemnation but salvation."[67] Jesus came into the world to save it. He lived out this mission in the life that he lived and in the death that he died.

10. Jesus Came to Testify to the Truth—John 18:37

> *"'You are a king, then!' said Pilate.*
> *Jesus answered, 'You are right in saying I am a king. In fact, for this reason I was born, and for this I came into the world, to testify to the truth. Everyone on the side of truth listens to me.'"*

There has been much written in today's postmodern world about the inability to discern truth in an age of relativism. Can we know truth today? Jesus answers, Yes. Jesus states that he came into the world "to testify to the truth." If you want to know truth, then look to Jesus. He is the revelation of truth, and one reason he came into the world was to give us truth.

Conclusion

We cannot truncate the mission and purpose of Jesus into one idea. He came into the world in order to accomplish many things. If we are to imitate the mission of Jesus, we need to become familiar with the reasons he came into the world. I have listed ten. You can find others. Some of my ten overlap; for example, Jesus came to save sinners and to call people out of the darkness into the light. Perhaps we can narrow the ten down to four. This is how I would combine them:

1. To preach, to call sinners, to lead people as a light to God, to testify to the truth, and to offer abundant life to people

2. To do God's will, i.e., to keep the saved, saved

3. To serve

4. To give his life as a ransom, to save the world

Of course, number four is something that only Jesus could do—only Jesus could give his life as a ransom to save the world from sin. That leaves three.

What about these other three? It seems to me that these should be reflected in our ministries.

1. We are to preach the Word and call sinners to repentance.
2. We are to do God's will, which Jesus expressly states is to help those who are saved to stay saved.
3. We are to embrace the ministry of service.

I believe we should focus our ministries on these three tasks.

Earlier, I mentioned that Jesus came preaching, teaching, and healing. These three participles describe his ministry. I find it interesting that the three aspects of the mission of Jesus fit nicely and neatly with these three participles.

Preaching equals #1: To preach, to call sinners, to lead people as a light to God, to testify to the truth, and to offer abundant life to people. This seems self-evident.

Teaching equals #2: To do God's will, i.e., to keep the saved, saved. A big part of the teaching ministry of the church is to equip the saints for works of service and to help disciples mature in Christ.

Healing equals #3: To serve. Jesus' healing ministry was about doing some good and helping people. The service ministry of the church is also about doing some good and helping people.

Now we need to ask ourselves: How are we doing in these three areas of ministry? I'll leave that for you to think about and to discuss.

Be Like Jesus
(GSK)

Jesus left heaven and came to earth.
Then he left earth and went back to heaven.
When he went back, he left a little of himself behind
In each of us.
Let's be his gentle hands
    his industrious feet
    his loving eyes
    his compassionate heart.
Be like Jesus on your part of earth.
Embrace his mission.
Model his ministry.
Be the change you seek to make on this earth.
Be like Jesus.

End Notes

49. Borg, *Jesus: Uncovering the Life, Teachings, and Relevance of a Religious Revolutionary*, 163.

50. Author's own translation

51. Henri J.M. Nouwen, *In the Name of the Father: Reflections on Christian Leadership* (New York: The Crossroad Publishing Company, 1992), 37–38.

52. Dale E. Galloway, *20/20 Vision* ([n.pl.]: Scott Publishing, 1986), 74.

53. Ibid.

54. Author's own translation

55. Gene Mims, *The Kingdom-Focused Church* (Nashville: B&H Books, 2003), 152.

56. Ken Blanchard and Phil Hodges, *Lead Like Jesus* (Nashville: Thomas Nelson, 2008), 26–27.

57. Author's own translation

58. R. T. France, Tyndale New Testament Commentaries, *Matthew* (Grand Rapids: Eerdmans, 1985), 104–105.

59. Kenneth Bailey, *Jesus Through Middle Eastern Eyes* (Downers Grove, IL: IVP Academic, 2008), 156.

60. Bailey, 165.

61. "Because He Loved Me So," Lyrics by A.H. Ackley. Music by B.D. Ackley, 1912. In the public domain.

62. R. L. Cooper, *Holman New Testament Commentary* vol. 2, *Mark* (Nashville, TN: Broadman & Holman Publishers, 2000), 171–172.

63. J. R. Edwards, The Pillar New Testament Commentary, *The Gospel according to Mark* (Grand Rapids, MI: Eerdmans/Leicester, England: Apollos, 2002), 326.

64. Edwards, 327.

65. Carson, *The Gospel According to John,* 377.

66. Ibid., 385.

67. W. Hendriksen and S. J. Kistemaker, "John 12:47" in *New Testament Commentary* vol. 1–2, *Exposition of the Gospel According to John* (Grand Rapids: Baker Book House, 1953–2001).

Chapter 6

The Dawn of the Kingdom as Seen in the Healing Ministry of King Jesus

Jesus' healing ministry is based upon the great value of each individual person.[68]

—Brad H. Young, NT scholar

One cannot read the Gospel accounts without the question arising, "Who is this man who is master of nature, disease and even death?" In Jesus' actions people saw a bold claim to a unique authority.[69]

—Robert H. Stein, NT scholar

Jesus went throughout Galilee, teaching in their synagogues, preaching the good news of the kingdom, and healing every disease and sickness among the people. News about him spread all over Syria, and people brought to him all who were ill with various diseases, those suffering severe pain, the demon-possessed, those having seizures, and the paralyzed, and he healed them. Large crowds from Galilee, the Decapolis, Jerusalem, Judea and the region across the Jordan followed him.

—Matthew 4:23–25

Defining "Miracle"

First, what is a miracle? My simple definition of the word goes: A supernatural act of God in our world. A miracle is supernatural in that God sets aside the laws of nature to perform the miracle. Natural law says that someone who has been dead for three days will not come back to life. When that occurs, it is a supernatural occurrence. When God is the cause of such an event, a miracle has occurred.

My bit more convoluted definition of "miracle" goes: A miracle is an event where God sets aside the laws of nature to work in a supernatural manner in order to authenticate his message or his messenger, or in order to manifest himself or his redemptive purpose to humanity. In other words, God acts in a supernatural way in our world.

There are four Greek words generally used for the miracles of Jesus in the New Testament. The first is δύναμις/*dunamis*, which can also be translated as "power." Perhaps you see the word "dynamite" inside this word. It is an anachronistic way of defining *dunamis*, but it does help some people associate *dunamis* with power. *Dunamis* can also be translated as "a mighty work," "a mighty deed," "a powerful act," or "a manifestation of power." It can be used in reference to God's character, such as "the power of God." When Jesus performed a mighty act, it was understood that he was demonstrating "the power of the Most High God" through that mighty act.

In John's Gospel the word used most frequently to denote Jesus' miracles is σημεῖον/*semeion*, often translated as "signs." The word implies that Jesus' signs were intended to designate Jesus as one who was endowed with the power of God.

The third word is τέρας/*teras*, which is usually translated as "wonders." *Teras* denotes something unusual or something that causes wonder and amazement.

A fourth word is sometimes used in John's Gospel. This word, ἔργον/*ergon*, means "work" or "works" and is often translated as "act" or "deed."

Jesus' miracles demonstrated an enormous range of power—healing illness, controlling nature, forgiving sin, overcoming demonic possession, and breaking the bonds of death. Marcus Borg writes:

> The synoptics contain thirteen stories of particular healings. The conditions include fever, leprosy, paralysis, withered hand, bent back, hemorrhage, deafness and dumbness, blindness, dropsy, severed ear, and a sickness near death or paralysis.[70]

This is just a list of the healing miracles and does not include miracles over nature, demon possession, or death. The varied miracles of Jesus demonstrate the fullness of his power.

Stephen T. Davis in his book, *Risen Indeed*, defines "miracle" in this way: "a miracle is an event that (1) is brought about by God and (2) is contrary to the prediction of a law of nature that we have compelling reason to believe is true."[71] Dr. Davis then differentiates between soft miracles and hard miracles. He writes, "A *soft miracle*, let us say, is a miraculous event that religious skeptics can consistently agree has occurred; it is just that they will disagree with religious believers on its cause and meaning."[72] When a terminal cancer patient becomes free of cancer, this is often viewed as a soft miracle. The patient, his or her family, and the doctors describe the change of condition as miraculous, but there are different opinions as to how the change happened. Dr. Davis goes on to write, "A *hard miracle* on the other hand, is one that is very difficult for religious skeptics to explain naturalistically, and so skeptics will not want to allow that it has occurred at all."[73] The resurrection of Jesus would fit into this category. It is difficult for a naturalist to believe that a man who has been dead for over forty-eight hours can come back to life. Naturalists do not accept *hard* miracles.

The Miracles of Jesus Christ Divided by Type of Miracle[74]

NATURE MIRACLES	Matthew	Mark	Luke	John
1. Stilling the Storm	8:23	4:35	8:22	
2. Feeding the 5000	14:13	6:30	9:10	6:1
3. Walking on the Water	14:25	6:48		6:19
4. Feeding the 4000	15:32	8:1		
5. Temple Tax in the Fish's Mouth	17:24			
6. Withering the Fig Tree	21:18	11:12		
7. Draught of Fish			5:1	
8. Turning Water into Wine				2:1
9. Second Draught of Fish				21:1

HEALING MIRACLES	Matthew	Mark	Luke	John
General Healings				
1. Cleansing of a Leper	8:2	1:40	5:12	
2. Healing a Centurion's Servant	8:5		7:1	
3. Healing Peter's Mother-in-Law	8:14	1:30	4:38	
4. Healing the Sick at Evening	8:16	1:32	4:40	
5. Healing a Paralytic	9:2	2:3	5:18	
6. Healing the Hemorrhaging Woman	9:20	5:25	8:43	
7. Healing Two Blind Men	9:27			
8. Healing a Man's Withered Hand	12:9	3:1	6:6	
9. Healing the Gentile Woman's Daughter	15:21	7:24		
10. Healing the Epileptic Boy	17:14	9:17	9:38	
11. Healing a Blind Men	20:30	10:46	18:35	
12. Healing a Deaf Mute		7:31		
13. Healing a Blind Man at Bethsaida		8:22		
14. Healing the Infirm, Bent Woman			13:11	
15. Healing the Man with Dropsy			14:1	
16. Cleansing the Ten Lepers			17:11	
17. Restoring a Servant's Ear			22:51	
18. Healing the Nobleman's Son (of fever)				4:46
19. Healing an Infirm Man at Bethesda				5:1
20. Healing the Man Born Blind				9:1

RESURRECTIONS	Matthew	Mark	Luke	John
1. Raising the Ruler's Daughter	9:18,23	5:22,35	8:40,49	
2. Raising of a Widow's Son at Nain			7:11	
3. Raising of Lazarus				11:43

CASTING OUT DEMONS	Matthew	Mark	Luke	John
1. Demons Entering a Herd of Swine	8:28	5:1	8:26	
2. Curing a Demon-Possessed Mute	9:32			
3. Casting Out an Unclean Spirit		1:23	4:33	
4. Curing a Possessed, Blind/Mute Man	12:22		11:14	

Did Jesus Perform Miracles?

My second question: Did Jesus really work miracles? This is a fair question. Many, if not most, members of the scholarly world over the last 200 years have answered this question with a resounding, No! Their reasoning goes, "The laws of nature are fixed and cannot be superseded. No one performs miracles today. If miracles cannot be performed today, then why would they have occurred 2,000 years ago?"

But the Gospel writers attribute over thirty miracles to Jesus. Many scholars believe the miracle stories were included in the text to make Jesus appear like a Greek or Roman god. These scholars go to great lengths to explain away the miracles of Jesus. They say, "Jesus didn't really walk on water. The setting sun caused a reflection on the water, and it just looked like he was walking on it." Or they write, "Jesus didn't really cast out demons; he counseled emotionally disturbed people back to reality in the same way that a competent psychologist might nurture someone back to health today." Some scholars paint Jesus as a holistic healer who cured people with natural, homeopathic remedies. In their minds, there was nothing supernatural about the healing work of Jesus.

But these arguments fail to explain how Jesus calmed a storm at sea or brought Lazarus back from the dead. They also fail to explain the most important miracle story in the New Testament—the resurrection of Jesus from the dead.

What we have here is a difference in worldviews—a naturalistic worldview versus a supernaturalistic worldview. Much of the tension that exists between liberal theology and evangelical theology comes from a difference in worldviews. Liberal theologians reject the possibility of miracles occurring. Liberal theologians follow the tenets of the Scottish philosopher David Hume (1711–1776) who, as a British Empiricist, rejected the possibility that God or anyone else could suspend natural law and work a miracle. In Hume's mind, miracles were a logical impossibility. Hume wrote, "A miracle is a violation of the laws of nature, and as a firm and unalterable experience has established these laws, the proof against miracle, from the very nature of the fact, is as entire as any argument from experience can possibly be imagined."[75] Thomas C. Oden comments on Hume's position, "If one takes the view of David Hume, that a miracle cannot by its very nature be authentically reported, then miracle must be *prima facie* removed in advance from all inquiry and all potential historical occurrences."[76]

To a naturalist, the miracles of Jesus can and must be explained within the realm of modern scientific convention. In other words, Jesus didn't really work miracles. To the naturalist, all of his "miracles" have a natural explanation: When Jesus healed people, he used herbs and homeopathic remedies. Many of the illnesses Jesus cured were psychosomatic;

therefore, when Jesus helped people psychologically, he cured their illnesses. Of course, it's more difficult to explain away resurrections, especially one like Lazarus's where he was dead for several days.

There were many other miracle workers in the Hellenistic and Roman periods. Perhaps Jesus' miracles were no different from those of other miracle workers of his day? Walter Grundmann in the *Theological Dictionary of the New Testament* mentions three ways the miracles of Jesus are distinguished from miracles performed by first-century miracle workers. Grundmann writes:

> a. The NT miracles of Jesus have no connection with magic, or with magical means and processes, like the majority of miracles outside the NT.... b. The miracles are evoked by the powerful Word of Jesus, which has nothing to do with magic.... c. The miracles presuppose the faith of the one who performs them and also of the one on whom they are performed. They are accomplished in a wholly personal relationship.[77]

The miracles of Jesus were qualitatively different from other supposed miracles of his day.

Could Jesus perform miracles? Why not? If you believe that Jesus was present in the creation of the world, then certainly Jesus had the power to work outside natural laws. William Jennings Bryan offers this argument concerning the possibilities of miracles, writing, "Can God perform a miracle?... A God who can make a world can do anything He wants to do with it."[78]

Do Miracles Still Happen Today?

Third, do miracles still happen today? Depends by what you mean by miracle. Yes, God works miracles through prayer. This is what Stephen T. Davis would classify as a "soft" miracle. I'm sure that we all have witnessed the answering of prayer. That doesn't make us miracle workers in the biblical sense. When our son, Daniel, was seven months old, he was admitted to hospital in Helsinki, Finland because of a strange allergic reaction to some medication. Prayers from the church in New York during its midweek assembly coincided with the exact time that Daniel's body started to heal in Helsinki. I consider that a miracle. Not everyone would.

At the same time, biblical miracles were done for a purpose—to demonstrate that God was moving in a powerful way. In the ministry of Jesus, miracles revealed that God was working through him.

The Bible teaches that God works miracles today through answered prayers. The Bible doesn't teach that people today have the ability to perform miracles with the laying on of hands as they did in the first century. Why? Because Jesus gave his disciples the ability to perform miracles so their testimony would be confirmed through miraculous signs (Mark

16:20). Since we have the word of God confirmed to us today through the written confirmation of the apostles' testimony in the New Testament documents, there is no need for miracles to accompany that testimony. The miraculous gifts of the early church were for a season (1 Corinthians 13:8–10). That season has passed. Now we have the power and authority of God revealed to us in his perfect law of liberty (James 1:22–25 ESV).

Why Did Jesus Perform Miracles?

Fourth, why miracles? Did Jesus work miracles to prove he was divine? Not completely. Remember that many other biblical figures performed miracles, and none of these people were looked upon as divine. Miracles in themselves do not prove divinity, although at times, the miracles of Jesus do underscore his divinity and his claim to be the Messiah.

Did he work miracles to instill faith? Not entirely. Remember that not everyone who saw a miracle responded with faith. Some, in fact, stumbled over the miracles of Jesus. At times, Jesus' signs and miracles did lead people to faith, and Jesus even commented that some would not believe unless they witnessed a miracle (John 4:48); but Jesus knew that not everyone who saw a miracle would believe in him. The purpose of miracles was not to overwhelm people with evidence that Jesus was the Christ. Miracles do not compel or force a person into faith. Some who asked Jesus to perform a sign were asking for the wrong reason. Jesus did not give signs to the Pharisees when they asked for them.

The miracles showed that Jesus was the Messiah. They caused people to ask the question, "Who is this person who can do such things?" but miracles didn't force them into a declaration of Jesus being the Messiah.

So we ask again, why miracles? Thomas C. Oden answers:

> Jesus appears not to have performed miracles miscellaneously or without purpose. Rather, each one responded to some special need or served some purpose in pointing to the coming reign of God. He did not draw attention to himself as a worker of miracles. Rather each miracle was a specific response to some personal, social, or contextual need."[79]

So there was no one reason why Jesus worked miracles. He worked miracles to meet needs. He worked miracles because he had a compassionate heart. He worked miracles because he was actively battling the powers of darkness. He worked miracles as a sign of the rule and reign of God being offered in his person and through his ministry.

Four Reasons Why Jesus Performed Miracles

1. To confirm his word or testimony

Mark 16:20 reads, "Then the disciples went out and preached every-where, and the Lord worked with them and confirmed his word by the signs that accompanied it." Hebrews 2:2–4 notes:

> *For if the message spoken by angels was binding, and every violation and disobedience received its just punishment, how shall we escape if we ignore such a great salvation? This salvation, which was first announced by the Lord, was confirmed to us by those who heard him. God also testified to it by signs, wonders and various miracles, and gifts of the Holy Spirit distributed according to his will.*

2. To draw out faith from people or to confirm their faith in Jesus

Miracles did not necessarily produce faith. Some saw the miracles of Jesus and stumbled over them, but others saw his miracles and believed that he was the Christ. John 20:30–31 reads, "Jesus did many other mirac-ulous signs in the presence of his disciples, which are not recorded in this book. But these are written that you may believe that Jesus is the Christ, the Son of God, and that by believing you may have life in his name."

3. To demonstrate his Lordship and to show that Jesus was Immanuel—God with us

When Nicodemus came to Jesus, Nicodemus said, "Rabbi, we know you are a teacher who has come from God. For no one could perform the miraculous signs you are doing if God were not with him" (John 3:2).

4. To demonstrate that Jesus is the Messiah as foretold in prophecy

At times the gospel writers connected the miracles of Jesus with prophecy concerning the coming of the Messiah, who was to work mir-acles. The Messiah was to heal the sick, cause the blind to see, and em-power the lame to walk (compare Luke 4:18–19 with Isaiah 61:1–2 and Matthew 8:16–17 with Isaiah 53:4).

A Prophet in Word and Deed

I'm sure that you've heard the saying, "Actions speak louder than words." Well, the fact is that both are important. Jesus proved he was a prophet through his words and his deeds. At the conclusion of his Gospel, the men walking to Emmaus reported, "[Jesus] was a prophet, powerful in word and deed before God and all the people. The chief priests and our rulers handed him over to be sentenced to death, and they crucified him" (Luke 24:20). Jesus was a prophet in word and deed.

At the close of the Sermon on the Mount, Matthew records the audience saying that Jesus taught with authority (Matthew 7:28–29). Fourteen times in this sermon Jesus says, "You have heard that it was said,...but I tell you." Jesus' words were filled with authority. They were powerful. Jesus was a prophet in word.

Another aspect of his powerful ministry was his mighty works; or, more properly, the mighty works of God through Jesus. When Jesus spoke the Word, people were immediately healed of their infirmities (Matthew 8:1–18). His words were accompanied by power. The miracles were a proof of the kingdom arriving in the person and work of Jesus. He was a prophet in deed.

This was the two-tiered ministry of Jesus—words and deeds. This should also be reflected in our ministry today. We must preach the truth in love, but we must also have a ministry that changes lives.

What Do Miracles Say about Jesus?

Fifth, what do the miracles say about who Jesus was? All miracles are Christocentric; they all point to Jesus as Lord and Christ (Messiah). Jesus is Lord over nature, over disease, over demons, over sin, over weakness, and over death. If you allow him, then he will be Lord over your life as well. Jesus is a caring and compassionate Messiah who cares for the hurts and needs of people, including you and me. He wants to heal people from the inside out. He came into the world to offer people wholeness (*shalom*—peace).

The miracles forced people to think about the nature of Jesus. When a miracle was performed, people began to see who Jesus was, or at least they began to ask questions about who he was. John 6:14 records, "After the people saw the miraculous sign that Jesus did, they began to say, 'Surely this is the Prophet who is to come into the world.'" The miracles prompted this response in the people. So what do the miracles tell us about Jesus?

Jesus Was a Compassionate Messiah: The Miracles over Sickness and Disease

The miracles of Jesus add evidence to his claim to be the Messiah. When John sent his disciples to Jesus to ask if he truly was the Messiah or if they should keep their eyes open for another (which hints of the fact that they were several "Messiah sightings" in the first century), Jesus sent John's disciples back with this word, "Go back and report to John what you hear and see: The blind receive sight, the lame walk, those who have leprosy are cured, the deaf hear, the dead are raised, and the good news is preached to the poor" (Matthew 11:4–5). The miracles acted as proof that Jesus was the Messiah.

Isaiah 35:5–6a prophesied that several types of miracles would accompany the coming Messiah:

Then will the eyes of the blind be opened

and the ears of the deaf unstopped.
Then will the lame leap like a deer,
and the mute tongue shout for joy.

The Messianic Age dawned in the miracles of Jesus' ministry. Isaiah 29:18 reads:

In that day the deaf will hear the words of the scroll,
and out of gloom and darkness
the eyes of the blind will see.

The prophets declared that in the Messianic Age, physical and spiritual healing would occur. The miracles pointed to the type of Messiah that Jesus would be: not a militaristic, warrior king; but a compassionate, benevolent, and loving king.

Why did Jesus heal the sick? He healed people because of his compassion. The English word "compassion" comes from two Latin words, *pathos* and *cum*, which mean "suffer" and "with," respectively. So, to have compassion for someone means "to suffer with" that person. In the Greek, the word for compassion (σπλάγχνον/*splagchnon*) can mean "womb, inner parts, entrails." Thus, feelings of compassion are associated with the womb of a woman and with the stomach, bowels, or loins of a man, so the Bible uses the image of the bowels being moved with compassion. When we suffer with someone, we sometimes feel pain in our gut. This is what it means to be moved by compassion. Jesus helped people because he was moved by compassion to help them.

In some early Jewish communities, the lame and diseased were outcasts; they were separated from the community. N. T. Wright notes:

> The evidence from Qumran suggests that, in some Jewish circles at least, a maimed Jew could not be a full member of the community. In addition to the physical burden of being blind, or lame, or deaf, or dumb, such a Jew was blemished, and unable to be a full Israelite. How far this was taken by Jewish society in Jesus' day it is difficult to assess. But we know that at least in Qumran it was a very serious matter. This means that Jesus' healing miracles must be seen clearly as bestowing the gift of shalom, wholeness, to those who embraced it, bringing not only physical health but renewed membership in the people of YHWH.[80]

Jesus offered his community and his fellowship to the blind, the lame, the deaf, and the dumb. Jesus offered wholeness to all people, even those who were cast out of other fellowships.

As we progress through our discussion of the miracles of Jesus, we are going to focus on Matthew 8. This chapter occurs after the Sermon on the Mount. In the Sermon on the Mount Jesus forms his community around his word, teaching them his ethical standard. Now, in Matthew 8, Jesus expands the reach of community to those who suffer from leprosy, to the sick, and to the demon-possessed. His community is expanded to embrace a Gentile who also happens to be a leader in the occupational forces of the Roman army. How does he reach out to these people? He reaches them through his deeds, his miracles.

Matthew 8 begins with healing of a leper. Jesus reaches out to touch the leper, offering the leper his hand in fellowship. Matthew 8:1–4 (cf. Mark 1:40–45, Luke 5:12–14) reads:

> *When he came down from the mountainside, large crowds followed him. A man with leprosy came and knelt before him and said, "Lord, if you are willing, you can make me clean."*
>
> *Jesus reached out his hand and touched the man. "I am willing," he said. "Be clean!" Immediately he was cured of his leprosy. Then Jesus said to him, "See that you don't tell anyone. But go, show yourself to the priest and offer the gift Moses commanded, as a testimony to them.*

In the first century, lepers were considered the walking dead. A leper was obligated to tell anyone who approached him that he was unclean. This leper was bold; his behavior was atypical of a leper. He should have kept his distance from Jesus and sounded the warning, "Unclean! Unclean!" Instead, he approached Jesus, kneeled before him, and made a request: "Lord, if you are willing, you can make me clean."

I wonder if the leper felt surprised when Jesus didn't pull away from him with disgust. Surely any other rabbi would have. Any other rabbi would not have dared to touch the leper for fear of becoming unclean. Any other rabbi would have castigated the leper for even approaching him. But Jesus was unlike any other rabbi. The hand of Jesus came closer and closer to the leper. I wonder if the leper cringed when Jesus' hand approached his skin. I wonder if he began to pull back. Then came the touch. Jesus should have become unclean from that touch. Instead, the leper became clean.

I appreciate the leper's boldness. Many of the miracle stories portray the person in need of healing as being bold; for example, the lady with the issue of blood who reaches out to touch Jesus' garment and the blind man who will not stop crying out, "Son of David, have mercy on me." Why were they bold? Because they were desperate to get help, and desperation makes a person bold.

Jesus healed the leper's physical illness, but he also healed the leper's social illness, restoring him to the community. Jesus was a compassionate Messiah.

In Matthew 8:5–13 (cf. Luke 7:1–10), a Roman centurion comes to Jesus seeking a miracle for his servant. Matthew writes:

> When Jesus had entered Capernaum, a centurion came to him, asking for help. "Lord," he said, "my servant lies at home paralyzed and in terrible suffering."
>
> Jesus said to him, "I will go and heal him."
>
> The centurion replied, "Lord, I do not deserve to have you come under my roof. But just say the word, and my servant will be healed. For I myself am a man under authority, with soldiers under me. I tell this one, 'Go,' and he goes; and that one, 'Come,' and he comes. I say to my servant, 'Do this,' and he does it."
>
> When Jesus heard this, he was astonished and said to those following him, "I tell you the truth, I have not found anyone in Israel with such great faith. I say to you that many will come from the east and the west, and will take their places at the feast with Abraham, Isaac and Jacob in the kingdom of heaven. But the subjects of the kingdom will be thrown outside, into the darkness, where there will be weeping and gnashing of teeth."
>
> Then Jesus said to the centurion, "Go! It will be done just as you believed it would." And his servant was healed at that very hour."

The main character in this second miracle was not a Jew, but a Roman. The centurion stood clearly outside of the community of the Jews. He was a Gentile and a military leader in the forces occupying Galilee. The centurion was aware of the fact that the only standing he had in the community came because of his authority as a military commander. He was also aware that Jesus, as a Jew, should not enter his home. Therefore, the centurion politely suggested that Jesus stay away. He mentioned that he wasn't fit to have Jesus come into his home. He didn't want to hurt Jesus' standing in the community. He didn't want Jesus to be stigmatized by having fellowship with a Gentile. But Jesus reached out to the centurion and offered him a place within the community of the faithful. He mentioned that the centurion had greater faith than anyone in all of Israel.

I appreciate how the centurion felt unworthy of Jesus' favor. He was used to ordering people around, but he didn't give Jesus an order; he made a request from him. Why? Because the centurion knew that Jesus had more authority than he did and felt unworthy of Jesus' grace.

Continuing in Matthew 8, we see that Jesus opened up his community to women. This was a very bold move on Jesus' part. We see this in the healing of Peter's mother-in-law. Jesus also opened the door of his community to anyone who came to him needing help and aid. Again we see the healing ministry of Jesus connected with his compassion. Matthew 8:14–17 (cf. Mark 1:30–34, Luke 4:38–41) records:

> When Jesus came into Peter's house, he saw Peter's mother-in-law lying in bed with a

fever. He touched her hand and the fever left her, and she got up and began to wait on him.

When evening came, many who were demon-possessed were brought to him, and he drove out the spirits with a word and healed all the sick. This was to fulfill what was spoken through the prophet Isaiah:
> *"He took up our infirmities*
> *and carried our diseases."*

Matthew is quick to connect the ministry of Jesus with OT prophecy. In this case, he connects the miracles of Jesus with one of four Suffering Servant poems in Isaiah. Isaiah 53:5–6 describes the Messiah as a suffering Messiah who would take onto himself the infirmities and weakness of the people. Why? So that they wouldn't have to suffer any longer. He would carry their diseases. Why? So that they wouldn't be diseased. Jesus was a compassionate Messiah. He helped his people. He wanted to make them whole. Because he died, others could be healed (in the here and now and in the hereafter).[81]

Luke stresses that Jesus had power to heal (Luke 4:36, 5:17, 6:19, 8:46). Another way to translate the word "disease" is to use the word "weakness." Jesus had power to heal weakness in others.

Jesus the compassionate Messiah healed the brokenness of people, and we need to embrace this ministry as well. This is the healing ministry of Jesus. It takes a compassionate heart to engage in this ministry. We have to see the hurt in people, then we have to respond in an appropriate manner to that hurt.

Jesus Was a Powerful Lord: Nature Miracles

If we continue our reading in Matthew 8, we come across a miracle of Jesus over nature. Matthew 8:23–27 (cf. Mark 35–41, Luke 8:22–25) reads:

> *Then he got into the boat and his disciples followed him. Without warning, a furious storm came up on the lake, so that the waves swept over the boat. But Jesus was sleeping. The disciples went and woke him, saying, "Lord, save us! We're going to drown!"*
>
> *He replied, "You of little faith, why are you so afraid?" Then he got up and rebuked the winds and the waves, and it was completely calm.*
>
> *The men were amazed and asked, "What kind of man is this? Even the winds and the waves obey him!"*

Jesus had the power to calm the chaotic evil of the turbulent sea. Marcus Borg writes:

> Central to these stories is 'the sea,' an image which reverberates with rich resonances

of meaning in the Hebrew Bible. The Hebrew word for "sea," derived from the name of the evil god in the Babylonian creation story, carried connotations of evil, a mysterious and threatening force opposed to God.[82]

Jesus' miracle over the storm at sea demonstrates the power of Jesus over the forces of nature. If Jesus has the power to still a raging storm on the Sea of Galilee, imagine what he can do to quiet the storms in your life.

Jesus Was a King Who Fought Against Darkness: The Exorcisms by Jesus

If we continue in Matthew, we next come across an exorcism by Jesus. Matthew 8:28–34 (cf. Mark 5:1–15, Luke 8:26–36) reads:

> When he arrived at the other side in the region of the Gadarenes, two demon-possessed men coming from the tombs met him. They were so violent that no one could pass that way. "What do you want with us, Son of God?" they shouted. "Have you come here to torture us before the appointed time?"
>
> Some distance from them a large herd of pigs was feeding. The demons begged Jesus, "If you drive us out, send us into the herd of pigs."
>
> He said to them, "Go!" So they came out and went into the pigs, and the whole herd rushed down the steep bank into the lake and died in the water. Those tending the pigs ran off, went into the town and reported all this, including what had happened to the demon-possessed men. Then the whole town went out to meet Jesus. And when they saw him, they pleaded with him to leave their region.

Exorcisms are unique in the Gospels. They signaled the battle between Jesus and the powers of darkness. In the story above, you see the desperation of the two men illustrated by the fact that they lived in the tombs and were so violent that no one would pass their way. Yet they understood what other people missed: that Jesus was the Son of God. They didn't want to have anything to do with him; they recognized that he had come to torment them. That Jesus came to battle the powers of darkness is seen in his exchange with demons.

N. T. Wright notes:

> The exorcisms are especially interesting in that they formed apart neither of the regular Old Testament predictions nor first-century Jewish expectations concerning healing and deliverance associated with the coming of the kingdom; nor were they a major focus of the life and work of the early church. They therefore stand out, by the criterion of dissimilarity, as being part of a battle in which Jesus alone was engaged. He seems to have seen himself as fighting a battle with the real enemy, and to have regarded the exorcisms—or healings of those whose condition was attributed to the work of Satan—as a sign that he was winning the battle, though it had not yet reached its height.[83]

Walter Grundmann writes:

> The miracles of Jesus are part of the invading dominion of God which Jesus brings with His own person in proclamation and act. They are the dominion of God overcoming and expelling the sway of demons and Satan. Like the whole history of Jesus, His miracles are an eschatological event."[84]

The miracles by which Jesus exorcized demons signaled the beginning of the *eschaton* (the last days) because Jesus was combating darkness in these events. Jesus had power over darkness, and his miracles demonstrated this power.

Why Do the Miracle Stories Contain Different Details?

What about the differences in the miracle stories? Was there one demoniac who approached Jesus, or two? Who asked Jesus to heal the servant girl, the centurion or his delegates?

Many scholars believe that Matthew and Luke shared two sources, Mark and Q (The Q Source=the Sayings of Jesus). Scholars believe that Matthew and Luke followed Mark's account but made changes to Mark's story. Does this mean that the gospel writers made up these stories? Does this mean the differences in the stories were contradictions and inaccuracies? In my estimation, the differences in the miracles do not negate the factuality of the stories. The differences come from the retelling of the story from different perspectives.

Matthew, Mark, Luke, and John all had far more material than they needed to write their gospels. There were many witnesses to the ministry of Jesus who could have provided source material. The Gospels are similar because they tell the same story, but differences appear because the individual writers focus on different aspects of the same story. For example, if three people see an automobile accident, they might retell what happened in the accident in three distinct ways. If you go over the accounts, it might look like each person saw a different accident. There was one accident, but you hear three versions of the accident because three people recount the story in their own unique way. The retelling of the accident doesn't change what really happened, even though the retelling of the event can make it seem like each person saw something different.

Look at the story of the quieting of the storm at sea as told by Matthew, Mark, and Luke. In this story, how did the disciples talk to Jesus when they woke him from his sleep? In Matthew, the disciples said, "Save, Lord; we perish" (ASV). In Mark they asked, "Teacher, don't you care if we drown?" In Luke, they declared, "Master, Master, [we] perish" (ASV). Which is right? All are right. They probably said more than this. I would have. The story is told from three different perspectives, but all are accurate.

The story followed different chronologies in the Gospels. Matthew recorded Jesus speaking first and then acting on the storm. Jesus invited them to think about what he was going to do, then he did it. In the other two gospels, Jesus acted and then he spoke. In these gospels, the words of Jesus sounded more like a rebuke. How can this be reconciled?

First, these men were speaking in Aramaic. All we have today are translations of the original event, thus we are at least one or two steps removed from what really happened. Second, both the disciples and Jesus said more than was recorded in the Gospels. Matthew, Mark, and Luke selected fragments from the event that told the story, but they were also teaching a lesson in the telling of the story. Matthew focused on their lack of faith. They had faith, but their faith needed to grow. Luke asked where their faith had gone. They had faith, but where was it now? In Luke, for those who were struggling, Jesus' message was "Find your faith." In Mark the message was: "Why are you afraid; do you not have faith? You disciples, you are acting like unbelievers." Mark was toughest on those who should know how to react with faith but didn't. When testing came, they failed the test.

Each writer was able to make a theological statement as they retold the story of Jesus calming the sea. Their theological retelling didn't change the story. The event transpired as it transpired: Jesus fell asleep in the boat, a storm rose on the sea, the disciples cried out, Jesus answered their cries, they continued to cry out, Jesus calmed the storm, and then Jesus challenged them for their lack of faith.

The different Gospel traditions don't take away from the facts of what happened in the miracle stories. In the retelling of the stories, the gospel writers are able to challenge us to think about our own lives in light of what happened in the ministry of Jesus. The retelling of the miracle stories from different perspectives doesn't weaken the power of the gospel message; it strengthens it.

*****

I want to close this section with a quote from the German theologian, Jurgen Moltmann, who writes, "Jesus' healings are not supernatural miracles in a natural world. They are the only truly 'natural' things in a world that is unnatural, demonized, and wounded."[85] I believe that Moltmann has the right perspective on the miracles of Jesus. Through the miracles of Jesus, we catch a glimpse of the world turned "right side up." We catch a glimpse of the rule and reign of God entering the world.

Bartimeus
Henry Wadsworth Longfellow

Blind Bartimeus at the gates
Of Jericho in darkness waits;
He hears the crowd;—he hears a breath
Say, "It is Christ of Nazareth!"
And calls, in tones of agony,
Ἰησου, ἐλἐησὸν με![86]

The thronging multitudes increase;
Blind Bartimaeus, hold thy peace!
But still, above the noisy crowd,
The beggar's cry is shrill and loud;
Until they say, "He calleth thee!"
Θαρσει ζγειραι , φωνει σε![87]

Then saith the Christ, as silent stands
The crowd, "What wilt thou at my hands?"
And he replies, "Oh, give me light!
Rabbi, restore the blind man's sight."
And Jesus answers, Ὑπαγε'
Ἡ πιστις σου σεσωκε σε![88]

Ye that have eyes, yet cannot see,
In darkness and in misery,
Recall those mighty Voices Three,
Ἰησου, ἐλἐησὸν με!
Θαρσει ἐγειραι, υπαγε!
Ἡ πιστις σου σεσωκε σε![89]

The Miracles of Jesus Based on the Number of Occurrences[90]

MIRACLES	Location	Matthew	Mark	Luke	John
NARRATED IN ONE GOSPEL					
Two blind men healed	Capernaum	9:27–31			
A dumb demoniac healed	Capernaum	9:32–34			
Coin in the mouth of the fish	Capernaum	17:24–27			
The deaf and dumb man healed	Decapolis		7:31–37		
A blind man healed	Bethsaida		8:22–26		
When Christ passed unseen through the multitude	Nazareth			4:28–30	
Draught of fish	Bethsaida			5:4–7	
Raising the widow's son	Nain			7:11–18	
Healing the woman with an infirmity	Jerusalem			13:10–17	
Healing the man with dropsy	Jerusalem			14:1–6	
Healing the ten lepers	Samaria			17:11–19	
Healing the ear of Malchus, servant of the high priest	Gethsemane			22:50–51	
Turning water into wine	Cana				2:1–11
Healing the nobleman's son of fever	Cana				4:46–54
Healing impotent man at Bethesda	Jerusalem				5:1–9
Healing the man born blind	Jerusalem				9:1–41
Raising of Lazarus	Bethany				11:1–44
Draught of fish	Bethsaida				21:4–6
NARRATED IN TWO GOSPELS					
Healing the Syrophoenician daughter	Tyre	15:21–28	7:24–30		
Feeding the four thousand	Gennesaret (?)	15:32–39	8:1–9		
Cursing the fig tree	Mt. of Olives	21:17–20	11:12–14		
Healing the centurion's servant	Capernaum	8:5–13		7:1–10	
The blind and dumb demoniac	Galilee	12:22–23		11:14–15	
The demoniac in a synagogue	Capernaum		1:23–28	4:33–37	
NARRATED IN THREE GOSPELS					
Stilling the storm	Sea of Galilee	8:23–27	4:35–41	8:22–25	
The Demons entering the swine	Gadara	8:28–34	5:1–16	8:26–36	
Healing of Jairus' daughter	Capernaum	9:18–26	5:21–43	8:40–56	
Healing woman with an issue of blood	Gennesaret	9:20–22	5:25–34	8:43–48	
Healing the man sick of the palsy	Capernaum	9:1–8	2:1–12	5:17–26	
Healing the leper	Gennesaret	8:1–4	1:40–45	5:12–14	
Healing Peter's mother-in-law	Bethsaida	8:14–15	1:29–31	4:38–39	
Healing man with withered hand	Capernaum	12:9–13	3:1–5	6:6–11	
Healing the demoniac child	Mt. Tabor (?)	17:14–21	9:14–27	9:37–43	
Healing the blind Bartimaeus	Jericho	20:29–34	10:46–52	18:35–43	
Walking on the sea	Sea of Galilee	14:22–33	6:45–52		6:16–21
NARRATED IN FOUR GOSPELS					
Feeding the 5,000	Bethsaida	14:15–21	6:32–44	9:11–17	6:1–13

End Notes

68. Brad H. Young, *Jesus the Jewish Theologian* (Peabody, Massachusetts: Hendrickson Publishers, Inc., 1995), 40.

69. Stein, 143.

70. Borg, *Jesus: Uncovering the Life, Teachings, and Relevance of a Religious Revolutionary*, 146.

71. Stephen T. Davis, *Risen Indeed: Making Sense of the Resurrection* (Grand Rapids: Eerdmans, 1993), 10.

72. Ibid., 11.

73. Ibid., 12.

74. Chart found at www.bcbsr.com/survey/jmrcls.html.

75. David Hume, Section X, *"Of Miracles" in An Enquiry Concerning Human Understanding* (Bobbs-Merrill, Library of Liberal Arts edition, 1748), 123.

76. Thomas C. Oden, *Systematic Theology,* vol. 2, *The Word of Life* (San Francisco: Harper Collins, 1989), 270.

77. Walter Grundmann, *"dunamai/dunamis,"* in *Theological Dictionary of New Testament Theology,* vol. 2, edited by Gerhard Kittel, translated by Geoffrey W. Bromiley (Grand Rapids: Eerdmans, 1964), 302.

78. William Jennings Bryan, *The Prince of Peace* (Chicago: Reily and Briton Company, 1909), 13–14.

79. Oden, 299–300.

80. N. T. Wright, *Jesus and the Victory of God,* 191–192.

81. The word for healed and the word for saved are often the same word in the Greek. As we are saved, we are also healed from the inside out.

82. Marcus J. Borg, *Jesus, a New Vision* (San Francisco: HarperCollins Publishers, 1987), 65.

83. N. T. Wright, *Jesus and the Victory of God,* 195.

84. Grundmann, 302.

85. Jurgen Moltmann, *The Way of Jesus Christ* (Philadelphia: Fortress Press, 1995), 99.

86. Translated, "Jesus, have mercy on me now."

87. Translated, "Do not fear. Get up. He calls you."

88. Translated, "Go. Your faith has saved you."

89. Translated:

> Jesus, have mercy on me.
> Do not fear. Get up. Go.
> Your faith has saved you.

90. B.W. Johnson, "Our Lord's Miracles," in *The People's New Testament,* 1 April 2002, 18 May 2009, <http://blueletterbible.org/study/pnt/pnt05.cfm>.

Chapter 7

The Teaching Ministry of Jesus, Part 1: The Sermon on the Mount

Jesus was from the peasant class. Clearly, he was brilliant. His use of language was remarkable and poetic, filled with images and stories. He had a metaphoric mind. He was not ascetic, but world-affirming, with a zest for life. There was a sociopolitical passion to him—like a Gandhi or a Martin Luther King, he challenged the domination system of his day. He was a religious ecstatic, a Jewish mystic, for whom God was an experiential reality. As such, Jesus was also a healer. And there seems to have been a spiritual presence around him, like that reported of St. Francis or the present Dalai Lama. And as a figure of history, Jesus was an ambiguous figure—you could experience him and conclude that he was insane, as his family did, or that he was simply eccentric or that he was a dangerous threat—or you could conclude that he was filled with the Spirit of God.[91]

—Marcus J. Borg, Jesus scholar

Aphorisms: The Short, Pithy Sayings of Jesus

We all know that Jesus taught in parables.[92] But Jesus also taught using aphorisms—short, pithy sayings that are easy to remember. Sayings like: "Blessed are the poor in spirit..." and "Give, and it will be given to you," and "Let the dead bury their own dead." Aphorisms include beatitudes, declarations, pronouncements, directives, and short analogies. Over one hundred of these are attributed to Jesus in the Gospels.

Aphorisms are very similar to proverbs. Marcus Borg differentiates between an aphorism and a proverb, noting:

Proverbs commonly express the folk wisdom, the conventional wisdom, of a culture—what everybody knows or should know. They are most often anonymous, the product of generations of experience and reflection....Aphorisms on the other hand express the fresh insight of a particular individual and often function to overturn or subvert conventional wisdom. They are surprising, arresting, and thought-provoking.[93]

Part of the genius of Jesus' teaching can be seen in his use of aphorisms, by which he turned conventional wisdom on its ear. Jesus gave his audience memorable phrases so that they could cling to his words long after he left their town or village, phrases that provoked thoughtful discussion, like "All who draw the sword will die by the sword."

He would have used these one-liners over and over in his ministry as he traveled from village to village. At times, he would string the phrases together to form long blocks of aphorisms. An example of this is his list of beatitudes at the beginning of the Sermon on the Mount (Matthew 5:1ff).

Jesus knew that his words were important. He called attention to what he was about to say by using introductory phrases, like "You have heard that it was said..., but I say to you...."[94] He said, "Truly, I say to you...." (ESV). It's much like a coach saying, "Hey, listen up," or a teacher saying, "Pay attention; this will be on the test." Rabbis quoted the wisdom of other rabbis. When it came time for them to pronounce their finding, they would say, "This is my ruling." Jesus did the same; but he added a note of authority to his ruling by saying, "Truly, I say to you." Or, "You have heard that it was said..., but I [myself] say to you...." Jesus' audience noted that he did not speak like the other teachers of his day. The difference? Jesus taught with authority (Matthew 7:28–29).

The Ethics of Jesus' Kingdom

The Sermon on the Mount presents the ethics of the kingdom of God. It was an ethic of the emerging community of Jesus at the beginning of his ministry. Matthew 5:1–2 states, "Jesus saw the crowds; he went up on the mountain, and after he sat down, his disciples came to him. Then he began to teach them, saying..." Jesus sat down and spoke to his disciples. He didn't direct his teaching to the entire crowd; he spoke to those who were interested in hearing what he had to say, to those who were interested in his kingdom.

Others heard the sermon. It filtered down the hillside to the crowds below. Matthew 7:28–29 reads, "When Jesus finished saying these words, the crowds were amazed at his teaching, for he taught them as one with authority and not as their scribes." But the crowds were not his primary audience. Jesus didn't mind who heard the message, but the message was directed to those following him.

There is one major problem with the Sermon on the Mount. Do you know what that problem is? It's not that it is too difficult to understand. Almost anyone can understand the sermon. The problem is that it is not livable. Surely even the most self-righteous, overly pious, most Pharisaic among us would say, "I have a difficult time living up to its standard." Jesus heightens the standard of the Old Covenant so that he is now, as Jeremiah's prophecies foretold, writing a covenant on the heart. The Sermon on the Mount presents an extremely high standard for the community of Jesus.

Perhaps we should see the Sermon on the Mount as a goal for us to shoot for in life. It is an unreachable goal in many ways, but it is a goal that will stretch us to be our best for God. The goal of life is to please God and give him glory by living like Jesus. The Sermon on the Mount is our roadmap to fulfill that goal. The Sermon is our challenging, upward call to be like Jesus and walk in his steps. We understand that it is unattainable, but it is still our goal.

In the Sermon, Jesus establishes his community. He wants his community to live by these ethics and then be salt and light to the world. That is also our goal. We will fall short, but when we do, God will be there to cover our failings with his grace.

The Beatitudes: The Blessings—Matthew 5:1–12

When Jesus saw the crowds, he went up on the mountain, and after he sat down, his disciples came to him. Then he began to teach them, saying:

"Fortunate are the humble in spirit, for theirs is the kingdom of heaven.
Fortunate are those who mourn, for they will be comforted.
Fortunate are the meek, for they will inherit the earth.
Fortunate are those whose who hunger and thirst for righteousness, for they will be filled.
Fortunate are the merciful, for they will receive mercy.
Fortunate are the single-minded, for they will see God.
Fortunate are the peacemakers, for they will be called the children of God.
Fortunate are those who are persecuted because of righteousness, for theirs is the kingdom of heaven.

"Fortunate are you when people insult you and persecute you and speak all kinds of evil against your falsely because of me. Rejoice and be glad, because your reward is great in heaven. For they persecuted the prophets before you in the same way."

The word "blessed" (μακάριος/*makarios*) can also be translated "happy." I follow Albright and Mann and translate *makarios* with the word "fortunate." They comment, "The word in Greek was used in classical times of the state of the gods in contrast to men."[95] The Greeks believed their gods lived in a plane above the world that was superior to the world. You see this belief expressed in the philosophy of Plato. Their gods were fortunate in this way. When we adopt the attitudes of the beatitudes, we elevate ourselves above the earthly existence of this world. We enter into a spiritual realm that calls us higher. In this way, those who follow the beatitudes are fortunate.

As Christians, we are fortunate because God has favored us by allowing us to have a relationship with him. Do we feel favored? Do people around us know that we are favored and happy? I remember a preacher once telling his audience, "If you're happy to be here today, notify your face." Our happy, vibrant attitude should distinguish us as disciples.

Disciples of Jesus are on a serious mission, but our relationship with God needs to keep us happy and content. We are the fortunate ones. But this does not mean that we should fake happiness. The world is an incredibly tough place, and bad things happen to disciples too. Jesus doesn't expect us to walk around all the time with a silly grin on our faces. He does expect us to face our struggles with faith. This faithful acceptance of even the most difficult matters of life will separate the disciple of Jesus from the nondisciple. And at times, it is even possible to keep a happy, positive, faithful attitude in the midst of difficult circumstances.

There is a progression in these beatitudes. The first one leads to the second and the second to the third, and so on.

3"Blessed [happy, fortunate] are the poor [humble] in spirit, for theirs is the kingdom of heaven."

What does it mean to be poor in spirit? The word usually translated "poor" can also mean "afflicted" or "humble." Spiritual poverty is our recognition of our need for God. This is where happiness starts. If we do not see our need for God, then we will never come to him. When you are poor, really poor, you are desperate. The poor in spirit are desperate for God.

4"Blessed are those who mourn, for they will be comforted."

This beatitude contains a paradox: How are those who mourn happy? Spiritual poverty leads to repentance. And when we repent, we hurt over the pain that our sin has caused God, others, and self. But once we confess our sin, God is quick to forgive; he turns sadness to joy.

In order to change, you have to be willing to admit that you have a problem, and spiritual poverty allows us to see that we have a problem. We mourn because we see that our sin has hurt God, others, and ourselves. This leads us to repentance, then joy comes from true repentance.

5"Blessed are the meek, for they will inherit the earth."

Meekness does not mean weakness, frailty, or passivity. Jesus is not speaking of groveling at the feet of others. He isn't talking about the person who is so insecure that he or she can't look others in the eye. He's not talking about being a pushover. That doesn't characterize Jesus, nor should it characterize his followers.

For Jesus, meekness is power under control. The word "meek" (πραΰς/*praus*) suggests gentleness and self-control. D. A. Carson writes about meekness:

> In general the Greeks considered meekness a vice because they failed to distinguish it from servility. To be meek toward others implies freedom from malice and a vengeful spirit. We must acknowledge our own bankruptcy (vs. 3) and mourn (vs. 4). But to respond with meekness when others tell us of our bankruptcy is far harder. Meekness therefore requires such a true view about us as will express itself even in our attitude toward others.[96]

Meekness does not come easily. It goes against what we are taught by the world. To become meek, we must look to Jesus.

Jesus exemplified meekness in his own life. He was the kind of person who could huddle up with children for a laugh or drive thieves and moneychangers from the temple courts. He was just as comfortable in the house of the poorest widow or the palace of the king. He could have called ten thousand angels to save him from the cross, but he bowed his head in submission and died for the sins of humanity. He had power under control.

This type of meekness inherits the earth. This type of meekness means thinking before answering, praying before responding, and asking, "What would Jesus do?" This type of meekness garners the respect of other people. Jesus, the meek King of kings, was willing to stretch out his arms and be nailed to a cross, suspended between heaven and earth, for the sins of humanity. Blessed are the meek.

6"Blessed are those who hunger and thirst for righteousness, for they will be filled."

Not many of us in the First World know hunger, real hunger. We sometimes put ourselves through self-imposed times of hunger by fasting, and by so doing can begin to experience hunger. Hunger produces an intense desire to grab any morsel of food and eat it. Thirst means you'll drink anything to quench that thirst. Hunger (like poverty) implies desperation. When we hunger and thirst for righteousness, we are desperate for righteousness.

I usually translate righteousness as "right living." When we are righteous, we are focused on doing right and acting right every moment of every day. We want even the least little detail in our lives to be right. We aren't doing and acting on our own power. That would be self-righteous, not righteous. We are doing and acting right because God gives us the power to do the right thing.

When we act the right way and do the right thing, God fills us with confidence because we know that we are in a good place. When we know we are living right, we feel full, content, and at peace. This is God's plan of righteousness.

7"Blessed are the merciful, for they will be shown mercy."

To receive mercy, we must give mercy. The Greek work for merciful is ἐλεέω/*eleao*. It can also mean to be sympathetic. To have mercy means to be filled with compassion or pity for someone. Jesus expects his disciples to have compassionate hearts and to empathize and sympathize with others. If we are going to receive mercy, then we must be merciful.

8"Blessed are the pure in heart, for they will see God."

Only the pure-hearted will see God. We usually think of purity as an absence of lust, especially sexual lust; but the term means so much more. Purity in the Bible means single-mindedness. Dietrich Bonhoeffer, in his excellent book, *The Cost of Discipleship*, answers the question: "Who is pure in heart?" by writing:

> Only those who have surrendered their hearts completely to Jesus that he may reign in them alone. Only those whose hearts are undefiled by their own evil, and by their own virtues too. Only they will see God, who in this life have looked solely unto Jesus Christ, the Son of God. For then their hearts are free from all defiling phantasies and are not distracted by conflicting desires and intentions.[97]

Purity is the ability to keep our focus on God and not let our eyes wander over to the distractions of the world. When God is our focus, then everything else in life is in the proper perspective.

9"Blessed are the peacemakers, for they will be called sons of God."

Shalom. It is a word of greeting meaning "hello" or "goodbye." It also means wholeness in life. When we greet others by saying *shalom*, we are telling them that we want them to experience a long, fulfilled, healthy, and happy life.

10"Blessed are those who are persecuted because of righteousness, for theirs is the kingdom of heaven."

Once again, we have a paradox—how can the persecuted be happy?

Happiness comes from knowing that just as Jesus and the prophets were persecuted, persecution places us in the company of men and women throughout history who were willing to stand up and do what was right. We do not take delight in the persecution—and we should never bring persecution on ourselves—but we delight in the fact that we have been included with Jesus and the prophets.

Every time we suffer for Jesus, we connect ourselves with the cross of Jesus. Bonhoeffer writes:

> The cross means sharing the suffering of Christ to the last and to the fullest. Only a man thus totally committed in discipleship can experience the meaning of the cross. The cross is there, right from the beginning, he has only got to pick it up; there is no need for him to go out and look for a cross for himself, no need for him deliberately to run after suffering. Jesus says that every Christian has his own cross waiting for him, a cross destined and appointed by God. Each must endure his allotted share of suffering and rejection.[98]

If we never sacrifice, never suffer, never put ourselves out for the kingdom, then we are disconnected from the cross. To be connected with the cross implies sacrifice.

Salt and Light—Matthew 5:13–16

> "You are the salt of the earth, but if salt loses its saltiness, how is it able to become salty again? It is good for nothing, except to be thrown out and trampled under men's feet. You are the light of the world. A city built on a hill is not able to be hidden. Neither do men light a lamp and place it under a bushel, but on a stand, and it shines to all who are in the house. Let your light so shine before men that they may see your good works and glorify your Father in heaven."

We are to be like salt. In the first century, salt was used primarily to preserve food. Contaminated salt was thrown on the roads and on the flat rooftops, where it would harden with the soil and be trampled under foot. Disciples are to make a difference in the world around them. We need to be the salt of the earth.

We are to be "the light of the world." As Christians, we are to be the spiritual light that allows the world to see spiritual truths. The light of our example will expose lies and darkness and show people what they need to change.

Jesus and the Law—Matthew 5:17–20

> "Do not think that I have come to destroy the Law or the Prophets. I have not come to destroy but to clarify the true meaning of Scripture. I tell you truthfully, until heaven and

earth pass away, not one letter or one stoke of a pen will pass from the law until all is accomplished. Therefore, whoever breaks one of the least of these commandments and teaches others to do the same, he will be called least in the kingdom of heaven. Whoever does and teaches these commandments, he will be called great in the kingdom of heaven. For I tell you, unless your righteous exceeds that of the scribes and Pharisees, you will not enter the kingdom of heaven."

Some would charge Jesus with not keeping the law. Some would say that he was changing the law. This was especially true of the Sabbath law. Jesus anticipates this here. He redefines what it means to keep the law. He doesn't want us just to obey, but he wants us to obey with the right attitude. Jesus is going for the heart. That is the difference between intrinsic and extrinsic motivation. Jesus wants us to know why we are doing what we do and to be motivated intrinsically. Jesus challenges the members of his kingdom community to do things for the right reason.

Jesus did not "come to abolish the Law or the Prophets [which to the Jewish mind meant the writings of the Old Testament]...but to fulfill [πληρόω/*pleroo*] them (NIV)." The word *pleroo* can mean "to complete," but it can also mean "to clarify." I believe the second meaning fits better with this context. Jesus came to heighten our understanding concerning the law. Throughout this section he uses the formula, "you have heard that it was said...but I say to you." Jesus takes ethical statements from the Old Testament and reinterprets them for his community.

The Pharisees and teachers of the law were concerned with keeping the letter of the law, but Jesus wants his disciples to understand the heart of the law. He heightens their perception of the law in six particular areas: anger, adultery, divorce, oaths, retaliation, and love of enemies.

Anger—Matthew 5:21–26

"You have heard that it was said of the ancients, 'Do not murder, and whoever murders will be liable to judgment.' But I say to you that everyone who is angry with his brother is liable to judgment. Whoever says to his brother, 'Raca,' is liable to the council. Anyone who says, 'Fool,' is liable to the Gehenna of fire.

"Therefore, when you bring your gift to the altar, if you remember your brother has anything against you, leave the gift before the altar and first go and reconcile yourself with your brother.

"Settle the matter quickly with your adversary on the way to court, or he may deliver you to the judge and the judge to the officer, and he will throw you in prison. I tell you the truth, you will not get out until you have paid the last penny."

The law said, "Do not murder," but Jesus says not to be angry with our brother. The focus here goes from the act of murder to the heart behind the act. If lies, hatred, prejudice, and anger are rooted out, then murder will not occur.

Jesus gets to the root of the problem of anger: We must not blame others; rather, we need to take the first step toward reconciliation. This should be an urgent action. Paul implores, "Do not let the sun go down while you are still angry" (Ephesians 4:26). Jesus underscores the importance of relationships. They must be guarded as precious gifts.

Adultery—Matthew 5:27–30

> *"You have heard that it was said, 'Do not commit adultery.' I say to you—everyone who looks at a woman in a lustful manner has already committed adultery with her in his heart.*
>
> *"If your right eye scandalizes you, tear it out and cast it from you. For it is better to lose one of your members than your whole body be cast into Gehenna. And, if your right hand scandalizes you, cut it off and toss it away, for it is better to lose your hand than your whole body be thrown into Gehenna."*

It was said, "Do not commit adultery," but Jesus is saying, "Do not lust after another person." In fact, he goes on to say that to lust after someone is to commit adultery in your heart. Here, Jesus heightens the ethic of moral purity within his community. To guard ourselves against adultery, we must not lust. Since sin begins in our minds, we must control what we put in our minds.

Jesus also gives a new, radical way of dealing with sin in our lives. He says, "If your right eye causes you to sin, gouge it out and throw it away" (5:29 NIV). Is Jesus advocating self-mutilation? Some have taken this literally (like Origen who castrated himself), but Jesus did not mean for it to be taken so. He is using a figure of speech called hyperbole, an exaggeration. Jesus is heightening our awareness of sin to say that if something is causing you to sin, then distance yourself from that temptation.

Divorce—Matthew 5:31–32

> *"It was said, 'Whoever divorces his wife must give her a certificate of divorce.' But I say to you, everyone who divorces his wife, except for marital unfaithfulness, makes her commit adultery, and whoever marries a divorced woman commits adultery."*

Jesus sensitizes us toward divorce by saying that it is only accepted in the case of marital unfaithfulness (πορνεία/*porneia*). Jesus is speaking to his covenant community, and he expects them to follow his standard. God does say, "I hate divorce" (Malachi 2:16), but he allowed divorce in Moses' day. Many will come into the kingdom having gone through divorce and remarriage. Paul states that they should be received in whatever state they find themselves when they enter the kingdom (1 Corinthians 7). For those who are already Christians, we should see that marriage is for life.

Jesus is striving to get those in his community to have a serious attitude about their marriage vows. In the ancient Greco-Roman world, divorce was rampant. Even within Judaism, divorce was commonplace. Some rabbis said that a man could divorce a woman for being a bad cook (burning bread). Jesus restates God's ideal: Marriage is for life.

Oaths—Matthew 5:33–37

"Again you have heard it said by the ancients, 'Do not swear falsely, but keep your oaths to the Lord.' I say to you, do not swear at all: neither by heaven, which is God's throne; neither by the earth, which is his footstool; nor by Jerusalem, which is the city of the great King. Do not swear by your head, because you are not able to make one hair white or black. Let your word be 'yes, yes' or 'no, no'—anything exceeding this is from the Evil One."

In the Old Testament, taking oaths was not prohibited, but if a person took an oath, he was expected to keep it. Jesus is not necessarily speaking against taking oaths, but against those who would take an oath and not keep it.

In the Jewish mind there were all types of oaths that could be taken. Some were considered more serious and binding than others. Some were too serious and should never be invoked. Jesus cuts through this pecking order and gets to the heart of the matter, namely: Be honest and keep your word. He tells his community to refrain from taking oaths and instead to let your "yes" be "yes" and your "no" be "no." In other words, always be truthful.

Retaliation—Matthew 5:38–42

"You have heard it said, 'An eye for an eye and a tooth for a tooth.' But I tell you, do not resist an evil person. But if anyone strikes your right cheek, turn the other to him. If someone wants to sue you for your tunic, give him your outer cloak as well. If someone forces you to go one mile, go two with him. Give to everyone who asks, and do not refuse anyone who wants to borrow from you. Love your enemies."

What do we do with the problem of evil? How does the community of Jesus handle evil in the world? Here, Jesus uses four illustrations of how we are to respond to evil.

1. One of the most difficult sayings in the Bible reads, "If anyone strikes your right cheek, turn the other to him" (5:39). To strike someone on the cheek was considered an insult, like slapping someone across the face with a glove in the nineteenth century. When insulted, how should we act? We should not insult the person back or return evil for evil. This is difficult, but it is the only way that we can live together in peace.

2. Jesus says, "If someone wants to sue you for your tunic, give him your outer cloak as well" (5:40). Under the Mosaic Law, the Jews were allowed to sue for the inner garment or tunic. The outer garment, however, was a possession that could not be taken away. Jesus says that when someone, even a supposed "believer," sues us for our tunic, we should go so far as to give the one who is suing us what he cannot legally take away—and give it to him freely. Yet, if someone asks us for our clothes, we need not give him everything until we have nothing left. This would be enabling him instead of helping him.

3. The third illustration describes the practice of Roman soldiers commanding non-Romans to carry their bags for them. Many would grudgingly carry the bags with venom and spite in each step of the journey. Jesus tells his community that their attitude must be different. If they are asked to carry the bag one mile, they should volunteer to carry it a second mile. Imagine the reaction of the Roman soldier as a disciple of Jesus picked up the soldier's bags with a smile on his face and walked past the one-mile marker, perhaps chatting amiably with the soldier along the way. We are to perform even the most menial tasks of service to the best of our ability with a good attitude in our hearts.

4. "Give to everyone who asks, and do not refuse anyone who wants to borrow from you" (5:42). Does this mean that we should give anything to anyone who asks? No. That would be enabling the person. Jesus is fighting against a legalistic interpretation of the OT teaching on giving. A disciple is to be generous. He should go beyond the letter of the law.

Love for Enemies—Matthew 5:43–48

> "You have heard it said, 'Love your neighbor and hate your enemy.' I tell you, love your enemies and pray for those who persecute you. Thus you will become children of your Father in heaven. He makes the sun rise on the evil and sends rain on the righteous and unrighteous. If you love those who love you, what reward do you have? Do not the tax collectors do the same? If you greet only your brother, what are you doing more than others? Don't even the pagans do that? Be true, therefore, as your Father in heaven is true."

The Old Testament does not contain any commands of God to "hate your enemies." But this had become the practice of many in first-century Judaism. The Zealots taught that the Jews should hate the Romans. The Qumran community also taught the principle of hating enemies. Yet, Jesus taught the opposite: "Love your enemies." His community was to be different. They were to do good to people who hated them. In this way they would be a spiritual light.

Jesus raised the standard for those in his community to a height that seems unattainable: "Be perfect, therefore, as your heavenly Father is perfect (NIV)." Literally translated, "You will be perfect, therefore, as your heavenly father is perfect." This is not just a demand, but it is a promise.

The word "perfect" (τέλειος/*teleios*) can also be translated "complete, mature, or full-grown." It can also mean "true, sincere, or genuine."

Jesus is not teaching the doctrine of Christian perfectionism, that is, after a person becomes a Christian, she or he can reach the level of moral perfection in life. Moral perfection is unattainable. Jesus challenges us to become perfect/mature in the way we treat people and in the way we respond when we are mistreated. We must imitate God who loves the unlovely and continues to love people even when they reject him. We must strive toward this high standard.

The Heart of the Matter—Matthew 6:1–18

One of the aspects of the Sermon on the Mount that I appreciate the most is how Jesus centers on the heart in his teaching. In this section on giving, praying, and fasting—the three most prominent acts of piety for the Jew—Jesus teaches that our motivation behind our actions must be right. In other words, we should not give to be seen by men, but because God sees us give. We must desire to please God in all that we do. God will not reward our "righteous actions" if we do them for show (6:1). We must check our hearts when we give, pray, or fast to make sure that they are in the right place. D. A. Carson outlines the structure that Jesus uses in discussing each action. He lists the following:

1. A warning not to do the act to be praised by men.
2. A guarantee that those who ignore this warning will get what they want but not more.
3. Instruction on how to perform the act of piety secretly.
4. The assurance that the Father who sees in secret will reward openly.[99]

Incidentally, Jesus says, "When you give...when you pray...when you fast...." He assumes that as his disciples we will be doing all these things. He does not teach against any of these acts when they are properly done, but he teaches against acting ostentatiously while we do them.

Giving—6:1–4

"Be careful of doing your righteous actions before men to be seen by them. If you do, you will have no reward from your Father in heaven.

"When you give to those in need, do not sound a trumpet before you, as the

hypocrites do in the synagogues and in the streets, so they can receive glory from men. I speak the truth, they have received their reward. But when you give to those in need, do not let your left hand know what your right is doing; thus your giving will be in secret. Your Father who sees in secret will reward you."

Jesus begins this section by talking about almsgiving. Giving to the needy was an important part of first-century Judaism. The apocryphal book of Tobit mentions, "It is better to give alms than to treasure up gold. For almsgiving delivers from death, and it will purge away every sin" (Tobit 12:8b–9a).

Scholars are unsure what the reference to sounding trumpets means. At times a trumpet would sound to notify people of a special need. In the temple, alms were placed in receptacles that resembled the bell of a trumpet. However, Jesus is probably just using a metaphor as a reference to calling attention to our actions when we give alms.

We are not to be like the hypocrites. The word ὑποκριταὶ/*hypokritai* means "actor" or "player" and is derived from a compound word meaning "a double face or a false face." On the Greek stage, actors portrayed different characters by holding masks in front of their faces. This way, one actor could play several parts. "Hypocrite" is taken from this practice of an actor using a mask. Jesus wants his disciples to be genuine—we are not to perform our acts of righteousness for show. A rabbi in the second century wrote that nine-tenths of all the hypocrisy in the world was found in Jerusalem. Jesus did not want his disciples falling into the trap of hypocrisy.

Albright and Mann suggest another definition for "hypocrite."[100] They state that the Greek definition above came later than NT times and should not be considered when defining the word. Instead, we must go to an earlier origin of the Greek word. In Homer, the verb *krinesthai*, from which the word "hypocrite" is derived, meant "to interpret (dreams)." This definition stresses a sense or capacity of discernment. It began by implying that someone had a critical, discerning mind. Later it developed the negative connotation of being hypercritical. Albright and Mann write:

> The Greek, *Kritikos*, is similarly neutral, implying a capacity for discernment. We may even carry the sense a step further and speak of someone as "hypercritical," intending to convey the idea that a person is given to fine, hairsplitting distinctions, but we do not at the same time accuse such a person of "being a hypocrite" in our modern sense.[101]

Albright and Mann go on to suggest that "hypocrite" should be translated as "over scrupulous" or "you casuists." The hypocrite was the person who was overly critical. He would use hairsplitting legalism against other people, put himself on a pedestal, and look down on others who were different from him.

When we give, we are to give in secret. This way, God who sees us in secret will reward us. Otherwise, he will not. We have to ask ourselves which do we desire more—the reward of men or the reward of God? The fact that God sees what we are giving should be our only reward.

Prayer—6:5–15

"When you pray, do not be like the hypocrites, who love to pray standing in the syna-gogues and street corners to be seen by men. I speak the truth, they have received their reward. When you pray, enter your room and close the door and pray to your Father, who is in secret. Then your Father, who sees in secret, will reward you. When you pray, do not act as the pagans who babble on and on, for they think they will be heard for their verbosity. Do not be like them, for your Father knows what needs you have before you ask him.

"You should pray like this:

Our Father who is in heaven,
Holy is your name,
Let your kingdom come,
Let your will be done,
On the earth as it is in heaven.
Give us today our daily food.
Forgive us our debts,
As we also have forgiven our debtors.
Lead us not into temptation,
But deliver us from the evil one.

"For if you forgive men their trespasses, your Father in heaven will forgive you. But if you do not forgive men their trespasses neither will your Father forgive your tres-passes."

Jesus discusses the second righteous act: prayer. He was not against public prayer (he prayed in front of his disciples), but he was against prayer for show. This was a problem in first-century Judaism. We know the Jews were devoted to prayer. They prayed the Shema Israel[102] in the morning and the evening, and in the morning, noon, and afternoon, they would pray another prayer also, so the devout Jew would pray five times a day. Therefore, the attention-seeking Jew could time his prayers so that he would be in public (in a synagogue or on a street corner) when the time of prayer arrived.

Jesus expected his disciples to pray in secret. He tells them to enter a room and close the door. He did not mean that they must literally go into a closet every time they prayed. He is teaching the principle that prayer is between each individual and God.

Jesus specifically mentions that we are not to pray like the pagans or Gentiles. They prayed lengthy prayers, believing their many words would gain the favor of their gods. The Greek word translated as "babble" is βατταλογέω/*battalogeo*. It was used for constant repetition or the stammering of words. The Gentiles also believed that if they said the name of their gods over and over, this would win the god to their cause. However, our God already wants to answer us—we do not have to impress him with flowery words or lengthy prayers. We must simply give God our hearts in prayer and state our needs.

Fasting—6:16–18

"When you fast, do not look dismal, like the hypocrites, for they disfigure their faces to show men they are fasting. I tell you the truth, they have received their reward. When you fast, put oil on your head and wash your face; thus your fasting will not be seen by men but by your Father who is in secret. For your Father who sees in secret will reward you."

Fasting is refraining from food so that we can better focus on spiritual matters. The key to fasting is to take time to really focus on God.

Fasting from food can be especially helpful in heightening our spiritual senses. Having gone on several fasts, I find that when I fast, I am more focused on the spiritual realm. For example, I can spend the time that I would have spent preparing food and eating meals in reading my Bible and praying.

Where Is Your Treasure?—Matthew 6:19–34

"Do not treasure up for yourselves treasures on earth where moth and rust destroy and where thieves break in and steal. Treasure up for yourselves treasures in heaven, where neither moth nor rust destroy, and where thieves do not break in and steal. For where your treasure is, there your heart will be.

"The lamp of the body is the eye. Therefore if your eye is sound, your whole body will be full of light. If your eye is evil, your whole body will be full of darkness. If then the light that is in you is darkness, how great is that darkness!

"No one is able to serve two lords; for he will either hate the one and love the other, or he will be devoted to one and despise the other. You cannot serve God and money.

"Therefore, I say to you, do not worry about your life, what you will eat or what you will drink, or about your body, what you will wear. Look at the birds of the heavens because they neither sow nor reap nor store in barns, and your heavenly Father feeds them. Are you not more valuable than they? Which of you by worrying is able to add a single hour to his life?

> *"And why do you worry about clothes? Watch how the lilies of the field grow. They do not labor or spin, but I tell you that Solomon in all his glory was not dressed like one of these. But if God thus clothes the grass of the field, which is alive today and tomorrow is cast into the fire, how much greater will he clothe you—you of little faith? Therefore, do not worry, saying, 'What will we eat?' or 'What will we drink?' or 'What will we wear?' For the pagans strive after all these things. For your Father knows that you need these things. But seek first of all the kingdom of God and his righteousness, and all these things will be given to you as well. So do not fret about tomorrow, for tomorrow frets on its own. Each day has its own troubles."*

Jesus makes it clear that where your treasure is, your heart is also there. So find your treasure, and you will find your heart. Or, find where your heart is, and you will find your treasure: They go hand in hand. What is your passion? What do you dream about? Where does most of your time and energy go? If you asked your closest friends, what would they say makes you really happy? If you asked your acquaintances at school or work, what would they say describes you best? The answer to these questions is your treasure, and thus it is your heart.

It is very easy for us to think of the "here and now" and difficult for us to think about the hereafter. We have the here and now in our faces all day long. "Buy this! Watch this! Read this! Wear this!" We need to get away from all that to think of the hereafter.

Jesus shows us the temporal nature of treasures on earth by pointing out that moth and rust consume them and thieves steal them. During Jesus' day, elaborate clothing was often used as currency, but moths could easily destroy this treasure. Precious metal was also used as currency, but rust could tarnish the metal, causing it to lose its value. Houses were made of mud brick, and thieves could easily break through these walls and steal a person's valuables.

In our day and time, earthly treasures are just as temporary. Styles change overnight. We hide our money inside bank safes and watch inflation eat away at it. The stock market is terribly fickle. The only really safe place to store our treasure is in heaven, where nothing can get at our treasure—not moth, rust, thieves, inflation, stock market scams, or even the taxman. Heaven is the only secure storage place for treasure.

Jesus is not against having a savings account or saving for your child's college education. He warns not to store up treasure "for yourselves," implying storing in a selfish manner. He also warns against storing up for self and leaving God out of the picture or storing up first for self and putting God second, or worse, putting God last. The disciple gives to God first and uses what he has left in a wise way.

Jesus draws a contrast between the good eye and the evil eye. In the first-century mind, the eye was the window to the soul. What we allow into our eyes will influence the way we live our lives. Jesus is using He-brew antithetical parallelism here by stating opposites. He defines what the evil eye is: selfishness and greed. The sound eye would be the oppo-site of that: generosity, giving, and selflessness. Greed brings darkness, while generosity brings the light of God into our lives. In the context of treasures, Jesus is teaching us that we need to have a generous spirit with what God has given us.

Jesus introduces a principle that he repeats throughout his ministry: We cannot serve two lords. In this context, one lord is the Lord God and the other lord is money. The Aramaic word *mammon* (μαμωνᾷ/*mamona* in the Greek) means "money, wealth, or possessions." You can literally translate it as "a thing we trust," or "a thing in which we trust." When we put our trust in possessions or things, those things become our god—a false god.

The word "serve" can also be translated "slavery." "To serve or be a slave of" implies total devotion. You cannot be totally devoted to two masters. You can serve one or the other, but not both. Jesus says we must make a choice between serving God or money.

If we serve God, will he take care of us? Jesus answers, Yes. We are not to worry about what we will eat, drink, or wear. To illustrate this, Je-sus uses two examples from nature. First, he mentions birds, which do not grow their own food, yet have plenty to eat from God's hand. Second, he mentions "the lilies of the field." These are purple flowers similar to the color of the royal robes that King Solomon wore. Yet Solomon's regal, elaborate dress paled in beauty next to the lilies. Therefore, Jesus reas-sures us that God will provide for us, so why should we worry? Worry does not add anything to our lives—in fact, it takes away.

Matthew 6:33 has not changed in the last twenty years (or the last 2,000). It still reads, "But seek first of all the kingdom of God and his righ-teousness, and all these things will be given to you as well." Jesus focuses on what is really important, on what our priorities should be.

One way to think of kingdom and righteousness is to view them as a synonymous parallelism. If so, then kingdom and righteousness would be the same thing and to seek the kingdom and righteous of God is the same as seeking God. In other words, are we God-focused? Are we preoccupied with God? Is God first in our lives?

The conclusion of this section is: Do not worry! Take each day one day at a time. Worry isn't helpful. It doesn't change anything. Therefore, don't worry.

Judge Not—Matthew 7:1–6

"Judge not, so you will not be judged. For in what judgment you use to judge, you will be judged. In what measure you use to measure, it will be measured to you.

"Why do you look for the splinter in your brother's eye and do not notice the log in your own eye? How can you say to your brother, 'Allow me to take the splinter from your eye,' when you have a log in your own eye? Hypocrite, first take the log out of your eye. Then when you can see clearly, you can take the splinter from your brother's eye.

"Do not give what is holy to dogs; do not cast pearls before swine. They will trample them under their feet and turn and tear you apart."

"Judge not." By judging, Jesus does not mean that we cannot discern right from wrong in the actions and teachings of others. If so, he would not tell us a little later to "beware of false prophets" (7:15). What does he mean? He wants us to guard against a critical, negative, cynical outlook that fails to find the good in people. He also wants us to guard against judging the motives of others. We cannot read hearts and must be very careful when we attempt to discern what is in the heart of another person.

Jesus paints a comical picture of the man who is a hypocritical judge. He is busy trying to take a speck of sawdust out of someone else's eye, while a huge two-by-four is stuck in his own eye. He can barely approach the other person with this gigantic plank in his own eye, but he does not let this stop him from being a critical judge. How ridiculous we look to God when we behave this way! There is nothing worse than a bitter, critical, judgmental hypocrite who is so busy looking at the minor faults of others that he cannot see the major flaws in his own life. Jesus warns us not to fall into this trap.

Jesus also warns us to be discerning when it comes to offering spiritual guidance and advice to people. He uses synonymous parallelism to illustrate this: "Do not give what is holy to dogs; do not cast pearls before swine." The pearls are being equated with what is holy because holiness is valuable. Yet, dogs and pigs would have no idea of the value of pearls. Therefore, before we give spiritual guidance to people, we need to make sure they want to receive it and understand its value.

This principle especially holds true with family and old friends who are not spiritually minded. I have made this mistake before. I remember years ago when some friends were asking a question about what to do in a particular situation. They were not looking for spiritual advice, but I thought I would give it anyway. This was a big mistake on my part! They definitely trampled my choice pearls into the ground.

Ask, Seek, Knock—Matthew 7:7–11

"Ask and it will be given to you; seek and you will discover; knock and the door will be opened for you. For everyone who asks receives. He who seeks discovers. And the one knocking on the door—it will be opened for him.

"Is there a person among you that if his child asks for bread, will give him a stone?

If he asks for a fish, will you give him a snake? If you, being evil, know how to give good gifts to your children, how much more will your Father in heaven give good gifts to those who ask him!"

Asking, seeking, and knocking are all metaphors for prayer. That the prayer is persistent is implied in the use of the present tense of the verb. Continual, persistent prayer will be answered.

Since God is a loving Father, he wants to answer our prayers. If earthly fathers are concerned about the needs of their children, think how much more concerned our heavenly Father is about our needs.

But we must not think that the spiritual journey to God is a walk in the park. It is absolutely the best life to live, but it is not an easy life. The easy life is the life that leads to destruction—it's a wide road and traveled by many. The way of the few, the way to life, is narrow and difficult. At the end of the difficult path is eternal life; therefore, it is the path worth taking.

Summary of Jesus' Ethics: The Golden Rule—Matthew 7:12

"So in everything, whatever you wish for men to do for you, you do for them. This is the Law and the Prophets (the Scripture)."

The sum of Jesus' ethics, as seen in the Sermon on the Mount, is found in the phrase, "Do to others what you would have them do to you (NIV)." Think of how different the world would be if all humanity lived by this one rule. Supposedly, the Roman Emperor Alexander Severus (AD 222–235) had this rule written in gold on his palace walls—thus, "The Golden Rule." The Golden Rule is unselfish love in action. It is the way we all want to be treated, and the way Jesus wants us to treat other people. It should be a distinguishing mark of a Christian.

Many religious teachers before Jesus had taught this rule in its negative form: "What you do not want done to you, don't do it to others." But apparently, Jesus is the first person to state the rule in its positive form, which makes a huge difference. To obey it in the negative requires us to do nothing, but to obey Jesus' Golden Rule requires action. We must actively treat people the way we want to be treated. This moves us to make the world around us a better place.

Two Roads—Matthew 7:13–14

"Enter through the narrow gate, because the gate is wide and the road is broad that leads to destruction. There are many who take it. But the gate is small and the road is narrow that leads to life, and few find it."

Perhaps Jesus now turns to those outside his community, those who have been "listening in" to the sermon, and he now has a word for them. He sets up a group of contrasts and choices: two roads, two trees, two types of followers, and two builders. He asks people to make a choice—which path are you going to follow?

There are only two paths in life. One leads to destruction and the other leads to life. The road to destruction is broad and easy—easy to navigate and well traveled. It is the way of comfort and complacency.

The road to life is completely opposite. It is difficult and challenging. Only a few travel on it. It is the road of discipleship, of placing the mission of Jesus above our own desires. Which road are you on?

Two Trees—Matthew 7:15-20

"Beware of false prophets, who come to you in sheep's clothing, but inside they are ravenous wolves. You will know them by their fruit. Do people pick grapes from thorns, or figs from thistles? Thus, every good tree produces good fruit, and the bad tree, evil fruit. A good tree is not able to produce evil fruit, nor is a bad tree able to produce good fruit. Every tree that does not produce good fruit is cut down and cast into the fire. Thus, you will know them by their fruits."

We can know people by their fruit. In this context, Jesus is telling us to be on our guard against "false prophets." False doctrine has flooded our world. We have to be careful to discern between false doctrine and sound doctrine, because false doctrine kills. Satan deceives many into believing what is false.

Next, Jesus warns that not everyone who says to him, "Lord, Lord" will enter the kingdom of heaven (Matthew 7:21). In fact, many that prophesy in his name, drive out demons, and work miracles are false teachers. Someone might ask, "Aren't these great works evidence that a person must be right with God?" Not according to Jesus. Jesus says *the* discriminating factor is whether or not a person is obeying God.

Just as there are two roads, there are also two types of trees and two types of fruit. One tree produces good fruit, and the other tree produces evil fruit. We cannot have good fruit and bad fruit growing on the same tree. By looking at our fruit, we can determine what type of tree we are. But make no mistake; there are only two types of trees: good and bad.

When I was a boy, I used to listen to an album by an old country preacher from Tennessee named Marshall Keeble. I remember Mr. Keeble talking about people telling him not to be judgmental in his preaching. They would say, "Mr. Keeble, the Bible says, 'Do not judge.'" Mr. Keeble would reply, "Soon after Jesus said, 'Do not judge,' he also said, 'By your fruit you will know them.'" Mr. Keeble then added, "I'm not a judge—I'm just a fruit inspector!"

Two Types of Followers—Matthew 7:21–23

"Not everyone who says to me, 'Lord, Lord,' will enter the kingdom of heaven, but only they who obey the will of my Father in heaven. Many will say to me on that day, 'Lord, Lord,' we prophesied in your name, in your name expelled demons, and in your name we performed powerful miracles.' And then, I will declare to them, 'I never knew you, go away from me, you lawless people.'"

There are two types of followers of Christ. One follower calls Jesus "Lord" and does his will. The other follower calls Jesus "Lord" but does not do his will.

To do the will of the Father is to follow the teachings of the Bible. We must do things God's way. We can do many great things, but if we fail to do them God's way, then they are unacceptable to him.

On the judgment day many will protest their innocence, essentially saying, "But we prophesied for you, cast out demons for you, and performed amazing miracles for you." Jesus will look at these people and call them evildoers. What they did was evil because it was outside God's will.

Two Types of Builders—Matthew 7:24–27

"Everyone who hears these words of mine and does them is similar to a wise man who built his house on the rock. And the rains fell, the floods rose, and the winds blew and beat against that house. The house stood because it was built on a rock.

"And everyone who hears these words of mine and does not do them is similar to a foolish man. He built his house on the sand. The rains fell, the floods rose, and the wind blew and beat against that house; and it fell with a great crash."

Jesus closes the Sermon on the Mount by emphasizing the need to put his word into practice. It is not enough to just hear the Word—we must change. This is illustrated in a masterful way with the Parable of the Wise and Foolish Builders. The difference between them was their choice of foundation: One built on the Word and the other on something else, like hedonism, Gnosticism, or stoicism. The difference in the foundations is that the wise man built by hearing the Word and putting it into practice, while the foolish man built by just hearing the Word. He didn't act on what he heard. Hearing is not enough: We must be doers of the Word. The proof of our faith is in the way we live our lives.

The Conclusion: Jesus as a Teacher—Matthew 7:28–29

When Jesus finished saying these words, the crowds were amazed at his teaching, for he taught them as one with authority and not as their scribes.

What did the people notice the most about Jesus as a teacher? Was it his beautiful ways of illustrating his points? Was it the flawless logic he used to reach his conclusion? Was it the immense vocabulary he showered upon them as he spoke? The one thing that impressed them the most was his authority—"He taught them as one with authority and not as their scribes." Authority and confidence are closely linked. Jesus knew who he was and he knew that his message came from God. For this reason, he spoke confidently about God, about the meaning of life, and about the nature of true spirituality—and people were impressed with his confidence.

Do we know who we are? Do people take note of something different in our lives? Do we live confident lives? What impresses people is a life that backs up words. Jesus had both the life and the words; therefore, people were impressed with him.

The Sermon on the Mount is the greatest of Jesus' ethical discourses and the greatest ethical discourse in the history of humanity, but Jesus taught many other wonderful lessons. We will explore some of these great teachings of Jesus in the following chapter.

End Notes

91. Borg, *Jesus: Uncovering the Life, Teachings, and Relevance of a Religious Revolutionary*, 164.

92. Parables will be discussed in a later chapter.

93. Borg, *Jesus: Uncovering the Life, Teachings, and Relevance of a Religious Revolutionary*, 155.

94. The author's own translation of Matthew is used throughout this chapter except where otherwise noted.

95. W.F. Albright and C.S. Mann, *The Anchor Bible,* vol. 26, *Matthew.* (Garden City, NY: Doubleday, 1971), 76.

96. Carson, *The Expositor's Bible Commentary with the New International Version,* 132.

97. Dietrich Bonhoeffer, *The Cost of Discipleship, 6th ed.* (London: SCM Press, 1959), 119.

98. Ibid.

99. Carson, *The Expositor's Bible Commentary with the New International Version,* 162.

100. Albright and Mann, 76.

101. Ibid.

102. Shema Israel means "Hear, Oh Israel," and it is the opening phrase of the prayer in Deuteronomy 6:4–5.

Chapter 8

The Teaching Ministry of Jesus, Part 2: Great Themes—Authority, Discipleship, Loving God and Loving Neighbor, and Prayer

In the teaching ministry of Jesus, he emphasized many different themes. Some he emphasized more than others. In this section, we will focus on four themes that Jesus highlighted in his teaching ministry: authority, discipleship, our love for God and neighbor, and prayer.

Jesus and Authority

What do you think of when you hear the word "authority"? Does it comfort you or make you afraid? People react differently to the term. Why? Because for some, their experience with authority has been encouraging, whereas for others, they have experienced the abuse of power. Authority can be good or bad depending on the people who wield it.

In Matthew 11 and 12 we see a clash of two different types of authority. We see the Pharisees, the Jewish religious leaders who hounded Jesus by testing him in an attempt to expose him as a false Messiah. When they couldn't file a legitimate charge against Jesus, they trumped up a charge against him and accused him of treason and sedition. In Matthew 12, they accuse Jesus of being in league with Beelzebub, the prince of demons.

On the other side is Jesus. Matthew presents him as the Lord of the Sabbath. If you doubt this fact, then watch as he heals a man on the Sabbath. He is the King who has come with his kingdom. If you doubt this, then watch as he casts out a demon, which has caused a man to be mute and blind. Jesus restores sight and speech to the man. Jesus has ultimate authority. You see it in his words, but also in his actions.

This clash between Jesus and the religious leaders occurs in Matthew 11 and 12, but it is a theme that runs throughout the Gospels. We see it again in Matthew 22:15–46. It comes to a head in Matthew 22–23 and in the Passion narrative of Matthew 26–27.

Who Is This Jesus of Nazareth?—Matthew 12:1–50, cf. Mark 2:23–3:35

The deepest aspects of a person's character are often revealed under stress. In chapter 12 a series of happenings placed Jesus in situations of stress, revealing His integrity, convictions, and personal discipline. When good confronts evil, the result is an increase of defensiveness which actually increases the expression of evil to its own ruin by extreme exposure.[103]

—*The Preacher's Commentary Series*

Jesus had just declared himself to be the one for whom John the Baptist, the Elijah, was preparing the way. He had denounced those who would not believe in him, and invited those who would believe in him to come to him and to know the Father through him. He was attracting the notice of many, including the Pharisees. "Who is this Jesus of Nazareth?" they must have been wondering. They came to him, not as loyal followers, but as religious leaders who feared losing followers. They came to Jesus in order to prove to the people that he was false. In the end, the tables were turned, and the Pharisees were the ones who were proven false.

Jesus Is the Lord of the Sabbath—Matthew 12:1–8, cf. Mark 2:23–28, Luke 6:1–5

At that time Jesus went through the grain fields on the Sabbath. His disciples were hungry and began to pick some heads of grain and eat them. The Pharisees saw this and said to him, "Look, your disciples are doing an unlawful act on the Sabbath!"

Jesus replied, "Have you not read what David did when he and his men were hungry? How they went into the house of God and ate the bread of Presence, which was not lawful for him or his men to eat, but only for the priests to eat? Or have you not read in the law that in the temple on the Sabbath the priests break the Sabbath, but are innocent? I say to you—one greater than the temple is here. But if you had known what this means: 'I desire mercy and not sacrifice,' you would not have condemned the innocent. For the Son of Man is the Lord of the Sabbath."[104]

Jesus is not just the Lord of nature and the Lord over sickness and death, but he is also the Lord of the Sabbath, a day holy to the Jews. Not only were the Old Testament regulations strictly enforced on the Sabbath, but many man-made regulations were enforced as well. The Pharisees kept especially stringent laws concerning the Sabbath. They followed not just the written law, i.e., do not work on the Sabbath, but they also followed a man-made oral code that specified what was to be considered forbidden or permissible on the Sabbath. If a person had a cotton swab in his or her ear and it fell out on the Sabbath, that person could not bend over, pick up the swab, and replace it in his ear. That was considered lifting a burden on the Sabbath. A person was not to spit on the Sabbath. The spit might be trampled under a sandal, thus causing the ground to be plowed on the Sabbath.

In this passage, the Pharisees view the plucking of wheat from the field as reaping, the rubbing of the grains of wheat between the palms as threshing, and blowing the chaff from the kernel as winnowing. In their minds, the disciples of Jesus were guilty of breaking the Sabbath law. Since Jesus was their rabbi, the Pharisees believed that Jesus should not have allowed his disciples to break the Sabbath code.

Jesus interprets the Sabbath according to the written law of God. He begins with "Have you not read?" This is a very important question. The Pharisees equated their oral tradition with the written law, seeing their oral code as just as authoritative as the written one. Jesus placed the written law above all tradition, seeing it as authoritative. He quotes from the written law, and his examples come from there. Today, what is your canon of Scripture? Is it the written Scripture alone? Are there any traditions or any man-made commands that you hold as equal to the Bible? Is so, then Jesus has a question for you—"Have you not read?"

Jesus refers first to a time when David and his men were fleeing for their lives from Saul to the town of Nob where the tabernacle was located (1 Samuel 21:1-6). They were hungry, so they ate the consecrated bread, which had been removed from the tabernacle. This bread was reserved for the priests, but David understood that the greater law of saving life meant he could eat it. Jesus also refers to the work that priests did in the tabernacle on the Sabbath, but they were not guilty of breaking the Sabbath. So God allowed certain work to be performed on the Sabbath.

Jesus interprets the law of the Sabbath in light of the scripture, "I desire mercy, not sacrifice (Hosea 6:6)." Perhaps if the Pharisees had paid more attention to the written law (actual Scripture) instead of their oral law (man-made traditions), they would have seen this as well. They measured Scripture by their tradition, instead of measuring their tradition by Scripture. We need to be careful not to make this same mistake.

In quoting Hosea 6:6, Jesus gets to the heart of what the Sabbath should be about—rest. The Sabbath should be a time where people are refreshed. The Pharisees with all their rules and regulations made the Sabbath a burden to people. In Mark 2:27, Jesus says, "The Sabbath was made for man, not man for the Sabbath." Therefore, Jesus opposed the man-made rules and regulations that the Pharisees heaped on top of people in reference to the Sabbath. He and his men were innocent of breaking the Sabbath law. Stuart Weber writes:

Jesus proclaimed his innocence, not defensively, but authoritatively. If the Pharisees had understood the centrality of mercy and compassion in the Sabbath law, they would not have attacked Jesus as a lawbreaker. Rather, they would have praised him for his consistency with the law's true meaning.[105]

Jesus also makes two bold claims here. First, "One greater than the temple is here." Wow. What a claim. If that isn't enough, then second, Jesus says, "For the Son of Man is Lord of the Sabbath." Jesus is the Son of Man; he is also the Lord of the Sabbath. These are outlandish statements. Outlandish, but true. These statements set the Pharisees on their ears. The Pharisees claim to have authority, but they are blind to the one who has real authority—Jesus. Since Jesus is the Lord of the Sabbath, he can judge if someone is guilty of breaking it, and he finds his disciples innocent. *The Preacher's Commentary Series* notes, "As greater than the temple and as Lord of the Sabbath, Jesus is the ultimate authority regarding service and worship in the will of God…. The conclusion places mercy above ritual, and love above law."[106]

Jesus Heals on the Sabbath—Matthew 12:9–14, cf. Mark 3:1–6, Luke 6:6–11

> *Leaving there he entered their synagogue, and a man with a withered hand was there. Looking for a reason to accuse Jesus, the Pharisees asked him, "Is it lawful to heal on the Sabbath?"*
>
> *He said, "Which of you, if you have a sheep and it falls into a pit on the Sabbath, will not seize it and lift it out? How much more valuable is a human being than a sheep? Therefore it is lawful to do good on the Sabbath."*
>
> *He then said to the man, "Stretch out your hand." And he stretched it out and it was restored, as healthy as the other. But the Pharisees took council about him, how they might kill him.*

The Pharisees were now looking for a way to trap Jesus. When Jesus entered the synagogue, a man was there with a withered hand. *The Preacher's Commentary Series* includes this interesting note about the man:

> We are told nothing about the man in the Gospels. However, in the noncanonical Gospel According to the Hebrews, we are told that the man requested Jesus to heal him. He is reported to have said, "I was a stone mason, seeking my living with my hands. I pray you, Jesus, to give me back my health, so that I shall not need to beg for food in shame." True or not, it is clear in the account that Jesus looked on the man with compassion while the scribes and Pharisees were not concerned about the man but about the minutiae of their regulations.[107]

The Pharisees asked Jesus a question that was often discussed by the rabbis: "Is it lawful to heal on the Sabbath?" Most of the rabbis agreed that if it were a life-or-death situation, then it was fine to provide medical help on the Sabbath. A withered hand did not fall into that category; this man's hand could be healed on Sunday. It could be healed Saturday night after the second star appeared in the sky (which would have ended the Sabbath). The Pharisees had laid a nice trap for Jesus. Would he heal this man on the Sabbath or wait a few hours in order to show respect for their Sabbath laws?

With impressive logic, Jesus answered the Pharisees' question with a question. This was typical of a rabbinical discussion. Rabbis often answered questions with questions to make students think. Jesus here presents himself as the teacher and the Pharisees as the students who need teaching. Jesus asks, "If you have a sheep and it falls into a pit on the Sabbath, will you not seize it and lift it out?" The implied answer is "Yes, we would." Even the law of the Pharisees allowed for planks to be placed before the sheep to help the sheep escape from the ditch. Jesus then leads the Pharisees to this conclusion: "How much more valuable is a human being than a sheep?" The implied answer is "Immeasurably more." Jesus finally concludes, "Therefore it is lawful to do good on the Sabbath."

Interestingly, the Essenes of Qumran wrote that if a sheep or other beast of burden fell in a pit, it was unlawful to remove the animal on the Sabbath. You see how seriously some people took the Sabbath. Jesus understood that the Sabbath was created for man and not man for the Sabbath. When legalism clashed with grace, Jesus sided with grace. He healed the man on the Sabbath. With a word, he heals the man's hand. Stuart Weber writes:

> There was no indication that Jesus used touch in this case. This method was even more dramatic than if he had used touch. Jesus commanded, "Stretch out your hand," and the man's compliance probably happened within a second or two. This brought into the scene the element of surprise, displaying the authority of Jesus' word. He was authenticating his right to the title, "Lord of the Sabbath."[108]

The man's hand was completely restored; it became the same as the other hand. This demonstrates the power of Jesus. He can fix what is broken. He can heal what is hurt. When he heals, he heals completely. He does it all with a word because Jesus' word is power—power and authority.

Jesus' actions and his statements upset the Pharisees. They went away and conspired how they might destroy him. Jesus made a man whole on the Sabbath; the Pharisees plotted an innocent man's death on the Sabbath. Who was really breaking the Sabbath? By an act of mercy to a crippled man, Jesus enters into a dispute with the Pharisees that will eventually lead to his crucifixion.

The Pharisees did not like the fact that Jesus escaped their trap. They realized that to get rid of him would take planning on their part, and they began to discuss how they could be rid of him once and for all. The tension between Jesus and the religious authorities would continue to mount from this point on.

Jesus Is the Fulfillment of Prophecy—Matthew 12:15–21, cf. Mark 3:7–12

Jesus knew what they were thinking, and left there. Large crowds followed him, and he healed all of them, and he ordered them not to tell what he was doing, so that the word of the prophet Isaiah might be fulfilled which says:

Lord, my servant whom I have chosen,
My loved one in whom my soul is pleased;
I will put my Spirit on him,
And he will proclaim justice to the nations.
He will not quarrel or cry out,
Nor will his voice be heard in the streets.
He will not break a bruised reed
And he will not put out a smoldering wick.
In his name the nations will hope.

Aware of what the Pharisees were thinking, Jesus withdrew to another area. *The Preacher's Commentary* states:

Jesus was courageous but not careless. Knowing the Pharisees were plotting to destroy Him, He withdrew from premature confrontation. This was not only a sound political course of action but was good psychology. On many occasions an issue can be dealt with better after a time of emotional adjustment and creative distance.[109]

The use of the verb γινώσκω/*ginosko* suggests that Jesus heard reports of what the Pharisees were planning. It doesn't have to imply a supernatural knowledge of the plans of the Pharisees.

As Jesus left, large crowds followed him. After healing them, he ordered them not to spread the news of his miraculous works. The Pharisees were laying plans to arrest him, and Jesus did not wish reports of his miracle working to hasten his arrest.

Matthew says this happened to fulfill prophecy, and he quotes from the first of four Servant Songs found in Isaiah (Isaiah 42). First-century Jews knew these songs to be highly Messianic in content. Matthew has used this "fulfillment formula" throughout his gospel to connect Jesus with Old Testament prophecy. This is the longest of the fulfillment prophecies in Matthew.

Isaiah speaks of the Messiah as being the redeemer of Israel, the servant of God. God would place his spirit on his servant, as God had done at Jesus' baptism. The servant would not quarrel, nor would his voice be heard in the street. This fits in nicely with the present context. Jesus tells those he heals not to spread word of his actions. He doesn't want to start a rebellion or draw undue attention to himself at this point in his ministry. Jesus humbly and quietly serves and heals people away from the limelight. That is the type of Messiah that he is.

Isaiah says, "A bruised reed he will not break, and a smoldering wick he will not snuff out." When the Pharisees tried to trap Jesus, he could easily have turned the crowds against the Pharisees and started a rebellion, but he did not stir up the crowds; he was following the path of the Suffering Servant of Isaiah.

Jesus Is Greater than Satan—Matthew 12:22–32, cf. Mark 3:20–28

Then they brought him a demon-possessed man who was blind and mute, and Jesus healed him, so that he could both talk and see. All the people were astonished and said, "Could this be the Son of David?"

But when the Pharisees heard this, they said, "It is only by Beelzebub, the prince of demons, that this fellow drives out demons."

Jesus knew their thoughts and said to them, "Every kingdom divided against itself will be ruined, and every city or household divided against itself will not stand. If Satan drives out Satan, he is divided against himself. How then can his kingdom stand? And if I drive out demons by Beelzebub, by whom do your people drive them out? So then, they will be your judges. But if I drive out demons by the Spirit of God, then the kingdom of God has come upon you.

"Or again, how can anyone enter a strong man's house and carry off his possessions unless he first ties up the strong man? Then he can rob his house.

"He who is not with me is against me, and he who does not gather with me scatters. And so I tell you, every sin and blasphemy will be forgiven men, but the blasphemy against the Spirit will not be forgiven. Anyone who speaks a word against the Son of Man will be forgiven, but anyone who speaks against the Holy Spirit will not be forgiven, either in this age or in the age to come.

The demonstration of the authority of Jesus continues to be pressed in this section. Now the Pharisees bring to Jesus a man who is possessed by a demon, a possession that has left the man blind and mute. The Pharisees have their trap set: If Jesus is unable to cast out the demon, then he is false. If he is able to cast out the demon, then he is in league with Satan.

In the *Star Trek* series, cadets training to become Star Fleet captains had to face a training episode called the Kobayashi Maru. In the exercise, a civilian vessel named the Kobayashi Maru is stranded in the Klingon Neutral Zone and the Star Fleet captain trainee is to respond to its distress signal. When he or she does, Klingon ships appear and attack the Star Fleet vessel, outgunning it and leaving it crippled in space. It is a no-win situation. The Pharisees were presenting Jesus with a no-win situation: a Kobayashi Maru. But Jesus does not believe in no-win situations.

Jesus heals the man, and the crowds begin to wonder if Jesus could really be the Son of David—the King/Messiah. Faith is starting to bloom in the hearts of some of the people, but not in the hearts of the Pharisees. They spring their trap. They claim that Jesus is casting out demons by Beelzebub, the ruler of demons.

Jesus answers their accusations by making three arguments stated as questions. First, can a kingdom that is divided against itself stand? Why would Satan be divided against himself and destroy his own work? It doesn't make sense. If Jesus were in league with Satan, then he would not cast out demons.

Second, if Jesus is casting out demons by Beelzebub, by whom do the Pharisees cast them out? The Pharisees had their own exorcists. If the only way to cast out a demon was to be in league with Satan, then what did that say about Jewish exorcists?

Third, can anyone ransack the house of a strong man without first binding him? Jesus had to first bind Satan to be able to cast out his minions. Jesus is saying, "I am stronger than Satan. I have authority over him. I cast out demons because I have power over Satan."

Jesus urges the Pharisees to recognize that the kingdom of God has come into the world. Verse 28 reads, "But if I drive out demons by the Spirit of God, then the kingdom of God has come upon you." This is clear evidence that a manifestation of God's kingdom came in the person and work of Jesus. He was King; his authority over demons demonstrated that. The Pharisees should have recognized that Jesus was the Messiah. Instead, they attributed his works to Satan. Jesus has thrown down the gauntlet. He is saying, "Since I cast out demons, the kingdom has come." What is implied is, "Are you going to be a part of this kingdom or not?"

Jesus warns the Pharisees not to speak against the Holy Spirit, warning them that their own words will either acquit or condemn them. He speaks of the unpardonable sin.

What is "the unpardonable sin?" We must consider the context of this verse to answer this question. Jesus has just healed a blind and mute man by casting out the demon that caused his illness. The Pharisees say that he did this by the power of Satan and not by God's power. Therefore Jesus says, "Anyone who speaks a word against the Son of Man will be forgiven, but anyone who speaks against the Holy Spirit will not be forgiven, either in this age or in the age to come." What is this sin against the Holy Spirit? Simply put, it is when someone claims that the mighty works of Jesus are a product of Satan and not of the Holy Spirit. When you claim that Jesus is working miracles because of Satan's power, then you have blasphemed the Holy Spirit.

Literally, to blaspheme the Holy Spirit is to attribute the works of Jesus to Satan. Before a person gets to that point, his heart has already rejected Jesus as Lord. *The Preacher's Commentary Series* reads:

> Jesus said that persons may not fully understand the man Jesus of Nazareth and, out of ignorance, may speak critically of what He was doing and yet have forgiveness. But where the truth of God comes through by the illumination of the Holy Spirit and men reject that truth, they place themselves beyond pardon. While some interpret this "unpardonable sin" as an act of attributing the work of the Spirit to Satan, it is much more an attitude than a single act; it is a state of willful sin. It is an attitude that closes one's mind and conscience to the convictions of the Spirit until the conscience becomes so hardened that the one voice which calls to God, the voice of the Spirit, can no longer get through. Such are then beyond pardon, beyond hearing the call to pardon.[110]

Some would say that since Jesus is not here in the flesh working miracles today, you cannot blaspheme the Holy Spirit today. *The Bible Knowledge Commentary* states:

> This specific sin cannot be reproduced today, for it required Jesus' presence on earth with His performing miracles through the Spirit's power. If, however, the leaders, acting on behalf of the nation, concluded that Jesus was empowered by Satan, they would commit a sin that would never find national or individual forgiveness (in this Age or in the Age to come). The consequences would bring about God's judgment on the nation and on any individual who persisted in that view.[111]

I personally would not be so quick to rule out this possibility today. I think this verse stands as a warning to us. We had better not get in such a wicked, corrupt place that we claim the work of Jesus is the work of Satan. When we get in that place, then we are past the point of returning to God; we have committed the unpardonable sin. This should be a word of caution for anyone who wants to attack the works of Jesus in today's world.

You Can Know Jesus by His Fruit—Matthew 12:33–37

"Produce a good tree and its fruit is good, or produce a bad tree and its fruit is bad. For the fruit knows the tree. You offspring of vipers, how are you able to speak good when

you are evil? For out of the abundance of the heart the mouth speaks. A good man brings good things out of the good treasured in him. An evil man brings evil things out of the evil treasured in him. I tell you that for every careless word that men speak, they will have to give account concerning that word on the Day of Judgment. By your words you will be condemned."

In the last section, a question was posed that must be answered—is Jesus in league with Beelzebub or is he the Son of David? How can this question be answered? Look at the works of Jesus. You can know a tree by its fruit. What is the fruit of Jesus' life? He enables the blind to see, the lame to walk, the deaf to hear, and the mute to speak. Jesus has produced only good fruit.

What is the work of the Pharisees? Evil. Instead of helping a man on the Sabbath, they plot the death of Jesus. Instead of recognizing the Spirit's power in Jesus, they attribute his work to Satan. They are an offspring of snakes, out to attack the good things that Jesus is doing.

Jesus teaches valuable principles here. First, if you want to know the character of someone, look at the person's actions and not his or her words.

Second, we produce whatever we have treasured inside us. Therefore, it is important to watch what we treasure in our hearts. What goes into our heart comes out in words and actions.

Third, we need to guard our speech. We must give an answer for every careless word on the Day of Judgment. This is a scary statement, one of the scariest in the Bible. Jesus says, "I tell you that for every careless word that men speak, they will have to give account concerning that word on the Day of Judgment. By your words you will be condemned." Does Jesus really say "every" careless word? Wow. That's radical. Why such a high standard for our language? Because our words reflect who we are. Our words reflect our attitude. They reflect our heart. If our words are careless, so is our heart. To keep a check on your words, first you have to guard your heart. After all, it is out of the abundance of the heart that the mouth speaks.

The Ultimate Test of Jesus' Authority: His Resurrection— Matthew 12:38–42

Then some of the scribes and Pharisees said to him, "Teacher, we want to see a sign from you."

He answered them, "A wicked and adulterous generation asks for a sign and it will not be given a sign except for the sign of the prophet Jonah. For as Jonah was in the belly of the great fish for three days and three nights, so the Son of Man will be in the heart of the earth for three days and three nights. The men of Nineveh will rise up at the judgment with this generation and condemn it because they repented at the preaching of Jonah, and behold one greater than Jonah is here. The Queen of the South will rise up at the judgment and condemn it because she came from the ends of the earth to listen to the wisdom of Solomon, and behold one greater than Solomon is here."

Even though Jesus had demonstrated his power through his teaching and his miracles, the scribes (the teachers of the law) and Pharisees were still not convinced that he was King. They asked Jesus for a sign that would demonstrate beyond a doubt that he was the Messiah. Jesus condemned them for asking, calling them a wicked and adulterous generation. This was the same language used by the prophets to speak to Israel when she turned away from God to follow idols. Their lack of faith condemned them.

The only sign he gave them was the sign of Jonah: "As Jonah was in the belly of the great fish for three days and three nights, so the Son of Man will be in the heart of the earth for three days and three nights." In Jewish reckoning, a part of a day counted as a whole day, so even though Jesus rose on Sunday morning, Sunday counted as a day and night in the Jewish mind. Here Jesus foreshadows his resurrection, the ultimate sign of his authority. If he was not who he claims to be, then produce his dead body. If he was who he claims to be, then he rose from the dead.

The resurrection is the greatest sign that Jesus is who he claimed to be. Jesus is the Lord of the Sabbath. He healed the sick. He is the King of the Messianic Kingdom. He exorcised demons. He had power over Satan. He manifested his authority in many ways in this section. But the ultimate manifestation of his authority would be his resurrection.

Jesus Challenges "This Evil Generation"—Matthew 12:43–45

"When an unclean spirit has been cast out of a man, it goes through dry places seeking a resting place, but does not find it. Then it says, 'I will return to my host that I left.' When it comes, it finds it empty, swept, and put in order. Then it goes and brings with it seven other spirits more wicked than itself, and they enter and live there, and the last condition of the man is worse than the first. Thus it is with this evil generation."

Jesus stated what he really thought of this evil generation: They were like an unclean spirit that had been cast out of a person. The spirit tried to find a resting place in the desert, but was unable to. So he returned to his old host, this time with seven other spirits who were worse. The condition of the man was worse than it was at first.

Jesus had been trying to sweep clean this generation. He had taught them, healed them, answered their questions, and walked among them. Even after all he had done and all they had seen, they failed to accept him as the Son of David. If they would not invite the Spirit of God into their lives, then the spirit of Satan would gladly take residence there. Their condition would be worse than when they started listening to Jesus.

Jesus' True Family?—Matthew 12:46–50, cf. Mark 3:21, 31–35, Luke 8:19–21

While Jesus was speaking to the crowds, his mother and brothers stood outside, wanting to speak to him. Someone said to him, "Look, your mother and your brothers are standing outside wanting to speak with you."

He answered, "Who is my mother and who are my brothers?" Pointing to his disciples, he said, "Look, my mother and my brothers. For whoever does the will of my Father in heaven is my brother and sister and mother.

The Pharisees didn't understand who Jesus was. They failed to perceive his greatness and authority. The unbelieving generation failed to see as well. They missed the authority of Jesus. Surely the family of Jesus would understand. Sadly, they miss it as well. Therefore, Jesus redefined family.

Jesus' mother and brothers wanted an audience with him. Mark tells us the names of Jesus' brothers: James, Joseph, Judas, and Simon. Mark also tells us that Jesus' family tried to seize him because they thought he was out of his mind (Mark 3:21). These are the people who should understand who Jesus was, but they failed to see Jesus as Lord.

So what did Jesus do? He redefined family. Jesus didn't look at family from a physical point of view. His family was made up of those who would do the will of the father. Stuart Weber writes:

Jesus loved and honored his physical family (e.g., John 19:25–27), and he intended no insult to them. However, their presence gave him the opportunity to define an even more significant family. The head of this new family is God, the heavenly Father. Membership in this family is determined not by blood but by a relationship with the Father through covenant faith, evidenced by obedience to his will.[112]

Conclusion

Jesus was Lord of the Sabbath and the King of his kingdom. He healed with a word. Some of those in the crowds were starting to understand this. Unfortunately, some of those who should have been most in tune with who Jesus was didn't understand. The scribes and Pharisees missed it. Sadly, his family missed it. What about you? That's where we are left after exploring this topic: How do you see Jesus?

Is Jesus your Lord? Do you honor him as King? Have you surrendered your life to his Lordship? Are you a part of his newly defined spiritual family?

Jesus and Discipleship

Christianity without discipleship is always Christianity without Christ.[113]
—Dietrich Bonhoeffer, theologian and writer

Those who aren't following Jesus aren't his followers. It's that simple. Followers follow, and those who don't follow aren't followers. To follow Jesus means to follow Jesus into a society where justice rules, where love shapes everything. To follow Jesus means to take up his dream and work for it.[114]
—Scot McKnight, NT scholar

If Jesus is who he claimed to be (and he claimed to be Lord), then when he calls people, they should follow. Following Jesus is also known as discipleship. The call to discipleship is a major theme that runs throughout the gospels.

What does Jesus expect of his followers? When a disciple followed a rabbi, he dedicated his life to learning what the rabbi had to teach. When the rabbi taught, the disciple took notes and memorized the teachings of the rabbi word for word. Also, the disciple served the rabbi. When the rabbi asked for water, the disciple ran to get water. If the rabbi was hungry, the disciple fried up some vittles. That's the nature of the disciple/rabbi relationship.

But Jesus was more than a rabbi. As we have seen, he was the Lord of the Sabbath and Lord of the universe. As such, discipleship to Jesus was set at an even higher commitment level than the disciple/rabbi relationship. We need to think of it as a slave/Master or servant/Lord relationship. Jesus was Lord; therefore, his disciples must obey his commands.

Lee Camp, author of *Mere Discipleship*, writes:

Jesus of Nazareth always comes asking disciples to follow him—not merely "accept him," not merely "believe in him," not merely "worship him," but to follow him: one either follows Christ, or one does not. There is no compartmentalization of the faith, no realm, no sphere, no business, no politic in which the lordship of Christ will be excluded. We either make him Lord of all lords, or we deny him as Lord of any.[115]

The decision to be a disciple of Jesus calls for the highest level of commitment. Before one accepts this invitation to follow Jesus and become his disciple, he or she must think through the ramifications of what that decision means.

In the Gospel of Luke, Luke focuses on the theme of discipleship. He includes several sections where Jesus calls various people to follow him/ to be his disciples. A look at these passages will help us understand what Jesus taught about discipleship in his ministry.

Luke 9:22–26 (cf. Matthew 16:21–28, Mark 8:31–9:1)

And he said, "The Son of Man must suffer many things and be rejected by the elders, chief priests and teachers of the law, and he must be killed and on the third day be raised to life."

Then he said to them all: "If anyone would come after me, he must deny himself and take up his cross daily and follow me. For whoever wants to save his life will lose it, but whoever loses his life for me will save it. What good is it for a man to gain the whole world, and yet lose or forfeit his very self? If anyone is ashamed of me and my words, the Son of Man will be ashamed of him when he comes in his glory and in the glory of the Father and of the holy angels."

Jesus lets the disciples know his future; namely, he must suffer, be rejected, die, and come back to life. Then he lets them know their future if they choose to follow him as disciples; namely, a cross. In both cases, a cross is involved.

"If anyone would come after me," is the call of discipleship. The call is the same for everyone. Jesus never acknowledged a clergy/laity system. He doesn't say there are normal disciples, super disciples, and super-duper disciples. The call of discipleship is a level playing field where everyone must (1) deny self, (2) take up the cross daily, and (3) follow.

1. Deny self. What does this mean? Discipleship implies sacrifice; the nature of discipleship is self-denial. We all have a selfish nature that wants to be our lord, and to follow Jesus, we must deny that selfish nature. Martin Luther said, "God creates out of nothing. Therefore, until a man is nothing, God can make nothing out of him."[116] Matthew Henry wrote, "The first lesson in Christ's school is self-denial."[117] Anyone who wants to be an apprentice of Jesus must deny self.

   What does this mean for you? In what ways are you selfish? What must you put to death in order make Jesus your Lord?

2. Take up the cross daily. In the first century, everyone knew what the cross symbolized: It meant death. Jesus was saying that his disciples must die daily. Discipleship is a daily decision, a daily commitment to die to self.

3. Follow. To be a disciple means that wherever Jesus leads, we follow. We know one place where Jesus is leading us. He mentions it right before he gives the call of discipleship: Jesus will suffer, be rejected, and die. He is heading for the cross. If we follow Jesus, then we must be willing to die on the cross as well.

Jesus gives three interesting statements about discipleship. The first is a paradox, or a statement that seems to be absurd or self-contradictory but which upon closer investigation proves to be true. The next two statements are a bit paradoxical in nature. They certainly create memorable images for the listener to ponder.

1. Jesus said, "For whoever wants to save his life will lose it, but whoever loses his life for me will save it." To be a disciple of Jesus, you have to die daily. People don't generally want to die; they want to save their lives. So the question arises, "How can I save my life?"

Jesus answers, "To save life, you have to lose it for me." That's the paradox. Life comes by giving up your life. Discipleship isn't easy. We want to find an easier way to save our lives. *The Believer's Bible Commentary* notes:

> The natural tendency is to save our lives by selfish, complacent, routine, petty existences. We may indulge our pleasures and appetites by basking in comfort, luxury, and ease, by living for the present, by trading our finest talents to the world in exchange for a few years of mock security. But in the very act, we lose our lives, that is, we miss the true purpose of life and the profound spiritual pleasure that should go with it![118]

There is no easy path of discipleship. If we are going to save our lives, we have to lose them for Jesus.

2. Jesus asked, "What good is it for a man to gain the whole world, and yet lose or forfeit his very self?" This second statement is a rhetorical question: What good is it to gain the whole world and lose your soul? The implied answer is, "It doesn't do any good at all." To wind up at the end of your life with all the possessions the world has to offer and lose your self or your soul in the process is foolish.

Jesus acknowledges that everyone has a choice. You have free will, and you can choose to follow him or put "self" before him. You can choose the world over discipleship and the cross. Is that a good choice? The implied answer is, "No, that's not a good choice."

Suppose you choose the world, and it works out so that you gain the whole world. You are Imperial Emperor of the World. That's not as cool as Supreme Monarch of the Universe, but it's still pretty cool. But if that title comes with the loss of your self or soul, what have you gained? Nothing. Therefore, choose discipleship.

Christ paints a picture. Imagine a guy holding the whole world above his head. He stands there with a satisfied smile looking up at the world above him. He thinks to himself, "I've got the whole world in my hands. I did it. I acquired the entire world." Then a wind begins to blow. It starts to blow the man apart like dust in a breeze. The wind begins at the feet, then it moves to the calves, the knees, and the thighs. The man's smile turns to a grimace. He realizes that he has the whole world, but he's not going to enjoy it. The wind continues to blow the man apart particle by particle until there is nothing left but the world floating in space. Then the whole world drops into blackness and everything fades to black.

Thus it is with anyone who seeks the world over discipleship.

3. Jesus said, "If anyone is ashamed of me and my words, the Son of Man will be ashamed of him when he comes in his glory and in the glory of the Father and of the holy angels." What is the paradox here? If you feel shame in the here and now because of Jesus, then you don't really know shame. Wait for the hereafter; then you'll know the real meaning of shame.

If you feel shame in following Jesus, then you aren't really a disciple. True discipleship means that you are fully invested, one hundred percent committed, and full hearted in your discipleship. There isn't any room for shame. There is no second-guessing.

If you are ashamed of being a disciple of Jesus now, then you are in a bad place. That is unacceptable to Jesus. You will find greater shame when Jesus returns with his angels and pronounces his shame over your choice of the world over discipleship. Therefore, choose discipleship.

Luke 9:57–62 (cf. Matthew 8:19–22)

> As they were walking along the road, a man said to him, "I will follow you wherever you go."
>
> Jesus replied, "Foxes have holes and birds of the air have nests, but the Son of Man has no place to lay his head."
>
> He said to another man, "Follow me."
>
> But the man replied, "Lord, first let me go and bury my father."
>
> Jesus said to him, "Let the dead bury their own dead, but you go and proclaim the kingdom of God."
>
> Still another said, "I will follow you, Lord; but first let me go back and say good-by to my family."
>
> Jesus replied, "No one who puts his hand to the plow and looks back is fit for service in the kingdom of God."

In Luke's gospel, Jesus has just stated what it means to be a disciple. Now Luke will illustrate what it means to follow Jesus by including three exchanges between Jesus and potential disciples.

1. As Jesus was walking down the road, a man said to him, "I will follow you wherever you go." But Jesus challenges that response with, "Make sure you know what you are saying. Even the Father's small animals have a home, but I don't. I don't know where I'm going to lay my head tonight.

Are you ready for that?"

This man doesn't know what he is asking. To be a disciple of Jesus implies that you will follow his lifestyle. Jesus senses that the man isn't ready for true discipleship and responds, "You don't know what you're asking. I have no home. Are you ready for that?" Jesus demands that if we are going to commit to follow him, then we need to think through that commitment and commit to him for the long haul.

How many of us are starters and stoppers? We start a project. Stop. Start another project. Stop. Start something else. Stop. We have unfinished projects all around us. When it comes to following Jesus, we can't be a starter-stopper. We have to start and finish. That's what Jesus is saying to this scribe. He's saying, "Think through this decision before you commit to it. Think before you speak. If you start, then I expect you to finish."

How many of us have started the journey of discipleship only to find ourselves right now in the present not as committed to Jesus as we were when we first started the journey? That's what Jesus is saying here. If you are going to start, then finish strong. Don't start and stop. Don't start, then coast. Don't start and punch the cruise control button and cruise the rest of the way. If you are going to start, then finish and finish strong.

2. Jesus says to another man, "Follow me." This is the call of discipleship. The man makes the excuse, "I've got to go bury my dead father." In that culture, this was the same as saying, "Let me take care of my dad's estate." This seems like a legitimate reason not to follow Jesus, but Jesus doesn't see it that way. The mission of Jesus is of utmost urgency. Jesus responds, "Those who are spiritually dead can do that. There is a bigger commitment here than family, and it's staring you in the face." If you are going to be a disciple, then the call of discipleship is more important than anything else in life.

3. A third man's response to Jesus is: "I'll be a disciple, but first let me say goodbye to my family." This again seems like a good reason not to follow. Jesus doesn't see it that way. He tells him, "If you are going to follow me, there is no looking back." What happens if you look back while you are plowing? Your rows become crooked. Your field becomes a mess. If we look back as a disciple, our lives become a mess. To follow Jesus means that we keep our eyes on him. He must be our sole focus.

Jesus is saying that there is no excuse that excuses you from discipleship. So follow. Follow to the finish. And when you finish, finish strong.

Luke 14:25–33

Large crowds were traveling with Jesus, and turning to them he said: "If anyone comes to me and does not hate his father and mother, his wife and children, his brothers and sisters—yes, even his own life—he cannot be my disciple. And anyone who does not carry his cross and follow me cannot be my disciple.

"Suppose one of you wants to build a tower. Will he not first sit down and esti-mate the cost to see if he has enough money to complete it? For if he lays the foundation and is not able to finish it, everyone who sees it will ridicule him, saying, 'This fellow began to build and was not able to finish.'

"Or suppose a king is about to go to war against another king. Will he not first sit down and consider whether he is able with ten thousand men to oppose the one coming against him with twenty thousand? If he is not able, he will send a delegation while the other is still a long way off and will ask for terms of peace. In the same way, any of you who does not give up everything he has cannot be my disciple."

Here Jesus gives a longer discourse on discipleship. He begins, "If anyone comes to me." Again, the standard of discipleship is the same for anyone and everyone.

Jesus knows that one of the greatest pulls to keep someone from be-ing a disciple can be family. Therefore, Jesus teaches that to follow him you must "hate" father and mother, wife and children, brothers and sis-ters. What does Jesus mean by "hate"? Didn't Jesus teach love, not hatred? Jesus is using hyperbole here. He states his point in an exaggerated way to give it more of a punch. Our love for God needs to be so great that any other love seems like hate.

Family isn't the only pull against discipleship. The greatest pull of all is self. Jesus says we must hate our own life. Again, this is hyperbole; Jesus doesn't teach self-hatred. But our love for him must be so great that any other love pales in comparison.

Jesus entreats his disciples to pick up their cross and follow him. This foreshadows what Jesus must literally do in the future. His follower might literally have to pick up a cross and follow, but every follower must do this spiritually. *The Bible Knowledge Commentary* notes:

When the Roman Empire crucified a criminal or captive, the victim was often forced to carry his cross part of the way to the crucifixion site. Carrying his cross through the heart of the city was supposed to be a tacit admission that the Roman Empire was correct in the sentence of death imposed on him, an admission that Rome was right and he was wrong. So when Jesus enjoined His followers to carry their crosses and follow Him, He was referring to a public display before others that Jesus was right and that the disciples were following Him even to their deaths. This is exactly what the religious leaders refused to do.[119]

Taking up the cross means that we publicly align ourselves with Jesus. Everyone sees us carrying the cross. We become identified with the cross of Jesus.

The cost of discipleship is a commitment to the lordship of Jesus.

Dietrich Bonhoeffer, the German minister and theologian who died during the Holocaust, wrote an engaging book entitled, *The Cost of Discipleship.* In his book, Bonhoeffer wrote about cheap grace. Cheap grace is when a person tries to claim the grace of God without offering any commitment of discipleship.

The invitation to pick up a cross is challenging. Therefore Jesus invites his disciples to think about their decision before they make it. He talks about estimating the cost. If you are going to build a tower, doesn't it make sense to make sure you have enough money to complete the tower before you embark on the project? In the same way, anyone who wants to be a disciple of Jesus should carefully think through his or her decision.

But if you are leaning toward deciding not to commit to Jesus' lordship, then consider this: You are about to wage war against God. If you are going to go to war, then you need to see if you can win the war.

In the martial art of Kung Fu, you learn how to spar against people. When you get ready to spar against someone, you try to determine how you can defeat your opponent. You begin by observing him to see how long his reach is and how good he is with his kicks. You try to see what he is most comfortable with—punches or kicks. You look for any weakness. You want to take advantage of his weaknesses.

In Jesus' story, he describes a no-win situation. If you fight against this king who has twice as many soldiers as you do, you are going to lose. Therefore, draw up terms of peace. Don't fight.

The point of Jesus' story is this—God is the king with twice as many soldiers. His arm is twice as long as yours and his punch is fast as lightning. His kicks come out of nowhere and sound like thunder. He has combinations that you haven't even thought about. Jab, cross, uppercut, haymaker, back fist, and hook. You can't win if you fight against God. Therefore, submit. Choose discipleship. The cost of nondiscipleship is much worse than the cost of discipleship.

Dallas Willard writes:

> The impression gained by most who hear about "counting the cost" of following Jesus is one of how terrible and painful that cost is. But to count the cost is to take into consideration both the losses and gains of all possible courses of action, to see which is beneficial. This done, Jesus knew, the trails of apprenticeship (discipleship) would appear to be the only reasonable path.... The cost of non-discipleship would then be seen for what it is—unbearable. This is why one would become able to sustain cheerfully the *much smaller* "cost of discipleship to him."[120]

When you write out the pros and cons of discipleship versus nondiscipleship, the choice is obvious: Choose discipleship.

To be a disciple of Jesus is costly. You have to go where he leads, and as the suffering Messiah, his path will lead to suffering. You have to make sacrifices, and the sacrificing won't stop until you get to heaven. Discipleship is costly, but it will cost you more not to be a disciple of Jesus. Choose Jesus. Choose discipleship.

Jesus' Teaching Concerning Loving God and Loving Neighbor

When we tell God we love him with all our heart, often we are just using words, making a speech that has no reality. From our childhood on, many of us have been taught to speak in such a way, and so we continue to do so when we have grown up—often without knowing what we are saying.

But to love God means to have no will other than his. It means to faithfully observe his holy law. It means to have a horror of sin. To love God means to love what Jesus loved—poverty, humiliation, suffering. It means to hate what Jesus hated—the world, our pride, our passions.[121]

—François Fenelon, 17th century French devotional writer

What did Jesus have to say about having a relationship with the Father? What did he teach about following the law versus having a heart for God? If Jesus were asked to pinpoint the most important aspect of having a relationship with God, what would his answer be?

The Greatest Commandment—Matthew 22:34–40, Mark 12:28–31, Luke 10:25–28

The context of this passage in Mark and Matthew is the same. Many of the religious leaders who excelled at following the way of legalism came to Jesus to test him and to question him about the law. The Pharisees tested him by asking a question about taxes. The Sadducees followed up by asking a question concerning the resurrection. Then a scribe (a lawyer or theologian) asked Jesus a question, "What is the greatest commandment?"

This was a question that was commonly debated in Judaism. One answer that was often given to this question was to quote the *Shema Israel* as found in Deuteronomy 6:4, "Hear, O Israel: The Lord our God, the Lord is one." This was a great propositional truth accepted by the Jewish people, a distinguishing mark of Judaism. But propositional truths do not equal relationship. Jesus wanted to go beyond propositional truth to talk about relationship. Therefore, he added, "Love the Lord your God with all your heart, soul, mind, and strength."

Jesus makes sure that we place great value on relationship and not just on propositional truth. Truth is important, but truth without relationship quickly evolves into legalism. M. Robert Mulholland, Jr., in his wonderful book *Invitation to Journey*, writes:

> The Christian's identity and value do not reside in the fragile order and tenuous control that she or he imposes upon life. Identity and value are found in a vital and living relationship with Christ as Lord. This relationship liberates Christians from dependence upon their little systems of order and fragile structures of control. Not that believers live without order or control, but they are liberated from dependency on those systems and structures for their sense of self.[122]

Jesus teaches that the greatest command is to love God. This love is *agape* love, an unconditional, committed love. It is love that knows no boundaries. It is a love that is a consuming fire. It overwhelms us. It is emotional, romantic, and intellectual.

Jesus teaches that our love for God must include our whole being. We must love him with all that makes us a person, withholding nothing from him. This love takes the whole of our heart (καρδία/*kardia*). In the first century, the heart was looked upon as the seat of the emotions. It includes our passion. Our love for God must include our soul (ψυχῇ/*psuche*). The soul is what makes us an individual person. It is our personality, our personhood; it is who we are as a person. We must give God the whole of our mind (διανοίᾳ/*dianoia*); God wants us to give him our intellect. He wants us to comprehend him on an intellectual level. He also wants the whole of our strength (ἰσχύος/*ischuos*). Our strength is our drive, our will, our desires, and our actions. All of these attributes make us who we are as a person. God wants all of us. To give him our intellect without our emotions isn't enough. To give him our emotions but to hold back our drive and will isn't pleasing either. He wants everything that we are.

R. T. France in his commentary on Matthew writes, "Heart, soul and mind are not different 'parts' of man, but different ways of thinking of the whole man in relation to God."[123] D.A. Carson echoes this sentiment in his two-volume commentary:

> From the viewpoint of biblical anthropology, 'heart,' 'soul,' and 'mind' are not mutually exclusive but overlapping categories, together demanding our love for God to come from our whole person, our every faculty and capacity.[124]

Is your whole person, every faculty and capacity of you, in love with God? Is this love a fully committed, unconditional love of God? This is the greatest commandment. We must be consumed by our love for God. This is basic and fundamental to Christianity.

Do We LOVE God?

The greatest question is not, "Do we love God?" The greatest question is, "Do we **LOVE** God?" We must **LOVE** God with an ἀγάπη/agape LOVE. He must consume us. We must **LOVE** God with every faculty of our being, with all the capacity of our love. Do we **LOVE** God?

Do you know what it is like to be consumed by love? Have you ever been so in love that it hurts? Have you ever been head over heals, crazy, punch-drunk, silly, stupid, madly in love with someone?

The first time I ever felt this way about someone was in college when I met Chippy Leigh Brewer. She was the prettiest girl I had ever seen. She had big, beautiful, hazel eyes; curly brown hair, a great smile, the craziest laugh that you ever heard in your life, and more personality than any one person was allowed to have. When we started dating, I was consumed by love for her. When I was in class, I would think of her. I got up for breakfast just to see her. I would say goodnight to her at her dormitory, walk back to my room and call her on the phone. I was consumed by love for her.

G.K. Chesterton wrote, "Romance is the deepest thing in life, romance is deeper even than reality."[125] The romantic love that I felt in college for the girl who would become my wife was the deepest emotion that I had ever experienced in life up to that point and would only get deeper the more I fell in love with her. I had never felt that type of love for God. I never thought of being in love with God that deeply; I never allowed myself to think about being romantically in love with God. I always thought of loving God in an intellectual way, but perhaps the truest connection that we can make with God is in a romantic way. This is what it means to be consumed by our love for God. Are you head over heels, crazy, nuts, silly about him? Are you so in love that your love doesn't have an off switch? Do you think of him all the time? Do you long for him? This is being in **LOVE** with God. We should have desire, heart, and passion. It should be magical, mystical, spiritual, unquantifiable, huge, ferocious, gigantic **LOVE**. It should be **LOVE** that is beyond us, special and extraordinary. Is this the kind of **LOVE** we have for God?

Oswald Chambers calls this type of love a "haunting." In his devotional classic, *My Utmost for His Highest*, he writes:

What are you haunted by? You will say—By nothing, but we are all haunted by something, generally by ourselves, or, if we are Christians, by our experience. The Psalmist says we are to be haunted by God. The abiding consciousness of the life is to be with God, not thinking about Him. The whole of our life inside and out is to be absolutely haunted by the presence of God. A child's consciousness is so mother-haunted that although the child is not consciously thinking of its mother, yet when calamity arises, the relationship that abides is that of the mother. So we are to live and move and have our being in God, to look at everything in relation to God, because the abiding consciousness of God pushes itself to the front all the time.

If we are haunted by God, nothing else can get in, no cares, no tribulation, no anxieties. We see now why Our Lord so emphasized the sin of worry. How can we dare be so utterly unbelieving when God is round about us? To be haunted by God is to have an effective barricade against all the onslaughts of the enemy.[126]

Agape **LOVE** is a haunting **LOVE**. This is the type of love that we must have for God.

Trading True Love for a Cheap Imitation

Some of us might have had a consuming love for God before, but traded it in for a cheap imitation—a legalistic love. This is where you trade being in **LOVE** with God for doing things for God. You change desire (I want to **LOVE** God) for ought (I ought to do this for God). This was the mistake of the Pharisees in Jesus' day (Matthew 23).

One way of doing this is to create a checklist of things that we ought to do instead of focusing on our desire to be close to God.

This checklist might include:

- Reading my Bible for twenty minutes each day
- Praying for fifteen minutes every day
- Meeting at least one new person every week
- Getting with a prayer partner every week
- Encouraging a weak brother or sister every day
- Serving someone this week

Obviously there is nothing wrong with any item on this list. In fact, these items should be the natural outpouring of our love for God. But we often trade a head-over-heels, consuming **LOVE** for God for a checklist of duty, service, doing, and acting.

This checklist makes life easier in the short term because we can check off what we think is expected of us. We do our duty; we fulfill legalistic righteousness; we feel good about checking items off the list. Yet in the long run, when we fail to meet the requirements of the list, we feel guilty. We begin to equate the checklist with our love for God. We honor God with our checklist, but our hearts are far from him.

Loving God should be about desire, heart, and a consuming **LOVE**. Brent Curtis and John Eldredge speak of the difference between having a checklist love for God and a consuming **LOVE** for God in their wonderful book, *The Sacred Romance.* They write:

The religious technocrats of Jesus' day confronted him with what they believed were the standards of a life pleasing to God. The external life, they argued, the life of ought and duty and service, was what mattered. "You're dead wrong," Jesus said. "In fact, you're just plain dead [whitewashed tombs]. What God cares about is the inner life, the life of the heart" (Matt. 23:25–28). Throughout the Old and New Testaments, the life of the heart is clearly God's central concern. When the people of Israel fell into a totally external life of ritual and observance, God lamented, "These people...honor me with their lips, but their hearts are far from me" (Isaiah 29:13). Our heart is the key to the Christian life.

The apostle Paul informs us that hardness of heart is behind all the addictions and evils of the human race (Romans 1:21–25). Oswald Chambers writes, "It is by the heart that God is perceived [known] and not by reason...so that is what faith is: God perceived by the heart." This is why God tells us in Proverbs 4:23, "Above all else, guard your heart, for it is the wellspring of life." He knows that to lose heart is to lose everything. Sadly, most of us watch the oil level in our car more carefully than we watch over the life of our heart.[127]

We must desire God's word, long to speak with him, be excited about loving people, loving worship, and loving the weak. We need a consuming *LOVE*.

Not the Easier Road, but the Right Road

A consuming love takes more effort than a simple checklist. Which is tougher?

- To read your Bible for twenty minutes or to hide God's word in your heart?

- To pray for thirty minutes or to pray without ceasing?

- To meet a new person every week or to love your neighbor as yourself?

- To show up at worship for two hours on Sunday or to present your body as a living sacrifice?

To put your heart into something is much more challenging than going through a checklist. We must look for God outside a checklist—outside the box. To love God requires heart and desire. Curtis and Eldredge write:

Indeed, if we will listen, a Sacred Romance calls to us through our heart every moment of our lives. It whispers to us on the wind, invites us through the laughter of good friends, reaches out to us through the touch of someone we love. We've heard it in our favorite music, sensed it at the birth of our first child, been drawn to it while watching the shimmer of a sunset on the ocean. The Romance is even present in times of great personal suffering: the illness of a child, the loss of a marriage, the death of a friend. Something calls to us

165

through experiences like these and rouses an inconsolable longing deep within our heart, wakening in us a yearning for intimacy, beauty, and adventure....

The true story of every person in this world is not the story you see, the external story. The true story of each person is the journey of his or her heart.[128]

When asked what is the greatest commandment, Jesus answered, "Love the Lord your God with all your heart, soul, mind and strength." This means that we must be consumed by our love for God.

We must redefine our love for God. I'm going to start by seeing it as a romance. Instead of thinking "I ought to love God," I'm going to desire to love him. Instead of "do, do, do," I'm going to "be, be, be." Instead of a checklist, I'm going to focus on a relationship. Let's have a consuming love for God and love him with all our heart, soul, mind, and strength. Ask yourself, "Do I **LOVE** God?"

The Second Greatest Command

When we review Matthew 22:34–40, Mark 12:28–31, and Luke 10:25–28, we see that Jesus didn't just answer the question about the greatest commandment and stop there. He went on to add that there was a second great commandment: to love your neighbor as yourself. As far as we know, Jesus is the only rabbi to tack this second commandment onto the first one. The first commandment was "Hear, O Israel: The Lord our God, the Lord is one. Love the Lord your God with all your heart and with all your soul and with all your strength." The second commandment was like it: "Love your neighbor as yourself." The first commandment was taken from Deuteronomy 6:4–5 and the second comes from Leviticus 19:18. Jesus not only added the second commandment to the first, he also noted that on these two commandments all the Law and the Prophets hang.

Why Is This Important?

Why is it important that Jesus on his own initiative adds the second commandment to the first? Because Jesus demonstrates that our love for God must be translated into love for people. This has always been a failing in religion—think of the Pharisees, the Judaizers, the Gnostics, the Catholic church of the Dark Ages, down to our own day. They all claimed to love God, but their treatment of people did not demonstrate the love of God. We should not claim to love God unless we love people.

1 John 4:20–21 reads, "If anyone says, 'I love God,' yet hates his brother, he is a liar. For anyone who does not love his brother, whom he has seen, cannot love God, whom he has not seen. And he has given us this command: Whoever loves God must also love his brother." To love God means that we must love people.

We see the importance of linking these two commands when Jesus says, "All the Law and the Prophets hang on these two commandments." That is like saying, "everything depends on this." D.A. Carson notes:

> These two commandments are the greatest because all Scripture "hangs" on them; i.e., nothing in Scripture can cohere or truly be obeyed unless these two are observed. The entire biblical revelation demands heart religion marked by total allegiance to God, loving him and loving one's neighbor. Without these two commandments the Bible is sterile.[129]

This has been proven true throughout the history of the church. If we don't have a consuming love for God and an unconditional/serving love for people (people both inside and outside the church), everything will fall apart. We can have many other aspects of the gospel in good working order—proper doctrine, total commitment, true sacrifice, biblical discipleship—but if we fail in loving God and loving neighbor, everything will come to a grinding halt. God will place his hand of discipline on us. It is like trying to drive your car without ever changing the oil. You can run for a while on old, used oil. You might be able to push the car 5,000 miles or 7,000 miles, but at some point you will begin to notice problems. If you keep pushing the car, it will come to a halt. You will burn out the engine. Loving God and loving people is the oil in the engine of the church. Without this oil, the church can make some advances, but eventually everything will come to a grinding halt.

In Matthew's gospel, Jesus answers the scribe's question concerning the greatest commandment just before he rebukes the Pharisees in chapter 23. This context is important because the Pharisees believed they were experts at keeping the law and honoring the prophets. They equated loving God with keeping the law (see Matthew 23:23–26 and Matthew 23:29–32). When we push to keep the commands of God without remembering our love for people, we are Pharisees. Loving God and loving people must appear in our lives simultaneously.

Consider the Example of Jesus

Jesus loved God and he loved people. We see Jesus' concern for people in Matthew 9:35–38:

> *Jesus went about all the cities and villages teaching in their synagogues and proclaiming the good news of the kingdom and healing every disease and every sickness. When he saw the crowds, he had compassion on them because they were harassed and helpless as sheep without a shepherd. Then he said to his disciples, "The harvest is plentiful, but the workers are few. Therefore ask the Lord of the harvest to send workers into his harvest."*

I've read this verse often while focusing on the ministry of Jesus. I've emphasized that Jesus was going, teaching, preaching, and healing. I've also taught that Jesus was doing this because he wanted a harvest. His sacrifice was all about the harvest, but I overlooked the real reason why he was doing those things: He had compassion on people. Jesus loved people deeply. That is why he went, taught, preached, healed, and prayed. He saw the crowds, and his compassionate heart went out to them because they were harassed and helpless, like sheep without a shepherd.

The going, teaching, preaching, and healing must come from our compassion for people. Leadership guru, John C. Maxwell, writes in his book *Be a People Person*:

> Jesus went, saw, felt and cared. It's only when we go and expose ourselves to various situations that we will see enough to develop the concern necessary to move us to action.
>
> It's difficult to become motivated to help people without first seeing and feeling their needs. The secret is to spend time with them. Only when you go and see will you feel and do.[130]

Do we love people? Do we love people the way Jesus did? Do we love people enough to go to them, see their need, feel their hurt, and care for them? This is how Jesus loved. He was moved by compassion for people. He loved God and he loved people.

Jesus and Prayer

George Buttrick asks, "Who can understand music but the musician, or prayer but the man who has long prayed?"[131] Jesus understood prayer like the master musician understands music. He understood prayer because he "long prayed." It was his natural connection with the Father. Therefore, Jesus can teach us about prayer. When it comes to prayer, what lessons does Jesus teach us?

1. The Need for Persistence in Prayer—Luke 18:1–8

> One should pray with such energy that he would wish all his limbs, and all his strength, his eyes, ears, mouth, heart, and all his senses were straining within him. He should not cease until he seems to have become one with Him who is present and to whom he prays.
>
> —Meister Eckhart, mystic

> *Then Jesus told his disciples a parable to show them that they should always pray and not give up. He said: "In a certain town there was a judge who neither feared God nor*

cared about men. And there was a widow in that town who kept coming to him with the plea, 'Grant me justice against my adversary.'

"For some time he refused. But finally he said to himself, 'Even though I don't fear God or care about men, yet because this widow keeps bothering me, I will see that she gets justice, so that she won't eventually wear me out with her coming!' "

And the Lord said, "Listen to what the unjust judge says. And will not God bring about justice for his chosen ones, who cry out to him day and night? Will he keep putting them off? I tell you, he will see that they get justice, and quickly. However, when the Son of Man comes, will he find faith on the earth?"

—*Luke 18:1–8*

What is persistence? In Luke 18, Jesus tells the parable of a persistent widow who was oppressed. She had been coming to an apathetic judge to ask him one request, "Grant me justice over my adversary." The judge was hardhearted to her cause and turned her away, but she kept coming and pleading with him. She kept seeking justice and would not let his apathy deter her. So the judge finally heard her case, saying, "Because this widow keeps bothering me, I will see that she gets justice, so that she won't eventually wear me out with her coming!"

Persistence is the willingness to keep asking even when you get "No" for an answer. Persistence is dogged determination. It means that you are unflappable. The persistent widow didn't care that she was bothering the judge or that he wanted to run the other way every time he saw her coming. She was going to keep coming until he heard her case. That is persistence.

Are you persistent in prayer? When God says "No" to your prayer, do you give up? What can we learn about persistence from this parable?

Persistence Has a Childlike Quality to It

If you are a parent, then you know how persistent a child can be. They just keep asking. "Daddy, can I have another cookie? Daddy, I want another cookie. Daddy, can I have another cookie? Daddy, just one, I only want one. Daddy, I'm hungry. Daddy, can I have another cookie?" Children are unrelenting. They are unflappable. They are intransigent. They keep on asking.

How many times has your child gotten what they wanted simply because they kept asking? This is the analogy Jesus used in Luke 18 to describe persistence in prayer. God is our father and we are his children. He wants to bless us. He expects us to ask for blessings. Because we are his children, we can ask in prayer. And we can keep asking.

Persistence Springs from Desperation

Notice in the story of the persistent widow that she was desperate for justice. She had an adversary who was pursuing her, so she desperately needed the judge to hear her case.

Desperation means that we will do anything to get an answer. The widow kept coming to the judge. Neil Lightfoot, author of *Lessons from the Parables*, writes, "Unless a prayer is uttered in dead earnestness it is not prayer."[132] Why have you stopped praying? Is it because you have lost your sense of desperation?

Persistence Is a Test of Character

Our character is tested when God says "No" to prayer. We have to stop and see if we are willing to fight through our doubts and insecurities. Think again of the widow. How would you respond if a judge rejected your case? You might doubt your case and yourself. You might feel personally rejected. You might question, "Is there justice?" But in the story, the widow keeps coming back to the judge. She doesn't doubt. She knows her cause is just. She is persistent. Do you have that type of character? Are you willing to say, "God, I'm just going to keep knocking!"

"Knock, knock, knock!" "Lord, it's me again. I'm still knocking. I'm going to keep knocking until you open the door."

Some prayers take this type of persistent devotion.

2. The Need for Faith in Prayer—Mark 11:22–24, cf. Matthew 17:20–21

> *"Have faith in God," Jesus answered. "I tell you the truth, if anyone says to this mountain, 'Go, throw yourself into the sea,' and does not doubt in his heart but believes that what he says will happen, it will be done for him. Therefore I tell you, whatever you ask for in prayer, believe that you have received it, and it will be yours.*

When we come to God persistently in prayer, we need to make sure that we are praying faithful prayers. Faith is often viewed as belief, and belief is often viewed as trust, and trust is often viewed as confidence.

I have faith in gravity. No matter how high I jump, I am always going to come back down. If I set a book on a table, I have confidence that the book will not float up and drift away. I can put my confidence in gravity.

When we have faith in someone or something, we have confidence in that person or thing. When we have faith in ourselves, we have confidence in ourselves. We believe in ourselves. Belief is powerful. When we have faith in a surgeon, we will let him or her operate on us. We place our faith in the pilot of the plane every time we get on a plane. We trust that she is competent in her skill. We trust that she is sober and ready to fly.

We place our faith in various people and things every day of our lives.

Faith places our focus on God. Why was Abraham faithful? Because he trusted God. Why was Moses faithful? Because he trusted God. We place our trust in God because he is worthy of our trust. Therefore, we pray with confidence.

If we don't pray with confidence, then we shouldn't expect God to say "Yes" to our prayers. Would you? For example, imagine praying, "Dear God, I know that you aren't going to answer this prayer, but I thought I'd ask anyway for the umpteenth time. I'm not sure why I'm asking again. I'm sure you are going to say, "No." No, no, no—that seems to be all I hear when I talk to you about this. But here goes, not that it really matters because you're not going to give this to me,..." That is a prayer without any confidence. We need to believe and not doubt.

Remember that prayer is friendship with God; therefore, when we pray, we are talking to a friend who has our best interests at heart, so we approach the throne of God with confidence.

3. The Need for Boldness in Prayer—Luke 11:5–13

Then he said to them, "Suppose one of you has a friend, and he goes to him at midnight and says, 'Friend, lend me three loaves of bread, because a friend of mine on a journey has come to me, and I have nothing to set before him.'

"Then the one inside answers, 'Don't bother me. The door is already locked, and my children are with me in bed. I can't get up and give you anything.' I tell you, though he will not get up and give him the bread because he is his friend, yet because of the man's boldness he will get up and give him as much as he needs.

"So I say to you: Ask and it will be given to you; seek and you will find; knock and the door will be opened to you. For everyone who asks receives; he who seeks finds; and to him who knocks, the door will be opened.

"Which of you fathers, if your son asks for a fish, will give him a snake instead? Or if he asks for an egg, will give him a scorpion? If you then, though you are evil, know how to give good gifts to your children, how much more will your Father in heaven give the Holy Spirit to those who ask him!"

Jesus is setting up a hypothetical situation. The NIV invites us to "suppose" this situation is true. In the Greek, this story begins with a formulaic question, "Which of you, if you have a friend...?" The question is rhetorical, and the answer is, "No one has a friend that would turn away another friend at midnight." You see, this sets up a situation that isn't true. It is a parable, a story.

Why does the unresponsive friend get out of bed and answer the door? Because of the boldness and audacity of the friend who keeps asking. This guy just keeps banging on the door until he gets what he came to get. This is the point of the parable: Be bold in prayer.

God has invited us to ask for anything in prayer. After the parable Jesus makes clear the meaning of the parable by inviting us to "ask," "seek," and "knock." He tells us that the true nature of God is in no way similar to the unresponsive friend in the parable. In fact, God is like a loving father who knows how to give good gifts to his children. God wants to give us good gifts. He invites us to be bold in prayer, so why don't we take him up on his invitation?

Praying the Lord's Prayer—Matthew 6:9–13, cf. Luke 11:2–4

"The Lord's Prayer" is a good model to follow when we pray. Jesus bids us to pray this prayer, but he does not expect us to quote the prayer word for word. The prayer gives us topics to be considered in prayer. If we quote the prayer without thinking about its meaning, then we are doing the very opposite of what Jesus wants us to do.

When we pray, we are usually quick to get to our requests, skipping over Jesus' example of addressing God with respect, praising him, and having a kingdom focus. But these other parts of prayer help us to line up our requests within the will of God. It is good to include each part of the Lord's Prayer when we pray and to keep the order of the prayer as well. Let's break it down into sections to see how we can follow this model.

Address: "Our Father in heaven."

At the beginning of the prayer, it is good to remember that we are praying to God in heaven. We often get caught up in the concerns of this world, but God is outside this world. When we speak to God, we are tapping into a power completely beyond us, an otherworldly power. In 2 Corinthians 4:7, Paul refers to this power as the "all-surpassing power" of God. As we begin our prayers, we need to pause for a moment and realize whom we are addressing: the Creator of the world, who lives in realms above and beyond us. Because of Jesus, we can approach his throne with confidence—but we cannot forget the power and the majesty of the One who occupies the throne.

Jesus uses the term *Abba* for father. This is the same term that a Jewish child would have used for his or her earthly father. There is no evidence in the Old Testament or Rabbinic literature for anyone before Jesus using this word to apply to God. As far as we know, Jesus was the first person to use *Abba* to address God, showing the unique relationship Jesus had with the Father.

However, it also shows that Jesus was teaching his disciples a new way to view God: God as Father. He instructs them to say "*our* Father in heaven" (Matthew 6:9, emphasis added). God is not just Jesus' Father, but he is the Father and *Abba* of the disciples as well. Additionally, "our" indicates that this prayer was to be prayed in fellowship with other disciples.

Interestingly, any time Jesus discusses the forgiveness of sin, he uses the term "your Father," but whenever he speaks of his Sonship or authority, he uses the term "my Father." Since he is here teaching his disciples to pray, he teaches them to say "our Father."

Praise: "Hallowed (holy) be your name."

In the ancient mind, to know someone's name was to know his character, which is why names were so important. Therefore, to know the name of God would be to know God. In the opening of our prayers, we should begin by extolling the greatness of God. His name is holy, and he deserves our praise.

We are not very good at praise. See how many ways you can praise God. The psalmists were very adept at this. By studying the Psalms, we can learn wonderful ways of praising him. When we praise God, we see where we stand in relationship to him: He is the Creator and we are his creation. We must keep this distinction always before us.

Kingdom focus: "Your kingdom come, your will be done on earth as it is in heaven."

It is important to have a kingdom focus in our prayers. Do we pray for the kingdom of God to reign in our lives? Are our prayers focused beyond the here and now of our everyday lives? Do our prayers have an eternal focus? Do we pray for God's kingdom to grow and be manifest among humanity as it is in heaven? Do we pray selfish prayers, or do we take time in prayer to focus on the needs of others? Our prayers need to lift others before the throne of God. Do our prayers have an otherworldly focus?

Requests: "Give us today our daily bread."

This sentence beckons us to lay our requests before God. There is nothing wrong with asking God for the desires of our heart. The apostle James wrote, "You do not have, because you do not ask God" (James 4:2), but we must be sure that we ask for what is within God's will and that we ask faithfully, without doubting. If we ask with doubt, then God promises to answer our request with a "No."

But again, let's not be selfish in our requests. The phrase "daily bread" implies that we are asking for necessities—for things that will sustain us in life. If we need a car, we should pray for a car, but perhaps we should refrain from praying that it be a new, bright yellow Mercedes convertible.

Asking for forgiveness: "And forgive us our debts."

Whenever we stand before the throne of God, we should remember that we are sinners. When Isaiah received his call in the presence of God, he protested that he was a man of unclean lips (Isaiah 6). This is to say that he saw his sins clearly. When we pray, we should remember that it is by God's grace that we have forgiveness of our sins, and this is not a gift to be taken lightly. When we lose appreciation for the lengths that God went to in order to offer us forgiveness, we are in a terrible place. By talking about our sinfulness whenever we pray, it keeps this idea in the forefront of our minds.

Forgiving others: "...as we also have forgiven our debtors."
As God has forgiven us, we should also forgive those who have wronged us. We need to think through and pray about these potentially difficult relationships.

Also, this is a good time to remember anyone who has trespassed against God and who has not yet been forgiven. We need to pray for those we know who are still living in their trespasses. They might be our friends, our family, our coworkers, our fellow students, or recent acquaintances.

Dealing with temptation: "And lead us not into temptation"
This could also be translated as "deliver us or save us from temptation." We need to pray that we will be victorious over temptation, remembering of course that God himself does not tempt us; rather, he tests us so that our character will be strengthened. We should not pray to avoid the tests of God, because it is through them that our character will change. Rather, we should pray that when Satan tempts us, God will deliver us from that temptation.

Closing: For yours is the kingdom and the power and the glory now and forever. Amen.
Many of us learned the Lord's Prayer with this doxology on the end. It is based on a prayer of David in 1 Chronicles 29:10–13 and is not found in the earlier, more reliable Greek New Testament manuscripts. It seems to have been added to some manuscripts in the fifth century.

If we close with this line, we end the prayer in the same way we began: by focusing on the otherworldly nature of God. And we need to try to keep this view of God with us as we face the world around us.

We have investigated four major themes found in the teaching ministry of Jesus. Let's now move on to explore another major area of Jesus' teaching ministry: his use of parables.

End Notes

103 Augsburger and Ogilvie, 18.

104. All scriptures from Matthew in this chapter are the author's own translation.

105. S. K. Weber, *Holman New Testament Commentary,* vol. 1, *Matthew* (Nashville, TN: Broadman & Holman Publishers, 2000), 171.

106. Augsburger and Ogilvie, 18.

107. Ibid.

108. Weber, 172–173.

109. Augsburger and Ogilvie, 18.

110. Ibid.

111. J. F. Walvoord, R. B. Zuck, and Dallas Theological Seminary. "Mt 12:30–37" in *The Bible Knowledge Commentary: An Exposition of the Scriptures* (Wheaton, IL: Victor Books, 1983).

112. Weber, 181.

113. Dietrich Bonhoeffer, *The Cost of Discipleship, 6th ed.* (London: SCM Press, 1959).

114. Scot McKnight, *The King Jesus Gospel* (Grand Rapids: Zondervan, 2011).

115. Lee Camp, *Mere Discipleship: Radical Christianity in a Rebellious World* (Grand Rapids: Brazos Press, 2003), 23.

116. http://www.thegracetabernacle.org/quotes/Self-Denial.htm.

117. Ibid.

118. W. MacDonald and A. Farstad, "Luke 9:24" in *Believer's Bible Commentary: Old and New Testaments* (Nashville: Thomas Nelson, 1997).

119. J. F. Walvoord, R. B. Zuck, and Dallas Theological Seminary, "Luke 14:25–27" in *The Bible Knowledge Commentary: An Exposition of the Scriptures* (Wheaton, IL: Victor Books, 1983).

120. Dallas Willard, *Renovation of the Heart* (San Francisco: Harper and Row, 1988), 87.

121. Fenelon, 81.

122. Mulholland, *Invitation to a Journey, revised ed.* (Nashville: Upper Room Books, 2000), 89.

123. France, 319.

124. Carson, *The Expositor's Bible Commentary with the New International Version,* 495.

125. Gilbert K. Chesterton, *Heretics,* 12th edition (Norwood, MA: Plimpton Press), Chapter XIV "On Certain Modern Writers and the Institution of the Family," http://www.bibleteacher.org/here7.htm (accessed March 22, 2006).

126. Oswald Chambers, *My Utmost for His Highest* (Westwood, NJ: Dodd Mead & Company, 1935), 112.

127. John Eldredge and Brent Curtis, *The Sacred Romance* (Nashville: Thomas Nelson, 1997), 9.

128. Ibid., 6–7.

129. Carson, *The Expositor's Bible Commentary with the New International Version,* 465.

130. John C. Maxwell, *Be a People Person* (Colorado Springs: Victor Books, 1994), 27.

131. George Buttrick, *Prayer* (New York: Abingdon Press, 1942), 27.

132. Neil Lightfoot, *The Parables of Jesus* (Grand Rapids: Baker, 1965), 74.

Chapter 9

The Teaching Ministry of Jesus, Part 3: The Parables

Jesus' stories, people say, were just "earthly stories with heavenly meaning." But that's just rubbish. Stories are far more powerful than that. Stories create worlds. Tell the story differently, and you change the world. And that's what Jesus aimed to do.[133]

—N.T. Wright, New Testament scholar

Jesus was a metaphorical theologian. That is, his primary method of creating meaning was through metaphor, simile, parable and dramatic action rather than through logic and reasoning. He created meaning like a dramatist and a poet rather than like a philosopher.[134]

—Kenneth E. Bailey, author and theologian

The importance of parables is evident when we realize that fully a third of Jesus' teaching in the Synoptic Gospels comes in parabolic form.[135]

—G. R. Osborne, professor of hermeneutics

What Is a Parable?

The preacher's definition of the word "parable" is: "An earthly story with a heavenly message." I remember Tom Holland, professor of homiletics at Freed-Hardeman College, teaching me this definition my freshman year. It's a nice, pithy way to describe the parables, but the parables are bigger than this definition.

The Greek root for the word "parable" (παραβολή/parabola) means "to throw alongside" or "to cast alongside." Parables are stories that are thrown alongside of life to get us to think about life. They are interactive stories that invite the listener to participate in the story and to think alongside the storyteller about deep matters of life.

Marcus Borg defines a parable in this manner:

Parables are made-up stories, fictional narratives, and their meaning does not depend upon their factuality....Parables work by being good stories. They draw the audience into the narrative. They need to be good stories not only to avoid being tedious, but because fanciful or unrealistic details would get in the way of the audience's entering the story. ...Parables invite the audience to make a judgment. Implicitly, the parables begin or end with, "What do you think?"[136]

Parables are allegories. Craig Blomberg writes that there are three purposes for allegories. These match very closely the purposes for which Jesus spoke in parables. According to Blomberg, the purposes of the parable are:

(a) to illustrate a viewpoint in an artistic and educational way, (b) to keep its message from being immediately clear to all its hearers or readers without further reflection, (c) to win over its audience to accept a particular set of beliefs or act in a certain way.[137]

Kenneth E. Bailey, author of the amazing book *Jesus Through Middle Eastern Eyes*, states that a parable is a metaphor. He writes, "A parable is an extended metaphor and as such it is not a delivery system for an idea but a house in which the reader/listener is invited to take up residence."[138] I like this idea. The parable is a house where we are invited to take up residence so we can meditate upon a truth of Jesus until it becomes a part of our lives. Osborne writes, "The parables encounter, interpret, and invite the listener/reader to participate in Jesus' new world vision of the kingdom."[139]

The use of parables is not original with Jesus. Allegories have been used throughout history. Many rabbis spoke in parables. Rabbi Phineas ben Jair wrote:

If a man loses a sela' or an obol [a small coin] in his house, he lights lamp after lamp wick after wick, till he finds it. Now does it not stand to reason: if for these things which are only ephemeral and of this world a man will light so many lamps and lights till he finds where they are hidden, for the words of the Torah which are the life both of this world and of the next world, ought you not to search as for hidden treasures (*Midrash Rabbah* on the Song of Songs 1.1, 9).[140]

Also, Rabbi Eleazar ben Azariah wrote:

He whose wisdom is more abundant than his works, to what is he like? To a tree whose branches are abundant but whose roots are few, and the wind comes and uproots it and overturns it... But he whose works are more abundant than his wisdom, to what is he like? To a tree whose branches are few but whose roots are many; so that even if all the winds in the world come and blow against it, it cannot be stirred from its place (*The Mishnah*, Aboth 3:18).[141]

Of course, Jesus had his unique take on telling parables. He told parables to prepare his disciples for the work ahead of them—kingdom work. Blomberg writes:

It remains undeniable that Jesus' parables are explicit illustrations and signs of the in-breaking kingdom of God, personally ushered in by his own ministry and message, in a way that applies to none of the rabbinical texts.[142]

Why Parables?

Why parables? Some would say parables were told to communicate clearly with people. The teacher would tell common stories that were easy to visualize so that the listener could picture them and grasp their understanding. But this is exactly the opposite of why Jesus said he spoke in parables. Matthew 13:11 reads, "The knowledge of the secrets of the kingdom of heaven has been given to you, but not to them." Jesus spoke in parables to conceal his meaning. N. T. Wright notes:

Jesus knew his kingdom-announcement was subversive. It would be drastically unwelcome, for different reasons, to the Romans, to Herod, and also to zealous Jews and their leaders, whether official or not. He must therefore speak in parables "so that they may look and look but never see." It was the only safe course. Only those in the know must be allowed to glimpse what Jesus believed was going on.[143]

Therefore we need to be careful in the way we read the parables and especially in the way we interpret the parables.

Matthew 13 gives the reason why Jesus speaks to the multitudes in parables, stating, "This is why I speak to them in parables, because seeing they do not see, and hearing they do not hear (v. 13 ESV)." Since they have a hard, callous heart, they fail to understand the parables. Although "he told [the whole crowd] many things in parables (vv. 2–3)," Jesus' parables were really meant for his inner circle of disciples, who would be willing to search for the meaning in them (see vv. 11–12).

However, we should recognize that many times his closest disciples did not understand the meaning of Jesus' parables, either. Consider Mark 7:14–20:

Again Jesus called the crowd to him and said, "Listen to me, everyone, and understand this. Nothing outside a man can make him 'unclean' by going into him. Rather, it is what comes out of a man that makes him 'unclean.' "

> After he had left the crowd and entered the house, his disciples asked him about this parable. "Are you so dull?" he asked. "Don't you see that nothing that enters a man from the outside can make him 'unclean'? For it doesn't go into his heart but into his stomach, and then out of his body." (In saying this, Jesus declared all foods 'clean.')
> He went on: "What comes out of a man is what makes him 'unclean.'"

If the parables are picture-book stories that clearly communicate a spiritual truth, then why did the disciples not understand the meaning of these stories?

Jesus did not mean for everyone to get the meaning of the parables. He spoke in parable so that the meaning of his words would not be clear to outsiders. Parables are spoken with insider language. Craig Blomberg writes:

> J.A. Baird has observed that over two-thirds of the parables which Jesus explained, however briefly, were addressed to his disciples, while most of those left unexplained were addressed to his opponents. This pattern fits in with Jesus' desire to make his teaching in some sense clearer to insiders than to outsiders.[144]

The parables contain "the secrets of the kingdom." Therefore they are what I like to call "kingdom speak." They are insider language meant for insiders. We have kingdom speak today. We use words like discipling, discipling partner, Bible Talk, and counting the cost. The parables were first-century "kingdom speak."

Parables cause you to think. They draw pictures for you to contemplate in your mind. You are to ruminate on them.

I also like to call the parables Jesus' love language for his own people. For the most part, the parables were meant for Jesus' disciples. When he explained the meaning of the parables, he explained them to a small circle of initiates, not to the masses. That's why I like to think of the parables as Jesus' love language for his inner circles of devoted followers. Having said that, the parables were recorded for posterity. Therefore, we are now a part of Jesus' inner circle of believers, and his love language is directed toward us.

Parables are illustrations; they are stories, but they are stories with a hidden meaning. Often a parable can mean many things depending on the context, so you have to pay attention to the context of the parable within the gospel story.

The Greek word for "parable" is παραβολὴ/*parabola*. This word is not only used for a parable, but also a riddle or a pithy saying. The Hebrew equivalent is a mashal, an oracle, a dark saying, or a taunt. A parable is a story that holds up a mirror to the real world so that we can take a look. C.H. Dodd said, "A parable is a metaphor or a simile taken from real life."[145]

We've heard them so often that we miss the wonder of the parables. Imagine hearing them for the first time—they were stories that caused the original hearers to pause and think.

The parables of Matthew and Mark are more about the kingdom of God. The parables of Luke tend to be about discipleship and are more about people. In Luke, most are found between 9:51 and 19:44. This section is called the travel narrative, and it is peculiar to Luke. Jesus is going to Jerusalem, and he trains his disciples along the way.

How Do We Interpret the Parables?

Without interpretation the power of the parable is lost, for every parable must be understood before it can be applied. Its "evocative power" is best discerned when seen as Jesus intended it; that is, in terms of its first-century background and in its Gospel context. Nevertheless, we should not relegate it merely to a word-by-word analysis. It must remain parable lest its ability to startle and move the hearer be lost.[146]

—G.R. Osborne

In the early church, parables were treated as allegories. The interpreter took the liberty to make every element of the story mean something. This found full expression in the work of the early church father Origen. For example, the following is a list of elements in the Parable of the Good Samaritan and Origen's designation for each element:

- The man who was going down to Jericho = Adam
- Jerusalem from which he was going = Paradise
- Jericho = this world
- Robbers = hostile influences and enemies such as mentioned in John 10:8
- Wounds = disobedience or sins
- Priests = Law
- Levite = Prophets
- Good Samaritan = Christ
- The donkey = body of Christ
- Inn = church
- Two denarii = knowledge of the Father and Son
- Innkeeper = angels in charge of the church
- Return of the Good Samaritan = second coming of Christ

Consider the Parable of the Prodigal Son:

- Father = God
- Prodigal = any sinner who turns away from God
- Older brother = self-righteous, hard-hearted Pharisee

- Ring = Christian baptism
- Banquet = Lord's Supper
- Robe = immortality/heaven
- Shoes = preparation for the journey to heaven

Adolf Julicher, a German scholar, criticized the allegorical method of interpretation. He rightly pointed out that no two interpreters come up with the same key or code for interpreting the parables. Surely this is not how Jesus meant for the parables to be taken. Also, most allegorical interpreters take the parable out of its first-century context and make it fit their own time. Allegorical interpreters aren't concerned in hearing the *ipsissima vox Jesu*, the authentic voice of Jesus. This is always a mistake.

Julicher contended that every parable has one point; therefore, we should look for the one point that Jesus is making in the parable. For example, in the Parable of the Prodigal Son, the point that Jesus was making was that God's forgiving love has no limits. He is always ready to forgive. In the parable of the Ten Virgins, the message was that disciples should always be prepared for the second coming of Jesus. The parable of the mustard seed taught that God's kingdom would have a wide influence in spite of its small beginning. The parable of the barren fig tree taught that there was a time when it is too late to repent.

This is how I was taught to interpret the parables. I was taught that I needed to analyze the parables with great care to see exactly what Jesus was teaching and that I should not go beyond that original meaning. I shouldn't labor over the characters of the parables or the ingredients of the story. I should look for the one kernel of truth in the story, meditate on that truth, and go no further.

Craig Blomberg in his wonderful book, *Interpreting the Parables,* says it is okay to allegorize the parables if you emphasize the right points. He calls this a restrained allegory.

How do you go about determining which points to emphasize and which should not be stressed? G.R. Osborne writes:

The task is to distinguish between "local color" (details not meant to carry spiritual meaning) and theologically loaded details (those which do have allegorical significance). This is determined on the basis of context, both macro (the larger context within which the parable is found) and micro (the parable itself), as well as the historical background of the details as seen in the story.[147]

This is the most important and difficult aspect of interpreting the parables. Blomberg makes four points concerning restrained allegory:[148]

1. The parables, as they stand in the Gospels, are much more allegorical than is usually acknowledged.

2. To avoid the errors of past allegorizers, modern interpreters must also assign meanings to the details of parables which Jesus' original audiences could have been expected to discern.[149]

3. Many parables probably make more than one point.

4. The presence of mysterious and unusual details in the parable, pointing to an additional level of meaning, is much more widespread than has usually been realized.[150]

Part of the beauty of the parables is that the Spirit of God is alive in the reading and rereading of them.

Some Keys to Interpreting the Parables

1. Interpret the parable in light of historical/cultural/geographical evidence.

Interpret considering the sociopolitical setting of the story. Consider the first-century historical setting of the parable. Hear the story like you were in the original audience. Before you make any application for today, sit at the feet of Jesus and hear the story like you were hearing it for the first time. Kenneth E. Bailey writes, "Historical interpretation is the key to unlocking the vault that contains the gold of theological meaning. Without that key the gold turns to brass."[151]

2. Uncover the need that prompted the parable.

In other words, consider the context. Is Jesus answering a question? Is he speaking to his disciples or to the Pharisees? This is often called the *Sitz em Leben*, the life setting of the parable. Read the parable in context to discover the reason why Jesus told the parable in the first place.

3. Analyze the structure and the details of the parable.

Who are the main characters? What is happening in the story? What is the point of the story?

4. Respond to the appeal that is made in the parable.

What can you learn from the parable? How does the parable speak to you personally? What does the parable say to you today?

5. Look for Jesus in each of the parables.

They are his stories and his "love language" to his people. Therefore, we need to see the stories as coming from his lips. We need to place our-selves in the first-century setting and try to understand what Jesus was saying.

Sometimes Jesus placed himself in the parables. In the Parable of the Sower, the sower is the Son of Man. In the Parable of the Prodigal Son, Jesus is seen in the Father figure. In Matthew 21, in the Parable of the Wicked Tenant Farmers, the son was killed; Jesus was the son. We need to search for Jesus in the parables.

Lessons from the Parables

We don't have time in this book to consider all the parables of Jesus. If you are interested in that type of book, then I suggest Neil Lightfoot's *Parables of Jesus*.[152] I read this book when I was a teenager and found it extremely valuable. I still use it today.

In this section, we will explore a selection of the parables so that we can apply some of the principles of hermeneutics to the parables and learn what they are teaching us. I've selected some of my favorites, fo-cusing on two chapters in the Gospels that I love—Luke 15, "The 'Lost' Chapter," and Luke 12, "The Parable of Bigger Barns."

Luke 15—The "Lost" Chapter

I call this chapter of Luke "The 'Lost' Chapter" because in it we find three parables with a similar element—a lost sheep, a lost coin, and a lost son. This is one of my favorite chapters in all the gospels.

In the first two parables, Jesus begins with a rhetorical question: What person losing his or her sheep or silver coin would not look for it? The question begs a negative answer: No one.

In the quest to seek the lost, Jesus uses two types of people who find themselves on the periphery of society—the shepherd and a woman. The shepherd was looked upon as a crook and a ruffian, and in first-century Palestine, women had no standing in society. Jesus uses these social out-casts to paint the picture of what it meant to have a God-like love for the lost. It is an interesting choice to choose a shepherd and a woman. Jesus doesn't pick a scribe or a Pharisee or a priest. He picks a despised shep-herd and a marginalized woman.

The third parable focuses on a lost son, who became lost by leaving home. It is also the story of a searching father and a second son who also is lost, though he never left home. It is one of the greatest stories ever told and deserves our attention.

Have you ever been physically lost? When I was a teenager, my friend and I went out in the woods one day and got so turned around that we were lost. It was not a good feeling. When we finally stumbled upon a road that led to safety, we felt a great sense of relief.

All of us have experienced the feeling of being spiritually lost. That's a horrible feeling. But God didn't give up on us. He sought us out. He found us and rejoiced. That's what God does.

Luke 15:1–2 reads, "Now the tax collectors and 'sinners' were all gathering around to hear him. But the Pharisees and the teachers of the law muttered, 'This man welcomes sinners and eats with them.'"

This sets up what is to follow. What personalities do you see involved in the opening verses? What's going on here?

Notice first that the tax collectors and sinners were "all" gathering around to hear Jesus. This shows his popularity. They weren't gathering around the Pharisees and scribes. Jesus had something that others wanted, and he still does. When people really learn who Jesus is, they are attracted to him.

The Pharisees and scribes were complaining because Jesus ate with sinners. Eating with someone was a big deal in the first-century Jewish culture. To recline and eat with someone was to have fellowship with them. It meant Jesus was accepting of sinners. He wasn't accepting of their sin, but he was accepting of them. He knew how to welcome people even with their shortcomings and failures. This is a real key to drawing people to God.

The Pharisees and scribes were too self-righteous to eat with sinners. They didn't want anyone to think that they were having fellowship with these people. In their minds, they believed sinners had forfeited their relationship with God because they were not faithful to God's law. A later Rabbinic source on Exodus 18:1 states: "Let not a man associate with the wicked, even to bring him near to the law."[153] This became the attitude of Jewish leaders toward sinners, but it was not Jesus' attitude. I'm not sure how the scribes and Pharisees expected to influence sinners if they were not going to be with them.

What can we learn here? We should not be judgmental toward people. That was the problem with the Pharisees and scribes. They acted as if God only loved the righteous and not sinners. D. L. Bock writes:

Jesus does not share the separatist mentality of the scribes and Pharisees (Mark 2:15 = Luke 5:32; 19:10). He is interested in befriending such undesirables, regardless of what others may think. His rationale is simple: he wishes to draw them to God.[154]

God loves everyone. He wants people to change, but he still loves them when they are a mess. You shouldn't forget how it wasn't too long ago when you were a mess as well. Someone spoke to you. Someone had a meal with you. Someone took time to study the Bible with you. Now you can pay it forward.

To demonstrate God's love for sinners, Jesus told three parables. One commentary notes:

> These stories were aimed directly at the scribes and Pharisees, who were never broken before God to admit their lost condition. As a matter of fact, they were as lost as the publicans and sinners, but they steadfastly refused to admit it. The point of the three stories is that God receives real joy and satisfaction when He sees sinners repenting, whereas He obtains no gratification from self-righteous hypocrites who are too proud to admit their wretched sinfulness.[155]

The Parable of the Lost Sheep—Luke 15:3–7

> *Then Jesus told them this parable: "Suppose one of you has a hundred sheep and loses one of them. Does he not leave the ninety-nine in the open country and go after the lost sheep until he finds it? And when he finds it, he joyfully puts it on his shoulders and goes home. Then he calls his friends and neighbors together and says, 'Rejoice with me; I have found my lost sheep.' I tell you that in the same way there will be more rejoicing in heaven over one sinner who repents than over ninety-nine righteous persons who do not need to repent."*

What happens when the shepherd loses a sheep? He leaves the ninety-nine to search for the one. Jesus speaks of a shepherd of modest means. Most herds had up to two hundred sheep, and a herd of three hundred sheep was considered a large herd. Being a shepherd was a common occupation in first-century Palestine. Sheepherders were not looked upon in a favorable way. Many were considered to be thieves and scoundrels. As I mentioned before, it is interesting that Jesus chooses a shepherd to illustrate his point about God's love for the lost.

A shepherd would count the sheep before retiring for the night. Sometimes we count sheep as we try to sleep, but that's altogether different. Here the shepherd is one short. He leaves the ninety-nine to go after the one. What does this tell us about the heart of the shepherd and the value of one sheep?

How long does the shepherd look for the sheep? Until he finds it. It doesn't mention how much effort the shepherd put into finding the sheep, but what is implied in the text is that he was not going to call off the search until the sheep was found. What effort did God put into finding his lost sheep? He sent Jesus into the world. He gave us his Word. He gave us his church. He commissioned his church to be a search party for lost sheep.

What could have happened to the sheep while it was away from the herd? Terrible things. The shepherd will keep looking until he finds the sheep or the remains of the sheep. In this case, the story has a happy ending. Not all stories of lost sheep end with happy endings, and this should make us even more urgent in the search.

When he finds the sheep, what does the shepherd do? First, he hoists the sheep on his shoulders and takes it home. He doesn't make the sheep walk ten steps behind him on the way home. He doesn't kick him all the way home, saying, "How could you have wandered away like that?" The sheep must have been tired and dehydrated. Picture that image—the shepherd with the sheep on his shoulders. Now realize this is what God has done for you.

Then the shepherd calls up everyone he knows and says, "Rejoice with me." What does that tell us about him? He is happy and wants to share his joy with others.

Jesus makes a comparison between the party thrown by the shepherd and the party in heaven over one sinner who repents. C.S. Lewis wrote, "Joy is the serious business of heaven."[156] I like that image. In heaven, God and the angels love it when sinners repent.

What brings you great joy in life? The Giants-versus-Patriots' Super Bowls brought me joy. Whenever I think about the pass from Manning to David Tyree (the miraculous helmet catch), I smile. When I think about the pass from Manning to Manningham (the perfect sideline pass and catch), I grin a silly grin. That those passes happened against the Evil Empire of Brady and Belichick makes it even sweeter. But joy over sporting events pales in comparison to the joy in heaven over a sinner who repents.

One point being made here is that it is good and right to leave the ninety-nine to search for the one. The one needs saving; the ninety-nine are safe. Wolves could mangle the one lost sheep. That doesn't mean that God doesn't care for the ninety-nine. He does, but the ninety-nine are safe. Why was Jesus hanging with tax collectors and sinners? Because he knew they needed to be saved. What are we doing to find the one?

The Parable of the Lost Coin—Luke 15:8–10

> Or suppose a woman has ten silver coins and loses one. Does she not light a lamp, sweep the house and search carefully until she finds it? And when she finds it, she calls her friends and neighbors together and says, "Rejoice with me; I have found my lost coin." In the same way, I tell you, there is rejoicing in the presence of the angels of God over one sinner who repents.

What happens when this woman in the parable loses one of her ten silver coins? She sweeps the house and searches carefully until she finds it. This drachma was a silver coin that was the equivalent of a denarius. It was worth a quarter of a shekel or a day's wage for the average worker at that time. That's a modest sum of money, but it's enough to make someone want to carry out a diligent search for the coin. Blomberg notes that the Hebrew word for "coin," zuzim, can also mean, "those that have moved away, departed."[157] Perhaps Jesus is deliberately using a play on words. People have rolled away, but they are still close enough to be swept back into the fellowship.

Notice how deliberate the woman is in her search. She is going to focus on this lost coin. She lights a lamp. Most houses did not have windows and were dark. The lamp would provide a bit of light, but not much. Most of the light from the lamp would go upward to the ceiling and not downward to the floor. So she gets her broom (probably made of palm leaves) and begins to sweep. She must listen carefully as she sweeps to hear the coin scrape across the floor. She's looking. She's listening. Her senses are heightened. She sweeps and sweeps until she finds the coin. She puts effort into her search.

What happens when she finds the coin? She calls her lady friends and female neighbors (both words are feminine). She asks them to rejoice with her. Why? What was lost is now found. That is cause for rejoicing. A comparison is made between the coin that was found and the one sinner who repents. When the sinner repents, the angels rejoice. Heaven celebrates. Wouldn't you love to see that celebration? High fives all around in heaven.

Both these parables teach us of God's heart for sinners. God is like the shepherd and the woman: He wants people to be saved.

But the parable is not just about God. A contrast is made between the Pharisees and Jesus. The Pharisees didn't make the effort to go after sinners. They grumbled that Jesus was eating with sinners.

Who are we most like? None of us would like to admit that we have the heart of a Pharisee, but what about our actions? If we don't actively search for the lost, then we are like the Pharisees. It's not the action of Jesus. Bock writes:

> The danger of seeking righteousness is that one can withdraw from the world in pursuit of heaven's blessings and the fellowship with those of like mind. The disciple is not to withdraw into a cocoon, inoculated from people of the world. Rather, part of the mission is to love people and draw them to God.[158]

Jesus is our model. We must leave the ninety-nine to go after the one. We must diligently search until the one coin is found.

How are you doing searching for the lost sheep or the lost coin? Are you talking to people about Jesus? Are you reaching out to people at your work, your school, your neighborhood, and your gym?

The Parable of the Lost Son—Luke 15:11–32

We come to what many consider to be the greatest parable of all. Charles Dickens, who knew how to write a great story, called it, "The greatest story ever told." Rembrandt was so moved by the story that he painted a masterpiece about it. Henri Nouwen was so moved by Rembrandt's painting of the story that he wrote a book about the painting. It's pretty incredible when a story inspires a painting about the story that is so good that it inspires a book about the painting about the story.

Let's not forget the context of this parable. Two types of people surround Jesus in 15:1–2: "Now the tax collectors and 'sinners' were all gathering around to hear him. But the Pharisees and the teachers of the law muttered, 'This man welcomes sinners and eats with them.'"

The younger brother in this story represents the tax collectors and sinners. The older brother is the Pharisees and scribes who have a conniption because Jesus fellowships with tax collectors and sinners.

The Younger Son—The Tax Collectors and Sinners

The Younger Son Leaves Home—15:12

> The younger one said to his father, "Father, give me my share of the estate." So he divided his property between them.

What is the story of the younger son? He is the rebel without a cause. He wants his independence. This is natural, a part of the process of growing up. But how he goes about getting his independence isn't so typical. He asks for his portion of the inheritance from his father, which would be one third of the estate. Since it was property, this meant the son sold off one third of the father's property. That would be a heavy blow to the father.

He insults the father by asking for his inheritance before the father's death. He spits upon their relationship, selfishly asking for his inheritance and quickly leaving home so that he can tout his independence of the father. Kenneth E. Bailey writes:

> In the Middle East when a young man asks for his inheritance while his father is still alive his request means "Dad, why don't you drop dead." The father is expected to get angry, slap the boy across the face and drive him out of the house. None of these things happens in the parable.[159]

Bailey might be pressing the point too far, but it is certain that the son is breaking social convention. More than that, he wants to leave home and get away from his dad.

Spiritually speaking, at some point in our lives, we all leave home. Edward Markquart writes:

> The broader interpretation is this: we as human beings, we take the inheritance that God has given to us. We take the money, the brains, the personality, the health, the resources; we take the inheritance that God has given to us. We say, "God, I don't want to have anything to do with you anymore. I am going to go and live my life as if you never existed." And so we take our God-given inheritance and we go and live as if God didn't exist or remotely exists. That's what this story is all about. Then, we finally come to our senses and we come home to God.... This is a story about us, about you and me, when we take our God-given inheritance and run away from God, living as if God does not exist. This story applies to all of us.[160]

The Younger Son Chooses Sin—15:13–14

> *"Not long after that, the younger son got together all he had, set off for a distant country and there squandered his wealth in wild living. After he had spent everything, there was a severe famine in that whole country, and he began to be in need.*

The younger son leaves home, converts his inheritance into currency and then squanders it in wild living. Διασκορπίζω/*diaskorpizō* means "to waste or to squander." Whenever we leave the home of the Father, we begin to waste our inheritance. The longer we stay away from home, the more we feel the pain, hurt, and guilt over wasting our inheritance.

We take our inheritance (everything God has given us as gifts—our intellect, our talent, our personality, and our personhood), and we leave the Father behind to pursue life without him. This leaves various scars on our person and our psyche. If we ever hope to be healed, we must understand that this is what all of us have done at one point or another. We all have been the younger son.

A big part of this story is told in reference to distance. The younger son goes to a distant country. Any time we leave God, we are headed into a distant country. The distant country looks like freedom, independence, parties, and good times, but really it is about wasting our inheritance (our gifts, talents, and abilities) while we are separated from God. You aren't at home in a distant country.

A severe famine comes into the land. The son could have been prepared for this famine if he had managed his money wisely. He hadn't, so now the famine causes his situation to go from bad to worse. He has nothing left; he can't afford shelter for the night. He can't even purchase a meal to soothe the pain of an empty stomach.

He searches and finds work on the farm of a Gentile, getting paid to take care of pigs. Imagine how low it must have seemed for this Jewish boy to be working with pigs. But he's going to sink even lower.

Verse 16 is the low point of the young man's life. It reads, "He longed to fill his stomach with the pods that the pigs were eating, but no one gave him anything." The young man was so hungry that he wanted to eat the slop that the pigs were eating. The pigs were better off than he was. They had food; he didn't. Ironically, he couldn't eat pigs, which were considered an unclean animal, but he could eat what the pigs were eating. He would have loved some pig slop; however, no one had compassion on him. He was alone in a distant land. He had hit rock bottom.

Rembrandt does a wonderful job in his painting of showing how beat up and destitute the younger son was. His once white clothes are now yellowed, soiled, and stained. They hang off his body because he has lost so much weight. His head is shaved and he has no beard (both were marks of shame and contempt in the ancient world).

The Younger Son Repents—15:17–20a

> *"When he came to his senses, he said, 'How many of my father's hired men have food to spare, and here I am starving to death! I will set out and go back to my father and say to him: Father, I have sinned against heaven and against you. I am no longer worthy to be called your son; make me like one of your hired men.' So he got up and went to his father.*

The text reads, "When he came to his senses." This is like a person who faints and starts waking up. He asks, "Where am I? What happened? How did I get here?" This is the beginning of self-realization for the younger son. He begins to understand how far he has fallen. He starts thinking about home. He reflects on how good he had it when he was back there. He realizes the hired workers of his father are better off than he is. They have bread. His father takes care of them. He finally begins to realize all that he left behind when he left home.

He decides to return home. He is going to close the distance between himself and the father. This begins with repentance. He admits, "I have sinned." That is the beginning of repentance.

The phrase, "against heaven and against you," demonstrates the younger son's admission that he sinned against God and against his earthly father. Sin doesn't just hurt you. The nature of sin is that it hurts other people as well. We often think, "I'm not hurting anyone but myself." That's the lie that Satan wants us to believe. Whenever you choose to sin, you hurt more than yourself. You hurt God. If you are married, you hurt your spouse because sin drives a wedge between you and your spouse. If you are a parent, your sin hurts your children because it keeps you from being the best parent you could be. That is the destructive nature of sin: We sin against God and people.

The younger son decides that he will return home and place himself at the mercy of his father. He knows he has given up his inheritance. He is no longer worthy to be called a son. Maybe, just maybe, his father will receive him back.

He'll ask his father to receive him as a day laborer. Darrel Bock explains the role of the day laborer. He writes:

> His request is simply for daily care and sustenance as a day laborer (μίσθιος, *mis-thios*...), the lowest of three classes of laborers. A slave (δοῦλος,/*doulos*; Luke 17:7–9) was like part of the family, although part of the lower class. The day laborer was hired only on special occasions for one day at a time, and so was less cared for. The son's request shows that he wants to be a minimal burden. He is prepared to be the lowest of the low.... He accepts the consequences of his choices. There are no excuses, only confession and a humble request. The picture shows what repentance looks like: no claims, just reliance on God's mercy and provision.[161]

A day laborer had no rights in the family and had to get hired out each day. When my family lived in the Holy Lands, we saw these day laborers standing on the street corners early in the morning hoping to be hired out for the day. They would approach any car or truck that looked like it might be searching for someone to do some work that day. This is what the younger son was willing to do when he returned home. He didn't expect to be accepted back into the family. He had no expectation whatsoever, but he did have a realization: "Being home with my father must be better than living here in this distant country." He felt the longing for home.

People hearing the story must have been thinking, "I wonder how the father will respond?" Obviously, we know the story. We know how the father responds, but for those hearing it for the first time, this question must have been on their minds. Let's look at the father's response.

The Loving Father—God

The father enters the story before verse 20. We saw him at the beginning of the story when he gave his son his portion of the inheritance and then watched him leave home. This must have been terribly difficult for the father. We understand that the father in the story represents God. God has given us free will. Even when our decisions aren't good decisions, he allows us to make our own choices in life.

The father also enters the story when the son is in the pigpen longing to eat the slop the pigs are eating. The son comes to his senses, and his father enters his mind. The son begins to realize, "There's no place like home." Home represented security, protection, food, and shelter. The son knew that the father was a loving father who took care of his family and his servants. This is the nature of God. James 1:16–17 reads, "Don't be deceived, my dear brothers. Every good and perfect gift is from above, coming down from the Father of the heavenly lights, who does not change like shifting shadows."

The Father's Reaction—15:20b–21

> "But while he was still a long way off, his father saw him and was filled with compassion for him; he ran to his son, threw his arms around him and kissed him.
> "The son said to him, 'Father, I have sinned against heaven and against you. I am no longer worthy to be called your son.'

The story turns to the reaction of the father when the son decides to return home. The son must have wondered how his father was going to respond when he saw him. He insulted his father by asking for his inheritance. He sold off a third of the property to get it, then squandered it in wild living. How would the father respond? That's the question on everyone's mind.

In that culture, most fathers would not have received the son back home. In fact, they would have already had some type of formal or informal funeral for their son and considered him dead. This is what the audience listening to the story is expecting. They are expecting the father to be angry and to put the son in his place, to be unforgiving and hard. Here comes a major twist in the story.

The father spotted his son coming home while the son was "still a long way off." Remember that distances are important in this story. If the father saw his son while he was still "a long way off," that means the father was looking in the distance for his son. He was looking out the window, awaiting his son's return. He must have looked out that window day after day, hoping. He has his eyes focused down the road where the road bends toward the house. This is his daily ritual. Then, he spots a figure off in the distance. He's not forgotten the silhouette of his son; he recognizes the figure walking down the road toward home.

When he sees his son return, he hoists up his robe and runs to him. Notice what happens with distance here. The father runs to his son, closing the distance between the two of them. When we take a step toward God, he comes running to us.

In the Middle East, older men don't run to their children, but this father is willing to look less than dignified. Why? He is rejoicing, and when you are rejoicing, you forget how you look. He gives his son a big hug and welcomes him back with a kiss. This goes against all Middle Eastern convention and protocol. The father doesn't care about convention or protocol. His lost son is coming home.

Here is a story from Edward F. Markquart that puts the parable in modern terms:

> The young son had gone to San Francisco. He was out of money, out of friends, out of options. He had hit the bottom and was at wits' end. This lost son wrote a letter home to his parents living in the Seattle area. He wrote, "Dear Mom and Dad, I have sinned deeply against you. I have sinned against you and I have sinned against God and I am not worthy to be called your son. There is no reason for you to love me or welcome me back home. I am at the bottom of the barrel and I need to come back home. I hope that you would welcome me. I have been given a ticket for a train, a ticket to get me back to Seattle. The train comes past our farm south of Seattle. The train comes around the bend and right past our farmhouse. If you want me to come home, please put a white towel on the clothesline, out in the back yard near the tracks. I will then know that you want me to come back home. If there is no towel there, I understand. I will understand that it is not right for me to come back home." The young man sent the letter, got on the train, and started heading north.
>
> As he came closer and closer to home, he became more nervous inside and was pacing up and down the center aisle of the train. As the train came closer and closer to his farmhouse, he couldn't bear it anymore. He was momentarily sitting next to a man, and he said to him, "Sir, around this next corner, this next bend, there is going to be a farm house on the left. A white house. An old red barn behind it. A dilapidated fence. There will be a clothesline in the back yard. Would you do me a favor and look and see if there is a white towel hanging on the clothesline? I know it sounds peculiar, but I can't bear to look."
>
> Well, the train came closer and closer to the bend and started to go around the bend, and the young man's heart was racing as fast as it could. The man said, "Look, look, look. Open your eyes." The whole clothesline was covered with white towels. The oak trees were covered with white sheets. The barn roof was covered with sheets. The old dilapidated fence was covered with white sheets. There were sheets everywhere. The father and mother so deeply wanted their son to come back home.[162]

Imagine the son's emotions when he sees his father running up to him. Imagine how that hug must have felt. Imagine the son's feeling when his father kissed him to welcome him back home. That's how we need to feel every day because we receive the father's love every day of our lives.

Many of us tend to beat ourselves up because of our shortcomings and our failures. We've been conditioned that way, but God wants us to feel his hugs and kisses. He wants us to know his love.

The son states the confession he rehearsed before he returned home. He admits his sin and rejects any claim to being a son, but he doesn't ask to be a day laborer. Some think the father interrupted the son before he could make the request. Some believe the father's reaction to the son's return was enough to allow the son to know that he was welcome to return as a son. We can't be certain why the son never got to the part where he asks to be a day laborer, but we can certain that the father would have rejected the offer. He received his son back as a part of the family.

The Father's Celebration—15:22–24

> *"But the father said to his servants, 'Quick! Bring the best robe and put it on him. Put a ring on his finger and sandals on his feet. Bring the fattened calf and kill it. Let's have a feast and celebrate. For this son of mine was dead and is alive again; he was lost and is found.' So they began to celebrate.*

If the son had any question about where he stood in the eyes of his father, the father makes it clear when he says to his servants,

> *"Quick! Bring the best robe and put it on him. Put a ring on his finger and sandals on his feet. Bring the fattened calf and kill it. Let's have a feast and celebrate. For this son of mine was dead and is alive again; he was lost and is found."*

He starts with the word "quick." The father doesn't want there to be any delay in restoring the son to the family. He wants to begin the celebration right away.

The father doesn't just request a robe; he asks for the best robe. The ring may have been a signet ring to symbolize the son was accepted back into the family with full rights and privileges of a family member. The son was barefoot, a symbol of destitution, so the father orders that sandals be placed on his feet. The father orders that the fattened calf be slaughtered. Fattened calves were saved for the high holy days and religious celebrations. This was a great sacrifice to make and symbolizes the importance of the occasion.

The father wants to celebrate. This repeats the joy over finding what was lost in the last two parables (the sheep and the coin). When the lost are found, there is cause for celebration.

What a lovely way for the story to end. You imagine this postscript, "And they all lived happily every after." But that's not the end of the story. If this were a movie, some ominous music might start right now. Like when Darth Vader enters the scene in Star Wars, the tuba begins to play: "Dum, dum, dum, pah dah-dum, pah dah-dum. Dum, dum, dum, pah dah-dum, pah dah-dum." Enter the elder brother.

The Elder Brother—The Pharisees and Teachers of the Law

Enter the Elder Brother—15:25–27

> *"Meanwhile, the older son was in the field. When he came near the house, he heard music and dancing. So he called one of the servants and asked him what was going on. 'Your brother has come,' he replied, 'and your father has killed the fattened calf because he has him back safe and sound.'*

Now, the third character, the tragic character: the elder brother. After I read this story in a Bible class, some students came up to me and said they felt sorry for the elder brother. Let's see if there is reason to feel sorry for him.

What do we know about the elder brother? He seems to be the dutiful son. He was out working in the field when his younger brother returned home. He was taking care of business on the farm. As the elder brother worked, was he close to the father? Seems like he was holding some bitterness toward the father in his heart.

He represents the Pharisees and scribes, the religious leaders of that day. One thing you can say about the Pharisees and teachers of the law— they were a hard-working and serious group of people. You can picture them working hard on the farm mending every fence and taking care of every detail. But their work wasn't God's work. They thought it was, but they had gotten off track because they forgot the Father's heart.

Look at some of what Jesus has to say to them in Matthew 23:

> *Then Jesus said to the crowds and to his disciples: "The teachers of the law and the Pharisees sit in Moses' seat. So you must obey them and do everything they tell you. But do not do what they do, for they do not practice what they preach. They tie up heavy loads and put them on men's shoulders, but they themselves are not willing to lift a finger to move them.*
>
> *"Everything they do is done for men to see: They make their phylacteries wide and the tassels on their garments long; they love the place of honor at banquets and the most important seats in the synagogues; they love to be greeted in the marketplaces and to have men call them 'Rabbi.'*
>
> *—Matthew 23:1–7*

> *"Woe to you, teachers of the law and Pharisees, you hypocrites! You shut the kingdom of heaven in men's faces. You yourselves do not enter, nor will you let those enter who are trying to.*
>
> *"Woe to you, teachers of the law and Pharisees, you hypocrites! You travel over land and sea to win a single convert, and when he becomes one, you make him twice as much a son of hell as you are.*
>
> *—Matthew 23:13–15*

> *Woe to you, teachers of the law and Pharisees, you hypocrites! You give a tenth of your spices—mint, dill and cummin. But you have neglected the more important matters of the law—justice, mercy and faithfulness. You should have practiced the latter, without neglecting the former. You blind guides! You strain out a gnat but swallow a camel.*
>
> *—Matthew 23:23–24*

No wonder the Pharisees and scribes failed to see that Jesus was the Messiah. They were at home with the Father, but they had forgotten the heart of the Father.

The older brother returns from a long day of work to hear the sounds of a celebration—music and dancing. He must wonder what is going on. What has he missed while he was out in the field taking care of the crops?

He calls a servant over and inquires about the music. The servant informs the older son that his younger brother has returned home. The father has called for a celebration because his son is back home safe and sound.

I can really relate to the elder brother because I grew up in a church that believed we were following the Bible word for word and line for line, but there was very little joy in our church. Most of the people had no heart for the lost. We were diligently working on the farm, but we were also very self-righteous and prideful. We would argue with anyone about the Scriptures, but we would do it in a way that would belittle people and make them feel small.

I remember a conference that I went to when I was a sophomore in college. The school invited a professor from another church in our fellowship to come and give some lectures on the Bible. He opened up his class for questions and comments. One man attacked him because he used the Revised Standard Version of the Bible. He laid him open, but the professor was so gracious to his attacker that it made me realize the difference between being self-righteous and righteous. It was good for me to see that.

When you think you have the truth of the Scripture figured out, then you have to make sure that you don't become like the older brother. He was tending to the farm, but he forgot to enjoy the time with his father.

The Elder Brother's Reaction—15:28–30

> *"The older brother became angry and refused to go in. So his father went out and pleaded with him. But he answered his father, 'Look! All these years I've been slaving for you and never disobeyed your orders. Yet you never gave me even a young goat so I could celebrate with my friends. But when this son of yours who has squandered your property with prostitutes comes home, you kill the fattened calf for him!'*

What do we notice about the elder brother here? The elder brother is upset, so upset that he won't go inside the house. Notice the distance here as the elder brother distances himself from the father. Without even knowing it, the elder brother has left home just like his little brother. He doesn't leave for a distant country like the younger brother, but he's outside the house nevertheless. His self-righteousness and pride have blinded him to the fact that he is just as lost as his younger brother was when he was away from home.

The father goes out to talk with the elder brother. Notice the spacing here. The older brother is outside the house so the father goes out to him. Both times, the father went to the son. This shows us something about the heart of God. He comes to us; he seeks us out. The father pleads with his older son to come inside and join the party.

This should remind us of how Jesus went to the religious Jews and offered them an invitation to the celebration. Jesus went to the Pharisees, the scribes, the Sadducees, and all the other Jewish leaders and gave them an opportunity to come into the kingdom. He offered them a personal invitation to the party, but they didn't accept it. This stands in contrast to the sinners and tax collectors who welcomed Jesus. He offended the Pharisees and teachers of the law by the company he kept. They were scandalized by it and wouldn't come to the party.

The elder son will have nothing to do with the celebration. He thinks it unjust. He has been home working diligently while his brother was out partying and wasting his birthright on prostitutes. The elder brother complains that his father hadn't killed so much as a goat for him, but when his brother returns, the father kills the fattened calf. He wants to know where the justice is in that. Shouldn't the father disown this disobedient, rebellious son, instead of throwing a party for him?

The elder brother is so busy searching for justice that he fails to see grace. The father didn't give the younger son what he deserved. He gave him grace. If the elder brother could see that, he would know how wonderful and gracious his father was and appreciate his father even more. But the elder brother can only think of himself. He is so self-consumed, so self-righteous, that he has no concern for the lost brother. Bock writes:

> A proper response is not to compare how you are treated in relationship to the penitent, but to remember that repentance yields the same gracious fruit for all, so it is just. Repentance also represents a new direction in life, and one might share in the joy of a changed direction. The brother is so consumed by the issue of fairness that he cannot rejoice at the beneficial transformation that has come to his brother.[163]

The Father's Response—15:31–32

> *"'My son,' the father said, 'you are always with me, and everything I have is yours. But we had to celebrate and be glad, because this brother of yours was dead and is alive again; he was lost and is found.'"*

The father tells his older son, "My son...you are always with me, and everything I have is yours." That is to say, "The return of your brother hasn't changed your status one bit. Everything I have is still yours. You haven't lost anything. There is plenty of my grace and bounty to go around."

The father adds, "But we had to celebrate and be glad, because this brother of yours was dead and is alive again; he was lost and is found." Celebration wasn't an option. When those thought to be dead are found, we celebrate. When the lost are saved, we celebrate. Note how the father speaks of the prodigal as "this brother of yours." He appeals to the elder brother's heart to receive the boy back as his brother.

The younger son was rebellious. The elder brother was self-righteous. We don't want to be rebellious or self-righteous. One writer compares and contrasts the two sons by writing:

> Rebellion uses people, just like this son used his dad. He just used him for the money. Those of you who are rebellious, you use people. You want your parents, family, friends, coworkers, boyfriend, girlfriend, husband, wife, church, government to just pick up your mess and pay your tab. You use people. Religious people don't use people, they judge people. "You're stupid, you're lazy, you're an idiot, you're not as good as me." That's exactly what the religious son does. Rebellion is unrighteous. . . . Religion is self-righteous. Rebellion is, "I'm my own person and I express myself and I'm a free spirit and I'm unique and I don't play by the rules and I do what I feel and I'm true to myself." And it's unrighteous. And religion comes along and says, "And I'm better than those people and I'm smarter than those people and I'm harder working and more compliant and I make a better contribution to society. They ruin everything and I'm the one holding it together." They're self-righteous. And the only thing in the story that the rebellious and the religious son hold in common? They're both using the father. Neither of them is loving him. . . . My question to you is this: which are you? Rebellious or religious? Are you more rebellious or religious? When your heart inclines one way or the other, which direction does it go?[164]

I appreciate the writer's point when he says, "They're both using the father. Neither of them is loving him." What we need to do is love and appreciate the father. That will keep us from being rebellious or self-righteous.

How does the elder brother respond? We don't know. The story doesn't say. Why? Because Jesus is speaking to the Pharisees and the teachers of the law. He leaves the story open ended so that they will think about themselves. How will they respond to the father's rebuke? Will they now go out and treat tax collectors and sinners with the love the father had for the younger son?

How will we respond to the father's rebuke? Will we have the heart of Jesus in the way we treat those outside the church? The parable asks each disciple to check his or her heart to see if we are like Jesus. *The Preacher's Commentary* notes:

> In His ministry Jesus sought the lost in all sorts of unlikely places. He offended the religious leaders by eating with the lost—those who were not righteous, not clean, not good. Jesus is the Great Physician, and a physician does not set a broken arm from across the street; he goes where the patient is.[165]

This is what God expects of us: He expects us to look for the lost sheep and the lost coin. He expects us to run out to the prodigal when he or she returns and throw a celebration. Do we have that heart, a heart for the lost? How will we respond?

Bigger Barns: The Parable of the Rich Fool—Luke 12:16–21, Luke 12:13–34

Let's look at a parable in Luke 12. The parable is found in verses 16–21, but to understand it better, we should look at verses 13–34 to get the context.

> Someone in the crowd said to him, "Teacher, tell my brother to divide the inheritance with me."
>
> Jesus replied, "Man, who appointed me a judge or an arbiter between you?" Then he said to them, "Watch out! Be on your guard against all kinds of greed; a man's life does not consist in the abundance of his possessions."
>
> And he told them this parable: "The ground of a certain rich man produced a good crop. He thought to himself, 'What shall I do? I have no place to store my crops.'
>
> "Then he said, 'This is what I'll do. I will tear down my barns and build bigger ones, and there I will store all my grain and my goods. And I'll say to myself, "You have plenty of good things laid up for many years. Take life easy; eat, drink and be merry." '
>
> "But God said to him, 'You fool! This very night your life will be demanded from you. Then who will get what you have prepared for yourself?'
>
> "This is how it will be with anyone who stores up things for himself but is not rich toward God."
>
> Then Jesus said to his disciples: "Therefore I tell you, do not worry about your life, what you will eat; or about your body, what you will wear. Life is more than food, and the body more than clothes. Consider the ravens: They do not sow or reap, they have no storeroom or barn; yet God feeds them. And how much more valuable you are than birds! Who of you by worrying can add a single hour to his life? Since you cannot do this very little thing, why do you worry about the rest?

"Consider how the lilies grow. They do not labor or spin. Yet I tell you, not even Solomon in all his splendor was dressed like one of these. If that is how God clothes the grass of the field, which is here today, and tomorrow is thrown into the fire, how much more will he clothe you, O you of little faith! And do not set your heart on what you will eat or drink; do not worry about it. For the pagan world runs after all such things, and your Father knows that you need them. But seek his kingdom, and these things will be given to you as well.

"Do not be afraid, little flock, for your Father has been pleased to give you the kingdom. Sell your possessions and give to the poor. Provide purses for yourselves that will not wear out, a treasure in heaven that will not be exhausted, where no thief comes near and no moth destroys. For where your treasure is, there your heart will be also.

I like to call this parable the Parable of the Bigger Barns. It is also known as the Parable of the Rich Fool. It is the story of a rich man who has an amazing harvest, so big that he builds bigger barns in which to store it. The man isn't storing grain to prepare for a famine; he is storing away his harvest because of greed. Bigger Barns is a story of greed.

In the United States of America, we live in a Bigger Barn culture. Our lives are brimming over with stuff. We have so much stuff that we don't know what to do with all of it. Americans spend twenty-two billion dollars each year on storage units. It's difficult to get your head around one billion. Think of this: a billion seconds ago it was 1959. That would make me two years old. A whole lot of seconds have passed since I was a two-year-old. Now consider this: A billion minutes ago Jesus was alive. A billion is a very large number. In the US we spend twenty-two billion a year on bigger barns.

For many people, a storage unit is a bigger barn. Tom Vanderbilt writes:

According to the Self Storage Association, a trade group charged with monitoring such things, the country now possesses some 1.875 billion (almost 2 billion) square feet of personal storage. All this space is contained in nearly 40,000 facilities owned and operated by more than 2,000 entrepreneurs....

What this translates into... is an industry that now exceeds the revenues of Hollywood (and doesn't have to deal with Tom Cruise). One in 11 American households, according to a recent survey, owns self-storage space—an increase of some 75 percent from 1995. Most operators of self-storage facilities report 90 percent occupancy, with average stints among its renters of 15 months. Last year alone saw a 24 percent spike in the number of self-storage units on the market.[166]

There is a television show called *Storage Wars* where people bid on stuff that others left behind in storage units. When someone wins the bid on a storage unit, they open it to see if they've found anything special. That's entertainment at its best.[167]

Bigger Barns

Preceding the parable, a man asks Jesus to settle a dispute between him and his brother concerning an inheritance. It is quite common for family members to fight over inheritances. Just these last couple of weeks I heard of three cases where this happened. I've heard it said, "Whenever there is an inheritance, ninety-nine percent of the people become wolves." Greed gets the better of us and we forget that we are family.

Jesus is asked to settle the dispute because he is a rabbi; the man addresses him as "Teacher." It was common in the first century for a rabbi to step in and settle this type of issue, but Jesus isn't that kind of rabbi. He isn't just going to step in and decide who should get what. He is going to speak to the heart of the issue. That's what Jesus does: He speaks to the heart. At the heart of the issue sits the old sin that dogs so many people—greed. Greed, simply put, is the desire to have more. Enough doesn't satisfy. Greed wants more, more, more.

That is the context of this parable. Jesus is telling it to illustrate the insidious nature of greed. Before he launches into the parable, he says, "Watch out! Be on your guard against all kinds of greed; a man's life does not consist in the abundance of his possessions." That's the theme of the parable. Then he tells the story of a man who thought that his life did consist in the abundance of his possessions.

After the parable, Jesus teaches directly concerning greed and hoarding possessions. He teaches some of the same lessons he taught in the Sermon on the Mount in Matthew 6. He says, "Life is more than food, and the body more than clothes." He adds, "And do not set your heart on what you will eat or drink; do not worry about it." He closes the discussion with a very direct command, "Sell your possessions and give to the poor. Provide purses for yourselves that will not wear out, a treasure in heaven that will not be exhausted, where no thief comes near and no moth destroys. For where your treasure is, there your heart will be also." The context is clear. Jesus is warning his followers about the sin of greed. Possessions, in and of themselves, are not wrong; but when we become greedy of our possessions, then we sin.

Let's look at the parable.

1. Greed begins when you forget God. The first verse in the parable sets up the story, "The ground of a certain rich man produced a good crop" (vs. 16). Nothing wrong here. This is a generic farmer who had a bountiful harvest. That's what we would all like in life. It's okay to work hard and to reap a bountiful harvest.

Then, as in all the parables, Jesus puts a twist in the story. Verse 17 reads, "He thought to himself, 'What shall I do? I have no place to store my crops.'" Here we see the first hint at what is going to be the Achilles heel of the man. He says, "I...I...my." "My crops." This theme of "I" and "my" pervades the parable. In the Greek there are fifty-one words. At least twelve of those words are a first person pronoun. There are eight I's and four my's. He forgets who gave him the crops. Where is God in all this?

The rich man makes the mistake of leaving God out of the picture. He acts as if he could grow crops without God, but could the rich man produce rain? Could he call the sun to rise in the sky? The problem is not the bountiful harvest; the problem is his perspective. Darrell Bock writes:

> He quite naturally wants to preserve his crops, but there is a hint of a problem in his perspective, for throughout these verses the major stylistic feature is the presence of the pronoun μου (*mou*, my), not to mention the numerous first-person singular verbs. The fruit of the land and other elements of the parable are repeatedly described with μου: my fruit, my barn, my goods, my soul. Such language suggests exclusive self-interest.[168]

Bock calls this "exclusive self-interest." Greed and self-interest often go hand in hand. God is left out of the picture, the kingdom of God is not in the picture, and others are not in the picture. The man is only thinking of himself.

He forgot God. It's not good to forget God. When we get old, we tend to get a bit forgetful. That's just part of getting old. I heard this story about three elderly sisters. I quote:[169]

> This week I read a story about three sisters—ages ninety-two, ninety-four, and ninety-six. These elderly siblings had never married and had lived together their entire LONG lives. One night, the ninety-six-year-old sister drew a bath for herself. She put one foot into the water, then paused and called out to her sisters asking, "Was I getting in the tub or out?" The ninety-four-year-old hollered back, "I don't know, sister, but I'll come up and see." She started up the stairs, but stopped halfway and with a perplexed look on her face called out to her siblings, "Was I going up the stairs or coming down?" The "little" sister—the ninety-two-year-old—was sitting at the kitchen table having tea, and she listened to her sisters' interchange with a smirk on her face. She shook her head and said, "I sure hope I never get that forgetful," and knocked on wood for good measure. Then she yelled out, "I'll come up and help both of you as soon as I see who just knocked at the door."[169]

Age can make us forgetful, but things can also make us forgetful. We mustn't forget God.

The best way not to forget him is to make sure that you stay connected with him every day. Begin your day with a prayer of gratitude to God for giving you life and for extending your life by at least one more day. Realize that every good thing you have in life comes from him. It is his gift to you.

2. Greed makes us foolish; it can turn any person into a fool. The story reads:

> *"Then he said, 'This is what I'll do. I will tear down my barns and build bigger ones, and there I will store all my grain and my goods. And I'll say to myself, "You have plenty of good things laid up for many years. Take life easy; eat, drink and be merry." '*
> *"But God said to him, 'You fool! This very night your life will be demanded from you. Then who will get what you have prepared for yourself?'*

God says to the man, "You fool." From all appearances this man seems to have it all. He seems to be a smart businessman, but God calls him a fool. Greed makes us foolish.

How does greed make us foolish? It makes us believe that our possessions are our lives. It makes us believe that the person with the biggest and best toys wins. It makes us believe that life is about our possessions. J.R. Miller writes:

> To look about, one would think a man's life *did* consist in the abundance of the things he possesses. Men think they become great just in proportion as they gather wealth. So it seems, too; for the world measures men by their bank account. Yet there never was a more fatal error. A man is really measured by what he *is*, and not by what he *has*.[170]

Allow me to repeat that last line, "A man is really measured by what he is, and not by what he has."

Success in life should not be measured by the amount or value of our possessions. Yet, too often we equate success with things. Some value possessions more than life itself. Consider this story:

> A rich young man was driving his Rolls Royce on a mountain road when he lost control and his car went over a cliff. The young man was thrown clear but his left arm was severed in the process. He stumbled to his feet, stood at the top of the cliff looking down at the burning wreck of his car, and cried out, "My Rolls! My Rolls!" The driver of another car stopped to help and heard him crying out like this. He gently grabbed the man and said, "Sir! You're in shock. Your arm has been severed! Let me help you." The young man looked down and when he saw that his arm was gone he cried out, "My Rolex! My Rolex!"[171]

Greed makes us foolish. It makes us equate things with worth. God doesn't look at the quantity of our possessions; he looks at the quality of our hearts.

How does greed make us foolish? It makes us believe that we are in control of our own destiny. It makes us believe that we can choose how our lives are going to be played out.

Look at the rich fool in this story:

> *"Then he said, 'This is what I'll do. I will tear down my barns and build bigger ones, and there I will store all my grain and my goods. And I'll say to myself, 'You have plenty of good things laid up for many years. Take life easy; eat, drink and be merry.'"*

What a fool. He thinks, "I've got my retirement all planned out. I'll rest on what I've made. I'll kick back, put on a movie, order up a pizza, grab some sweet ice tea, and enjoy life."

This is exactly the life that many Americans dream of having when they hit retirement age. They want to kick back somewhere near a golf course where they can play eighteen holes in the early morning, take a swim in the afternoon, and play cards with their friends into the night.

The problem is not the retirement fund. The problem is acting as if we are in control of our futures. We act like we write the script to our lives. We act as if we are in control of time. That is how greed makes us dumb. We stash all this stuff away, and we have no control over whether we will ever get to enjoy it or not.

Only God knows your future. Only he knows how much time you have left here on the earth. Only he knows what will happen to your possessions. Therefore, doesn't it make sense to think of God first in our lives?

Where is God in this picture? Where are others in this picture? Where are the lost? Where are the poor? Where is the neighbor who has been out of work for six months and is in need of food?

The rich fool chooses the easy life, which for him is the selfish and self-centered life. His life became his possessions. That is true of so many people today.

This man made the mistake of thinking that he was in control of his destiny and of thinking he had all the time in the world to kick back and enjoy his things. He thought about his things, but he didn't think about eternity.

Sooner or later, God will enter the picture. Whether you like or not, he will enter the picture. You might as well let him in now; now is better than later, but sooner or later, God *will* enter the picture. That's what God does. You're sitting there in your Laz-E-Boy chair, wrapped up in your snuggly, watching the NBA finals on your flat-screen TV, and God enters the picture. And his first words are, "You fool!" You fool with an exclamation point. The word is Ἄφρων/*aphrōn*. It is used consistently of the person who lives life without thinking of God. For example, Psalm 14:1 and Psalm 53:1: "The fools says in his heart, 'There is no God.'" God says to the man, "There is a God. Here I am. You forgot about me. You forgot about eternity. You were so busy collecting your things and building bigger barns that you never considered that you might not live long enough to enjoy your success."

How does greed make us foolish? It makes us think this life is all there is to life. Greed makes us forget eternity.

God says, "This very night your life will be demanded from you." The word for "life" (ψυχή, *psyche*) could just as easily be translated "soul." God says, "This very night your soul will be taken from you." The man was so caught up in things, in possessions, in kicking back and enjoying the easy life, that he forgot that he had a soul. For him, it's all about life in the here and now.

Then comes a haunting question, "Then who will get what you have prepared for yourself?" Who's going to enjoy your things once you are gone? Bock writes, "In this 'you can't take it with you' parable, Jesus shows that to focus on possessions and not be concerned with spiritual things is a grave, long-term error. Though riches may be enjoyable in the short term, they do not exist in the long term."[172]

Jesus warns us all, saying, "This is how it will be with anyone who stores up things for himself but is not rich toward God." The problem is not things. Possessions are neutral. The problem is storing up things for self out of greed. The problem is not being rich toward God. There is a contrast in this verse: storing up things for self (greed and selfishness) versus being rich toward God (benevolence and selflessness).

Again, the problem is not things. The problem is not even wealth. The problem is where the wealth is directed—toward self or toward God. Paul says in 1 Timothy 6:17–19:

> *Command those who are rich in this present world not to be arrogant nor to put their hope in wealth, which is so uncertain, but to put their hope in God, who richly provides us with everything for our enjoyment. Command them to do good, to be rich in good deeds, and to be generous and willing to share. In this way they will lay up treasure for themselves as a firm foundation for the coming age, so that they may take hold of the life that is truly life.*

Compared to the rest of the world, almost all of us are wealthy. The problem isn't wealth. The question is: Are you rich toward God? Trent Butler writes:

> Riches have one major weakness. They have no purchasing power after death. They cannot buy the currency needed to get to heaven. Do not try to be rich in regard to the bank or barn. Be rich in relationship to God. Through prayer, study, obedience, and practice of the word, be sure you are part of the kingdom of God.[173]

What does it mean to be rich toward God? Warren Wiersbe answers this by writing, "It means to acknowledge gratefully that everything we have comes from God, and then make an effort to use what He gives us for the good of others and the glory of God."[174] God allows us to have things so that we can use them for his glory. I heard a preacher say, "I have good news and bad news. The good news is that the church has all the money it needs. The bad news is that it is still in your wallets."

We should check our hearts. The problem isn't possessions; it is greed. Do you love things too much? Is "enough" enough for you, or do you constantly want more? Do you enjoy giving to others? Are you selfish or selfless?

Let's decide that we are going to be rich toward God.

Conclusion

This concludes our focus on the teaching ministry of Jesus. We have investigated the Sermon on the Mount, four main themes in the teaching ministry of Jesus (five if we count the section on the kingdom of God), and the parables of Jesus. There is so much more that we could consider, but perhaps that will appear in a future book.

Jesus was the greatest spiritual teacher ever to walk the face of the earth. His lessons are deep, brimming over with excellent theological thought; yet they are simple and practical so that everyone can understand them. The older I get, the more all I want to do is spend time in the Gospels listening to the words of Jesus. Why is that? Perhaps it's because I believe that when I listen to the words of Jesus, I clearly hear the voice of God.

Now we will turn to explore Jesus' ministry as he continues to train his disciples. There are valuable lessons that we can learn from the discipling ministry of Jesus.

End Notes

133. Tom Wright, *The Original Jesus*, 36.
134. Kenneth E. Bailey, 279.
135. G.R. Osborne, *The Hermeneutical Spiral: A Comprehensive Introduction to Biblical Interpretation, revised and expanded*, 2nd ed. (Downers Grove, IL: InterVarsity Press, 2006), 291.
136. Borg, *Jesus: Uncovering the Life, Teachings, and Relevance of a Religious Revolutionary*, 152.
137. Blomberg, *Interpreting the Parables*, (Grand Rapids: IVP Academic, 1990), 53–54.
138. Bailey, 28.
139. Osborne, 296.
140. Taken from Blomberg, 60–61.
141. Taken from Blomberg, 61.
142. Blomberg, 67.
143. N. T. Wright, *Jesus and the Victory of God*, 237.

144. Blomberg, 41.

145. C. H. Dodd, *The Parables of the Kingdom* (New York: Charles Scribner's Sons, 1961).

146. Osborne, 303.

147. Osborne, 294.

148. Blomberg, 20–21.

149. Blomberg, 166.

150. Blomberg, 45.

151. Bailey, 281.

152. Neil Lightfoot, *Lessons from the Parables* (Grand Rapids: Baker, 1976).

153. Mekilta de Rabbi Ishmael, tractate Amalek 3.55–57.

154. D. L. Bock, *Baker Exegetical Commentary on the New Testament,* Luke Volume 2: 9:51–24:53. (Grand Rapids: Baker, 1996), 1299.

155. W. MacDonald and A. Farstad, "Luke 15:1–2" in *Believer's Bible Commentary: Old and New Testaments* (Nashville: Thomas Nelson, 1997).

156. C.S. Lewis, *Letters to Malcolm: Chiefly on Prayer* (San Diego: Harvest, 1964), 92–93.

157. Blomberg, 180.

158. Bock, 1304–1305.

159. Bailey, 281.

160. http://www.sermonsfromseattle.com/series_c_the_prodigal_son.htm.

161. Bock, 1313.

162. http://www.sermonsfromseattle.com/series_c_the_prodigal_son.htm

163. Bock, 1318.

164. marshill.com/2011/03/08/the-parable-of-the-prodigal-son-sermon-notes-luke-65

165. B. Larson and L. J. Ogilvie, *The Preacher's Commentary Series,* vol. 26, *Luke.* (Nashville, Tennessee: Thomas Nelson, 1983), 237.

166. Tom Vanderbilt, Slate, "Self–Storage Nation," http://www.slate.com/articles/arts/culturebox/2005/07/selfstorage_nation.html

167. My tongue is firmly planted in my cheek as I write this.

168. Bock, 1151–1152.

169. http://www.redlandbaptist.org/sermons/sermon20090111.php

170. J. R. Miller, "Come Ye Apart," reading for June 10, as found in W. MacDonald and A. Farstad, "Luke 12:15" in *Believer's Bible Commentary: Old and New Testaments* (Nashville: Thomas Nelson,1997).

171. http://www.redlandbaptist.org/sermons/sermon20090111.php

172. Bock, 1154.

173. T. C. Butler, *Holman New Testament Commentary,* vol. 3, *Luke.* (Nashville, TN: Broadman & Holman Publishers, 2000), 204.

174. W. W. Wiersbe, "Luke12:13" in *The Bible Exposition Commentary* (Wheaton, IL: Victor Books, 1996).

Chapter 10

Jesus Prepares His Disciples for Ministry

Jesus' plan for his ministry did not include the goal of converting the whole world during his lifetime. Obviously, that was his heart, but that wasn't his plan. His plan was to die for the whole world and to train twelve men who would continue his ministry after he was gone. That was his "Plan A." He had no "Plan B."

Jesus focused on a few. His "few" included an inner circle of three and a larger circle of twelve. His focus was to prepare his disciples for the event of the cross and to train them to carry on his ministry. Both elements were crucial in the training of the twelve. The plan included (1) walking with the disciples so they could see how he ministered to people, (2) repeating the same lessons over and over (because the disciples needed to hear the lessons over and over), and, finally, (3) dying and rising from the dead (so they could understand who he was).

How Jesus Prepared His Disciples for Ministry

How did Jesus train his chosen disciples? He walked with them as a first-century rabbi walked with his students. It was the role of the rabbi to teach; it was the place of the student/disciple to watch and learn.

Jesus taught his disciples to pay attention to the needs of the people around them. He looked at the crowds as lost, harassed, and helpless. He taught his disciples that the crowds were like sheep without a shepherd and to have compassion for people.

Jesus instructed his disciples concerning their mission, which included seeking and saving the lost. He said to them, "Pray that the Lord of Harvest will send forth workers into the harvest field."[175] Then, in almost the next breath, he told them, "Go." He told them, "Pray for workers; and, by the way, you are the workers." As Jesus sent his disciples into the harvest field, he gave them instructions pertaining to their mission.

Jesus had been preparing them for this moment. He had shown them the way of ministry. Now it was time for them to be involved in the work of the ministry. But first, one more lesson. Jesus gave his disciples a few last directives before they left on their mission. As we explore these directives, let's see what we can learn concerning the mission of Jesus that will help us continue his ministry today.

The Calling of the Twelve—Matthew 10:1–4, cf. Mark 6:7, Luke 9:1–2

> *Jesus called his twelve disciples to him and he gave them authority over unclean spirits to cast them out and to heal all disease and every sickness.*
>
> *The twelve apostles' names are these: first, Simon called Peter, Andrew his brother and James the son of Zebedee and John his brother. Philip and Bartholomew, Thomas and Matthew the tax collector, James, the son of Alphaeus and Thaddaeus. Simon the Zealot and Judas Iscariot who betrayed him.*

This is the first and only time Matthew refers to the twelve as "apostles." The word ἀπόστολος/*apostolos* means, "one sent on a mission."

The list of the twelve is found in all four gospels. When you compare the different lists of apostles, certain facts begin to emerge.

1. Peter always begins the list of the apostles. Matthew begins his list by saying "first, Simon called Peter." Peter seems to have been the natural leader of the apostles, but "first" here probably means first among equals.

2. The first four names in each list are always the two pairs of brothers: Peter and Andrew, James and John.

3. Judas Iscariot is always the last person named in each list.

4. Simon the Zealot is the same person as Simon the Canaanite.

5. Judas the son of James is the same person as Thaddaeus.

6. Bartholomew is often identified with Nathanael of John 1:46.

7. Thomas is also known as Didymus, which means "twin."

D.A. Carson has made an interesting observation after comparing the lists of the apostles in the four gospels. He writes:

> In each list there are three groups of four, each group headed by Peter, Philip (not to be confused with the evangelist), and James the son of Alphaeus respectively. But within each group the order varies even from Luke to Acts!), except that Judas is always last. This suggests, if it does not prove, that the Twelve were organizationally divided into smaller groups, each with a leader.[176]

This seems (to me) to be a very valid insight. It suggests that Jesus began his ministry with a practical structure—the twelve divided into three groups of four with a leader over each group. I want to suggest a transcultural application here. If you are leading a ministry, your ministry needs to have structure. I've heard leaders say, "I'm a leader and not a manager." But every leader has to have at least a little manager in them or nothing will ever get done. Find a structure that suits your ministry and your leadership style.

Without structure, people get frustrated. Their needs will not be met. To grow big, you have to break it down small. Don't be afraid of structure. It can be the leader's best friend.

The Mission: Ambassadors of Peace—Matthew 10:5–15, cf. Mark 6:8–11, Luke 9:3–5

Jesus sent out the twelve on a mission, instructing them, "Do not go the way of the Gentiles and do not enter the town of the Samaritans. Go rather to the lost sheep of the house of Israel. Go and preach saying: The kingdom of heaven is near. Heal the sick, raise the dead, and cast out demons. You received freely; freely give. Do not take any gold or silver or copper in your belts, no bag for your journey and don't take two tunics, or sandals, or a staff. For the worker is worthy of his keep.

Whatever town or village you enter, search for some worthy person in it and stay there until you leave. As you enter the house, greet it. If the house is worthy, let your peace remain on it. If it is not worthy, let your peace return to you. Whoever does not welcome you or listen to your words, shake the dust off your feet when you leave that house or town. I tell you the truth—it will be more tolerable for Sodom and Gomorrah on the day of judgment than for that town."

Why does Jesus send his disciples only to the lost sheep of Israel? Why not send them to everyone in the world? Why in other places of the gospel does Jesus send them to everyone (Matthew 28:18–20)? Why not just go ahead and give the great commission? Why give a limited commission?

When you see something you don't understand in the Bible, ask a few questions. First, make sure the translation is accurate. Perhaps the misunderstanding comes from a faulty translation of the text.[177]

Second, check the sociopolitical, historical, and cultural context of the passage. You will need to step outside the text and do some extra reading to ascertain this information. Begin by doing some cross-referencing of the scripture. Check parallel passages. Read the specific passage in light of the whole of the Bible. I heard a minister say, "You can make any single passage of the Bible say almost anything you want it to say, but you cannot make the whole Bible say anything you want it to say." Each passage of

Scripture must be weighed alongside the whole of the biblical text. Then look for additional clarity in Bible handbooks, Bible encyclopedias, Bible dictionaries, and commentaries, of which there are many online. Always, search the Bible first and then appeal to other sources.

Third, see if there is any transcultural meaning in the message. Ask, "What is the author saying that applies to all people around the world at every moment of human history? What is being said that transcends culture?" Stop and meditate on this point. It is here that you will find what the scripture is saying for you, in your life, today.

Let's consider this passage. First, the passage is translated properly. You don't have to trust me on that point. You can do the work yourself, but I've translated the text, and I believe it is an accurate translation.

Second, let's consider the sociopolitical, historical, and cultural context. In this context, the disciples of Jesus were all Jewish. As of yet, there is no cross, no resurrection, no forgiveness in the name of Jesus, and no church. This would mean that if the disciples were to reach out to Gentiles, the disciples would have to convert the Gentiles to Judaism. Instead, Jesus sent his fellow Jews to other Jews to speak of the Messiah.

Also, the Jews did not relate to the Gentiles all that well. One rabbinical teaching concerning the Gentiles said that if a Jew came across a drowning Gentile, the Jew was under no obligation to save the drowning person. After all, the Gentile was lost and evil, so to save the Gentile would allow evil to continue to exist in the world. So Jesus sent his disciples first to the Jews. This is a good transcultural principle: First, go to the people you know.

The charge to the disciples was clear: Jesus is saying, "Go and do to others as I have done to you." Their ministry was to be a ministry of word and action. They were to preach the word and do some good. Today, our ministry should be the same. It should be a ministry of word and action. Let's preach the word and do some good.

The message was simple: The kingdom of heaven is near. The Jews were expecting the arrival of the Messianic kingdom, and the apostles were to prepare them for it. As they went, they were to perform good works to demonstrate the power of God: healing the sick, raising the dead, and casting out demons. Jesus told them, "You have received freely; freely give." This could be a practical admonition not to take money for their miraculous signs (although they could accept hospitality), or it could be an admonition to have a certain attitude—we have been given much; therefore, we are to give freely to people around us.

Then Jesus directed the seventy-two that if they were received into a home, they should bring peace to that home. If they were turned away, they should leave in peace but not leave their peace behind.

Peace is a wonderful thing. The Old Testament concept of peace (*shalom*) means "wholeness in life." It is contentment, security, and confidence.

The admonition to shake the dust off your feet demonstrates the urgency of the mission. Some would say this lacks compassion. They ask, "Shouldn't you stick around forever?" But there are consequences to rejecting the message. Give them the message and let God work on their hearts. The message needs to reach as many people as possible.

Great Motivation and Great Authority—Matthew 10:16–25

Indeed, I am sending you on a mission as sheep in the midst of wolves. Therefore be wise as serpents and innocent as doves. Be on your guard against men. They will hand you over to councils and flog you in their synagogues. And you will be brought before governors and kings because of me to testify to them and to the nations.

When they hand you over, do not worry about how you will speak, for I will give you in that hour what you will say. For it is not you who speak, but the spirit of your Father speaking through you.

Brother will betray brother to death and a father his child and children will rebel against their parent and have them killed. And because of my name all will hate you. But he who remains steadfast unto death will be saved. When they persecute you in one town, flee to another; I tell you the truth—you will not have gone through all the towns of Israel before the Son of Man comes.

A student is not above his teacher, nor a servant above his Master. It is enough for the student to be like his teacher and the slave his Lord. If they have called the master of the house "Beelzebul," how much more those in his household.

As we go into the world, Jesus does not want us to be naive. The world is a tough place. Not everyone will have your best interest at heart. He warns his disciples, "Be on your guard against men." Jesus gives the instruction to be as shrewd as snakes. What does this mean? Jesus is telling his disciples to be wise. Avoid trouble. Don't make a spectacle of yourself. There is no glory in persecution that comes because of stupidity. And we all have the tendency to be stupid at times. Be innocent like a dove. Speak the truth and speak it plainly, but be wise in your conversation and manner of life. The goal is to reach as many people as possible.

Do Not Fear Men—Matthew 10:26–33

"Do not fear them. There is nothing concealed that will not be revealed or nothing secret that will not become known. What I tell you in the dark, speak in the light, and what you hear whispered, proclaim from the rooftops. Do not fear those who kill the body but cannot kill the soul. Fear him who can kill body and soul in Gehenna. Are two sparrows not sold for a penny? And not one of them falls to the earth apart from your Father's

> *will. Even the hairs of your head are all counted. Do not fear. You are of greater value than all the sparrows.*
>
> *Everyone who confesses me before men, I will confess before my Father in heaven. Everyone who denies me before men, I will deny before my father in heaven."*

Persecution will come. Times will get tough, but we should not fear men, who can kill the body but cannot kill the soul. The one we should fear is God, because he is able to destroy both body and soul. *Gehenna* was the Hinnon Valley just south of Jerusalem. It was the site of human sacrifices in Old Testament times and became a continually burning garbage dump in the time of Jesus. *Gehenna* became synonymous for hell, the place with unquenchable fire.

If God takes care of the birds of the air, will he not take care of you? This is a rhetorical question. The answer is implied: "Yes, of course he will take care of you. After all, God keeps count of all the hairs on our head." This shows how much value we have in God's eyes. One of my favorite devotional books is *Shout for Joy* by David Head. In his book, Head places these words in the mouth of an angel:

> 10,467; 10,464; 10,463 (steady, man; anger won't get you anywhere); 10,390...
> Lord, counting hairs as they fall out is the dullest of occupations. But if doing this helps one of Thy anxious children to know his value in Thy sight, I will not begrudge the labor. By his knowledge that I count, may he know he counts![178]

We do count. And we can count on God's promise that no matter how intense things get around us, he will take care of us.

Therefore we should confess Jesus before men fearlessly. We need not be intimidated. God watches out for us. He knows every time a hair falls from our head. No one knows us like God does, and no one cares for us like God does.

Not Peace, But a Sword—Matthew 10:34–39

> *"Do not think I have come to bring peace to the earth. I have not come to bring peace, but a sword. For I have come to turn—*
> *A son against his father*
> *A daughter against her mother*
> *A daughter-in-law against her mother-in-law.*
> *A man's enemies will be of his own household.*
> *Anyone who loves father or mother more than me is not worthy of me. Whoever loves son or daughter more than me is not worthy of me. Anyone who does not take up his cross and follow me is not worthy of me. Whoever finds his life will lose it, and whoever loses his life for my sake will find it."*

Jesus did not come to bring peace, but a sword. Most Jews believed that the Messiah was going to restore the past glory to Israel and usher in a time of peace. The Messiah would do this with a sword. Jesus is saying, "Not so." Jesus came bringing spiritual peace, but he never guaranteed physical peace.

The peace that Jesus brought would be disruptive, especially within the family. Jesus knew that in this culture, family ties were tight. Sons were expected to follow the traditions of their fathers. Daughters were expected to please their mothers. Extended families lived in a single home. When a child got married, an extra room was built onto the house for the new couple. Often a funeral was performed for someone who went against the wishes of the family. Family pressure was intense. Jesus said it would be that way. He even felt it from his own family. We must realize that the message of Jesus is a disruptive message.

Rewards—Matthew 10:40–42

Whoever welcomes you welcomes me; and whoever welcomes me welcomes he who sent me. Whoever welcomes a prophet in the name of a prophet will receive a prophet's reward. And whoever receives a righteous man in the name of a righteous man will receive a righteous man's reward. Whoever gives even a cup of cold water to one of these little ones in the name of a disciple, I tell you the truth, will not lose his reward.

Jesus closes his second discourse with encouraging words about the positive reception that his disciples will receive and the reward they can expect. Although the mission will be tough, some people will welcome them as prophets and will receive a prophet's reward.

Conclusion

Jesus came preaching, teaching, and healing. He preached to the multitudes. He healed the sick in the towns and villages. He taught his disciples. He singled them out for specific lessons because his plan to win the world rested on their shoulders. He taught them about ministry and missions. Next, we will see, he taught them about discipleship and the cross.

End Notes
175. The author's own translation of Matthew is used throughout this chapter.
176. Carson, *The Expositor's Bible Commentary with the New International Version.*
177. This is why it is a good idea to have a working knowledge of Hebrew and Greek. If you can't work in the original languages, then you are at a disadvantage in terms of exegesis because you are one step away from the original text.
178. David Head, *Shout for Joy* (New York: Macmillan, 1962), 54.

Chapter 11

Jesus Prepares His Disciples for the Cross

As Jesus got closer to the cross, he spent more time away from the crowds with his circle of disciples. He specifically taught them about his crucifixion and his resurrection, but when Jesus described the cross, his disciples were slow to understand what he was saying.

The disciples had a preconceived idea of what the Messiah should be. They wanted a Messiah who was a warrior like King David and one who would advance the stature of Israel and Jerusalem like King Solomon. They wanted a sword-wielding Messiah who would ride into Jerusalem on a white stallion and kick the Romans out of their city and their land. They wanted freedom from Roman oppression and taxation. They were looking for a Messiah who would usher a time of peace and prosperity into the land. If they had to choose between peace and prosperity, they probably would have chosen prosperity. They were longing for a Messiah who would put food on the table and money in their pouches.

But Jesus was not going to be this type of Messiah. He was a spiritual King who inaugurated a spiritual kingdom. He did not come to kill Romans and rid the land of Roman occupation. Jesus came as a servant Messiah. He submitted to Roman occupation. The disciples expected something different in the Messiah. Therefore, Jesus took time to educate his followers about his mission, but his disciples were slow. They didn't understand. Perhaps they didn't want to.

So what did Jesus do? He kept explaining it to them. Not just once, not just twice, but over and over again. The fact is that the disciples never really comprehended what Jesus was trying to tell them until after his resurrection. Certainly not before his death. Jesus did try; he explained over and over to them the type of Messiah he was and the death that he would die. He kept working with his guys. Finally, they got it.

In a brilliant section in Mark's gospel (my favorite section in all the gospels), Mark takes us through this process of Jesus getting his disciples ready for the cross. This section opens and closes with a blind man. Between the two stories of the blind men, the disciples are blind to who Jesus is. In the first story, Jesus gives the blind man of Bethsaida a second touch of grace so that he can see clearly. This is what Jesus will do to his disciples throughout this section. He will give them a second and third touch of grace so that they can understand his mission. He prepares them for his death and his resurrection. Through these stories Mark is asking us to open our eyes to see Jesus as he really is.

The Yeast of the Pharisees and Herod—Mark 8:14–21, cf. Matthew 16:5–12

The disciples had forgotten to bring bread, except for one loaf they had with them in the boat. "Be careful," Jesus warned them. "Watch out for the yeast of the Pharisees and that of Herod."

They discussed this with one another and said, "It is because we have no bread."

Aware of their discussion, Jesus asked them: "Why are you talking about having no bread? Do you still not see or understand? Are your hearts hardened? Do you have eyes but fail to see, and ears but fail to hear? And don't you remember? When I broke the five loaves for the five thousand, how many basketfuls of pieces did you pick up?"

"Twelve," they replied.

"And when I broke the seven loaves for the four thousand, how many basketfuls of pieces did you pick up?"

They answered, "Seven."

He said to them, "Do you still not understand?"

The disciples often forgot things. Here they forgot bread. Over the next few chapters they will forget what Jesus teaches about his death and resurrection. They will also forget what type of Messiah Jesus was going to be, but he keeps teaching them and working with them.

Jesus warns his disciples of the yeast of the Pharisees and of Herod. The Pharisees and Herod both wanted to control people by a system they had created. This was very different from the kingdom that Jesus ushered into the world.

The disciples misunderstand Jesus. They think he is talking about literal yeast and literal bread. These next two chapters are about the disciples misunderstanding Jesus. They misunderstand what type of Messiah he will be, what type of death he will die, and what he means when he tells them, "In three days, I will return."

The words of Jesus in this section foreshadow the next two chapters. Jesus says, "Do you still not see or understand?" David McKenna writes, "After being witnesses and doers of miracles, they still are deaf, dumb, and blind to spiritual truth. How patient Jesus is with them."[179] This foreshadows the blind man of Bethsaida and blind Bartimaeus, who see Jesus better than his own disciples see him.

Jesus says, "Are your hearts hardened?" Their hearts will certainly appear to be hardened as Peter rebukes Jesus when Jesus predicts his death. Jesus calls Peter "Satan" because of the hardness of his dull heart and his lack of understanding. The disciples seem to have hard hearts when they argue about who will be greatest immediately after Jesus predicts his death for the second time. James and John appear to have hard hearts when, immediately after he has predicted his death for the third time, they ask Jesus to allow them to sit on his right and left when he comes into glory.

Jesus asks, "Do you have eyes but fail to see?" They certainly seem blind. Jesus heals two blind men in these chapters. At the end of the day, these two men see Jesus more clearly than the disciples do: They are blind, but they clearly see Jesus is the Messiah.

The Healing of a Blind Man at Bethsaida—Mark 8:22–26

They came to Bethsaida, and some people brought a blind man and begged Jesus to touch him. He took the blind man by the hand and led him outside the village. When he had spit on the man's eyes and put his hands on him, Jesus asked, "Do you see anything?"

He looked up and said, "I see people; they look like trees walking around."

Once more Jesus put his hands on the man's eyes. Then his eyes were opened, his sight was restored, and he saw everything clearly. Jesus sent him home, saying, "Don't go into the village."

This is one of two miracle stories that bookend a section in Mark's gospel where Jesus is emphasizing the nature of who he is as Messiah. He is also taking time in this section to teach his disciples how he must die and rise from the dead. The disciples don't understand. Mark uses the stories of these two blind men to highlight the blindness of the disciples.

Bethsaida was a fishing village north of Capernaum on the Sea of Galilee. It was part of the evangelical triangle—three cities that Jesus visited and taught often in his ministry, namely, Capernaum, Corazin, and Bethsaida. Some people brought a blind man to Jesus so that he could heal him. Jesus takes the blind man outside the village, probably to keep the miracle from becoming a public spectacle. He spits on the man's eyes, puts his hands on him, and asks, "Do you see anything?"

The man sees, but not clearly. He sees people, but they look like trees. This is the only miracle of Jesus where the person isn't healed instantly and completely. It seems strange that Mark would include this miracle.

After all, it might bring up questions about Jesus' authority and ability. Mark uses the story to teach a point about how Jesus works with the man to help him to see. Jesus will work with his disciples in the same way to help them see who he is. David McKenna writes, "Spiritual maturity is never instantaneous. Even though the person whom Christ forgives is free from sin, the growth line is just beginning."[180]

Jesus doesn't leave the man with blurred vision. He gives him a second touch of grace. He places his hand on the man's eyes a second time. This time, the man was able to see clearly. His sight was restored.

Mark uses this miracle story to frame what will happen next in his narrative. Jesus will tell his disciples who he is and what must happen to him. In the story before this one, Jesus asks his disciples, "Do you still not understand?" He also says they have eyes but fail to see. The disciples are like the blind man of Bethsaida. They need a second touch of grace. David McKenna explains:

> Mark, I believe, has yet another meaning in mind. He has just reported Jesus' question, "Having eyes, do you not see?..." (8:18). Ever so patiently, the Lord leads His disciples back through the miracles of feeding the multitudes so that their eyes will be opened to see who He is and understand what He does. Through the partial sight given to the blind man, the disciples see themselves. Slowly, their spiritual vision is clearing, but the message remains opaque and the Man remains a mystery. To see clearly and far, they need a second touch upon their eyes.[181]

Although his disciples miss it, Jesus continues to work with them.

Peter's Confession of Christ—Mark 8:27–30, cf. Matthew 16:13–20, Luke 9:18–21

> *Jesus and his disciples went on to the villages around Caesarea Philippi. On the way he asked them, "Who do people say I am?"*
>
> *They replied, "Some say John the Baptist; others say Elijah; and still others, one of the prophets."*
>
> *"But what about you?" he asked. "Who do you say I am?"*
>
> *Peter answered, "You are the Christ."*
>
> *Jesus warned them not to tell anyone about him.*

We reach the center point of Mark's gospel. This is where Mark has been taking his readers for the first eight chapters. Many scholars believe that this is the most crucial story in Mark's narrative, the pivot point. It is where Mark answers the question: "Who is Jesus?" and then begins to answer a second question: "How will Jesus be the Messiah?"

Jesus reveals who he is to his disciples: He is the Messiah. The disciples are happy to hear this revelation, but then Jesus begins to explain the type of Messiah that he will be. The disciples aren't ready for this revelation; they don't want to accept it. Therefore, Jesus will continue to explain it to them in the next couple of chapters. He will give them a second and third touch of grace.

Jesus takes his disciples twenty-five miles north from Bethsaida to the area of Caesarea Philippi. This is an idyllic setting at the base of Mt. Hermon with streams that feed the Jordan River. The town was build by Philip in honor of Caesar, thus the name, Caesarea Philippi. It was a bastion of foreign worship with a plethora of temples dedicated to foreign gods. These temples lined the base of Mt. Hermon. You can visit the ruins of these temples today and picture the scene from the first century.

The patron god of the city was Pan, the god of nature. The town was also called Panias, which in Aramaic (and Arabic) was corrupted to Banias. It was believed that behind the majestic temple dedicated to Caesar Augustus was the Gates of Hades. The temple backed up to a cave, and at the bottom of that cave were the gates to the Hadean realm (or so people believed). From the cave flowed a stream. Sacrifices were made in the temple and blood was thrown into the stream in the cave. If the blood flowed from the cave into the front of the temple, the sacrifice was accepted. If not, the sacrifice was refused. In Caesarea Philippi the worship of idols was the commerce of the town; it was literally built on the worship of false gods.

This was a fitting place for Jesus to reveal who he was to his disciples. He was different from the gods of the Roman religion; he was superior to those gods. Jesus was the Messiah, the Son of the living God, but he was a different Messiah from what the disciples were expecting.

Jesus asks his disciples, "Who do people say I am?" They give answers from what they have heard others say about Jesus, "John the Baptist, Elijah, one of the prophets." So Jesus says, "What about you?" He wants to hear what *they* think. Peter is quick to answer, "You are the Christ." Christ is the Greek equivalent of the Hebrew "Messiah." This was the Old Testament title for the "Anointed One" of God. It also means "King." Technically, Peter gets the answer right, but he doesn't really understand what type of Messiah Jesus was going to be.

Jesus warned his disciples not to tell anyone about him. This seems opposite of his mission, but Jesus did not want people thinking he was a nationalistic Messiah who had arrived in order to kick the Romans out of the land. Better for them to wait and see who he was through his death and resurrection.

Jesus Foretells His Own Death and Resurrection— Mark 8:31–33

He then began to teach them that the Son of Man must suffer many things and be rejected by the elders, chief priests and teachers of the law, and that he must be killed and after three days rise again. He spoke plainly about this, and Peter took him aside and began to rebuke him.

But when Jesus turned and looked at his disciples, he rebuked Peter. "Get behind me, Satan!" he said. "You do not have in mind the things of God, but the things of men."

Jesus asked, "Who do you say I am?" Peter answered correctly, "You are the Christ, the Son of the living God (Matthew 16:16)." But what type of Messiah would Jesus be? Mark spends the next half of his Gospel demonstrating what type of Messiah he was. He focuses on the question: "How would Jesus be Messiah?" David McKenna writes:

To human minds, the truth is a contradiction. The Christ who serves cannot be the Son of Man who suffers. So, when Jesus voices the paradox of truth openly and honestly, He finds Himself quite alone. The disciples slip back into their blindness and Satan goes on the offensive.[182]

Jesus began to teach them that the Son of Man must suffer many things, be rejected by the religious authorities, be killed, and after three days rise again. He was plain in his speaking. He wanted his disciples to understand what type of Messiah he would be—but they failed to understand.

Peter answered correctly when he said Jesus was the Messiah, but here we see that Peter really didn't understand what he was saying. After he hears Jesus' plain teaching on his death and resurrection, Peter takes Jesus aside and rebukes him.

Jesus turns to look at the disciples. He wants all of them to hear what he is about to say to Peter, who gets the worst rebuke that Jesus ever gave anyone: "Get behind me, Satan!" Peter isn't thinking like a disciple. He is thinking like Satan. Jesus says to him, "You do not have in mind the things of God, but the things of men." Anyone who doesn't accept Jesus as the suffering Messiah who must die on the cross is Satanic.

The disciples constantly stumbled over this topic—the death of Jesus. We will see Jesus predict his death two more times in the next two chapters, and each time the disciples fail to understand him. Mark clearly demonstrates the dullness of the disciples in this matter. He begins here with Peter.

The Cross and Self-Denial—Mark 8:34–9:1, cf. Matthew 16:24–28, Luke 9:23–27

> *Then he called the crowd to him along with his disciples and said: "If anyone would come after me, he must deny himself and take up his cross and follow me. For whoever wants to save his life will lose it, but whoever loses his life for me and for the gospel will save it. What good is it for a man to gain the whole world, yet forfeit his soul? Or what can a man give in exchange for his soul? If anyone is ashamed of me and my words in this adulterous and sinful generation, the Son of Man will be ashamed of him when he comes in his Father's glory with the holy angels."*
>
> *And he said to them, "I tell you the truth, some who are standing here will not taste death before they see the kingdom of God come with power."*

Jesus now looks at the crowds and his disciples and teaches them about discipleship. To be a disciple you must deny self, take up your cross, and follow.

Peter had just rebuked Jesus for predicting the cross. Now Jesus tells everyone ("If anyone") who wants to be his disciple that not only will he die, but they must die as well. Their death is a matter of self-denial. Aside from the physical cross and other forms of execution they will face in the future, the cross Jesus refers to here is figurative, symbolizing the death of one's own dreams and ambitions. To save your life, you have to lose it. You must die to self-centeredness. This will become a major theme of Jesus from this point on. He is teaching his disciples the cost of discipleship.

Jesus emphasizes his point by saying that he/she must take up his/her cross and follow him. Bearing one's cross is a symbol of dying to self. *The Bible Knowledge Commentary* writes:

> Cross-bearing was not an established Jewish metaphor. But the figure was appropriate in Roman-occupied Palestine. It brought to mind the sight of a condemned man who was forced to demonstrate his submission to Rome by carrying part of his cross through the city to his place of execution. Thus "to take up one's cross" was to demonstrate publicly one's submission/obedience to the authority against which he had previously rebelled.[183]

Jesus goes on to say, "If you want to save your life, you have to lose it." "Life" here is *psyche*. It can also be translated as "self." If you want to find your true self, the only way to do that is to lose yourself in Jesus.

Jesus also heightens the role of the Son of Man here. The "Son of Man" is Jesus' favorite way to refer to himself. It is a theologically neutral term to the disciples; therefore, it is less likely that they will misconstrue its meaning. The term "Messiah" was a theologically and politically loaded term. Therefore, Jesus refers to himself most often as the Son of Man.

Here he notes that the Son of Man will initiate the judgment scene. He will come with his angels to judge the deeds of humanity. Since Jesus will oversee judgment, it makes sense to make him Lord in the here and now. It makes sense to make his standard our standard every single day.

Jesus makes reference to the kingdom of God coming in glory. He says this will occur while some of the disciples (and the crowd) are still alive ("some who are standing here will not taste death"). Therefore, the kingdom of God coming in power will be visible to some of them.

We have to understand this reference in relation to other instances when Jesus speaks of the kingdom as being present in his person. For example, Luke 11:20: "But if I drive out demons by the finger of God, then the kingdom of God has come to you."

Jesus could be speaking of two different manifestations of the kingdom. In Luke 11:20, the kingdom is present with Jesus because he is King. The kingdom is also future because the kingdom will be manifest in the church. Jesus could be talking about the future arrival of the kingdom coming in the church in Acts 2.

However, there is a different way of understanding Mark 9:1. Jesus could be speaking of something that would happen in his ministry with the disciples: He could be speaking of what will happen in the story that Mark includes next in his narrative. Verse 2 intimates that the stories are connected because Mark writes, "After six days Jesus took..." Some of his disciples were alive to experience Jesus being transfigured in glory, proving that he was a greater lawgiver than Moses and a greater prophet than Elijah. Jesus was King of Kings and Lord of Lords. I believe that in Mark 9:1 Jesus is referring to his transfiguration.

The Transfiguration—Mark 9:2–8, cf. Matthew 17:1–8, Luke 9:28–36a

After six days Jesus took Peter, James and John with him and led them up a high mountain, where they were all alone. There he was transfigured before them. His clothes became dazzling white, whiter than anyone in the world could bleach them. And there appeared before them Elijah and Moses, who were talking with Jesus.

Peter said to Jesus, "Rabbi, it is good for us to be here. Let us put up three shelters—one for you, one for Moses and one for Elijah." (He did not know what to say, they were so frightened.)

Then a cloud appeared and enveloped them, and a voice came from the cloud: "This is my Son, whom I love. Listen to him!"

Suddenly, when they looked around, they no longer saw anyone with them except Jesus.

Jesus chose an inner circle from the disciples, and he allowed them to see things that the other nine did not. Peter, James, and John were taken on a high mountain to witness the transfiguration of Jesus. A practical point that can be drawn from this scene is that Jesus had friends, but he also had his inner circle—some very close friends with whom he shared more intimate parts of his life.

Each of us can only get close to so many people. We should have a plethora of friendships in the kingdom, but we should also have some friends that we are close to in a special way and with whom we can share our inmost feelings. These friends become our counselors. These are the friendships that we trust and value most of all. Although Jesus did not depend on his inner circle in the same way that we do, the fact that he picked out a few from the twelve with whom to share more intimate times is a principle that we can imitate.

For many years the high mountain in this passage was identified with Mt. Tabor close to the Sea of Galilee. This is the traditional site for the location of the transfiguration. Mt. Tabor is barely a mountain, and it certainly is not a high mountain. The last location of Jesus before the transfiguration was Caesarea Philippi in Northern Galilee. There is a high mountain close to Caesarea Philippi, namely, Mt. Hermon. Mt. Hermon is the highest point in Israel, rising up to 9,000 feet above sea level. It is much more likely that this was the site of the transfiguration.

The word for "transfigured" is the Greek *metemorpho*. This word means "to change," or "to transform." We derive our English word "metamorphosis" from this word. It is also used in the Bible to describe the change that occurs in a person's life when she or he becomes a disciple of Jesus. That person is transformed.

Moses and Elijah appeared on the mountain with Jesus. The voice of God was heard declaring, "This is my son whom I love. I am pleased with him. Listen to him (Matthew 17:5)." Moses represents the law and Elijah represents the prophets. God singles out Jesus and declares that we should listen to him; that is to say, Jesus is above the law and the prophets.

Peter misunderstands the significance of what is going on. He sees, but he is still blind, in this case, blinded by fear. The text says he did not know what to say because of his fear. Fear does that: It causes us to lose perspective. Jesus always fought to drive fear out of men's hearts.

How did Peter respond to the transfiguration? He refers to Jesus as "Rabbi." What happened to the earlier declaration that Jesus was the Christ? Peter doesn't understand the meaning of what he is seeing. Always a man of action, he says, "Let us put up three shelters." This is to say that Jesus is on an equal plane with Moses and Elijah. But Jesus is greater than Moses and Elijah; he is greater than the law or the prophets. This is the point of the transfiguration of Jesus. Peter sees what is happening, but he is blind to its real meaning.

This time a voice from a cloud gives Peter a second touch of grace. The voice is the *Kol Yahweh*, the voice of Yahweh, which says, "This is my Son, whom I love. Listen to him!" God places his stamp of authority on Jesus, who is greater than the law or the prophets. "Listen to him" is synonymous with "obey him."

Elijah and the Suffering Son of Man—Mark 9:9–13, cf. Matthew 17:9–13, Luke 9:36b

> As they were coming down the mountain, Jesus gave them orders not to tell anyone what they had seen until the Son of Man had risen from the dead. They kept the matter to themselves, discussing what "rising from the dead" meant.
>
> And they asked him, "Why do the teachers of the law say that Elijah must come first?"
>
> Jesus replied, "To be sure, Elijah does come first, and restores all things. Why then is it written that the Son of Man must suffer much and be rejected? But I tell you, Elijah has come, and they have done to him everything they wished, just as it is written about him."

Jesus again warns the disciples not to tell anyone what they have seen until he has risen from the dead. This is the last warning to silence mentioned in Mark. It is given with a time limit, namely, the resurrection.

Notice that while they were walking they discussed the meaning of "rising from the dead." They still did not understand. Even after the transfiguration, they were still blind.

This reference to the Son of Man brings the role of Elijah to the minds of the disciples. They want to know, "Isn't Elijah to come first?" Jesus answers, "Elijah does come first," in fact, "Elijah has come," and "they have done to him everything they wished." Jesus links the fate of Elijah and John the Baptist with his own fate, to suffer much and be rejected. Peter, James, and John are groping to understand what happened at the transfiguration with the appearance of Moses and Elijah. Although they fail to understand, Jesus continues to work with them.

The Healing of a Boy with an Evil Spirit—Mark 9:14–29, cf. Matthew 17:14–20, Luke 9:37–43a

> When they came to the other disciples, they saw a large crowd around them and the teachers of the law arguing with them. As soon as all the people saw Jesus, they were overwhelmed with wonder and ran to greet him.
>
> "What are you arguing with them about?" he asked.
>
> A man in the crowd answered, "Teacher, I brought you my son, who is possessed

by a spirit that has robbed him of speech. Whenever it seizes him, it throws him to the ground. He foams at the mouth, gnashes his teeth and becomes rigid. I asked your disciples to drive out the spirit, but they could not."

"O unbelieving generation," Jesus replied, "how long shall I stay with you? How long shall I put up with you? Bring the boy to me."

So they brought him. When the spirit saw Jesus, it immediately threw the boy into a convulsion. He fell to the ground and rolled around, foaming at the mouth.

Jesus asked the boy's father, "How long has he been like this?"

"From childhood," he answered. "It has often thrown him into fire or water to kill him. But if you can do anything, take pity on us and help us."

"'If you can'?" said Jesus. "Everything is possible for him who believes."

Immediately the boy's father exclaimed, "I do believe; help me overcome my unbelief!"

When Jesus saw that a crowd was running to the scene, he rebuked the evil spirit. "You deaf and mute spirit," he said, "I command you, come out of him and never enter him again."

The spirit shrieked, convulsed him violently and came out. The boy looked so much like a corpse that many said, "He's dead." But Jesus took him by the hand and lifted him to his feet, and he stood up.

After Jesus had gone indoors, his disciples asked him privately, "Why couldn't we drive it out?"

He replied, "This kind can come out only by prayer."

This next story, the healing of the boy with the evil spirit, continues the theme that Mark has been stressing in this section—the revelation of who Jesus was and the failure of the disciples to understand.

Jesus returns from the transfiguration to find the rest of his disciples surrounded by a crowd and arguing with the scribes. He inquires as to the subject of their argument.

A man reveals that he has brought his boy to the disciples, but they failed to heal him. Back in 6:7, Jesus had given the disciples authority over evil spirits. They should have been able to help this boy, but they lacked faith, and their lack of faith is later connected with a lack of prayer (verse 29).

The plight of the father illustrates that this is a hopeless situation. The boy is demon possessed. He is mute because of the demon. It causes him to fall down, foam at the mouth, and grow rigid. The demon has troubled the boy since childhood. It has even tried to kill him by throwing him into fire and water. This is a terrible situation. Jesus' disciples had already tried to cure the boy, but were unable. Mark highlights the fact that Jesus can help in situations that appear to be helpless.

The man says to Jesus, "If you can do anything, take pity on us and help us." Jesus' reply to this is: "If you can? Everything is possible for him who believes." Jesus says, "There are no 'if's' in faith." The father's replies,

"I do believe; help me overcome my unbelief!" He is asking for a second touch of grace. He believes, but not enough to drive out this demon. He needs the second touch that only Jesus can give.

The fact that the disciples were unable to help the boy demonstrates that they did not believe and were still blind. Jesus rebukes them for their lack of faith. He calls their generation both unfaithful and perverse, and adds, "How long must I be with you? How long must I put up with you?" (Matthew 17:17). Jesus could tolerate many things from his disciples—ingratitude, a lack of compassion, pride, selfish ambition—but there was one thing that Jesus could not tolerate: a lack of faith.

Why was this? Our lack of faith keeps God from powerfully working in our lives. God often works in spite of our pride and in spite of our lack of compassion, but he will not work through us if we lack faith. Faith is *the* crucial ingredient to allow God to work through us.

Jesus rebukes the evil spirit and heals the boy. The boy looks dead, but in fact, he is more alive than he has been for years.

Jesus and the disciples enter a house and the disciples want to know why they were unable to help the boy. Jesus gives them a second touch of grace through teaching. He says, "This kind can only come out by prayer." The disciples had not faithfully connected to God in prayer over the boy. Perhaps they had trusted past success? While Jesus was up on the mountain during the transfiguration, the disciples might have grown lax in their prayers.

It is so easy to forget our connection to God in prayer. Jesus reminds them of the importance of this and that their lack of faith is connected to their lack of prayer. David McKenna writes:

> The lesson is profound because it is so simple. We can be called and gifted, prepared and ordained, to be the disciples of Jesus Christ, but if we do not remain in constant contact with the source of our power, we will fail in crisis.... When the father brings his demon-possessed son to the disciples for healing, they fail in the face of a "critical incident" because they lack the resources of spiritual power that are sustained only through constant prayer."[184]

Jesus Again Foretells His Own Death and Resurrection— Mark 9:30–32, cf. Matthew 17:22–23, Luke 9:43b–45

They left that place and passed through Galilee. Jesus did not want anyone to know where they were, because he was teaching his disciples. He said to them, "The Son of Man is going to be betrayed into the hands of men. They will kill him, and after three days he will rise." But they did not understand what he meant and were afraid to ask him about it.

Jesus spends time teaching his disciples. The text says, "Jesus did not want anyone to know where they were." He wanted to give the disciples some focused attention. We don't know what Jesus concentrated on in his teaching, except we do know that Jesus again predicts his death and resurrection. This is the second time he has spoken to his disciples about his death. He reiterates, "The Son of Man is going to be betrayed into the hands of men. They will kill him, and after three days he will rise." Jesus is trying to prepare his disciples for what is about to come.

Jesus kept repeating his lessons for his disciples. We learn through repetition. When I studied Kung Fu, one of our mantras was, "Repetition is the mother of skill. The more you do it, the better you get." The disciples were slow learners, but Jesus was a patient teacher. David McKenna writes:

> The first time that He makes this prediction, the disciples stop their ears and Peter rebukes Him. Yet, the influence of His words remains just below the level of consciousness, ready for recall. After the Transfiguration, Jesus brings the subject up again, piquing the curiosity of Peter, James, and John. When He takes the epileptic boy by the hand and lifts him up from apparent death, the disciples see a symbol of the Resurrection, so when Jesus repeats His prophecy, He tugs at the thread of continuity between His teaching and the events which the disciples witnessed. It cannot be said too frequently: the teaching of truth must be a repetitive and consistent experience engaging mind, emotion, and will in all the aspects of life."[185]

Do the disciples finally grasp what Jesus is saying? Not yet. We see their lack of understanding in the discussion that follows.

Who Is the Greatest?—Mark 9:33–37, cf. Matthew 18:1–5, Luke 9:46–48

> They came to Capernaum. When he was in the house, he asked them, "What were you arguing about on the road?" But they kept quiet because on the way they had argued about who was the greatest.
>
> Sitting down, Jesus called the Twelve and said, "If anyone wants to be first, he must be the very last, and the servant of all."
>
> He took a little child and had him stand among them. Taking him in his arms, he said to them, "Whoever welcomes one of these little children in my name welcomes me; and whoever welcomes me does not welcome me but the one who sent me."

Immediately after Jesus predicts his death for the second time, where are the minds of the disciples? They are arguing about which one of them was the greatest. How blind can they be? Jesus doesn't rebuke them; he instructs them.

Who is the greatest? This question has posed problems for humanity for centuries. Jesus takes time to teach the disciples about the sin of pride. The pursuit of greatness has caused countries to be destroyed and has led people to cheat and defraud others. It has caused uncountable heartache and ruin.

Greatness in itself is not wrong. Jesus was a great person, and he did nothing wrong. The early apostles were great men. They stumbled at times, but they got back up and accomplished great things for God.

Jesus teaches his disciples about greatness. He says, "If anyone wants to be first, he must be the very last, and the servant of all." "Servant" is not δοῦλος/*doulos* or slave, but it is διάκονος/diakonos, our word for minister or deacon. A slave has to serve; a diakonos chooses to serve. If you want to be first, learn how to serve. We must learn to be last.

To illustrate his point, Jesus brings a child into their circle. He puts his arms around the child and welcomes him. In that society, a child had no place in a circle of adults and certainly no place in the discussion of a rabbi with his disciples, but Jesus opens his circle to those who have no place. In fact, he welcomes them with open arms. He is teaching his disciples to do the same. In doing so, they would become great.

Do we open our arms wide for those marginalized by society?

Whoever Is Not Against Us Is for Us—Mark 9:38–41, cf. Luke 9:49–50

> *"Teacher," said John, "we saw a man driving out demons in your name and we told him to stop, because he was not one of us."*
>
> *"Do not stop him," Jesus said. "No one who does a miracle in my name can in the next moment say anything bad about me, for whoever is not against us is for us. I tell you the truth, anyone who gives you a cup of water in my name because you belong to Christ will certainly not lose his reward. . . .* [186]

John brings an issue to Jesus. He reports that they stopped a man who was driving out demons because he was not one of them. Look at the contrast here—this man was successful in driving out demons while the nine were not. Here is someone outside the circle of disciples who seems to have more faith and a better understanding of Jesus than the disciples, who are still blind.

Jesus Predicts His Death for the Third Time—Mark 10:32–34, cf. Matthew 20:17–19, Luke 18:31–34

> *They were on their way up to Jerusalem, with Jesus leading the way, and the disciples were astonished, while those who followed were afraid. Again he took the Twelve aside*

*and told them what was going to happen to him. "We are going up to Jerusalem,"
he said, "and the Son of Man will be betrayed to the chief priests and teachers of the
law. They will condemn him to death and will hand him over to the Gentiles, who will
mock him and spit on him, flog him and kill him. Three days later he will rise."*

Now Jesus leads the disciples to Jerusalem, the city where prophets
go to die. He leads them to the cross.

Why were the disciples astonished and the crowd afraid? Perhaps
the disciples thought Jesus was leading them to triumph in Jerusalem
while the crowds understood that Jesus was headed to his death? If so,
then Mark demonstrates how the disciples are still blind to Jesus' mission
and purpose.

Jesus takes the twelve aside to instruct them about what would soon
happen to him. This is the third prediction of his death. He is more clear
and precise in the details surrounding his coming death than he was in
the earlier predictions. He uses eight future-tense verbs to describe what
will happen to him in Jerusalem. The future tense implies certainty. These
aren't conditional words; this was going to happen. Jesus tells them, "I'm
going up to be betrayed, condemned, handed over, mocked, spit upon,
flogged, and killed. Three days later I will rise." It's very difficult to miss
what Jesus is saying here. Surely the disciples must have understood what
was about to happen to Jesus. According to the response of James and
John in the next story, they still didn't understand. They were still blind.

The Request of James and John—Mark 10:35–45, cf. Matthew 20:20–28

*Then James and John, the sons of Zebedee, came to him. "Teacher," they said, "we want
you to do for us whatever we ask."*

"What do you want me to do for you?" he asked.

*They replied, "Let one of us sit at your right and the other at your left in your
glory."*

*"You don't know what you are asking," Jesus said. "Can you drink the cup I drink
or be baptized with the baptism I am baptized with?"*

"We can," they answered.

*Jesus said to them, "You will drink the cup I drink and be baptized with the bap-
tism I am baptized with, but to sit at my right or left is not for me to grant. These places
belong to those for whom they have been prepared."*

*When the ten heard about this, they became indignant with James and John.
Jesus called them together and said, "You know that those who are regarded as rulers of
the Gentiles lord it over them, and their high officials exercise authority over them. Not
so with you. Instead, whoever wants to become great among you must be your servant,
and whoever wants to be first must be slave of all. For even the Son of Man did not come*

to be served, but to serve, and to give his life as a ransom for many."

James and John ask Jesus to seat them on his right and left in glory. Do they still think that when Jesus gets to Jerusalem that he will establish an earthly kingdom? They seem to.

Jesus asks them, "Can you drink the cup I drink or be baptized with the baptism I am baptized with?"

They answer, "Yes, we got this." Were they asleep when Jesus said that he would be mocked, spit upon, flogged, and killed? No, they weren't asleep. They were dull, blind. Perhaps they thought Jesus was speaking of initiating some type of apocalyptic battle to usher in the kingdom, but Jesus was speaking of the cross.

The other ten become indignant with James and John. They don't seem to be upset that James and John made the request, but that they didn't think of asking first. Jesus pulls them together and does more teaching, as he constantly did. He tells them they shouldn't look for positions of authority like the Gentiles do. Instead, they must become servants. Jesus will set them this example when he dies on the cross.

Blind Bartimaeus Receives His Sight—Mark 10:46–11:1a, cf. Matthew 20:29–21:1, Luke 18:35–19:29

> *Then they came to Jericho. As Jesus and his disciples, together with a large crowd, were leaving the city, a blind man, Bartimaeus (that is, the Son of Timaeus), was sitting by the roadside begging. When he heard that it was Jesus of Nazareth, he began to shout, "Jesus, Son of David, have mercy on me!"*
>
> *Many rebuked him and told him to be quiet, but he shouted all the more, "Son of David, have mercy on me!"*
>
> *Jesus stopped and said, "Call him."*
>
> *So they called to the blind man, "Cheer up! On your feet! He's calling you." Throwing his cloak aside, he jumped to his feet and came to Jesus.*
>
> *"What do you want me to do for you?" Jesus asked him.*
>
> *The blind man said, "Rabbi, I want to see."*
>
> *"Go," said Jesus, "your faith has healed you." Immediately he received his sight and followed Jesus along the road.*
>
> *As they approached Jerusalem...*

Jesus leads his disciples to Jericho, the lowest inhabited city on the earth. As they were leaving and heading to Jerusalem, a blind man, Bartimaeus, hears that Jesus is approaching. He begins to shout, "Jesus, son of David, have mercy on me!" Although Bartimaeus is blind, he sees Jesus more clearly than any of the disciples do, referring to him as the Son of David. What is the significance of that title? It says that Jesus is King. This is the first time that this title, "Son of David," has been used in the open. A blind man who sees Jesus better than anyone else makes this declaration. Some tried to quiet Bartimaeus, but he shouted all the more. Jesus calls Bartimaeus to him and heals him. He says, "Go, your faith has healed you." Then Mark records that immediately he received his sight. Faith and sight go hand in hand. The disciples failed to see Jesus because of their lack of faith. Here, a blind man sees Jesus clearly because of his faith and then he is given physical sight.

Mark mentions that Bartimaeus followed Jesus "along the road." Where was the road going? To Jerusalem. What would happen to Jesus in Jerusalem? Suffering and a cross. When Bartimaeus follows Jesus, where will the road take him? To suffering and a cross. That is the ultimate destination of every disciple of Jesus.

Jesus worked with his disciples to get them to see what a blind man saw. He was the Messiah, but he was the Messiah who would die on a cross. What did that mean for his disciples? To be a disciple of Jesus, you must be willing to pick up your cross and follow.

Jesus gave his disciples a second and third touch of grace so that they would see who he was, but they remained blind. Let's make sure we aren't so dull in our faith that we fail to see Jesus as he really is. He is the suffering Messiah who died on the cross for the sins of the world.

Later the disciples would understand, but they had to experience the death and resurrection of Jesus to comprehend what he was saying. Jesus now takes them on that journey.

End Notes

179. D. L. McKenna and L. J. Ogilvie, *The Preacher's Commentary Series, vol. 25, Mark* (Nashville, Tennessee: Thomas Nelson Inc., 1982), 165.

180. Ibid., 167.

181. Ibid., 167–168

182. Ibid., 173

183. J. F. Walvoord, R. B. Zuck and Dallas Theological Seminary. "Mk 8:34" in *The Bible Knowledge Commentary: An Exposition of the Scriptures* (Wheaton, IL: Victor Books, 1983).

184. McKenna and Ogilvie, 184

185. Ibid.

186. These three dots indicate that we are about to skip to Mark 10:32. Mark includes Jesus' warning against causing others to sin, Jesus' teaching on divorce and remarriage, the incident of Jesus and the little children, and the conversation between Jesus and the rich young ruler. Although these are important sections in Mark's gospel, they would be better treated in a commentary on Mark. I want to follow Mark's thread concerning Jesus' predictions of his death and resurrection and the response to that teaching by his disciples.

The Beginning of the Passion Week: The Parables of the Passion; Jesus Answers His Opposition

We turn now to the beginning of the Passion of Jesus. Passion means "suffering." We often think that Jesus' suffering began when he was arrested on the eve of his crucifixion, but Jesus' sufferings began when he entered Jerusalem before the Passover.

Jesus' last week was spent in and around Jerusalem. The time was April, six days before the Passover. He entered Jerusalem from the old Jericho road, which ascended from 1,300 feet below sea level to 2,500 feet above sea level and was seventeen miles long. He entered the city during the day, teaching and preaching. During the night, he stayed in Bethany on the southeastern slope of the Mount of Olives. This was the home of Lazarus, Mary, and Martha. It is very likely that Jesus stayed at their home during this last week. Bethany afforded Jesus a beautiful view of the city of Jerusalem. It is still the most spectacular entrance to the city. He arrived in Bethany on Friday before the Sabbath and made his triumphal entrance into Jerusalem on Sunday.

He faced opposition that entire week. The religious authorities were laying a trap for him. They were gathering false witnesses to bring charges of treason against him. It was during the last few days before the Passover when the opposition toward Jesus really grew intense. Throughout the ministry of Jesus, he encountered opposition—from Herod the Great at his birth, from Satan at the beginning of his ministry, from his own family members, and from the Jewish religious leaders. Why? Jesus was a rabbi who did not act like a traditional rabbi. He was a good Jew, but he was an unconventional rabbi.

To the Sadducees who had the most political clout, Jesus was a problem because he drew large crowds to him. They were jealous. Jesus' movement was a growing one, and this frightened the Sadducees. If the movement got out of control, the Romans would blame them. If Jesus drew too many people to his favor, then they would lose authority. To them, Jesus was a false messiah who had to be stopped.

What did Jesus do that upset the Pharisees? He didn't cling to their Sabbath traditions. He exposed their hypocrisy. His implicit and explicit claims of deity also upset them. People marveled at his teaching, and this made them jealous. Jesus didn't hold to social conventions. He ate with sinners and spoke to women. He cleansed the temple. He spoke his mind to the Pharisees, and on more than one occasion he embarrassed them. The Pharisees could not tolerate this, so they colluded with the Herodians (a secular group that they disdained) in order to see Jesus executed.

The Triumphal Entry—Matthew 21:1–11, cf. Mark 11:1–11, Luke 19:29–44, John 12:12–19

> When they came near Jerusalem, they came into Bethphage located on the Mt. of Olives. Jesus sent two of his disciples, saying, "Go into the village and immediately you will find a donkey tied there and a colt with him. Untie them and bring them to me. And if anyone says anything to you, just say to him, 'The Lord needs them.' And he will immediately send them. This happened that the word of the prophet might be fulfilled:
>
> > Tell the daughter of Zion,
> > Behold the King comes to you
> > Humble and riding on a donkey
> > And on a colt, the foal of a donkey.
>
> His disciples went and did just as Jesus directed them. They brought the donkey and the colt and placed garments on them and he sat on them. A very large crowd spread their garments on the road, and others cut branches from the trees and spread them on the road. The crowds that went ahead of him and followed him cried out, saying:
>
> > Hosanna to the Son of David;
> > Blessed is he who comes in the name of the Lord.
> > Hosanna in the highest.
>
> And he went into Jerusalem. The whole city was in turmoil, asking, "Who is this?" And the crowds declared, "He is the prophet, Jesus of Nazareth in Galilee."[187]

Jesus entered Jerusalem from Bethany. He sent two of his disciples ahead to Bethphage to acquire a donkey and a colt. Since the colt was young, the older animal was needed to guide it. Jesus is preparing for his entrance into Jerusalem. When someone inquired about the animals, the disciples were to respond, "The Lord needs them." This implies that the owner of the animals was also a disciple of Jesus.

Jesus did not ride into Jerusalem on a stallion or a regal battle horse. He came into the city of peace on a symbol of peace.

This event must be understood as a prophetic symbol of the king entering his capital. Jesus entered Jerusalem as a messianic king, but not the king for whom the people had hoped and prayed. Jesus was no military king with a standing army and weapons. Jesus was a Messiah of peace. He was a humble, servant Messiah.

The passage goes on to say that garments were placed on the animals and on the road. People also cut branches from trees and set them on the road. This was a traditional way to welcome a king or an august visitor into a town.

They also cried out *Hosanna*, which literally means "Save us." By the first century this term had become a note of praise, "Praise to the God who saves." When the crowd says, "Hosanna to the Son of David," this was a nationalistic cry for a new king. It is very likely that the crowd was hoping to propel Jesus toward declaring his earthly kingship in the lineage of David as a military king. It's not likely that they were embracing him as the Messiah of peace.

The title "Son of David" shows that there were some who understood that Jesus was the Messiah. The phrase "he who comes in the name of the Lord" also points toward the messianic nature of Jesus. Since the crowds changed these shouts of joy into shouts of derision in a few short days, it is clear that they did not understand the type of Messiah that Jesus was.

Jesus probably entered the city at what is today known as St. Stephen's Gate or the Lion's Gate on the northeastern corner of the city. The crowds were stirred to excitement as he entered the city, and many wanted to know who he was. The followers of Jesus identified him as a prophet from Nazareth in Galilee.

Here we have the beginning of the coronation of Jesus as King, but the coronation leads not to a golden throne in a majestic palace on a hillside in Jerusalem. It leads to a cross, and his crown would be a crown of thorns. Jesus would become king through his suffering.

Jesus Cleanses the Temple—Matthew 21:12–17, cf. Mark 11:15–18, Luke 19:45–48

Jesus went into the temple and he cast out all who were buying and selling in the temple, and he turned over the tables of the moneychangers and the seats of those selling doves. He said to them, "It has been written:

'My house shall be called a house of prayer
But you have made it a den of robbers.'"

> *The blind and the lame came to him in the temple, and he healed them. The chief priests and scribes saw the amazing things he did and heard the children crying out in the temple: "Hosanna to the Son of David." They became angry and said to him, "You hear what they are saying!"*
>
> *But Jesus said to them, "Yes. Have you not read—out of the mouths of children and infants you have prepared praise?" And he left them. He went out of the city to Bethany and spent the night there.*

The Synoptic Gospels place the cleansing of the temple at the end of Jesus' ministry, while John places this event at the beginning of his ministry (John 2:13–22). Most scholars believe that Jesus only cleansed the temple once and that John placed the cleansing at a different place in his gospel for theological reasons. Jesus could have cleansed the temple twice; he could have cleansed it to inaugurate his ministry and three years later cleansed it again to begin the Passion Week.

The outer court of the temple was the Court of the Gentiles. It is the only place where the Gentiles (God-fearers) could go to worship in the temple area, but the outer court of the Gentiles had been transformed from a place of prayer to a market. The religious authorities placed money tables and market stalls close to the Royal Stoa at the southern wall of the temple. The moneychangers exchanged Greek and Roman coins into temple currency and charged for their services. They also sold sacrifices that were required of the pilgrims who had come to worship. Many brought their own sacrifices on the journey to the temple. They were animals that they had raised and were affordable sacrifices, but these would be found unworthy. The pilgrims were then charged exorbitant prices for worthy sacrifices. Thus the temple had become a "den of robbers" instead of a "house of prayer."

After Jesus cleansed the temple, the blind and lame came to him and he healed them, then the children were praising God saying, "Hosanna to the Son of David." This infuriated the chief priests. They wanted Jesus to quiet the crowd. He answered them by referring to Psalm 8:2. God has prepared this praise to come from children and infants. If God prepared the praise, who are they to try and stop it? Jesus then goes to Bethany to spend the night.

Jesus Curses the Fig Tree—Matthew 21:18–22, cf. Mark 11:12–14

> *In the morning, when he returned to the city, he was hungry. He saw a fig tree on the side of the road and he approached it and found nothing on it except leaves, and he said, "May you never bear fruit again." Immediately the fig tree withered.*

> When the disciples saw this, they were amazed and said, "This tree withered immediately. How is that possible?"
>
> Jesus answered, "I tell you the truth—if you have faith and do not doubt, not only will you do what was done to this fig tree, but you can say to this mountain, 'Go be thrown into the sea,' and it will be done. Whatever you request in a faithful prayer, you will receive."

Matthew places the cursing of the fig tree on the morning after the cleansing of the temple. Mark splits the story in half as a framework for the cleansing of the temple. According to Mark, Jesus curses the fig tree, cleanses the temple, and then teaches about the withered fig tree. Some scholars believe that Mark is following an exact chronology of the events where Jesus visits the temple on Sunday and cleanses the temple on Monday. They think Matthew is using a topical approach and condenses the events.

Which Gospel writer is correct, Mark or Matthew? Some scholars maintain that both are correct. Mark is right chronologically and Matthew is correct topically. We use the same freedom in our writing today. Other scholars say that Matthew agrees with Mark and places the cleansing of the temple on Monday. But Matthew does not mention the cursing of the fig tree on the day before; he includes the cursing and the withering of the fig tree together on Tuesday morning. His lack of concern for the exact chronology does not mean he is mistaken. He is trimming, condensing, and abbreviating Mark's account for topical reasons.

Jesus was hungry, and he approached a fig tree looking for fruit. By April, the fig tree should have begun to produce fruit that would ripen by August. Although this fruit was not highly desirable, it was edible. D.A. Carson writes:

> That it was not the season for figs explains why Jesus went to this particular tree, which stood out because it was in leaf. Its leaves advertised that it was bearing, but the advertisement was false. Jesus, unable to satisfy his hunger, saw the opportunity of teaching a memorable object lesson and cursed the tree, not because it was not bearing fruit, whether in season or out, but because it made a show of life that promised fruit yet was bearing none.[188]

Because the tree was barren, Jesus cursed it, and it immediately withered. The disciples were astonished at how quickly the tree withered. Jesus used this occasion to teach them about faith. If they had faith and didn't doubt, they could do what he did. In fact, they could say to a mountain "be thrown in the sea," and it would happen. This is the power of faithful prayer.

Many wonder why Jesus would curse the fig tree. Jesus performed a prophetic symbol here. He acted out a parable. He used the tree to teach his disciples about faith. The barren tree represented barren Israel. The Jews should have had faith in Jesus, but they didn't. Since they didn't, God would curse them, but those who believed (had confidence) in Jesus would be able to do amazing things.

Jesus Squares Off Against the Religious Authorities— Matthew 21:23–22:46

This is one of my favorite sections in Matthew's gospel. The religious authorities attempt to trap Jesus by asking him questions. The questions come from many different directions as different types of religious authorities question him. Each time, Jesus baffles them with his answer. At the end of their questions, Jesus asks them a question. He goes on the offensive, then the questions stop. Mark places these questions on Tuesday of the Passion Week.

The Authority of Jesus Questioned—21:23–27, cf. Mark 11:27–32, Luke 20:1–6

> When Jesus entered the temple courts, the chief priests and the elders of the people came to him as he was teaching and said, "By what authority are you doing these things and who gave you this authority?"
>
> Jesus answered, "I will ask you a question. If you answer me, I will tell you by what authority I am doing these things. The baptism of John—from where did it come—heaven or man?"
>
> They argued with one another saying, "If we say, 'From heaven,' he will say to us, 'Why did you not believe him?' If we say, 'From men'—we fear the people for they think of John as a prophet."
>
> So they answered Jesus, "We don't know."
>
> He said to them, "Neither will I tell you by what authority I do these things."

The chief priests and elders approached Jesus seeking his authority for his actions in regard to the events of the triumphal entry, the cleansing of the temple, and the healing in the temple court. These priests represented the Sanhedrin who had authority over the temple area. Jesus used the rabbinical formula and answered a question by asking a question. He asked them if the baptism of John was from heaven or from man. The religious authorities had to step aside and discuss the answer to this question. Jesus had left them with no out. If they said "from heaven," then they should have followed John. Also, John pointed to Jesus so they should follow Jesus. If they said "from men," then the crowd would be upset. So they answered, "We don't know." Since they wouldn't answer Jesus' question, he did not tell them by what authority he had done these things.

The Question about Paying Taxes—Matthew 22:15–22, cf. Mark 12:13–17, Luke 20:20–26)[189]

> Then the Pharisees went and planned how they might trap Jesus in his words. And they sent their disciples, with the Herodians, saying, "Teacher, we know that you are honest and you teach the way of God in truth and you are not anyone's pawn because you are not partial to anyone. Tell us, therefore, what do you think—is it lawful to pay taxes to Caesar or not?"
>
> But Jesus knew the evil they planned, and he said, "Why do you test me, you hypocrites? Show me the coin used for the tax." They brought him a denarius. He asked them, "Whose image is this and whose inscription is on it?"
>
> "Caesar's," they answered.
>
> "Then give to Caesar what is Caesar's, and to God what is God's," he said. When they heard this, they were amazed. And they departed from him.

Jesus has told three parables directed at the Jewish religious authorities. Different sects of the Jews now bombard Jesus with questions in an attempt to trap him. They hope to engage him in an argument that will expose a flaw in his character. The word "trap" was used in hunting, referring to trapping or snaring an animal. Each time the leaders engage Jesus in debate, he answers their questions and leaves his critics baffled.

The Pharisees and the Herodians were the first to lay their trap. These two groups are strange bedfellows. The Pharisees were anti-Rome, and the Herodians supported the alliance with Rome. The Sadducees worked closely with the Herodians, but the Pharisees did not. That these two groups should come together against Jesus demonstrates that a cross section of Jewish leadership was against him.

The opponents of Jesus begin by flattering him. They address him as "Teacher," or "Rabbi." They speak of his integrity and his teaching the truth of God. They say that Jesus was not concerned with being popular with people. Then they ask the question that is meant to ensnare him: Is it right to pay taxes to Caesar or not?

The trap is obvious. If Jesus says "No, it is not right," then the Herodians who are in favor of Rome will report him to the Roman authorities. If he says "Yes," then the Pharisees will announce to the people that Jesus is pro-Rome. He will lose his audience, because how could the Messiah be pro-Rome?

But Jesus answers their question with great wisdom. He asks them to show him a coin used for the Roman poll tax. This tax had to be paid in Roman currency by every foreign subject from puberty until age sixty-five. It was a reminder that the nation was under the rule of the Roman Empire. They hand Jesus a silver denarius, a coin equal to a day's wage. Jesus asks whose image is on the coin, and what is inscribed on it. The coin bore the image of the Emperor's head along with an inscription that read, "Tiberius Caesar, son of the divine Augustus" on one side, and *"pontifex maximus,"* which means high priest, on the other. It is easy to see why this coin offended the Jewish people. The Emperor is referred to as being divine and as being the high priest.

Jesus then makes his rabbinic pronouncement, "Give to Caesar what is Caesar's, and to God what is God's." One of the greatest aspects of true biblical Christianity is that it can exist under any political system. This will come as a shock to many politically charged believers, but Christianity is apolitical. Jesus did not come to overthrow the government. He was not concerned with sweeping social reform. He was concerned with individuals. Jesus wanted to better the lives of people, one person at a time. Thus he spent his days in the backwaters of the Roman Empire, in a secluded part of Judea known as Galilee. He never spoke to the Roman Senate or appeared before Caesar.

But Jesus also adds, "Give to God what is God's." When the government comes in conflict with one's ability to serve God, one must serve God. For a while the early church enjoyed the favor of all the people. They did not attempt to stir things up politically; they went around helping individuals. But in time, the Roman government started to clamp down on the freedom of the early church to worship Jesus. They demanded that the Christians bow to Caesar and worship him. At this point, the Christians had to say No to the government. They had to give their allegiance to God.

The Herodians and Pharisees saw the wisdom of Jesus' statement and were amazed by it. They turned and left.

The Question about the Resurrection—22:23–33, cf. Mark 12:18–27, Luke 20:27–40

On the same day the Sadducees came to him saying there is no resurrection. They asked him, "Teacher, Moses said, 'If a man dies without children, his brother should marry his wife and have children for his brother.' There were seven brothers, and the first married and died without children, leaving his wife to his brother. Likewise the second and the third—until the seventh. Finally, the woman died. Now in the resurrection, out of the seven brothers, whose wife will she be? For all had been married to her."

Jesus answered them, "You are wrong because you do not know the Scriptures or the power of God. For in the resurrection they are neither married nor given in marriage, but are all as the angels in heaven. But concerning the resurrection of the dead, have you not read the word of God when it says, 'I am the God of Abraham, the God of Isaac, and the God of Jacob'? God is not the God of the dead, but of the living."

And when the crowd heard this they were astounded at his teaching.

It was now the Sadducees' turn to attempt to trap Jesus. The Sadducees believed only in the Pentateuch, the first five books of the Old Testament. They were the higher-class, more influential leaders. They did not believe in angels or the resurrection, so they asked Jesus a question that was used to stump people who believed in the resurrection. They brought up the law of levirate marriage, established to take care of widows. It was part of the Old Testament social system that if a man died and left his wife without a son, his brother must marry her (Deuteronomy 25:5–10). The book of Ruth is an illustration of this principle at work.

The question that the Sadducees posed to Jesus was hypothetical. What if a married man had seven brothers? He died, leaving his wife alone to fend for herself. His brother now would become her husband. What if this happened seven times? We would certainly feel sorry for this woman and her bad luck. We might investigate the situation to see if any foul play occurred. But the Sadducees ask, "Since she was married seven times, who will be her husband in heaven?"

How many times had the Sadducees trapped advocates of the resurrection by this question? Jesus answers them directly: You are wrong on two counts; you don't know the Scriptures or God's power. In heaven, they are like the angels. This argument would trouble the Sadducees, since they did not believe in angels. When we die, we are transformed. Life as we know it changes. Marriage is no more. This does not mean that God will wipe away all memories of our marriages or our children. The Bible doesn't really speak to this issue. It is possible that all pleasant thoughts of our past life will exist with us in heaven. Love will exist in heaven. Since we will be in the presence of God, our love will be perfected. We will love on a level that we have never experienced.

Jesus then turns to the Scripture to answer the Sadducees. Since they only believe the books of Moses (the Pentateuch), Jesus answers using the book of Exodus. God says, "I am...the God of Abraham, the God of Isaac and the God of Jacob" (Exodus 3:6). Jesus bases his argument on the tense of a verb (present tense, "I am...the God"). This shows that Jesus believed in the inspiration of Scripture. He is willing to base his argument for the resurrection on the tense of a verb. The thought is that Abraham, Isaac, and Jacob are still alive, and God is still their God. Since they are alive, the resurrection is true. God is the God of the living.

Matthew mentions that the crowds were amazed at the teaching of Jesus. The exclusion of the Sadducees' response leads us to assume that they were less than impressed with this teaching. This is another example of their rejection of Jesus as the Messiah.

The Greatest Commandment—Matthew 22:34–40, cf. Mark 12:28–34

When the Pharisees heard that he had silenced the Sadducees, they gathered together and one of them, a lawyer, questioned him (putting him to the test): "Teacher, which is the greatest commandment in the law?"

He answered him, "Love the Lord your God with the whole of your heart and with the whole of your soul and with the whole of your mind. This is the greatest and the first commandment. And the second is similar: Love your neighbor as yourself. These two commandments sum up all the law and the prophets (all the Scriptures)."

Jesus had answered the questions of the Herodians, the Pharisees, and the Sadducees. Now it was time for the scribe-lawyers to question him. The scribes were well versed in the laws. They knew several languages and copied official documents for the people. The lawyer asked Jesus: What is the greatest commandment in all the law? This was a typical inquiry of the scribes, although many scribes taught that all aspects of the law were equal; therefore, there could not be a "greatest" command.

Jesus answered them by quoting the opening of the Shema Israel. This was a prayer that was prayed three times a day by religious Jews and is found in Deuteronomy 6:4–5. The greatest command was to love God with all your heart, soul, and mind (NASB). The heart is the seat of the emotions or our will. The soul is what makes us an individual. The mind is our intellect. Together these are to be taken as the whole of man. We are to love God with our whole being. This is the greatest commandment.

But after this, Jesus goes on to talk about the commandment that is the next greatest: to love your neighbor as yourself. The religious authorities were quick to point out the need to love God with our whole being, but they would often mistreat their neighbor. Jesus shows that loving people must follow our love for God. He is perhaps the first to combine these two commandments in this way. He closes by saying that the law and the prophets can be summed up in these two commandments.

The Question about David's Son—Matthew 22:41–46, cf. Mark 12:35–37a, Luke 21:38, 20:41–44

While the Pharisees were gathered together, Jesus asked them a question, saying, "What do you think of the Christ/the Messiah? Whose son is he?"

They said to him, "David's."

Jesus replied, "How then did David by the Spirit call him 'Lord' saying:

Say to my Lord
Sit at my right hand
Until I put your enemies
Under your feet.

If David calls him Lord, how is he his son?"
    And no one was able to answer his question, nor did anyone dare ask him more questions from that day.

Jesus has answered the questions of the religious authorities, but he did not stay on the defensive. He let his attackers ask him questions, but he also asked them a question. I think this concept is very important for us in today's world. Christianity is always being attacked. Science, philosophy, and the media all attack it. Instead of staying on the defensive against these attacks, as Christians we should go on the offensive. We should ask science, "If the world just evolved over time, then how do you explain morals and ethical values?" We should ask the philosophers, "If you have all the answers, then show us how humanity can get along with humanity." We should ask media, "You constantly attack Christianity, but do you even know what you are attacking? Have you ever read the Bible or studied the teachings of Jesus?" Jesus defended himself, then he took a stand. We must be willing to stand for the truth.

Jesus asked, "What do you think of the Messiah? Whose son is he?" They answered, "David's." Jesus then adds, "Then why did David call him Lord?" Since he is the Lord of David, he is greater than David. The religious leaders rejected the type of Messiah that Jesus represented. They wanted a messiah along the lines of King David, a military king who would bring a powerful political kingdom into existence. But Jesus is a Messiah who is greater than David. Since he is greater, his kingdom will be superior to David's. It will not be a military kingdom, but a spiritual kingdom.

Jesus' questions to his critics silence them. They have no more questions for him. He has answered them brilliantly on every turn and posed a question to them that made them think about their views of the Messiah. He has proven that he was both the Son of David and the Lord of David.

This would not be the last time Jesus would face his critics. Next, he would face them in a mock trial where trumped-up charges were levied against him. Before the trial, Jesus would let his followers know that at some point in the future everyone must stand trial before the Lord. Next we turn to the eschatological teachings of King Jesus.

End Notes

187. Scriptures from Matthew in this chapter are the author's own translation.

188. Carson, *The Expositor's Bible Commentary* with the New International Version, 445.

189. To highlight the dialogue between Jesus and the religious leaders, I have omitted the discussion of three parables in this section: The Parable of the Two Sons, Matthew 21:28–32; The Parable of the Wicked Tenants, Matthew 21:33–46; and The Parable of the Wedding Banquet, Matthew 22:1–14.

Chapter 13

The Passion Week, Continued: Eschatological Teaching; Preparation for Passover

He who loves the coming of the Lord is not he who affirms it is far off, nor is it he who says it is near. It is he who, whether it be far or near, awaits it with sincere faith, steadfast hope, and fervent love.

—Augustine of Hippo, theologian

We must never speak to simple, excitable people about "the Day" without emphasizing again and again the utter impossibility of prediction. We must try to show them that that impossibility is an essential part of the doctrine. If you do not believe our Lord's words, why do you believe in his return at all? And if you do believe them must you not put away from you, utterly and forever, any hope of dating that return? His teaching on the subject quite clearly consisted of three propositions. (1) That he will certainly return. (2) That we cannot possibly find out when. (3) And that therefore we must always be ready for him.[190]

—C. S. Lewis, British author and literary critic

Matthew 24–25 is the fifth great discourse of Jesus in Matthew.[191] Chapter 24 includes both a prediction of the fall of Jerusalem and the destruction of the temple, which would occur within the lifetime of many of the followers of Jesus. It also includes an eschatological teaching concerning the end of time. However, over the years, many people have found it difficult to distinguish between the two.

Critical scholars see this material as written after the destruction of the temple in AD 70. In general, these scholars do not believe in predictive prophecy; therefore, they date these writings after the destruction of the temple. They also believe the details are too precise and must have been written after the destruction of Jerusalem. But the language that Jesus uses comes from Old Testament prophecy and not from details of the destruction of Jerusalem.

We need to pay attention to the questions that the disciples ask Jesus as they leave the temple. They are gawking over the buildings of Jerusalem. The newly refurbished temple was considered an architectural wonder in the ancient world. Jesus says of the temple structure, "Not one stone here will be left on another." The disciples ask three questions: "When will this happen? What will be the sign of your coming? What will be the sign...of the end of the age?" In the Greek, it is two questions: "When will this happen? What is the sign of the end of the age?" The disciples had one question in mind: "When will Jerusalem fall?" They were primarily concerned with the destruction of the temple, the end of Judaism. Jesus, however, uses this as a teaching opportunity to speak to his second coming. He mostly speaks about the destruction of the temple, then shifts to speak about his parousia.

The tricky part of this passage is in understanding when Jesus answers the first question and when he answers the second question.

Verses 4–35 are directed to the question, "When will Jerusalem fall?" Verse 34 reads, "This generation will not pass away until these things occur." These verses apply to the fall of Jerusalem and the destruction of the temple. For the Jews, the fall of Jerusalem and the destruction of the temple were the equivalent of the last days of Judaism. What were the signs that would signal that the end was near?

1. False Christs claiming, "I am the Messiah"
2. Wars and rumors of wars
3. Famines and earthquakes
4. Persecutions
5. The love of many would grow cold
6. The abomination of desolation

Notice that Jesus says, "Flee." This can't refer to his second coming. There is no fleeing at the second coming of Christ, but when the Romans approached Jerusalem, the Jewish Christians could get out of the city. In fact, many did. They fled across the Jordan River to Pella and began a community there. Archaeologists have uncovered this community and have dated it to the time of the Roman invasion of Jerusalem.

What about verse 29? What is happening here? The sun is darkened and the moon will not give its light. These are images from Daniel and Isaiah. The prophets used these images to speak of the fall of Babylon. This is apocalyptic language that should not be taken literally. Figuratively, the sun was darkened and the moon failed to give light when Jerusalem was destroyed because this was a day of judgment against Jerusalem and the Jewish religious authorities who failed to receive Jesus as the Messiah. Perhaps the sun was literally darkened. It's possible. Perhaps a shadow did come over the land. We can be certain that it was a dark day for Jerusalem when the Romans entered the city and destroyed the temple.

As I just mentioned, Matthew 24 includes images and language that are apocalyptic in nature. Ἀποκάλυψις/*Apokalypsis* is from a Greek word that means "to reveal what is hidden or to make known." It is used in Revelation 1:1 in reference to the revelation of John. Apocalyptic writing uses symbols and metaphors to disclose information to a specific group of people who were usually undergoing persecution or were in need of encouragement. Apocalyptic literature is full of images that are highly symbolic. For the initiated, these symbols are clearly understood, but for those outside the circle of the initiates, the symbols are unclear. Imagine if you don't know anything about baseball and you turn on the radio to hear, "With two men out, it's a three-two pitch." Would you find meaning in that? How about, "The runner steals third base and now he's on his way home!" If you don't know baseball, then it seems the runner ought to be arrested for being a thief.

In the same way, the symbols and numbers, images and references of apocalyptic literature may seem strange to us, but they were familiar to their intended audiences in the first century. Once you have a basic grasp of the "game"—in this case the culture of Jewish apocalyptic writings—then the "code language" is easily understood as well.

In verse 36, Jesus moves on to answer the second question: When will the Son of Man come? Jesus says there will be no signs concerning this event. No one knows the day or hour of the coming of the Son of Man. Also, when Jesus uses the term "that day," this is a specific phrase that refers to the Day of Judgment, the *Yom Yahweh* of the Old Testament (see Matthew 7:22 and Luke 10:2). When Jesus speaks of his second coming, the concern is not when he will come, so he gives no clues about the time of his coming. In fact, this event will surprise everyone. Since you don't know when he will come, be ready all the time for him. That's the point here. Our focus should not be directed toward trying to figure out when he will come, but on being prepared when he does come.

The temple in Jerusalem was one of the wonders of the ancient world. Herod the Great (37–4 BC) began construction on the temple complex in 20–19 BC, and the construction went on for some eighty years. The new temple complex was completed only a few years before it was destroyed in AD 70. Herod's temple is known as the second temple, though in actuality it is the third (it is often referred to as Herod's temple). It is viewed as a reconstruction of the temple of the exiles, but the changes and expansion to the temple and the temple site were so vast under Herod that it is best to think of Herod's temple as a completely new structure. He expanded the temple on the north, west, and south—the eastern edge of the temple fell too steeply into the Kidron Valley to allow any expansion. He completely buried any remains of Solomon's temple or of the Post-Exilic temple as he rebuilt the new one. The new temple mount covered thir-ty-five acres. It was an impressive site, larger than the Acropolis in Greece.

When the disciples left the temple they pointed out to Jesus the beautiful buildings of the temple complex. Jesus predicted that the temple would be destroyed. Not a single stone would be left standing. This prediction would come true in AD 70 when Titus, the general of the Roman army, marched into Jerusalem and destroyed the temple.

The disciples approach Jesus later as he is sitting on the Mount of Olives and ask him two questions. It is important to see that, even though they had only the end of Judaism in mind, Jesus responds to two different questions. The first has to do with the destruction of the temple—when will this happen? The second has to do with the second coming (*parou-sia*) of Jesus—what will be the sign of the second coming and the end of the age? Jesus will spend the rest of chapter 24 answering not one, but two questions.

He begins in verses 4 through 35 by answering the first question—when will the temple be destroyed? Before the temple is destroyed, many false prophets will appear. Many will say, "I am the Messiah." They will deceive people, but Jesus lets his disciples know that the time for the destruction of the temple is not to come yet. There will also be famines and earthquakes in various places. All of these are signs that the destruction is still to come.

"Then you will be handed over to be persecuted and put to death" refers to the disciples. This would come before the destruction of the temple. By the time the temple was destroyed in AD 70, almost all of the original twelve disciples of Jesus had died martyrs' deaths because of their faith in Jesus. Many of the early followers stumbled when persecution first hit the church, but those who died clinging to their faith would be saved. The whole world would hear the proclamation of the kingdom before the end (of the temple) would come. According to Paul, the gospel was preached to every creature under heaven in his lifetime (Colossians 1:23).

Much has been written about "the abomination of desolation." Those who believe that Jesus is speaking of the end of the world in this section are still looking for the abomination of desolation. We must remember that we are reading apocalyptic literature here. It is highly symbolic. So what does the abomination of desolation symbolize? Jesus is still answer-ing the first question here—when will the temple be destroyed? Taking these thoughts in consideration, the abomination of desolation refers back to a prophecy in Daniel 11:31 that was fulfilled by Antiochus Epiph-anes in 168 BC when this Seleucid ruler erected an altar to Zeus over the altar of burnt offering in the temple area. He then offered a pig (an unclean animal) on this altar. This was the "abomination of desolation."

Before the temple was destroyed, this defiling act would happen again. It happened when Titus and the Roman army marched into the temple courts. Before the temple was burned to the ground, Titus entered the Holy of Holies. This was the most sacred room of the temple that could only be entered by the High Priest, and he could only enter it once a year on the Day of Atonement. When Titus entered into the Holy of Holies, the abomination of desolation occurred.

The early Christians heeded Jesus' words, and when the Roman armies came into Jerusalem, they fled. Because they understood, trusted, and obeyed the words of Jesus, they escaped the Roman sword. The Jews who did not heed Jesus' warning stayed behind and were executed. Josephus, the Jewish historian, notes that the Romans killed so many Jews at the temple that blood flowed in streams through the streets of Jerusalem.

Jesus uses apocalyptic language to describe the suffering that occurred in the days before and following the destruction of the temple. Did the moon darken? Did stars fall from heaven when the temple was destroyed? Perhaps not literally, although we weren't there and don't know, but these are words of judgment. God judged the city of Jerusalem in AD 70. In that way, the Son of Man did appear. He appeared as the judge over the city of Jerusalem and the Jewish religion. Judaism failed to receive Jesus as the Messiah. Therefore, Jesus came in power and judged Jerusalem. The elect were gathered away from Jerusalem and were spared the judgment of the city.

Jesus moves on to answer the second question—what will be the sign of your second coming and the end of the age? Jesus says concerning that time no sign will be given. No one knows the day or the hour when he will come. The angels don't know. The Son doesn't even know. Only the Father knows. Since only the Father knows the day or the hour of the Son of Man, it is ludicrous for anyone to attempt to predict when Jesus will come. He will come as a surprise. Like the people in Noah's day were surprised by the flood, people will be surprised when Jesus comes. One will be taken from a field and one left. When Jesus comes, the elect will meet him in the air. Those "left" does not refer to a group that will be left behind to face the anti-Christ. It means they will receive judgment after God judges the elect.

The point Jesus makes is that we should be alert. Since we don't know when he will come, we should be ready at any moment for his return. He will come as a thief, unannounced. No matter how much we would like to predict when Jesus will return, it simply is not possible. Jesus will surprise us; therefore, we must be vigilant, always ready for his return.

What is the point of Jesus giving no clue as to when he will come again and saying that he will come like a thief? It can be summed up in three words: "Therefore keep watch."

Parables Concerning the End of Time—Matthew 25:1-46

Jesus continues his thoughts concerning the end of time in chapter 25 of the Gospel of Matthew. Remember, the early copies of the Scriptures had no chapter divisions; there would have been no break between chapters 24 and 25.

Jesus tells two parables that each have something to say about the end of time. The Parable of the Ten Virgins (25:1-13) is a reminder to always be on watch for the return of the Messiah. He will return unannounced to surprise those who are not ready for his coming.

The Parable of the Talents (25:14-30) reminds us that we will be judged according to how we have used the gifts that God has given us. Have we made good use of our gifts, or have we used them selfishly? When the Messiah returns, he will have something to say about how we have used our talents.

Jesus gives us his greatest portrayal of the final judgment scene in verses 31-46. Here Jesus (the Son of Man) sits upon a throne of judgment before all of humanity. He divides everyone into two groups based upon how each person treated others while they were living.

This is the scene of final judgment. There is no hint of anyone being given a second chance here, nor is there any mention of purgatory. You live your life, you die, and then you face judgment. Your eternal destiny will be determined by how you live your life in the here and now.

The Parable of the Ten Maidens—Matthew 25:1-13

> "Then the kingdom of heaven will be like ten bridesmaids who took their lamps and went to meet the bridegroom. Five of them were foolish and five wise—for the foolish took their lamps, but did not take any oil with them. But the wise took jars of oil with their lamps. As the bridegroom was delayed, all of them became tired and fell asleep.
>
> "At midnight there was a shout, 'Look, the bridegroom is here! Come out and meet him!'
>
> "Then all the bridesmaids woke up and trimmed their lamps. The foolish said to the wise, 'Give us some of your oil; our lamps are going out.'
>
> "But the wise answered, 'No. There will not be enough for you and us. Rather go to the dealers and buy some for yourselves.'
>
> "But while they were going to buy it, the bridegroom came. Those who were ready went in with him to the wedding banquet, and the door was shut.
>
> "Later the others came, 'Sir! Sir! Open up for us.'
>
> "But he answered, 'I tell you the truth, I do not know you.'
>
> "Keep alert then, because you know not the day, nor the hour."[192]

What is the point of this parable? Simply put, it is this, "If Jesus were to come back today to judge the world, would you be ready to meet him?" Are you ready?

Curtis Mayfield (yes, the same guy that wrote "Superfly") wrote a Gospel song entitled "People Get Ready." The lyrics go:

> People get ready, there's a train comin'
> You don't need no baggage, you just get on board.
> All you need is faith to hear the diesels hummin.'
> You don't need no ticket, you just thank the lord.[193]

The main point of the Parable of the Ten Maidens is this: *Are you ready?* But the parable makes other points as well. In his book on the parables, Craig Blomberg draws three teaching points from this parable. He writes:

> (1) Like the bridegroom, God may delay his coming longer than people expect. (2) Like the wise bridesmaids, his followers must be prepared for such a delay—discipleship may be more arduous than the novice suspects. (3) Like the foolish bridesmaids, those who do not prepare adequately may discover a point beyond which there is no return—when the end comes it will be too late to undo the damage of neglect.[194]

Let's take a closer look at the parable and see what lessons we can learn from it.

1. In this life and for the afterlife, preparation is key. "Then" or "At that time" joins this parable of the ten maidens with the preceding story of the second coming of Jesus and the fact that Jesus will come at an unexpected time. Jesus introduces the parable by saying ὁμοιωθήσεται ἡ βασιλεία τῶν οὐρανῶν/*homoiothasetai ha Basileia ton ouranon*, "At that time the kingdom of heaven will be like." This is to say that this is how it will be for those in the kingdom when Jesus comes; some will be ready and some will not. So Jesus isn't talking about people in the world versus people in the church. He is talking about the kingdom. Within Jesus' community, some will be ready when he returns and some will not.

The story portrays a wedding procession. In that culture, the groom would go to the bride's home dressed in his wedding garb. He would bring the bride back to his home where there would be a wedding banquet. There would be a wedding procession from the bride's house to the wedding banquet at the groom's house.

The maidens were to walk with the bridegroom and his bride to the wedding banquet. They were to carry lamps to light the way in this procession. It was an honor to be able to light the way in the wedding procession.

What was the difference between the wise maidens and the foolish ones? There was one difference, and it made all the difference: preparation. That's it. The wise were prepared. They brought oil. The foolish weren't prepared. No oil.

I remember getting ready for a groom-honoring party some twenty-five years ago in New York. A large number of brothers met on the top of an apartment building where we were going to share our hearts with the groom. We had lots of sodas and about a dozen pizzas. We were ready to celebrate.

But the groom was late. We waited and waited. We went ahead and started eating pizza because we didn't want it to get cold. Still, no groom. Eventually, one brother leaned over to me and said, "You did invite the groom, didn't you?"

I said, "Nope, I didn't invite him. Did you?"

He answered, "Nope." We got everyone's attention and asked, "Did anyone invite the groom?" Silence. Blank stares. We had done everything except the most important thing. We failed to invite the very person we were honoring. Lack of preparation can make you look pretty foolish.

Are you prepared? If Jesus were to come right now, would you be ready?

2. Jesus might tarry longer than you think, so be ready for the long haul. In this story, there is a twist. Remember, in the parables, look for the twist. The twist is that the bridegroom is delayed and the ten maidens have to wait for him before they can go to the banquet. While they wait, they sleep. Both of the groups sleep, so sleep isn't the problem. When they hear the cry and wake up, only one group is prepared with oil.

Again, this parable must be interpreted in light of what was just said. Jesus said, "Be alert." You don't know when the bridegroom will come. He might come earlier than you think. Or he might tarry and come later than you think. Therefore, be in a continual state of preparedness. The cry comes at midnight, "Here comes the bridegroom." Only the wise maidens have enough oil when the groom arrives. Only the wise are prepared for his arrival.

You don't know how long it will be before Jesus calls you home. All of us should be ready to live ten, twenty-five, or fifty years for Jesus. Are you ready for the long haul?

Discipleship is like running a marathon, not a sprint. In a marathon, you have to pace yourself. You have to stay hydrated. You have to eat while you are running to keep energy in your body. You have to push through pain and set your mind that it's not over until it is over. It's a long race. Discipleship is a journey, and you have to set your mind that you are in it for the long haul.

Discipleship isn't easy. Martin Luther said, "A religion that gives nothing, costs nothing, and suffers nothing, is worth nothing." What are you willing to do to be a disciple and stay a strong disciple of Jesus? What are you willing to do to make sure your faith doesn't waver and your zeal doesn't fail?

You have to set your mind that nothing will keep you from your goal of reaching heaven.

3. Be prepared. There is a distinction between the wise and the unwise: The wise maidens have lamps and oil. The unwise have their lamps, but no oil. The wise are prepared. When the bridegroom arrives, they will be ready. He will not catch them unaware. Hendriksen and Kistemaker demonstrate the contrast between the two groups, writing:

> But though the ten resemble each other in so many outward points, their dissimilarity is even more striking. It is basic. It is what really counts: five were foolish, five sensible. The foolishness of the first group consisted in the fact that they were totally unprepared to meet the bridegroom; for, though they had taken lamps, *they had taken no oil.* That is what the text plainly indicates. ...They had lamps but no oil. They were careless, not forward-looking, guilty of inexcusable and senseless neglect, shortsighted, thoughtless. The sensible girls, on the contrary, were equipped with a generous supply of oil. They were fully prepared.[195]

No need to interpret the text in an allegorical manner. No need to attach meaning to the oil or the sleeping girls or the reason the bridegroom tarried. The parable has one big idea: When the bridegroom comes, be prepared. Donald A. Hagner writes, "The focus of the parable is the simple matter of preparedness versus unpreparedness and the tragic character of the latter."[196]

We should consider one question: Why did the wise girls not share their oil with the unwise? Their answer is adequate: "There might not be enough oil if we share it with you." Each person is responsible for his or her own preparedness. When the bridegroom returns, we must each be ready. If we aren't, then we find ourselves on the outside of the wedding banquet longing to get in, but the door will be shut. Jesus concludes the parable with these words: "Keep alert then, because you know not the day, nor the hour."

Are you ready? Is there anything going on in your life right now that would keep you from going to heaven? Any sin you haven't repented of? Any person you haven't forgiven? Anything you need to make right with someone?

The onus is on you to make it right. You are responsible to get yourself ready for eternity.

4. There is a point of no return. The unwise hurried off to buy oil in the village. Even though it was late at night, they were able to purchase oil, but their lack of preparation had already spelled their doom. When

they arrived at the wedding banquet, the door was shut. The unwise maidens pleaded for the door to be opened. They cried, *"Kurios, Kurios,"* which can be translated as "Sir, Sir" or "Lord, Lord." It reminds the reader of Jesus' stern warning in Matthew 7:21, "Not everyone who says to me, 'Lord, Lord,' will enter the kingdom of heaven, but only he who does the will of my Father who is in heaven."

A frank refusal comes from the other side of the door, "ἀμὴν λέγω ὑμῖν, οὐκ οἶδα ὑμᾶς/*amen lego humin, ouk oida humas,* "I tell you the truth, I do not know you." Hagner writes, "The symbolism of the shut door points to the time when it is too late to alter the division between the saved and the lost."[197] Once Jesus comes, that's it. Your fate is sealed. That is why it is so important to live in a state of constant preparedness.

The parable ends on a sad note. The unwise maidens are left out in the cold, unable to enter the banquet. One commentary notes, "Three of the saddest sayings in the parables of Jesus are found here: (1) "Our lamps are gone out"; (2) "The door was shut"; and (3) "I do not know you." This is illustrative of God's judgment, which is unequivocal and irreversible.[198]

Think of what they miss because they weren't prepared: the banquet. If only they had been prepared, they could have enjoyed the feast. Instead, they stand outside the gate, listening to the music, smelling the food, and hearing the laughter of everyone inside, all the while knowing that, with a little forethought and preparation, they too could have been inside enjoying the festivity.

The passage ends by stating the main point of the parable: "Γρηγορεῖτε οὖν, ὅτι οὐκ οἴδατε τὴν ἡμέραν οὐδὲ τὴν ὥραν/*gragoreite oun, hoti ouk oidate tan hameran tan horan,* "Keep alert then, because you know not the day, nor the hour." Stay alert. Watch. Be vigilant. William Hendriksen says the main point of the parable is this: "Preparedness is essential, for the time is coming when getting ready will no longer be possible; the door will be shut."[199]

How do we stay alert? How do we keep watch? Augustine writes, "Thus did the Gospel close; 'Watch, for ye know neither the day nor the hour.' But if we are all to sleep, how shall we watch? Watch with the heart, watch with faith, watch with hope, watch with charity, watch with good works."[200] We watch by being vigilant in every area of our spiritual lives.

What helps you to stay alert? For me, it's Bible study. What is it for you? Perhaps prayer? Or fellowship? Maybe evangelism? Whatever it is, drink deeply of that well. We need to always be alert for the return of the bridegroom. We don't want to be locked outside the banquet.

The Parable of the Talents—Matthew 25:14–30

"For it is as a man going on a journey who called his slaves and entrusted his property to

them. He gave one five talents of money, another two, and another one—each according to his ability. Then he left. The one who received the five talents left and traded with them, and made five more talents. Likewise, the one with two talents of money made two more. But the one who received the one talent went and dug a hole in the ground and hid his master's money.

"After much time, the master of the slaves returned and settled accounts with them. The one who had received the five talents of money came forward and brought five more saying, 'Master, you gave me five talents. See, I have made five more.'

"His master said to him, 'Well done, good and faithful servant, you have been faithful in the little things; I will put you in charge of many things. Enter into the joy of your master.'

"The man with the two talents came forward and said, 'Master, you gave me two talents; see, I have gained two more.'

"His master said, 'Well done, good and faithful servant; since you have been faithful in the small things, I will put you in charge of many things. Enter into the joy of your master.'

"The man who was given one talent came forward, saying, 'Master, I knew you were a hard man, reaping where you did not sow, and gathering where you did not scatter. I was afraid and went and hid your talent in the ground. See, you have what is yours.'

"His master answered him, 'You wicked and lazy servant! You knew I reap where I have not sown and gather where I have not scattered. Then you should have put my money in the bank, so when I returned I would have received it back with interest.

"'Take the talent from him and give it to the one with ten talents. For to all who have, they will be given more. And he will have in abundance. Whoever does not have, even what he has will be taken away. And cast this worthless slave in the outer darkness, where there will be weeping and gnashing of teeth.'"

The parable of the talents also highlights the importance of using the time before the parousia wisely. In this parable, just before a landowner takes a journey, he leaves his money in the care of his servants. To the first servant he gives five talents, to the second he gives two talents, and to the third he gives one talent, each according to his ability. In our day a talent would be worth about a thousand dollars. Not a small sum of money. Hendriksen and Kistemaker write:

Basically a "talent" is a measure of weight. ...The same word "talent" is, however, also used to indicate a unit of coinage. The value differed from one place and time to another, and also with the metal that was used, whether copper, silver, or gold. ...An Attic talent amounted to no less than six thousand denars. It would take an ordinary laborer almost twenty years to earn one. It is clear, therefore, that in the present parable we are dealing with a rich businessman. Naturally he does not want his money to lie idle during his absence. It must be used so that he may make a profit. The owner of all this wealth is not only rich but also sagacious. He realizes that not all servants (or "slaves") have equal business skill. So, figuring with each man's ability, he lets one servant have five talents, another two, and another one. Then he goes on his way.[201]

When the man returns, he asks the servants to account for what they did with the money. The first two have doubled their return. The master gives them high praise: "Well done, good and faithful servant, you have been faithful in the little things; I will put you in charge of many things. Enter into the joy of your master." The third hides his master's money in the earth. When the man returns, he calls the third servant to account for his money. The servant defends his decision to hide the talent: "Master, I always knew that you were a hard man, reaping where you did not sow, and gathering where you did not scatter; so, being afraid, I went away and hid your talent in the ground." This is not an accurate description of the master. He is not a hard taskmaster. He distributed the talents based on each man's abilities. He was a thoughtful man who entrusted his servants with responsibility.

The master responds by calling the servant "wicked." He tells him, "Even if I were as bad as you say, you still ought to have invested my money with a banker so that it would have earned interest. Instead, you did nothing." The word "wicked" is appropriate here. Hendriksen and Kistemaker write:

This man was wicked because he deliberately misrepresented both his master and himself. He falsely accused his master of being cruel. He also lied, namely, when he said, "Look (here) you have what is yours," for he actually owed his employer not only that one talent but also whatever it would have earned had he been faithful. But instead of admitting his guilt, he acts as if the master should have given him credit for having been so cautious and for having returned the entire talent intact. This shows that he was indeed an utterly wicked and selfish individual.[202]

The man takes the talent from his servant and gives it to the one with ten. He then orders the servant be cast into outer darkness, where there is weeping and gnashing of teeth.

Final Judgment: The Separation of the Sheep from the Goats—Matthew 25:31–46

"When the Son of Man comes in his glory and all the angels with him, then he will sit on his throne of glory. All the nations will be gathered before him, and he will separate the people one from another as a shepherd separates the sheep from the goats. He will put the sheep on his right hand, and the goats on his left.

"Then the King will say to those on his right, 'Come you blessed by may Father, inherit the kingdom prepared for you from the creation of the world. For I was hungry *and you gave me food, I was thirsty and you gave me drink, I was a stranger and you welcomed me, I was sick and you cared for me, I was in prison and you visited me.'*

"Then the righteous will answer him, 'Lord, when did we see you hungry and give you food, or thirsty and give you drink? Or when did we see you as a stranger and welcome you in, or naked and clothe you? And when did we see you sick or in prison and visit you?'

"The King will answer, 'I tell you the truth, when you did it to one of the least of these brothers of mine, you did it to me.'

"Then he will say to those on his left, 'You accursed ones, depart from me into the eternal fire prepared for the devil and his angels. For I was hungry, and you gave no food, I was thirsty and you gave me no drink, I was a stranger and you did not welcome me in, naked and you gave me no clothing, sick and in prison and you did not care for me.'

"They will answer, 'Lord, when did we see you hungry or thirsty or a stranger or naked or sick or in prison, and did not care for you?'

"He will reply, 'I tell you truthfully, when you did not do it for one of the least of these, you did not do it for me.'

"Then they will go away to eternal punishment, but the righteous into eternal life."

When I was in seminary, my New Testament professor, Dr. Richard Spencer, called this passage of Scripture the Mt. Everest of the New Testament. It is a dramatic presentation of the last judgment. The Son of Man will return with his angels to sit on the throne of judgment. All nations will be gathered, then the sheep will be separated from the goats. What standard will be used to distinguish the sheep from the goats? Their treatment of people who were hurting in life will determine their placement in judgment. The Son of Man personalizes their treatment of people in need, saying, "For I was hungry and you gave me food, I was thirsty and you gave me drink, I was a stranger and you welcomed me, I was sick and you cared for me, I was in prison and you visited me." The sheep question the King, "When did we see you in this circumstance?" The Son of Man answers, "Inasmuch as you did this to the least of my brothers, you did it to me."

This should make us look at people differently. How we treat people is how we treat Jesus. Mother Teresa of Calcutta, who served the poorest of the poor, said that she saw Jesus in the eyes of everyone she helped. Do we see Jesus in the eyes of the poor? Do we see Jesus in the eyes of the prisoner? Do we treat people as if they were Jesus?

This passage seems to say that we are judged based on our works. Well, of course we are. How could we not be? We are saved by grace, but the life of a disciple must be filled with good works. If not, then he or she isn't a disciple.

The sheep go away to everlasting life. The goats go to the everlasting fire prepared for the devil and his angels. This is described as everlasting punishment. Hendriksen and Kistemaker write:

> Nowhere—not even in Rev. 10:6—does Scripture support the notion that either after death or after the judgment day there will be no more time. Nowhere does Scripture eternalize or deify the inhabitants of the coming aeon. And since here in 25:46 the same adjective is used in both clauses, the word to be used in the translation should make clear in which respect the two, namely, punishment for the wicked and life for the righteous, are the same.[203]

This judgment scene gives the disciples of Jesus a revelation as to what God means for his people to be. If a person strives for righteousness, then he must pay strict attention to the lesson taught in this passage. William Barclay writes, "The lesson is this—that God will judge us in accordance with our reaction to human needs."[204]

Our concept of a relationship with God can get so warped by carrying on traditional standards of what it means to be a Christian that we can forget the example of Jesus and his definition of righteousness. New Testament professor Malcolm Tolbert comments:

> Sometimes we equate faithfulness to Jesus with attendance on religious services and giving money to support the institution. We honor Jesus who never said anything at all about building buildings by erecting larger and more magnificent structures. If we do take his words seriously, we shall surely testify to it by a shift of our emphasis from statistics and buildings to people in their need. The Lord is not going to ask, 'How many buildings did you build?' According to the passage, he is going to ask: How many hungry people did you feed? How many sick people did you visit?[205]

Jesus' words should help us focus our gaze on the helpless, poor, and suffering.

Whenever we find it difficult to get out of ourselves and meet the needs of others, Jesus' words should come ringing into our ears. Dr. Martin Luther King, Jr. wrote, "When we, through compassionless detachment and arrogant individualism fail to respond to the needs of the underprivileged, the Master says, 'Inasmuch as ye have done it not to one of the least of these my brethren, ye have done it not unto me.'"[206] Search and find the eyes of Jesus in every poor and helpless person.

Even though we look for the poor and rejected person, the true Christian is not searching to gain credit for himself. Christian service is to be uncalculating. We should be able to ask, "Lord, when did we see you in need?" Human suffering should awaken our compassion to the point of service, but our motives should be to minister and help without any type of ulterior motive. Our response to the needy must be instinctive within our own Christian character for it to be pleasing to God.

The Master's Eyes
(GSK)

Someone looks and sees the tears of loneliness
As they trickle down the corner of
Bright blue eyes.
Another gazes and sees the cold, blank,
Disease-ridden stare of death in
Dark brown eyes.
Still another looks and wipes crusted
Sleep from brilliant, newborn,
Hazel eyes.
And someone stares into dimly lit,
Uncontrolled and functionless
Almost colorless eyes.
Look closer into these eyes.
Someone looks back.
And they call him Jesus.

End Notes

190. C. S. Lewis, *The World's Last Night and Other Essays* (Mariner Books,1973).

191. Compare Mark 13 and Luke 21.

192. Scriptures from Matthew in this chapter are the author's own translation.

193. http://www.lyricsmania.com/people_get_ready_lyrics_curtis_mayfield.html.

194. Blomberg, 195.

195. Hendriksen and Kistemaker, 875–876.

196. D. A. Hagner, *Word Biblical Commentary, Vol. 33B, Matthew 14–28* (Dallas: Word, Incorporated, 1998), 728.

197. Hagner, 728.

198. Augsburger and Ogilvie, 18.

199. Hendriksen and Kistemaker, 875.

200. Augustine of Hippo, "Sermons on Selected Lessons of the New Testament," R. G. MacMullen, translated in A Select Library of the Nicene and Post-Nicene Fathers of the Christian Church, first series, vol. 6, Saint Augustin: Sermon on the Mount, Harmony of the Gospels, Homilies on the Gospels, edited by P. Schaff (New York: Christian Literature Company, 1888), 405.

201. Hendriksen and Kistemaker, 879–880.

202. Ibid., 882.

203. Ibid., 891–892.

204. William Barclay, *New Testament Words* (London: SCM Press, 1964), 36–37.

205. M. O. Tolbert, *Good News from Matthew* (Nashville: Broadman Press, 1975), 213.

206. Martin Luther King, *Strength to Love* (Glasgow: William Collins Sons, 1964), 19.

The Passover and the Crucifixion

Everything in Christ astonishes me. His spirit overawes me, and his will confounds me. Between him and whoever else in the world, there are not possible terms of comparison. He is truly a being by himself. I search in vain in history to find the similar to Jesus Christ, or anything, which can approach the gospel. Neither history, nor humanity, nor the ages, nor nature, offer me anything with which I am able to compare it or to explain it. Here everything is extraordinary.

—Napoleon

The Preparation for the Passover and the Celebration of the Passover Feast

Before we consider the account of the crucifixion of Jesus, let's look at the material leading directly to it.

The Anointing by the Woman of Bethany—Matthew 26:6–13, cf. Mark 14:3–9, John 12:2–8

Although the disciples of Jesus failed to grasp what would happen to Jesus in a couple of days, one woman did understand. She walked up behind Jesus while he was at supper and anointed his head with very expensive perfume worth 300 denarii (300 days' wages).

How did Judas respond? He talked about the waste of money in this woman's act. Part of the motivation of Judas was greed. We see in the next section that Judas asked the Jewish leaders, "What are you willing to give me if I hand him over to you?" A handful of silver coins was worth 100 denarii—the price of a slave. This is one third of what the woman's oil and jar were worth. Judas must have been incredulous at this waste. None of the disciples spoke up to defend the woman. Why? Because they didn't understand what she had done.

Jesus defended her. He said:

> *Why are you bothering this woman? For it is a beautiful thing she has done to me; for the poor you always have with you, but me you will not always have. I solemnly assure you, wherever this gospel is preached in the whole world, also what she has done shall be told in memory of her.*[207]

Of course Jesus had a heart for the poor, but the opportunities to honor Jesus in this way were running out. The woman recognized this fact, and she honored Jesus with her gift. The way she honored Jesus is a lesson for all of us to give him the honor he deserves.

Judas and the Chief Priests Reach an Agreement— Matthew 26:14–16, cf. Mark 14:10–11, Luke 22:3–6

This passage stands in stark contrast to the preceding one. Mary anointed Jesus for burial. Judas plotted to betray Jesus. Judas betrayed Jesus for a handful of coins, the price of a slave.

The Passover—Matthew 26:17–35, cf. Mark 14:12–31, Luke 22:7–39

Thursday arrived, the 14th of Nisan, the first day of the Feast of Unleavened Bread. A lamb was sacrificed and sauce was made for the feast. Peter and John were sent into Jerusalem to secure a room for the event. They were to look for a man carrying water, not a typical job for men in Jerusalem. He was probably a disciple of Jesus. They were to tell the man that the Master had need of a room for the Passover. In Jerusalem during Passover, if anyone had an extra room, that person was to provide the room without charge during the feast for those who needed it.

Jesus washed the disciples' feet and taught them a lesson on humility. Then they reclined at the table. Jesus predicted that one of them would betray him. They protested, "Surely not I." Jesus let them know that Judas was the man.

Jesus then celebrated the Passover with his disciples. He broke the bread, gave thanks, and said, "This is my body." He took the fruit of the vine, gave thanks, and said, "This is my blood of the covenant, which is poured out for many for the forgiveness of sins."

His body symbolized the blood of the paschal lamb. Hendriksen and Kistemaker write:

At this point Passover passes over into the Lord's Supper; for it was while, toward the close of the Passover meal, the men were all eating freely (see on verse 21) that Jesus instituted the new sacrament that was to replace the old. A few more hours and the old symbol, being bloody—for it required the slaying of the lamb—will have served its purpose forever, having reached its fulfillment in the blood shed on Calvary. It was time, therefore, that a new and unbloody symbol replace the old. Nevertheless, by historically linking Passover and Lord's Supper so closely together Jesus also made clear that what was essential in the first was not lost in the second. Both point to him, the only and all-sufficient sacrifice for the sins of his people. Passover pointed forward to this; the Lord's Supper points back to it.[208]

After Jesus and his disciples ate, they sang a hymn and headed to the Mount of Olives. Then Jesus let them know that the time had come. He warned them that they would all deny him that night. For Peter, he was specific: "You will disown me three times." Peter objected. They all objected, but when the time came, they all fled (v. 56).

Jesus predicted his resurrection for the fourth time. He let them know that he would go into Galilee ahead of them. The disciples still didn't understand. They would not stand with Jesus; they left him to face the cross alone. But what happened over the next three days would shake up their world and shake up the history of humanity as well. Now we turn to the cross and the resurrection of Jesus.

The Account of the Crucifixion

Four words are used to describe why Jesus was crucified on the Cross:

1. *Ransom* (redeem, redemption, *ludr*)—used in commerce in connection with purchasing goods. Jesus ransoms us. We are slaves to sin, slaves to self, slaves to death, slaves to our flesh, and slaves to the devil. We cannot get out of this slavery on our own; we are trapped in it. Jesus comes and ransoms us from slavery.

2. *Justification*—an idea connected to the law court. The evidence is brought against us and presented to the Judge. The judge is going to pass his judgment, and the evidence is overwhelmingly against us. However, the Judge declares us innocent because the righteousness of Jesus covers our guilt. The Westminster Confession of Faith says,

   Justification is an act of God's free grace toward sinners. It is an act of grace toward sinners in which He pardons all their sins and accepts them as righteous in His sight only because of the righteousness of Christ imputed to them and received by faith alone.[209]

3. *Propitiation*—used in connection with the temple and worship. God holds us accountable for our sins. He has a righteous anger against sin, and something must be done to appease his anger. A sacrifice must be made, and Jesus is that sacrifice.

4. *Reconciliation*—used in terms of relationship. There is a chasm between two people, and this hurt needs to be healed. The offender needs to apologize. In God's case with us, he is the injured party, yet he takes the steps necessary to heal the grievance.

Not one of these concepts when left alone tells the whole story of the sacrifice of Jesus. In fact, not all of them together tell the whole story. These are pictures to help us grasp the unfathomable: Jesus died for sinners, of which each of us is chief.

Gethsemane—Matthew 26:36–46, Mark 14:32–42, Luke 22:40–46, John 18:1

Matthew 26:39 reads, "My Father, if it is possible, may this cup be taken from me." Why would Jesus want the cup taken away? Did he lapse in his conviction? Did he forget who he was? Jesus realized that he was going to have to bear the consequences of sin on the cross. He would take on the sin of humanity. 2 Corinthians 5:21 states, "God made him who had no sin to be sin for us." He probably wasn't concerned about the physical punishment of the cross, but the unbearable burden of bearing the sins of all humanity must have been intense.

The lesson of Gethsemane is the lesson of prayer. Jesus teaches us the need to pray to bolster our courage before times of suffering and distress. It is also the beginning of the agony for Jesus. Before he endured the physical abuse of his arrest and crucifixion, he endured the emotional distress of Gethsemane. The phrase "my soul is overwhelmed with sorrow" can also mean "so sorrowful that it is to the point of death." Fritz Rienecker writes, "It implies a restless, distracted, shrinking from some trouble or thought of trouble, which nevertheless cannot be escaped."[210] Jesus was in anguish. Which is more painful, the physical pain or the emotional pain? They were both draining. Gethsemane was a dark night for Jesus.

Gethsemane is an olive garden just across the Kidron Valley from Jerusalem. The word "gethsemane" means "olive press." Part of the garden still exists today and is a "must see" for anyone who visits Jerusalem. When our family lived in Jerusalem, it was one of our favorite spots to visit. It is still the favorite site of my wife and daughter. My daughter, Chelsea, had a favorite olive tree that she would climb into and perch on a limb to pray. We named that tree "Chelsea's tree."

Just outside of the Garden of Gethsemane is a small grotto or cave that contained an olive press in the first century. Jesus might have gone into this cave when he separated himself from his disciples to pray.

Jesus struggled to surrender his will to the will of the Father. Perhaps he was not asking for a way out, but for another way to accomplish what needed to be accomplished. Was there another way to redeem the world? His agony in the garden demonstrated that Jesus understood that the crucifixion would be an agonizing death. He voluntarily endured the agony of the cross for us. He had to set his mind for the events that were about to transpire.

Three times Jesus prayed the same prayer to the Father. Each time he returned to find his disciples asleep. How disappointing it must have been for Jesus to find his disciples sleeping. Has anyone asked you to stay awake with them during a traumatic time? Perhaps they were in the hospital where they were afraid and needed encouragement. What if your wife was up all night having labor pains because she was about to deliver your child? Did you go to bed and let her endure the pain alone? You found a way to stay awake. You paced back and forth, threw cold water on your face, or made a pot of coffee.

But these three friends, Jesus' closest friends, were tired. Their eyes were heavy, but it isn't that difficult to stay awake for a few hours. (Apparently it was not even midnight yet). The fact that they fell asleep shows that they still did not understand what Jesus was about to endure. He came to them with his soul "overwhelmed with sorrow," and they were callous to his condition. Let's pray that our hearts will never be so callous.

The agony of the cross began for Jesus long before he was nailed to it. The last week of Jesus' life is called the Passion week because he suffered all week long. It was a week with long hours and little rest. It was a week when he tried to get his disciples to understand what he was about to endure, but they never really understood it until after the resurrection. It was a week of disappointment in the people who were closest to him. We see his agony in Gethsemane: Jesus was overwhelmed to the point of death. He knew what he was about to endure. If there had been a way out, he would have taken it, but he submitted to the will of the Father. He did not want to die, but he had to die to pay the price for forgiveness. He willingly paid that price.

At any moment in the process of his trial and crucifixion, Jesus could have called twelve legions of angels to rescue him. As he was being mocked, beaten, spit upon, and nailed to the cross, all he had to say was the name of the archangel, "Michael," and twelve legions of angels would have arrived. How do you fight an angel? And a legion is 6,000. Jesus had an out—he was not tricked into dying on the cross. He willingly went to the cross for us. He had a way of escape, but instead of escape, he chose to die on our behalf. He took the most courageous path that anyone has ever taken, the path to the cross. The way of suffering for Jesus was the path to our forgiveness.

The Arrest—Matthew 26:47-56, cf. Mark 14:43-52, Luke 22:47-53, John 18:2-12

Many pilgrims would have been in the garden that night, and so it was necessary for Judas to identify Jesus with a sign. The kiss was on the hand or foot and was a kiss of honor. R.T. France elaborates on Judas' choice to betray Jesus with a kiss:

> For a Rabbi's disciple to kiss his master (on hand or foot) was not an everyday greeting, but a mark of special honor. Nor dare the disciple take this initiative uninvited; to do so was a "studied insult." The greeting of Jesus as Rabbi in this context is therefore heavily ironical (see vs. 35, the only other use of this address in Matthew, again by Judas). Judas' action thus not only identifies Jesus to the arresting party, but also marks his own public repudiation of Jesus' authority.[211]

Jesus responds to Judas with the word "friend." Instead of resisting, he invites Judas to hurry and finish what he has started. The scene demonstrates that Jesus is in charge of what is occurring. He has set his mind in prayer and is ready for the events that are about to transpire.

One of Jesus' disciples grabs a sword and cuts off the ear of one the high priest's servants. John lets us know that it was the impulsive Peter who cut off the ear of Malchus. The proverb "all who draw the sword will die by the sword" must be taken in context. It is not a blanket statement teaching pacifism, but is a way that Jesus restates that he did not come to begin an armed revolution.

Jesus again demonstrates that he is the one who is in control at his arrest. He asked, "Why have you come to arrest me like an insurrectionist?" He reminds them of all the times he taught in their temple courts without an incident. What is happening is the fulfillment of Scripture. Jesus places his trust in God and allows the guard to arrest him.

The Trial—Matthew 26:57-68, Mark 14:53-65, Luke 22:54-65, John 18:12-24

The first place Jesus was taken after his arrest was to Caiaphas, the high priest. Archaeologists believe that Caiaphas and other religious leaders lived across the Kidron Valley from the Mount of Olives on Zion's hill. Today this is located just outside of Zion Gate on the Southeastern side of the Old City of Jerusalem. Church tradition has identified a house located around the church of St. Peter of Galicantu (the crowing rooster) as the home of Caiaphas. If this is true, and it very well could be, then the trial and confinement of Jesus the night before his crucifixion occurred here. Today you can walk through these ruins into a cellar (a water reservoir) that has been identified as the place where Jesus was confined for the night. We do not know if this is the actual place where Jesus was imprisoned, but it is likely that Jesus spent his night in a cellar (a makeshift jail cell) underneath the house of Caiaphas guarded by the Jewish guard.

Much has been written about the trial of Jesus. It has often been described as a "mock trial," because the Jewish authorities did not adhere to many of the legal regulations of a fair hearing before the Sanhedrin. Today some scholars have labeled the Gospel writers as anti-Semitic because of their portrayal of the Jewish authorities at the trial and crucifixion of Jesus, but the early church had no reason to invent the inconsistencies of the Sanhedrin. Matthew was attempting to reach a Jewish audience with his Gospel. Why would he include facts that would incite them against the church if the facts were not true? Also, in the minds of the Gospel writers, everyone was guilty of the death of Jesus. To them, you and I who are 2,000 years distant from the event of the cross are just as guilty as any of the Jewish or Roman authorities. As Matthew describes the events of the trial of Jesus, he is not trying to assign guilt to the Jews or the Romans. He is accurately depicting how despised and hated Jesus was by the Jewish leaders. They wanted to rid themselves of him. If they needed to cut a few legal corners, they were willing to do that.

What illegal actions did the Sanhedrin take?

1. It was illegal for them to try a capital case at night.

2. The charge of blasphemy did not meet the legal criteria for that charge. To commit blasphemy you had to pronounce the name of God in your statement.

3. To execute someone, the testimony of every witness had to agree. The Sanhedrin could not find even two witnesses that agreed.

4. The trial should have been held at the Royal Stoa in the temple area and not at Caiaphas' house. The Royal Stoa was the usual meeting place for the Sanhedrin.

5. Jesus was not given a defense attorney.

6. A minimum of two days was required to decide a capital offence. The trial of Jesus was rushed through in one night.

Let me also note that the Sanhedrin was the most powerful ruling council in Judaism, and they had the power to cut corners where they saw fit. If they feared mob violence, this would hasten their action. For them to execute Jesus before the Sabbath, they needed to try the case during the night and present it to Pilate the next morning (Friday morning). In their minds, their actions were appropriate. They were cutting corners that had to be cut to take care of a matter of supreme importance. This was a matter of national security, so the laws of a fair trial were secondary.

Pilate-Herod-Pilate—Matthew 27:11–31, Mark 15:1b–20, Luke 23:1–25, John 18:28–19:16

On Friday morning, the Sanhedrin met again to discuss what should be done with Jesus. After their discussion they handed him over to Pilate. Pilate had the power to execute Jesus, but he did not want to give the order for Jesus' execution, so he passed him over to Herod. Herod also didn't want to execute Jesus, so he passed him back to Pilate. Jesus was paraded back and forth between Pilate and Herod.

The discussion with Pilate could have occurred at the Royal Stoa on the Temple complex, as the Sanhedrin normally met there. Jesus would have been escorted from Caiaphas' house across a bridge into the temple area. We are uncertain where the events of Friday transpired. Some believe that Pilate was stationed at Herod's palace near the Jaffa gate, and some believe that he was at the Antonia Fortress overlooking the temple complex. Tradition places him at the Antonia Fortress. If tradition is correct, then the movements of Jesus on Friday would have been:

1. From Caiaphas' house to the Royal Stoa in the temple complex.

2. From the Royal Stoa to the Antonia Fortress to meet with Pilate.

3. From the Antonia Fortress to Herod's Palace to meet with Herod.

4. From Herod's Palace to the Antonia Fortress to meet again with Pilate.

5. Taken away to be crucified (either outside the northern gate of the city or on the Mount of Olives).

Peter's Denial—Matthew 26:69–75, Mark 14:66–72, Luke 22:54b–62, John 18:25–27

All four gospels record the event of Peter's denial of Christ. I have always been impressed with how the Bible is willing to portray the foibles of its major figures. Peter is the unofficial leader and spokesman for the disciples, yet here he denies Jesus. We should not forget that all the disciples denied Jesus. No one stood beside him during his darkest hour.

The Synoptic Gospels and John's Gospel differ in the order of the first two denials. We noted earlier a similar phenomenon in retelling of the testing of Jesus in the wilderness (Matthew 4). One retelling follows the chronological events as they occurred and the other follows a topical retelling. In the case of Peter's denial, it is difficult to determine which retelling is chronological and which is topical.

The Crucifixion—Matthew 27:32–56, Mark 15:21–41, Luke 23:26–49, John 19:16–37

When I Survey the Wondrous Cross
Isaac Watts (1674–1748)

When I survey the wondrous Cross
Where the young Prince of Glory died,
My richest gain I count but loss,
And pour contempt on all my pride.

Forbid it, Lord, that I should boast
Save in the death of Christ, my God;
All the vain things that charm me most,
I sacrifice them to his blood.

See from his head, his hands, his feet,
Sorrow and love flow mingled down;
Did e'er such love and sorrow meet
Or thorns compose so rich a crown?

His dying crimson like a robe
Spreads o'er his body on the Tree,
Then am I dead to all the globe,
And all the globe is dead to me.

Were the whole realm of nature mine,
That were a present far too small;
Love so amazing, so divine,
Demands my soul, my life, my all.

Crucifixion in the Ancient World[212]

To understand the crucifixion of Jesus, we need to understand something of crucifixion in the ancient world. We are going to look at references from the literature of the ancient Middle East to see what we can learn about the practice in the ancient world.

First, we see that crucifixion was very common. It wasn't just a Roman practice. It was practiced across the Middle Eastern world as a deterrent to crime, especially a crime against royalty. Crucifixion was a public spectacle. Therefore, as people witnessed an execution, they would be put on notice that anyone found guilty of a similar crime would meet a similar end.

As early as the Code of Hammurabi (c. 2250 BC), we find a reference to crucifixion. In the following quote, we see the punishment for a barber if he is guilty of freeing slaves (you can also read "doctor" in place of barber, since barbers often served as doctors or surgeons because of their skill with razors). The text reads:

> If a barber has excised a slave's mark without (the knowledge of) his owner so that he cannot be traced, they shall cut off the fore-hand of that barber. If a man has constrained the barber and he excises the slave's mark so that he cannot be traced, they shall put that man to death and shall hang him at his (own) door; the barber may swear 'Surely I excised (it) unwittingly', and he then goes free.[213]

The phrase, "hang him at his door," is a reference to a crucifixion. This public execution would stand as a deterrent to others who were thinking about freeing slaves.

A reference to crucifixion is found very early in the Old Testament. In Genesis 40:18–19, as Joseph reveals the meaning of the dreams of the butler and baker, he says to the baker, "Within three days Pharaoh will lift off your head [most likely a reference to decapitation], and hang you on a tree. And the birds will eat away your flesh." Not a conventional form of crucifixion, but crucifixion nonetheless. So in this reference, we see a form of crucifixion being practiced in Egypt c. 1880 BC.

We read a little later in Deuteronomy 21:22–23 (c. 1200 BC in Judea):

> If a man guilty of a capital offense is put to death and his body is hung on a tree, you must not leave his body on the tree overnight. Be sure to bury him that same day, because anyone who is hung on a tree is under God's curse. You must not desecrate the land the LORD your God is giving you as an inheritance.

For a man who was judged guilty of a capital offense in the ancient Hebrew culture, the punishment was death. After the criminal was put to death, his body was to be hung on a tree. This is a type of crucifixion. In the Old Testament tradition, the body was not to remain on the tree overnight.

Later in Joshua 8:29, we read:

> [Joshua] hung the king of Ai on a tree and left him there until evening. At sunset, Joshua ordered them to take his body from the tree and throw it down at the entrance of the city gate. And they raised a large pile of rocks over it, which remains to this day.

Here Joshua follows the directive of Deuteronomy 21 by making sure that the body of the King of Ai was buried before the day ended.

In the book of Esther we read the story of Haman who hated the Jews and devised a scheme to annihilate the Jewish people throughout his homeland. Through God's providence, Haman's scheme backfires and he is executed on the gallows that he had prepared for the Jews. Esther 7:9–10 reads:

> Then Harbona, one of the eunuchs attending the king, said, "A gallows seventy-five feet high stands by Haman's house. He had it made for Mordecai, who spoke up to help the king."
>
> The king said, "Hang him on it!" So they hanged Haman on the gallows he had prepared for Mordecai. Then the king's fury subsided.

In this verse the word for "gallows" can also be translated as "tree" or "pole." The word "hang" can also be translated as "crucify" or "suspend," so this form of execution could have been a crucifixion. Imagine how the Jews of the first century must have felt about crucifixion understanding that Haman wanted to crucify the Jews just for being Jews. Crucifixion was the punishment Haman wanted to use to wage genocide against the Jewish people.

After the death of Jesus, we see other crucifixions in Jerusalem. As Titus went into Jerusalem to quell the Jewish uprising in AD 70, he crucified dozens (if not hundreds) of people. Josephus records:

> When caught, they [Jews who were trying to escape from Jerusalem] were driven to resist, and after a conflict it seemed too late to sue for mercy. They were accordingly scourged and subjected to torture of every description, before being killed, and then crucified opposite the walls. Titus indeed commiserated their fate, five hundred or sometimes more being captured daily; on the other hand, he recognized the risk of dismissing prisoners of war, and that the custody of such numbers would amount to the imprisonment of their custodians; but his main reason for not stopping the crucifixions was the hope that the spectacle might perhaps induce the Jews to surrender, for fear that continued resistance would involve them in a similar fate. The soldiers out of rage and hatred amused themselves by nailing their prisoners in different postures; and so great was their number, that space could not be found for the crosses nor crosses for the bodies.[214]

From the references just cited, we can understand that crucifixion was practiced by many ancient civilizations from very early times. Crucifixion was used as a deterrent to crime. It made a public spectacle of the criminal, forcing others to see what would happen if they were caught in the same crime. A negative stigma was associated with crucifixion, and the Hebrew people viewed that stigma as a curse of God.

Second, crucifixion took many forms. When we think of crucifixion, we think of someone hanging on a t-shaped cross, but this was not always the case. In ancient times, the cross was shaped in many forms. At the height of the power of the Assyrian kingdom in the Middle East, one of their great kings was Tiglath-pileser III. He destroyed Lachish and then captured Jerusalem during the time of King Hezekiah. On the Nimrûd Slab Inscription of Tiglath-pileser III (c. 734 BC) there is a description of how Tiglath-pileser III executed the king of Bit-Shilani. The text reads:

> Bît-Shilâni, in its entirety, I smashed like a pot. Sarrabânu, their great royal city, I destroyed [so that it was] like a ruin [left by] the flood. I carried off its plunder. Nabû-ushabshi, their king, I hung up in front of the gate of his city on a stake. His land, his wife, his sons, his daughters, his property, the treasure of his palace, I carried off.[215]

Here we see crucifixion performed by impaling this king on a stake, but in an earlier case cited, the victim was hung on a door. So crucifixion was common and it took many forms.

Seneca wrote, "I see crosses there, not just of one kind, but made in many different ways: some have their victims with head down to the ground; some impale their private parts; others stretch out their arms on the gibbet."[216]

Third, crucifixion was usually saved for crimes that were considered serious. Crucifixion was considered to be a horrible death that should be saved for ruthless criminals. Let's look at some examples. Plutarch writes in *Moralia* 554a-b, "...every criminal who goes to execution must carry his own cross on his back...." Here you have a reference that demonstrates that the condemned must carry his own cross. You also see that the person being crucified was a criminal. Crucifixion was saved for people who were thieves, robbers, thugs, or felons.

To understand how Roman citizens viewed crucifixion, consider a quote from Cicero. In *Against Verres*, he writes, "To bind a Roman citizen is a crime, to flog him is an abomination, to slay him is almost an act of murder: to crucify him is—what? There is no fitting word that can possibly describe so horrible a deed" [II.v.66 (170)].[217]

This death was meant for extreme criminals. It was death without dignity, meant to humiliate the criminal and to make an example of him. The convict was stripped naked and suspended on wood at a major intersection. He was hung in the air for all to see. This was to be the grand deterrent to crime. It was a torturous death, the severity of the torture dependent only on the whim of the executioners. Seneca writes a realistic account of crucifixion in his *Epistles:*

Can anyone be found who would prefer wasting away in pain, dying limb by limb, or letting out his life drop by drop, rather than expiring once for all? Can any man be found willing to be fastened to the accursed tree, long sickly, already deformed, swelling with ugly tumors on chest and shoulders, and draw the breath of life amid long-drawn-out agony? I think he would have many excuses for dying even before mounting the cross![218]

The Romans excelled at executions. To keep the Roman Peace (*Pax Romana*), they ruled with an iron fist. They listed the ways they executed criminals and placed crucifixion at the top of the list calling it the *"summum supplicium"* (the supreme [Roman] penalty).[219] After crucifixion, the Romans used burning and decapitation as means of execution. Decapitation was looked upon as a more humane means of execution. It was illegal to crucify a Roman citizen; when a Roman citizen was executed, he was decapitated. This was the penalty inflicted upon the Apostle Paul in Rome. Hanging was also looked upon as a more humane punishment than crucifixion. Isidore of Seville wrote, "But hanging is a lesser penalty than the cross. For the gallows kills the victim immediately, whereas the cross tortures for a long time those who are fixed to it."[220]

Crucifixion was the supreme penalty handed out to the lowest class of society. It was for non-Romans. At the gladiatorial games in Rome, crucifixion was often used for entertainment. Crosses were placed at public venues, often outside city gates or at major intersections, so that many people could witness the execution. The executioners were professional. They knew how to keep a person alive for hours so that multitudes of people could witness the event.

Crucifixion was often saved for high crimes and for treason. The Romans wanted to make an example of the most severe criminals, and no crime was more severe than treason. Therefore an added stigma was placed on crucified people; you were more than a common criminal—you were an enemy of the state. Hengel writes, "Crucifixion was also a means of waging war and securing peace, of wearing down rebellious cities under siege, of breaking the will of conquered peoples and of bringing mutinous troops or unruly provinces under control."[221]

The Romans viewed crucifixion as the punishment for slaves. In fact "the slaves' punishment" is found in ancient literature to describe crucifixion. When slave owners could not control their slaves, they often had them crucified as an example to other slaves. If a slave owner was murdered, every slave in his house was executed by crucifixion. That way, any murderous talk among slaves was more likely to be reported by a slave who wanted to protect himself. The typical punishment for rebellious slaves was crucifixion. After the slave rebellion of Spartacus was crushed, six thousand slaves were crucified on the *Via Appia* (Appian Way) between Rome and Crassus.[222]

The knowledge that crucifixion was viewed as the slaves' punishment adds meaning to Philippians 2:6–11. Paul teaches that Jesus willingly became a slave and also became obedient to death, even death on the cross, the slave's punishment. How far was Jesus willing to go with his acceptance of slavery? He went all the way with it, even unto death. But this Jesus who became a slave and died a slave's death was in actuality the Lord of the universe.

Crucifixion and the Early Church
How did members of the early church view crucifixion, and what type of stigma did a crucified person bear? The early Christians worshiped a God/man who had been crucified. How did the Jews and Greeks react to this? Until recently I had never thought much about this. I knew what Paul wrote in 1 Corinthians 1:23, that the cross is "foolishness (μωρία/ moria) to the Gentiles and a stumbling block (σκάνδαλον/*skandalon*, a scandal) to the Jews." But I never realized the degree to which the Gentiles viewed the cross as absolute foolishness and the Jews viewed anyone who died on a cross as a scoundrel and thug. Martin Hengel's book, *Crucifixion*, opened my eyes to the folly of the message of the cross in the ancient world.[223]

How did the ancient world view crucifixion? First, the story of a religion saying its founder was crucified is unique in ancient literature. No other religion was based upon a leader (or a god) who had been crucified.[224] In fact, although many of the Greek gods had foibles, the Greeks celebrated the immortality of their gods. Yet the Christians worshipped a God who had died. He not only died, but their deity died a shameful death on a cross. It was difficult for the Greek mind to accept this. How could a god die? Why would a god die such an ignoble death? This distinguished Jesus from all other religious leaders and all other gods. To the Greco-Roman mind, this was foolishness and they could not grasp it.

Another aspect of this foolishness was the fact that Jesus willingly accepted this shameful death and did not fight against it. He predicted it would happen. He willingly accepted his arrest and did not defend himself at his trial. He humbly and obediently accepted death. Humility and obedience did not characterize the pagan pantheon. That Jesus had these characteristics was foolishness to the Greeks.

Second, the early church was attacked because of the cross. A major attack on the church came from the Gnostics, a group of philosophers who accepted Plato's teaching that the material world was evil. How then is it possible that God could come into the evil world and take on the evil flesh through the incarnation? How is it possible for God to die through the crucifixion? Gnostics taught that Jesus only seemed to be human (docetism). They also taught that Jesus did not die on the cross, he only seemed to die. Gnostics felt that Jesus must have escaped before his arrest or before the crucifixion. Someone else (a replacement) endured the suffering of the imprisonment and crucifixion of Jesus. To them the cross was foolishness. It was impossible that God would suffer as Jesus had suffered.

One such Gnostic was Celsus. He wrote many polemics against the church. Celsus wrote the following about Jesus: "And you, do you not believe that the son of God sent to the Jews is the most ridiculous makeshift of all?"[225] Celsus believed that Jesus had the perfect opportunity to demonstrate his divinity at his trial. If he had transported himself away from the suffering, he would have proven his deity. By staying, he disproved it, since no god would undergo the physical torment that Jesus went through. To Celsus, the story of the cross was illogical. Martin Hengel notes the protests of the Gnostics.

> To believe that the one pre-existent Son of the one true God, the mediator at creation and the redeemer of the world, had appeared in very recent times in out-of-the-way Galilee as a member of the obscure people of the Jews, and even worse, had died the death of a common criminal on the cross, could only be regarded as a sign of madness.[226]

To the mind of the Gnostic, the cross was unacceptable.

A discovery by archaeologists illustrates that the early church was ridiculed because of its teaching of the cross. Archaeologists found a first-century drawing of a man being crucified. In the drawing the crucified man is wearing a donkey's head, and underneath this drawing is the inscription: "Alexamenos worships god."[227] This graffito poked fun at the Christian belief that the Jesus who died on the cross was God. This belief was foolishness to the Gentile and a scandal to the Jews.

An interesting note here: Many Muslims do not believe that Jesus died on the cross. They worship Jesus as a great prophet but do not believe in his crucifixion. The cross is foolishness to them. Although this is not taught in the Koran, many believe that a substitute for Jesus went to the cross and that the substitute was Judas, who died on the cross instead of Jesus. I learned this teaching from my dialogue with Muslims about the crucifixion when I lived in Jerusalem.

Conclusion

To the first-century mind, crucifixion was the most barbaric, degrading, dehumanizing, and humiliating death that a person could suffer. It was saved for the lower classes. It was inflicted on traitorous criminals. It was "the slave's punishment." To the Roman, crucifixion was the *summum supplicium,* the supreme penalty. The Greco-Roman mind could not conceive of a deity undergoing this punishment. To them it was just foolishness to think this way.

To understand how the ancients thought about this, think about how the same ideas would strike us today. Imagine someone who has been arrested on the suspicion that he wanted to start a revolution and topple the United States government. After 9/11, it is not difficult to imagine this happening. He is placed on trial and convicted of a capital crime against the United States of America. He appeals to all the sources that he can appeal to, but he is still found guilty. It seems that some evidence was trumped up, but the conviction stands. He is executed for treason.

But you know the man. You know that he is not guilty and that he wanted the best for America and the American people. Some of his words had been taken out of context and he was executed unjustly, so you take up his cause. You parade around the country telling everyone that the man who was arrested, tried, convicted, and executed as a traitorous criminal was actually a good man. It is a tough sell, but you take it a step further. You declare that this man who was killed by the authorities was not a man at all, but the Son of God and divine. Imagine how people would react to this. They would think you were insane. Many reacted to the early disciples in the same way. The message of the cross was foolishness to the Gentiles and a stumbling block to the Jews. How did the early church win so many to their cause with this scandalous message? It was their commitment to the message that won many people over.

In 1 Corinthians 1:21–25, Paul writes:

> *For since in the wisdom of God the world through its wisdom did not know him, God was pleased through the foolishness of what was preached to save those who believe. Jews demand miraculous signs and Greeks look for wisdom, but we preach Christ crucified: a stumbling block to Jews and foolishness to Gentiles, but to those whom God has called, both Jews and Greeks, Christ the power of God and the wisdom of God. For the foolishness of God is wiser than man's wisdom, and the weakness of God is stronger than man's strength.*

What Can We Learn from the Cross?

1. Jesus literally became a slave for us, and in response we must become a slave for him.
Philippians 2:5–8 reads:

> *Your attitude should be the same as that of Christ Jesus:*
> *Who, being in very nature God,*
> *Did not consider equality with God something to be grasped,*
> *But made himself nothing,*

Taking the very nature of a servant,
Being made in human likeness.
And being found in appearance as a man,
He humbled himself
And became obedient to death—
Even death on a cross!

Jesus did not just act the part of a slave; he literally became a slave for us. He served humanity in everything he did and gave himself to humanity every day. But the ultimate example of his servant nature was his willingness to die the slave's death on the cross.

In Luke 9:23, Jesus directs his disciples, "If anyone would come after me, he must deny himself and take up his cross daily and follow me." What does he mean by "take up his cross daily"? In our culture today, we can water this down until it is meaningless, but in the time of Jesus to take up a cross meant one thing: to die. Not to die just any death; no, it meant to die the slave's death. We must be a slave for Jesus every single day and crucify our selfish nature every day. Some might protest that Jesus was directing this message to his closest circle of disciples, but he begins the sentence by saying, "If anyone would come after me..." The call of discipleship is the same for everyone. You cannot follow Jesus without a cross, and the cross is for death, a slave's death. To follow Jesus you must die to yourself every day and become a slave for him.

2. He died on the cross for us.

The Apostle Paul in Romans 8:32 states, "He who did not spare his own Son, but gave him up for us all—how will he not also, along with him, graciously give us all things?" Hengel comments on Paul's statement:

> Jesus did not die a gentle death like Socrates, with his cup of hemlock, much less passing on old and full of years like the patriarchs of the Old Testament. Rather, he died like a slave or a common criminal, in torment, on the tree of shame. Paul's Jesus did not die just any death; he was given up for us all on the cross in a cruel and a contemptible way.[228]

If we do not stumble at the cross or mock it as foolish, then the cross makes us appreciate the sacrifice of Jesus all the more. Jesus did not die for himself; he died for us. He took our place. We deserve the criminal's death on the cross, but Jesus died that death for us.

The Death and Burial of Jesus—Matthew 27:50–66, Mark 15:37–16:1, Luke 23:46–56, John 19:30–42

The death of Jesus is marked by one simple sentence: "And when Jesus had cried out again in a loud voice, he gave up his spirit." Death by crucifixion usually occurred by suffocation. As one hung upon the cross, the lungs would cease to function and carbon dioxide would saturate the blood. The body would long for oxygen. To take a breath, you would have to push up with your legs and fill your lungs. Since Jesus' feet were nailed to the cross, this would be a very painful undertaking. It would be during this time that Jesus would have made his seven statements from the cross.

After some time, the legs would begin to cramp and the pain from the nails would be intolerable, so the victim would slump back down and place his weight on the nails in his palms. He would begin to suffocate again because he would not be able to breathe with the pressure on his lung cavity. He would endure suffocation as long as possible, and then reflexively lift himself back up by the nails in his feet. Often the soldiers would hasten death by breaking the legs of the victim. If they could not push up with their legs, then they could not breathe, and they would quickly suffocate on the cross.

This is the type of agonizing death that Jesus endured. After such a painful ordeal, the Bible notes the death of Jesus simply as "he gave up his spirit." Jesus who was in full control up to this point, in his arrest, in his trials, is still in control. He "gives up" his spirit.

When Jesus died, the curtain of the temple was torn in two. The temple had an outer curtain and an inner curtain. The inner curtain separated the holy place from the most holy place. Matthew is referring to the curtain inside the temple. It tore from top to bottom, signifying that God did the tearing. The curtain separated the priests from the Holy of Holies where the presence of God resided. Only the high priest was allowed to go into the Holy of Holies, and he could enter only once a year. God now tears down this dividing partition. The curtain no longer separates us from the presence of God. We can now approach God directly.

Matthew concludes his narrative of the crucifixion with the reaction of an eyewitness to the event. The eyewitness is the centurion who oversaw the execution. He exclaims, "Surely he was the Son of God!" What the Jewish authorities failed to see, the centurion saw. What Jesus' disciples had a difficult time understanding, the centurion comprehended. The centurion saw with eyes of faith. Will the cross be a stumbling block to you? Will you consider it foolishness? Or will you see Jesus with eyes of faith?

End Notes

207. Scriptures from Matthew in this chapter are the author's own translation.

208. Hendriksen and Kistemaker, 908.

209. *The Westminster Confession of Faith* (P & R Publishing, 2nd edition, 2003).

210. Rienecker, Fritz, translated by Cleon L. Rogers, Jr., *A Linguistic Key to the Greek New Testament.* (Grand Rapids: Zondervan, 1976), 78.

211. France, 385.

212. Much of the material in this section is based upon Martin Hengel's classic study on crucifixion, *Crucifixion* (Philadelphia: Fortress Press, 1977). For a fuller, deeper study of the topic, see Hengel's work.

213. As quoted in Hengel.

214. Josephus, *Jewish Wars* 5.449–451, as quoted in Hengel.

215. As quoted in Hengel.

216. As quoted in Hengel, 90.

217. From Hengel.

218. As quoted in Hengel, "Seneca," 101.

219. Hengel, 90.

220. As quoted in Hengel, 92.

221. Hengel, 94.

222. Ibid.

223. Hengel.

224. Ibid., 6.

225. As quoted in Hengel, 25.

226. Ibid.

227. Hengel., 46.

228. Ibid.

Chapter 15

The Resurrection

Up from the Grave He Arose
Text and music: Robert Lowry (1826–1899)

Low in the grave he lay, Jesus my Savior,
Waiting the coming day, Jesus my Lord!

Refrain:
Up from the grave he arose
With a mighty triumph o'er his foes;
He arose a victor from the dark domain,
And he lives forever, with his saints to reign.
He arose! He arose! Hallelujah! Christ arose!

Vainly they watch his bed, Jesus my Savior.
Vainly they seal the dead, Jesus my Lord!
Refrain

Death cannot keep its prey, Jesus my Savior;
He tore the bars away, Jesus my Lord!
Refrain

The Meaning of Easter

I find that the Holy Week is draining; no matter how many times I have lived through
his crucifixion, my anxiety about his resurrection is undiminished—I am terrified
that, this year, it won't happen; that, that year, it didn't. Anyone can be sentimental
about the Nativity; any fool can feel like a Christian at Christmas. But Easter is the
main event; if you don't believe in the resurrection, you're not a believer.[229]

—John Irving, American writer

That Jesus succeeded in changing a snuffling band of unreliable followers into fearless evangelists, that eleven men who had deserted him at death now went to martyrs' graves avowing their faith in a resurrected Christ, that these few witnesses managed to set loose a force that would overcome violent opposition first in Jerusalem and then in Rome—this remarkable sequence of transformation offers the most convincing evidence for the Resurrection. What else explains the whiplash change in men known for their cowardice and instability?[230]

—Philip Yancey, author of *The Jesus I Never Knew*

Easter Joke:

Three guys died and are at the pearly gates of heaven. Now these three guys weren't the sharpest knives in the drawer; their elevator didn't go quite to the top; they were a few bricks shy of a load; they didn't drink their allotted portion of Smart Water. They were a little on the shallow side.

They arrive at the pearly gates of heaven. St. Peter tells them that they can enter the gates if they can answer one simple question. St. Peter asks the first not-so-smart man, "What is Easter?" He replies, "Oh, that's easy! It's the holiday in November when everyone gets together, eats turkey, and is thankful..." "Wrong!" replies St. Peter. Peter presses a button that releases a trap door and the man drops down a gigantic chute to the other destination for the afterlife.

Peter proceeds to ask the second not-so-smart guy the same question, "What is Easter?" The second one replies, "Easter is the holiday in December when we put up a nice tree, exchange presents, and celebrate the birth of Jesus." St. Peter looks at the second man, shakes his head in disgust, and tells him that he's wrong. He pushes the button, releases the trap door. "Whoosh," the man is gone.

Peter then looks at the third not-so-smart man and asks, "What is Easter?" The third man smiles confidently and looks St. Peter in the eyes. "I know what Easter is." "Oh?" says St. Peter, incredulously. "Easter is the Christian holiday that coincides with the Jewish celebration of Passover. Jesus and his disciples ate the Last Supper. Judas betrayed Jesus and turned him over to the Romans. The Romans crucified him. They hung Jesus on a cross by driving nails through his hands; they made him wear a crown of thorns; they stabbed him in the side with a spear; and they pronounced him dead. Jesus was buried in a nearby cave which was sealed off by a large boulder." St. Peter smiles broadly with delight. Then the not-so-smart man continues, "Every year the boulder is moved aside so that Jesus can come out...and, if he sees his shadow, there will be six more weeks of winter."[231]

It seems that Easter is greatly misunderstood. So, what is the meaning of Easter?

I've had two life events that have greatly influenced my view of the meaning of Easter. The first is my religious upbringing. The second is the year that my family and I lived in Jerusalem. I'll mention both of these.

First, my religious upbringing. I grew up in a very conservative church in Middle Tennessee that believed in following the Bible literally. We lived by Thomas Campbell's slogan, "Speak where the Bible speaks and be silent where the Bible is silent." When it comes to celebrating Easter, the Bible is silent. The word "Easter" is not in most translations of the Bible. You can find it in the King James Version of 1611. The KJV translates Acts 12:4 as: "And when he had apprehended him, he put him in prison, and delivered him to four quaternions of soldiers to keep him; intending after Easter to bring him forth to the people." The Greek word here is πάσχα/ *Pascha*, the word for Passover. Every modern translation that I could find translates πάσχα/*Pascha* as Passover. The writers of the King James Version wanted to legitimize the celebration of Easter, so they stuck Easter in their translation of Acts 12:4. My little conservative church in Middle Tennessee knew that Easter wasn't celebrated in the first-century church as a religious holiday. The earliest primary source that gives a reference for Easter comes from a mid-second-century sermon attributed to Melito, the bishop of Sardis (died c. 180), who characterizes the celebration of Easter as a well-established one. Due to the lack of evidence for the celebration of Easter by the earliest disciples, we did not celebrate Easter as a religious holiday in my home church in Tennessee.

The earliest Jewish Christians continued to celebrate the Passover feast. Passover was a commemoration of the passing over of the death angel, sparing the Jewish firstborn in Egypt, and the subsequent freeing of the Jewish people from Egyptian slavery. The earliest Jewish Christians could easily incorporate a celebration of the resurrection of Jesus into this festival, but there is no direct evidence that demonstrates this hypothesis.

The date for the celebration of Easter was seriously debated until the emperor Constantine in the Council of Nicaea (AD 325) decided that Easter would be celebrated on the first Sunday following the full moon of the spring equinox. Thus, Easter falls between March 22nd and April 25th.

The word "Easter" comes from a pagan, not a Christian, origin. The mother goddess of the Saxon people in Northern Europe was Eostre. The historian Bede, (672–735) a Christian scholar, made the claim that Easter was named after Eostre (a.k.a. *Eastre*). Also, the word might derive from a Scandinavian mother goddess, Ostra. Also, the Teutonic goddess of fertility was known as Eostra or Eostre. It has been surmised that her name is a derivative of *eastre*, the ancient word for spring. Thus Easter was a celebration of the arrival of spring, and many images have been carried over from that celebration (for example, the Easter bunny symbolizes fertility and the Easter egg symbolizes new life).

I never heard the phrase "Happy Easter" until I moved to an Italian neighborhood in Brooklyn when I was in my mid-twenties. On the streets of Carroll Gardens, my neighbors greeted me with "Good Friday" or

"Happy Easter." I wasn't sure of the correct response to their greetings, so I usually just smiled and said, "Thanks."

So to speak frankly, when I'm asked, "What is the meaning of Easter?" my answer must be: "To me, Easter as a religious celebration doesn't really mean that much." I'm not from the Orthodox tradition. I'm not even from a mainstream Protestant tradition. I don't celebrate Easter as a religious holiday. I don't disparage those who do celebrate Easter as a day to honor the resurrection of Jesus. I just choose, along with the church I was raised in, to celebrate the resurrection of Jesus every day, and, in a special way, to meditate upon and celebrate it each and every Sunday during the taking of communion.

The second life event that has informed me as to the meaning of Easter came during my year of living in Jerusalem, one of the most amazing cities in the world. I love the way that three active world religions exist side by side within the walls of the Old City of Jerusalem. The Old City is divided into four quarters: The Armenian Quarter, the Jewish Quarter, the Muslim Quarter, and the Christian Quarter. It was my custom every Friday to walk the streets of the Old City of Jerusalem.

Once on Good Friday, I decided to walk the Via Dolorosa, the traditional last steps of Christ as he headed toward the cross. There was one intersection where just before noon, a procession of Christians carrying crosses began to head up the Via Dolorosa toward the church of the Holy Sepulcher. At the same time, Muslims were headed toward their Friday prayers at the Al Aksa Mosque. The Christians were headed south to north and the Muslims were headed east to west at this one intersection in the road (which was more like a sidewalk than a road). To try to keep order in this chaos, Jewish soldiers carrying machine guns and automatic weapons were stationed at the intersection. It was a microcosm of the centuries-old conflict between the peoples representing the three major religions that occupy that city.

As I mentioned, Easter is associated with a celebration commemorating the resurrection of Jesus. The image of the empty tomb is one of the most important images in Christianity. The Apostle Paul wrote, "And if Christ has not been raised, your faith is futile; you are still in your sins" (1 Corinthians 15:17). The resurrection implies an empty tomb. In Jerusalem, Christians point not to just one empty tomb, but to two empty tombs. The orthodox churches, including the Catholic Church, say the empty tomb of Jesus is within the confines of the Church of the Holy Sepulcher. This could be the site where Jesus was buried, because first-century burial shelves have been found within the church; however, the Holy Sepulcher itself could not be the site of the empty tomb because the sepulcher dates back only to the 1800s. Protestant churches point to a different location for the empty tomb, suggesting a location just outside the Damascus Gate in what is known as the Garden Tomb. This again is a first-century tomb. It is picturesque and lovely, a more serene and contemplative setting than the Holy Sepulcher, but we cannot know with any certainty at all if this was the actual tomb of Jesus.

My time in Jerusalem taught me this: All this business by both the Orthodox and Protestant churches about locating and identifying an empty tomb that was used for a short period of time by Jesus of Nazareth demonstrates how important the Easter story is to Christianity. So even though I don't celebrate Easter as a religious holiday, I do celebrate the importance of the Easter story.

Why is the Easter story so important? Restoration minister, Walter Scott, wrote concerning the resurrection of Jesus in his book, *The Messiahship, Or, Great Demonstration,* noting:

> I handle this great subject (the resurrection) tremblingly, I confess, not, however, because I think the fate of our religion depends on my poor piece; nor because I think the resurrection still problematical; nor that the awful and eternal interests suspended on it are yet unsettled; nor because the river of sin and death still continues to stream through the race; nor that the problem of humanity is yet unsolved; nor the designs of the Almighty are still dark and unlovely, nor that we are still without God and without hope in the world; but I tremble lest Satan or his ministers, or what is still more to be deprecated, the ministers of Christ themselves, deceiving and being deceived, should have taught the reader to set lightly by the evidence of the fact, and so have turned him away from the testimony of holy apostles, on which it was designed by Almighty God, or should rest for faith in that fact on some fanciful and mysterious source of belief utterly unrecognized by the source of proof—the "word of God which liveth and abideth forever."[232]

The Resurrection—Matthew 28:1–15, cf. Mark 16:2–14, Luke 24:1–43, John 20:1–23

> *After the Sabbath, at dawn on the first day of the week, Mary Magdalene and the other Mary went to see the tomb.*
>
> *Behold, a great earthquake began, and an angel of the Lord descended from heaven, rolled back the stone and sat on it. His appearance was as lightening and his clothes as white as snow. The guards were afraid of him and shook and became as dead men.*
>
> *But the angel said to the women, "Do not be afraid; I know you are looking for Jesus who was crucified. He is not here, for he rose just as he said. Come see the place where he lay. Go quickly and tell his disciples—he has risen from the dead and is going ahead of you into Galilee. You will see him there. Indeed I have told you this."*
>
> *They left the tomb quickly. With fear and great joy, they ran to report this to his disciples. Jesus met them suddenly, saying, "Greetings!" They came to him, took hold*

of his feet and worshipped him. Jesus said to them, "Do not be afraid; go and tell my brothers to go into Galilee. They will see me there."[233]

The resurrection is the most central and crucial event in all Christianity. It is what sets Jesus apart from other religious teachers. If Jesus rose from the dead, then his message is true. If he did not rise from the dead, then his message is a hoax. The resurrection made the difference in the disciple's lives. Before the resurrection they were a weak, faithless, defeated group. After the resurrection, they turned the world upside down for Jesus. Stephen T. Davis, professor of philosophy at Claremont McKenna College, writes, "It is probable that apart from the belief of Jesus' followers that he had been risen by God, there would exist today no Christian faith or Christian church. Possibly no one today would ever have heard of the man Jesus of Nazareth."[234]

The Apostle Paul experienced the resurrection of Jesus and wrote about that experience in 1 Corinthians 15. He staked a great deal on the factuality of the Jesus' resurrection. He writes in 1 Corinthians 15:12–19:

But if it is preached that Christ has been raised from the dead, how can some of you say that there is no resurrection of the dead? If there is no resurrection of the dead, then not even Christ has been raised. And if Christ has not been raised, our preaching is useless and so is your faith. More than that, we are then found to be false witnesses about God, for we have testified about God that he raised Christ from the dead. But he did not raise him if in fact the dead are not raised. For if the dead are not raised, then Christ has not been raised either. And if Christ has not been raised, your faith is futile; you are still in your sins. Then those also who have fallen asleep in Christ are lost. If only for this life we have hope in Christ, we are to be pitied more than all men.

Paul said that if the resurrection were not true, then we as believers would be above all men most to be pitied (1 Corinthians 15:19) and that if Jesus has not been raised, then our preaching is in vain and our faith is in vain (1 Corinthians 15:14). He said that if the resurrection is not true, then we are still in our sins (1 Corinthians 15:17). Paul is saying that if the resurrection of Jesus is not true, then Christianity is based on a lie and the practice of it is pointless. But if the resurrection is true, then Christianity is true and should be practiced. If the resurrection is true, then we can tap into the resurrection power of Jesus to change our lives. If the resurrection is true, then we have hope of a future life with Jesus in eternity. The resurrection is the pivotal event of Jesus' life.

When I was in seminary working on my master's degree, I had a New Testament professor who attempted to explain away all the miracles of Jesus as we came across them in the text. He explained that Jesus' walking on the water was an optical illusion. Many parts of the Sea of

Galilee are very shallow and with the bright sun reflecting off the water it would look as if Jesus were walking on the surface of the water. He explained away the miracle stories by saying that Jesus was a holistic healer who had extensive knowledge of homeopathic remedies, which he used to cure people. He explained away every miracle in this fashion. But as we approached Easter, we came to the story of the resurrection in the text. I remember him saying, "I will explain away every miracle in the Bible except the resurrection. Because if Jesus did not rise from the dead, then we have no Christianity. If Jesus did not rise, then we have no hope of resurrection. As Paul said, 'we are above all men most to be pitied.'"

We were all a bit shocked at the professor's adamant attitude toward the resurrection. One of my friends raised his hand and asked, "But professor, how is it that you can believe in the resurrection and fail to believe the other miracles of the Bible? After all, which is harder to believe, that Jesus rose from the dead or that he changed water into wine?" The professor had no answer to this except to restate his earlier claim, "If Jesus did not rise from the dead, then we have no Christianity." Even my liberal professor from seminary recognized the importance of the resurrection of Jesus.

There are only a handful of possible explanations for the resurrection story/Easter story. Here are the possible scenarios, as I see them.

1. The body of Jesus simply vanished into thin air. Perhaps it was a case of post-mortem spontaneous human combustion. Except that not everything was consumed. His death shroud remained in the tomb. Also, Jesus appeared to people after his death.

2. The disciples of Jesus stole his body, thus fabricating the hoax of his resurrection. The disciples were certainly disappointed that Jesus died and didn't understand his death. But would they be willing to perpetrate a hoax on themselves, their families, and their fellow believers? Would they be willing to hold to this lie when they, their wives and children, and their fellow believers were persecuted, tortured, and executed? Without the resurrection, the disciples had no reason to believe Jesus, much less die for his cause.

3. Perhaps the opponents of Jesus stole his body. But the opponents had no reason to steal the body. In fact, to make sure the body wasn't stolen they placed guards at the tomb. If the opponents did steal the body, they must have forgotten where they placed it. Why else would they fail to produce the body of Jesus once rumors of his resurrection began to circulate? If you want to squash rumors of a resurrection, produce the dead body. Parade the corpse in the streets for a few days. That would squash a resurrection hoax.

4. Jesus didn't die on the cross; he was drugged or he swooned, appearing as dead.

> But the Romans were thoroughly trained at the art of execution. They would have known when their job was done. Also, if Jesus did wake up in the tomb, how could he have unwrapped the burial linen, removed the stone from the face of the tomb, and overpowered the Roman guards? If he did wake up and escape the tomb, how could he begin this hoax of his resurrection and still be considered a moral person? What good, moral person would allow people who believe in them to die for a lie?
>
> 5. Perhaps the women went to the wrong tomb or they met someone other than Jesus. If so, this would have been discovered soon enough. Certainly, Thomas would have uncovered the imposter when he asked to see his wounds.
>
> 6. The disciples spiritualized the event. They made an unbelievable event seem real in their minds. They hallucinated the event. But people have hallucinations as individuals and not as a group. Also, why didn't the opponents of Jesus produce the body and thus discredit the disciples?
>
> 7. Jesus rose.

Today, there are a number of scholars who: (1) simply evade the historicity of the resurrection saying that there is no way to know if Jesus rose from the dead or not—they accept a Jesus of faith and don't care if in fact he rose or stayed in the grave, (2) attack the historicity of the resurrection by saying that gospel accounts are unreliable and cannot be trusted, or (3) are naturalists, not supernaturalists, and reject the resurrection because they do not believe that God acts in this world in a supernatural, miraculous way. If someone denies the reliability of the Scriptures or the possibility of miracles, then it is difficult to convince them of the resurrection.

Other scholars do defend the historicity of the resurrection. N. T. Wright, biblical scholar and author, mentions three arguments for an empty tomb and the resurrection of Jesus. I quote from his book, *Surprised by Hope.*[235]

> 1. Jewish tombs, especially those of martyrs, were venerated and often became shrines. There is no sign whatever of that having happened with Jesus' grave.
>
> 2. The early church's emphasis on the first day of the week as their special day is very hard to explain unless something striking really did happen then....
>
> 3. The disciples were hardly likely to go out and suffer and die for a belief that wasn't firmly anchored in fact.

What Is the Meaning of Easter?

Let's ask, "What does the resurrection of Jesus mean for us today?" If the resurrection means nothing for our lives today, then what good does it do to believe in it? Stephen T. Davis raises these questions in his important book, *Risen Indeed: Making Sense of the Resurrection.*[236] Dr. Davis posits four crucial implications of the resurrection that apply to our lives today. Think of the first three of these ideas in terms of what the resurrection did in the past, what it does today, and what it will do in the future.

1. The resurrection posits that Jesus is Lord.

If Jesus rose, then everything he claimed to be and to do is true. What did the resurrection do in the past? It validated Jesus. Marcus Borg writes:

> What did Easter mean to the early followers of Jesus? . . . First, the followers of Jesus continued to experience him after his death. . . . Indeed, they experienced him as a divine reality, as one with God. Second, Easter meant that God had vindicated Jesus. As Acts 2:36 puts it, 'This Jesus whom you crucified, God has made him both Lord and Messiah.' Easter is God's 'yes' to Jesus and God's 'no' to the powers that killed him. Jesus was executed by Rome and vindicated by God. To put these two meanings as concisely as possible, Easter meant 'Jesus lives' and 'Jesus is Lord.'[237]

Jesus made many bold claims in his ministry. He claimed that he could forgive sin and that he could heal disease and raise the dead. He claimed that he was the one, true pathway to God, and that no one could get to the Father except through him (John 14:6). He claimed to be the Son of God (John 10:30) and that his word was truth. He claimed that he would die and come back to life within three days.

Either these claims are true or false. There is no middle ground. Disprove any one claim, and the rest fall like a house of cards. So if Jesus did not come back to life within three days, then all his claims are false. Therefore, produce his dead body and prove that he was a hoax. But if he rose, then all his claims are true.

We nicknamed one of my grandfathers, "Pa-Pa." He died way back in 1969 of stomach cancer. His funeral was the first one I ever attended. What if my Pa-Pa walked through the door and into the room saying, "Steve, I've got something very important to tell you. You need to listen very carefully to what I say and do exactly what I tell you to do." I'd have a choice to make. After I got over the initial shock, I'd either check myself into a psychiatric hospital for evaluation, or I'd listen to my Pa-Pa and do exactly what he said. Why? Because if he came back from the dead, then his words carry extra weight.

Since the resurrection is true, we need to heed the words of Jesus. Some of us are doing that and some of us aren't. If you're not, then you'd better wake up. This isn't some nice self-help program that we're talking about. This isn't like a course that you audit in school but don't get a grade. This stuff is real. It makes a difference now and for eternity.

2. The resurrection posits that God will win.

Dr. Davis focuses here on the afterlife, but I want to focus on the power of the resurrection in the present, in the here and now. If Jesus rose, then "Hoorah!" we can experience resurrection power in our own lives.

For many people the value of something lies in what they can gain from it right now. Does the resurrection mean anything for me in this real world?

We don't have to wait until after we die to experience the resurrection of Jesus; we can experience his resurrection in the here and now. Paul describes this process in Romans 6:1–7, writing:

> What shall we say, then? Shall we go on sinning so that grace may increase? By no means! We died to sin; how can we live in it any longer? Or don't you know that all of us who were baptized into Christ Jesus were baptized into his death? We were therefore buried with him through baptism into death in order that, just as Christ was raised from the dead through the glory of the Father, we too may live a new life.
>
> If we have been united with him like this in his death, we will certainly also be united with him in his resurrection. For we know that our old self was crucified with him so that the body of sin might be done away with, that we should no longer be slaves to sin—because anyone who has died has been freed from sin.

As Christ was raised, we can live a new life. Have you ever wanted a restart in life? Ever wanted a do-over? When I'm bored, I'll break out my phone and play checkers. It's tough to beat the computer, but I have an advantage that the computer doesn't have. If I make a bad move, then all I have to do to push the "undo" button and I get to redo that move. Through the power of the resurrection, Jesus offers a new start in our lives.

3. The resurrection posits that we too will rise from the dead.

If Jesus rose, then "Hip, hip, hoorah!" we have hope of eternal life with God. Let's go back to Paul's teaching on the resurrection in 1 Corinthians 15:20–26. He writes:

> But Christ has indeed been raised from the dead, the firstfruits of those who have fallen asleep. For since death came through a man, the resurrection of the dead comes also through a man. For as in Adam all die, so in Christ all will be made alive. But each in his own turn: Christ, the firstfruits; then, when he comes, those who belong to him. Then the end will come, when he hands over the kingdom to God the Father after he has destroyed all dominion, authority and power. For he must reign until he has put

all his enemies under his feet. The last enemy to be destroyed is death.

Death is inevitable—death and taxes. Death liberates us from paying taxes, but what liberates us from death? Paul says the resurrection of Jesus does. Calvin Miller writes:

> Paul grew rapturous when he considered the power of the Resurrection over death. "O death where is your sting?" he asked (1 Corinthians 15:55). Since Jesus had come, his Resurrection provided ultimate hope.... The ultimate fear of humankind has always been death. The resurrection story, therefore, is not a mere exaltation of what Jesus was able to achieve in walking out of the tomb. The resurrection story is the message of hope. [238]

The resurrection story is the story of victory over death, not just for Jesus, but for us all. Jesus is the firstfruit of the resurrection. The firstfruit is the first harvest. This implies there will be a second harvest. We will participate in that second harvest.

I have a friend in North Carolina who said he likes to walk through cemeteries just to give him a reminder that that's where he's going to end up some day. He even lay down in a casket just to try it out. Death doesn't scare him. He embraces it because he believes in the resurrection.

4. The resurrection posits that we will share the resurrection with others.

The resurrection gives us boldness to preach the message of Jesus. After all, if Jesus came back from the dead, doesn't everyone need to know about that miraculous event? After the crucifixion, the disciples of Jesus were downhearted and hopeless. Ever felt that way? Some of us can relate. You know what it's like to try your best at something, but it just doesn't work out like you thought it would. That's how they were feeling. They had given up at least three years of their life, their energy, their hopes, their dreams, and their aspirations to this kingdom movement led by Jesus, and now they were sitting together in a room with their heads in their hands wondering what they were going to do next. Have you ever been in that situation?

But they changed. Look at this contrast. John 20:19–21 reads:

> *On the evening of that first day of the week, when the disciples were together, with the doors locked for fear of the Jews, Jesus came and stood among them and said, "Peace be with you!" After he said this, he showed them his hands and side. The disciples were overjoyed when they saw the Lord.*
>
> *Again Jesus said, "Peace be with you! As the Father has sent me, I am sending you."*

Acts 4:13–20 states:

When they saw the courage of Peter and John and realized that they were unschooled, ordinary men, they were astonished and they took note that these men had been with Jesus. But since they could see the man who had been healed standing there with them, there was nothing they could say. So they ordered them to withdraw from the Sanhedrin and then conferred together. "What are we going to do with these men?" they asked. "Everybody living in Jerusalem knows they have done an outstanding miracle, and we cannot deny it. But to stop this thing from spreading any further among the people, we must warn these men to speak no longer to anyone in this name."

Then they called them in again and commanded them not to speak or teach at all in the name of Jesus. But Peter and John replied, "Judge for yourselves whether it is right in God's sight to obey you rather than God. For we cannot help speaking about what we have seen and heard."

The disciples of Jesus went from fearful to courageous, from not wanting to leave the upper room because of their fear to standing up to the Sanhedrin and saying, "You can't shut us up."

Sometimes we get fearful of evangelism. Sometimes we stay in our rooms and don't get out and share. We need to remember the resurrection of Jesus and his promise, "I am with you always." Whenever we share about Jesus, he is right there with us sharing with people.

Conclusion

What is the meaning of Easter? For me, Easter as a religious holiday doesn't mean much, but Easter as a symbol of the empty tomb and the resurrection of Jesus has great meaning.

What does Easter mean to you? You will have to work this out in your own thinking. I hope that this chapter has at least given you a perspective of what Easter can mean.

I'll close with Mark's account of the first Easter and the first retelling of the story of the empty tomb in Mark 16:1–6.

When the Sabbath was over, Mary Magdalene, Mary the mother of James, and Salome bought spices so that they might go to anoint Jesus' body. Very early on the first day of the week, just after sunrise, they were on their way to the tomb and they asked each other, "Who will roll the stone away from the entrance of the tomb?"

But when they looked up, they saw that the stone, which was very large, had been rolled away. As they entered the tomb, they saw a young man dressed in a white robe sitting on the right side, and they were alarmed.

"Don't be alarmed," he said. "You are looking for Jesus the Nazarene, who was crucified. He has risen! He is not here. See the place where they laid him."

Easter–Day
Henry Vaughan (1621–1695)

Thou, whose sad heart, and weeping head lies low,
    Whose cloudy breast cold damps invade,
Who never feel'st the sun, nor smooth'st thy brow,
    But sitt'st oppressed in the shade,
    Awake, awake,
And in his Resurrection partake,
    Who on this day (that thou might'st rise as he,)
    Rose up, and cancell'd two deaths due to thee.

Awake, awake; and, like the sun, disperse
    All mists that would usurp this day;
Where are thy palms, thy branches, and thy verse?
    Hosanna! Hark; why dost thou stay?
    Arise, arise,
And with his healing blood anoint thine eyes,
    Thy inward eyes; his blood will cure thy mind,
    Whose spittle only could restore the blind.

End Notes

229. John Irving, *A Prayer for Owen Meany: A Novel* (New York: Ballantine Books, 1997).

230. Philip Yancey, *The Jesus I Never Knew* (Grand Rapids: Zondervan, 1995).

231. Easter joke found at http://ucapmatters.com/holidays/easter.htm.

232. Walter Scott, *The Messiahship, Or, Great Demonstration: Written For The Union Of Christians, On Christian Principles, As Plead For In The Current Reformation* (Kansas City, Missouri: Old Paths Book Club, 18 [n.d.]), 197.

233. Scriptures from Matthew in this chapter are the author's own translation.

234. Davis, viii.

235. N. T. Wright, *Surprised by Hope* (New York: HarperOne, 2008), 62.

236. Davis, 191–209.

237. Borg, *Jesus: Uncovering the Life, Teachings, and Relevance of a Religious Revolutionary*, 276.

238. Calvin Miller, ed., *The Book of Jesus* (New York: Simon & Schuster, 1996), 410.

Chapter 16

The Great Commission

God gives all Christians a commission. We are not to sit idly by, doing nothing but daydreaming about the glories to come. Far from a denial of this life, the Christian message of resurrection is an affirmation of life here and now. This world is important. It is a gift, and a mission field, that God has given us. Our job as Easter Christians is to tell people, as Mary did, that the Lord is Risen.[239]

—Stephen T. Davis, author of *RISEN INDEED*

Elements of the Great Commission—Matthew 28:16–20, cf. Mark 16:15–18, Luke 24:44–49

"All authority in heaven and on earth has been given to me (by God himself)."[240]

Jesus as king is giving his disciples a divine commission before he leaves them. This is the last charge that he gives his followers.

"Therefore, make disciples of all nations."

This is the central command. Reproduce yourself. Don't just make Christians; make disciples.

How we are to make disciples:

1. "As you are going." Don't wait for people to seek you out, you go find them. Go to where the people are.
2. "Baptizing them in the name of the Father, Son, and Holy Spirit."
3. "And teaching them to obey everything—whatever I have commanded."
4. "And surely I am with you always, even to the end of the age." Jesus assures us that he will be with us.

Conclusion

This is what the local church should be. It should be a disciple-making church, a church that is going, baptizing, and teaching.

Why Do We Preach Jesus?

1. Because Jesus Gives Us a Better Life in the Here and Now.
   Jesus adds quality to our lives.

"The thief comes only to steal and kill and destroy; I [Jesus] have come that they may have life, and have it to the full."

—John 10:10

Notice that Jesus says there are thieves and robbers that break in to steal the sheep. In our lives there are many thieves and robbers all around us that steal from our quality of life. What are some of these thieves and robbers? Stress. Economic worries. Addictive behavior. Sin. Insecurity.

But Jesus stands in contrast to the thieves and robbers. He says, "I have come that they might have life and have it to the full." Jesus came to offer abundant life. How can he do this?

For stress—1 Peter 5:7:

Cast all your anxiety on him because he cares for you.

For economic worries—Matthew 6:31–33:

So do not worry, saying, 'What shall we eat?' or 'What shall we drink?' or 'What shall we wear?' For the pagans run after all these things, and your heavenly Father knows that you need them. But seek first his kingdom and his righteousness, and all these things will be given to you as well.

For addictive behavior and sin—Romans 8:37–39:

No, in all these things we are more than conquerors through him who loved us. For I am convinced that neither death nor life, neither angels nor demons, neither the present nor the future, nor any powers, neither height nor depth, nor anything else in all creation, will be able to separate us from the love of God that is in Christ Jesus our Lord.

For insecurity—Philippians 4:13:

I can do everything through him who gives me strength.

Jesus wants to help us manage life in the here and now, but sometimes we seem to lose sight of this. It's as if we feel we need to apologize to people for offering them Jesus. Jesus does shake up our lives at times, but he does so when we need to be shaken to the foundation. He is here to help us. Why preach Jesus? Because he is here to help and because he will give you a qualitatively better life in the here and now.

2. Because Jesus Gives Us Life in the Hereafter—Luke 12:16–21

Remember the story of the rich fool in the Parable of the Bigger Barns? He prepared for life here. He was packing stuff away so that at some point he could say, "Take life easy; eat, drink and be merry." But he never got to enjoy all those things he had stored away, because he was called away to eternity.

Jesus doesn't just help us in the here and now; he gets us ready for the hereafter. If you really believe in eternity, if you really believe that people will face judgment after this life is over, if you really believe in heaven and hell, and if you really believe that in order to go to heaven you have to have a relationship with Jesus, then compassion for people dictates that you will share Jesus with people.

We don't know how much time we have here. The rich fool thought he had many years ahead of him to enjoy his riches, but he didn't. You can count your riches, but you can't count your tomorrows. That's why there needs to be a sense of urgency in getting our lives right with God.

James 4:13–15 reads:

> Now listen, you who say, "Today or tomorrow we will go to this or that city, spend a year there, carry on business and make money." Why, you do not even know what will happen tomorrow. What is your life? You are a mist that appears for a little while and then vanishes. Instead, you ought to say, "If it is the Lord's will, we will live and do this or that."

Remember what Peter said in Acts 4:12: "Salvation is found in no one else, for there is no other name under heaven given to men by which we must be saved."

The early disciples had a sense of urgency in their preaching. Acts 8:30–39 records the conversion between Philip and the Ethiopian Eunuch. It concludes with:

> As they traveled along the road, they came to some water and the eunuch said, "Look, here is water. Why shouldn't I be baptized?" And he gave orders to stop the chariot. Then both Philip and the eunuch went down into the water and Philip baptized him. When they came up out of the water, the Spirit of the Lord suddenly took Philip away, and the eunuch did not see him again, but went on his way rejoicing.

Acts 16:22–34 records Paul and Silas' conversion with the Philippian jailer. Verses 31–34 read:

They replied, "Believe in the Lord Jesus, and you will be saved—you and your household." Then they spoke the word of the Lord to him and to all the others in his house. At that hour of the night the jailer took them and washed their wounds; then immediately he and all his family were baptized. The jailer brought them into his house and set a meal before them; he was filled with joy because he had come to believe in God—he and his whole family.

The Ethiopian stopped the chariot to experience baptism. When the jailor realized he needed to be baptized, he was baptized immediately. Can you sense the urgency?

Do we believe that we are helping people prepare for eternity? We need to see things from God's perspective. God sees every death. He sees every unprepared soul that enters eternity.

If we really believe that "there is no other name under heaven given to men by which we must be saved," then we must feel compelled to share what we know about Jesus with others. We must not delay.

Have you ever stood by a fast-moving stream or a rushing river and watched the water flow by? The water rushes by without ever stopping. It just flows and flows. If you try to follow a floating leaf, you see it for a few seconds, then it is gone.

Now imagine that you could float just above the atmosphere of the earth and watch the souls of dying people float up and away into eternity. Almost two people die per second on the earth. If you could see souls floating away from the earth they would look like a stream of water that never stops flowing.

Here's another way to look at it: Let me ask how you feel when you hear that about every four seconds one person dies from hunger. It probably moves you inside. You would like to do something about that. How do you feel when you hear that every second almost two people die without really knowing Jesus? Does that move you inside? Think about it.

> 1.8 people die each second.
> 1.8 x 60 seconds = 108 people per minute.
> 108 x 60 minutes = 6,461 people per hour.
> 6,461 x 24 hours = 155,060 people per day.
> 155,060 x 365 days = 56,597,034 people per year.

That's close to the population of Great Britain. Great Britain basically dies each year!

People are dying every day without Jesus. What are we going to do about that? What are we willing to do to help people get to know him? Why preach Jesus? Because Jesus commanded us to do so. Because the early disciples went everywhere preaching Jesus. Because Jesus will change people's lives for the better. Because Jesus will prepare people for eternity.

End Notes

239. Davis, 208.
240. Scriptures from Matthew in this chapter are the author's own translation.

Chapter 17

Conclusion

The older I get, the more all I want to know is Jesus, all I want to study is Jesus, all I want to read about is Jesus, all I want to preach is Jesus, and all I want to share about is Jesus. I love the entire Bible (every page, every verse, and every word), but nothing floats my boat like the four Gospels. I especially love the Synoptic Gospels. They help me see Jesus like no other books in the New Testament. That's why I love them.

In my teen years my mother introduced me to a short novel by Charles Sheldon entitled, *What Would Jesus Do?* The book made a major impression on me. [Spoiler alert.] It's a story of a preacher who was too busy with his sermon preparation to help a homeless man. The next day, the homeless man comes walking down the center isle of the church building as the same preacher is preaching his Sunday sermon and drops dead in the center aisle. The preacher feels guilty for ignoring the homeless man, so he realigns his life by asking a simple question before every decision, "What would Jesus do?" He asks his church to commit to following the same practice. The rest of the book follows the changes in the congregation as every member lives his or her life by asking, "What would Jesus do?"

More recently this question has been abbreviated to four letters, "WWJD?" You might have seen bracelets with these initials printed on them, or seen the movie of the same name. People wear these bracelets as a reminder that before any decision they should ask themselves, "What would Jesus do?"

That single question has really helped me in my life. It has caused me to pause before major decisions and think about Jesus. I'm grateful I learned this simple little formula early in life, but as I've grown older, I've realized the formula is too simplistic. It's a good starting point, but I have to grow beyond it, to move beyond asking, "What would Jesus do?" before each decision to asking, "How can I live like Jesus every moment of every day?" It should be that my entire life, all my thoughts, dreams, wishes, everything I do and say, every moment of every day is enveloped and engulfed in Jesus.

This was Paul's sentiment in Galatians 3:26–27, "You are all sons of God through faith in Christ Jesus, for all of you who were baptized into Christ have clothed yourselves with Christ." Everyone who has been baptized has been clothed in Christ. Other words for "clothed" are "wrapped" or "enveloped." We need to envelop ourselves in Christ.

For most parents, a few minutes after your baby was born, a nurse took your baby aside and gave him or her a little sponge bath. Babies come out of the womb a bit yucky and need a little bath. Then the nurse wrapped your newborn in a fresh blanket and presented your baby back to you like a finely wrapped package. When I saw how our first child and only daughter was wrapped, I thought, "What an amazing job that nurse did wrapping this baby." I thought, "How did she do that? I'll never be able to do that." It was the coolest wrapping job I had ever seen. Why do newborns get wrapped so nicely? The blanket provides security for the baby. They feel safe, like they were back in the mother's womb. That's why they envelop the baby in a blanket.

Are you enveloped in Jesus? Are you clothed in Christ?

Being clothed in Jesus means that Jesus surrounds us all day long. We don't just think of Jesus when we have a tough decision to make. He is with us every moment of every day. This is the "God with us" life represented in the name Immanuel. This is what it means to be enveloped or clothed in Christ. This is the "with Jesus" life.

Are you enveloped in Jesus? Is King Jesus with you at every moment of every day?

The "With Jesus" Life[241]

Jesus through the night.
Jesus at sunrise.
Jesus when the alarm rings.
Jesus with the first cup of coffee.
Jesus in our quiet time.
Jesus in our morning workout.
Jesus as we leave the house.

Jesus on the morning commute.
Jesus in the work place.
Jesus on the campus.
Jesus when we take a test.

Jesus at lunchtime.
Jesus during the afternoon slump.

Jesus on the commute home.
Jesus at the dinner table.
Jesus on a relaxing evening.

Jesus on the golf course.
Jesus on the football field.
Jesus playing X-Box.
Jesus at the movies.
Jesus at Starbucks.
Jesus at the mall.

Jesus in the living room.
Jesus when we're far from home.

Jesus when we are surfing the Net.
Jesus when we answer email.
Jesus in our text messages.
Jesus when we're on the phone.

Jesus when we serve the poor.
Jesus when we encourage a friend.

Jesus when we go to bed.
Jesus when we sleep.
Jesus when we dream.
Jesus when we wake up.
Jesus for each new day.

Jesus in every single thing we do.
Jesus in every word.
Jesus in every conversation.
Jesus in every joke.
Jesus in every comment.
Jesus when we sneeze.

Jesus in every moment.
Jesus in every space.
Jesus in every place.

Jesus in every relationship.
Jesus with Mom and Dad.
Jesus with our spouse.
Jesus with our kids.
Jesus with our neighbors.

Jesus in every action.
Jesus in every inaction.

Jesus when we're alone.
Jesus with our enemies.
Jesus with our friends.

Jesus when we're up or down.
Jesus when we're gray or blue.
Jesus when we are on top of the world.
Jesus when the world's on top of us.

Jesus in good times.
Jesus in bad.
Jesus in feast.
Jesus in famine.
Jesus in joy.
Jesus in sorrow.
Jesus in ecstasy.
Jesus in tragedy.
Jesus in pleasure.
Jesus in pain.
Jesus in strength.
Jesus in weakness.
Jesus in smiles.
Jesus in frowns.

Jesus up,
Jesus down,
Jesus right,
Jesus left,
Jesus forward,
Jesus behind,
and Jesus in between.
Jesus inside,

Jesus outside,
Jesus upside down.
Jesus three-sixty.
Jesus twenty-four/seven.

Jesus with us.
The "with Jesus" life.

Jesus, Jesus I love thee.
What a friend we have in Jesus.
Tis so sweet to trust in Jesus.
Jesus is all the world to me.
Jesus loves me, this I know.
Jesus keep me near the cross.
Take the world but give me Jesus.
Jesus, lover of my soul.
Anywhere with Jesus I can safely go.
Safe in the arms of Jesus.
Stand up, stand up for Jesus.
I have decided to follow Jesus.

Clothed in Jesus.
Wrapped in Jesus.
Enveloped in Jesus.
Encircled in Jesus.
Enmeshed in Jesus.
Engulfed in Jesus.
And even embalmed in Jesus.

Maranatha.
Come, oh Lord.
Come quickly, King Jesus.

End Notes

241. I based these thoughts on the conclusion of a sermon by Ray Pritchett of Keep Believing Ministries. You can find the original at http://www.keepbelieving.com/sermon/2004-09-05-Get-Your-Mind-in-Gear/.

The Life and Teachings of Jesus the Messiah as Told Through the Fourfold Gospel

I believe that the closer we get to the original Jesus—to the storytelling Jesus, the healing Jesus, the welcoming Jesus, the Jesus who declared God's judgment on those who rejected the ways of peace and justice—the closer we come to the kingdom-of-God Jesus, the closer we are to recognizing the face of the living God.[242]

—N.T. Wright, New Testament scholar

The Synoptic Gospels

Synoptic" means "with a common eye or common view." Matthew, Mark, and Luke all cover the same basic material in the life of Jesus. However, they each have their own distinctive characteristics.

The Distinctive Aspects of the Synoptic Gospels

The Gospel of Mark

1. Authorship

John Mark, a disciple of Peter, wrote Mark. Irenaeus, an early church leader who died around AD 200, wrote that after the death of Peter and Paul (AD 64–65), Mark, the associate of Peter, handed down the preaching of Peter in the Gospel of Mark. Another early church leader, Papius, (c. 115) was quoted by the church historian Eusebius as saying:

John the Presbyter also said this—"Mark, being the interpreter of Peter, whatsoever he recorded he wrote with great accuracy, but not, however, in the order in which it was spoken or done by our Lord, for he neither heard nor followed our Lord, but as before said, he was in company with Peter, who gave him such instruction as was necessary, but not to give a history of our Lord's discourses: wherefore Mark has not erred in anything, by writing some things as he has recorded them; for he was carefully attentive to one thing, not to pass by anything he heard, or to state anything falsely in these accounts."[243]

New Testament scholar, Merrill Tenney, summarizes:

From these considerations it may be concluded that this Gospel is the product of one of the junior preachers of the apostolic age, who was thoroughly acquainted with the message concerning Jesus and who recorded it as he heard it, without elaboration or embellishments of any kind. He made no attempt at a biographical interpretation; he merely allowed the facts themselves to speak for him.[244]

2. Date and Place of Writing

Mark was written in Rome. This is supported by the early church father Clement of Alexandria. His Gospel was most likely written from Rome during the time of the persecutions of Nero, who executed both Paul and Peter around the year 65. Between 63 and 70, the Christians in Rome faced severe persecution. Over half of Mark's gospel contains material about Jesus facing the cross. This theme would have strengthened those disciples who were facing Nero's persecution.

Most scholars date this Gospel between 65 and 70. This would be some time after the death of Peter and before the destruction of Jerusalem.

3. Audience

Mark was writing to the Gentile Christians in Rome. New Testament scholar F. F. Bruce states:

The life-setting in which this Gospel was published was probably the Emperor Nero's attack on the Christians of Rome in the months following the devastation of that city by fire in A.D. 64. Shaken and nearly demoralized by the suddenness and ferocity of this attack, they sorely needed to be reassured of the validity of their faith.... If they had to suffer for Christ's sake, they were but following in the steps of their Lord, who himself had suffered at the hands of the Roman power.[245]

This setting matches the theme of Mark's gospel—the theme of discipleship.

4. Purpose

Mark was writing to explain to the Gentile world the nature of Jesus. He was correcting the Hellenistic "divine man" image of Jesus. In Mark 1:1–8:26, Mark portrays Jesus as miracle worker. In Mark 8:27–16:8, he pictures Jesus as the suffering Son of Man.

Mark's gospel also serves as a guide to strengthen fellow Christians who are undergoing persecution. Just as Jesus went to the cross, his followers must take up their cross and follow him. In the first century, the cross only had one meaning—it meant death. The disciples of Jesus had to be ready to die for their faith.

5. Characteristics

Mark's style is energetic, brisk, and full of action. He uses the historical present (the present tense used as past action) 151 times. Mark uses the word "and" often. In the Greek of chapter 3, twenty-nine out of the thirty-five verses begin with the word "and." He uses the word "immediately" some forty-one times in his Gospel. In it, Jesus "gallops" from one place to the next doing the work of God.

Mark is a very Gentile gospel written to the Gentiles of Rome. He does not use many Jewish terms, and when he does, he explains them to his Greek audience.

The Gospel of Luke

1. Authorship

Luke was a traveling companion of Paul. The "we" sections in Acts (16:10–17, 20:5–15, 21:1–18, and 27:1–28:16) are a travel diary of Luke with Paul. Luke was a physician and historian. His prologue in Luke 1:1–4 describes how he wrote his Gospel. Merrill Tenney believes that Luke was an Antiochian Gentile who accompanied Paul on his second journey. Luke remained an evangelist in Philippi, then he accompanied Paul on his third journey. Colossians mentions that he was not a Jew (Colossians 4:10–14). This makes Luke the only non-Jewish writer of the New Testament. Eusebius says that he was from Antioch in Syria. Tenney writes:

> Accordingly, the author of Luke-Acts may have been an Antiochian Gentile, converted in Antioch not more than fifteen years after Pentecost. He became a friend and associate of Paul and traveled with him on the second journey after meeting him at Troas (Acts 16:10). He remained at Philippi as evangelist of the church while Paul pursued his itinerant ministry in Achaia and visited Antioch in Asia Minor (18:22, 19:1–41). When Paul returned to Philippi on the third journey, the author again joined his company (20:6). He went with him to the mainland of Asia, and then accompanied him to Jerusalem.[246]

2. Date and Place of Writing

Luke was written shortly after Mark's Gospel. He could have written it around 67–68. Some scholars would date it earlier, c. 57–60 (many would say around AD 64). Tenney states:

It must have been written before Acts.... Acts was probably composed prior to the close of Paul's first imprisonment at Rome, since the abrupt ending of the book intimates that the author had no more to say.... Perhaps AD 60 would serve as a median date, for by that time Luke would have been a Christian at least ten years or more, and would have traveled in Palestine, where he could have met many of those who had known Jesus in the flesh. [247]

The place of writing is unknown. It was written somewhere in the Hellenistic world (that is, outside of Palestine).

3. Audience

Luke was a Gentile writer writing to a Gentile audience. His Greek is excellent. He was an educated man who had a great grasp of the language.

4. Purpose

In Luke 1:1–4, he states that his purpose was to write an orderly account of what happened in the life and ministry of Jesus. Luke was attempting to attract and win cultured citizens in the Gentile world. He gave a picture of God's saving work in the world. He was writing a form of "salvation history." He gave his audience (Theophilus=lover of God) enough material to decide whether he wanted to be a Christian.

5. Characteristics

When the Gospel of Luke is placed alongside Acts, Luke gives a comprehensive history of the ministry of Jesus and the early church. His writing is the longest in the New Testament, making up twenty-seven percent of the New Testament material.

His message was very people oriented. Luke spoke of women and children (chapter 8), money and the poor, the good Samaritan, the rich young ruler, and Zaccheus. Luke especially includes the stories of the poor, the less fortunate, and the oppressed.

Luke includes the theme of prayer often in his work. He also has more references to the Holy Spirit than Matthew and Mark combined. Luke uses sixty percent of Mark's material, which makes up forty percent of his gospel. Twenty percent of Luke comes from a source that is common with Matthew. The other thirty-eight percent is found only in Luke. He writes like a historian. No other Gospel writer gives us historical references like Luke. His Gospel is very literate. Luke is the most readable of the Gospels. His vocabulary is rich and varied.

The Gospel of Matthew

1. Authorship

The Apostle Matthew wrote the Gospel of Matthew. In AD 130, Papius wrote, "Matthew composed the logia in the Hebrew tongue."[248] Irenaeus stated that Matthew composed his gospel in Hebrew. He states, "Matthew also issued a written gospel among the Hebrews in their own dialect, while Peter and Paul were preaching at Rome and laying the foundations of the church."[249] The early church leader, Ignatius of Antioch, quotes only the Gospel of Matthew. For this reason, many scholars believe it was written from Antioch.

Matthew was also known as Levi. He was a tax collector whom Jesus called to be an Apostle (Matthew 9:9–13, 10:3). After the listing of his name in Acts 1:13, we know nothing of him.

2. Date and Place of Writing

Most scholars date Matthew between 80 and 85. They place it after the temple was destroyed and after Mark's gospel. Most scholars date it after Luke, but there is no reason to date it this late. It could have been written at the same time as Luke's Gospel—around AD 67–68. It should be placed somewhere between 50 and 70.

The traditional place of writing is Palestine, as Matthew is a Jewish gospel, but it could have been written to Jews outside of Palestine. Two New Testament scholars, B.H. Streeter and Merrill Tenney, believe that it was written in Antioch of Syria. Tenney writes:

> The place of writing could be Antioch.... this first Gospel was probably the favorite of the Syro-Jewish church. Furthermore, the church at Antioch was the first to have a markedly Gentile constituency that spoke Aramaic and Greek.... It may, therefore, have been composed some time between A.D. 50 and 70 and have been circulated by those who worked in and from the church of Antioch.[250]

3. Audience

Matthew was writing to Jewish Christians in the second half of the first century. His is the only Jewish gospel. It contains approximately forty fulfillment citations. Matthew uses several Hebrew phrases, which he does not bother translating. He also uses the uniquely Jewish phrase "kingdom of heaven" instead of the Gentile "kingdom of God."

4. Purpose

Matthew's gospel is apologetic in nature; he was writing to convince Jewish readers that Jesus was the Messiah—the son of the living God. The birth/infancy narratives defend the birth of Jesus as miraculous and legitimate. In his resurrection account he includes the bribery of the guards to demonstrate that Jesus' body was not stolen.

Matthew also wants to show that the church is the true Israel. Jesus came to fulfill the Law of Moses. In doing so, he ushered in a new kingdom, a spiritual kingdom. Matthew attempts to show the Jewish people that Jesus is the king of a different type of kingdom. Everyone should become a part of this new kingdom, part of the church.

5. Characteristics

Matthew's writing is very concise. His is the only Gospel to mention the word "church." Matthew uses ninety percent of Mark, which makes up about fifty percent of Matthew. Twenty-seven percent of Matthew comes from a common source with Luke. Twenty-two percent of Matthew is from his own source. Matthew quotes from the Old Testament over sixty times. He uses direct quotes and a formula quotation: "This took place to fulfill what was spoken through the prophet..." Matthew is keen to demonstrate that Jesus is the fulfillment of Old Testament prophecy.

Matthew also emphasized Jesus as teacher. His gospel contains the longest block of teaching material found in the Gospels: the Sermon on the Mount (chapters 5–7). The teaching discourses of Jesus comprise three-fifths of Matthew's material.

Several aspects of Matthew are distinctive to his gospel. He uses the term "kingdom of heaven" thirty-three times. Only five times does he speak of the kingdom of God. Matthew is the only writer to include the following stories:

- The visit of the Magi
- The flight to Egypt and massacre of the infants
- After the crucifixion, the ground shakes, the tombs open, and holy people go into the city
- The bribery of guards at the tomb
- The miracle of the two blind men
- The healing of the dumb demoniac
- The story of the coin in the fish's mouth
- The longest single discourse of Jesus, Matthew 5–7

The Gospel of John

1. Authorship

The Apostle John was the last surviving Apostle. He was one of the sons of Zebedee, a fisherman of Galilee. His mother was Salome, probably a sister of Mary, Jesus' mother (Matthew 27:56, Mark 15:40, John 19:25). John was a fisherman by trade. He may have belonged to the first disciples of John the Baptist.

John was known as one of the "sons of thunder," also translated, "sons of tumult" (Mark 3:17). He was in the inner circle of Jesus, occupying the place of privilege and intimacy at the last supper (John 13:23). Jesus committed his own mother to John's care while he was on the cross (19:26–27). John was one of the first visitors at the empty tomb. He lived many years after Jesus' ascension. He probably died at the end of the first century. John was known as "the apostle of love."

2. Date and Place of Writing

John wrote his gospel during his final years in Ephesus. The Gospel has been dated anywhere from AD 40 to 140. The liberals dated it into the 200s until the John Ryland fragment was found. This fragment from John's Gospel was dated around AD 135. Therefore, the Gospel had to be written before 135. Most conservative scholars date it late in the first century, around AD 90.

3. Audience

John addressed a wide range of Gentile Christian readers who were scattered across the Mediterranean World.

4. Purpose

John 20:30–31 reads, "Jesus did many other miraculous signs in the presence of his disciples, which are not recorded in this book. But these are written that you may believe that Jesus is the Christ, the Son of God, and that by believing you may have life in his name." John is the only Gospel to tell us why it was written: to create faith in Jesus.

John was apologetic in his writing. He defends Jesus against the teachers of gnosticism and docetism. The Gnostics believed that the world was evil and wicked by nature. God's Son could not become flesh without being contaminated by the evil of the material world. Therefore, Jesus only seemed to become flesh (docetism comes from the Greek word meaning "to seem"). But John states clearly that the Word became flesh and dwelt among us (1:14). John portrays Jesus as fully human and fully divine.

John demonstrates the divine nature of Jesus in the "I am" statements that he scatters across his gospel. These statements tie in with the identity of God given to Moses before the burning bush in Exodus: "Say to the Israelites: 'I AM has sent me to you.'" Jesus uses this phrase to identify himself in several passages:

- I am the bread of life—6:35
- I am the light of the world—8:12, 9:5
- I am the gate (of the sheepfold)—10:7
- I am the good shepherd—10:11, 14
- I am the resurrection and the life—11:25
- I am the way, the truth, and the life—14:6
- I am the true vine—15:1

5. Characteristics

Several characteristics separate John from the synoptic gospels:

- John is arranged by feasts in which Jesus travels from Galilee to Jerusalem (north to south).
- Belief and faith are used ninety-eight times in John. In John, belief is equivalent to obedience.
- John is written is a more narrative style than the synoptic gospels.
- John's gospel is more theological than the synoptics.
- The two most important words for understanding John are:
  1. "Believe"—used ninety-eight times in John (only thirty-four in the synoptics)
  2. "Life"—used thirty-six times in John (only sixteen in the synpotics)
- John is writing so the reader will believe in Jesus and by believing experience a qualitative change in life.
- As Merrill Tenney states, "John contains no parables and only seven miracles, five of which are not recorded elsewhere."[251]

End Notes

242. Tom Wright, *The Original Jesus,* 83.

243. Found in Eusebius' *History of the Christian Church.*

244. Merrill Tenney, *New Testament Survey, Revised* (Grand Rapids: Eerdmans, 1985), 163.

245. F.F. Bruce, *The Message of the New Testament* (Exeter, England: The Paternoster Press, 1972), 19–20.

246. Tenney, 177.

247. Ibid., 179.

248. Tenney, 150–151.

249. Ibid.

250. Ibid.

251. Ibid., 188.

Appendix 2

Biblical and Extrabiblical Sources Related to Jesus

People often ask, "Was Jesus mentioned outside the New Testament?" There are a few extrabiblical sources that refer to Jesus as Christ.

Roman/Greek Sources

The Roman historian Tacitus (c. AD 60–120) wrote this reference to Jesus around AD 115 in his *Annals*:

> Christus, the founder of the name, had undergone the death penalty in the reign of Tiberius, by sentence of the procurator Pontius Pilatus, and the pernicious superstition was checked for a moment, only to break out once more, not merely in Judea, the home of the disease, but in the capital itself, where all things horrible or shameful in the world collect and find a vogue. (*Annals* 15.44).[252]

Pliny the Younger, a governor of the Roman province of Bithynia, wrote a letter (dated c. 121) to Emperor Trajan, which we have in a collection named *Epistles*. In this letter Pliny writes about trials held against the Christians in his region. He writes about the Christians, saying:

> They were in the habit of meeting on a certain fixed day before it was light [Sunday], when they sang in alternate verses a hymn to Christ, as to a god, and bound themselves by a solemn oath, not to any wicked deeds, but never to commit any fraud, theft or adultery, never to falsify their word, nor deny a trust when they should be called upon to deliver it up; after which it was their custom to separate, and then reassemble to partake of food—but food of an ordinary and innocent kind.[253]

Also, the Roman historian Suetonius (c. AD 75–60), in his *Lives of the Twelve Caesars* (c. AD 120), writes this line concerning the emperor Claudius, "Since the Jews constantly made disturbances at the instigation of Chrestus, he expelled them from Rome."[254] Many scholars believe that "Chrestus" is a misspelling of "Christus," meaning Christ.

Ancient Sources

Josephus, a Jewish historian writing around AD 90, mentions a time when Pontius Pilate ruled his Jewish homeland. He writes:

About this time there lived Jesus, a wise man, if indeed one ought to call him a man. For he was one who wrought surprising feats and was a teacher of such people as accept the truth gladly. He won over many Jews and many of the Greeks. He was the Messiah. When Pilate, upon hearing him accused by men of the highest standing amongst us, had condemned him to be crucified, those who had in the first place come to love him did not give up their affection for him. On the third day he appeared to them restored to life, for the prophets of God had prophesied these and countless other marvelous things about him. And the tribe of Christians, so called after him, has still to this day not disappeared.[255]

The Babylonian Talmud reads:

On the eve of the Passover *Yeshu* was hanged. For forty days before the execution took place, a herald went forth and cried, 'He is going forth to be stoned because he has practiced sorcery and enticed Israel to apostasy. Any one who can say anything in his favor, let him come forward and plead on his behalf.' But since nothing was brought forward in his favor he was hanged on the eve of the Passover—Ulla retorted: Do you suppose that he was one for whom a defense could be made? Was he not a Mesith [enticer], concerning whom Scripture says, *Neither shalt thou spare, neither shalt thou conceal him?* With *Yeshu* however it was different, for he was connected with the government [or royalty, i.e., influential]. Our Rabbis taught: *Yeshu* had five disciples, Mattai, Nakai, Nezer, Buni, and Todah.[256]

End Notes
252. Tacitus, Annals 15.44.
253. Pliny the Younger, Epistles.
254. Suetonius, Life of Claudius 25.4.
255. Josephus, The Antiquities of the Jews, Book 18.3.3.
256. The Babylonian Talmud, b. Sanhedrin 43a.

Appendix 3

New Testament Background:
The Land and the People of the Land

The Land

The history of any land and people is influenced to a considerable degree by their geographical environment. This includes not only the natural features such as climate, soil, topography, etc., but also the geopolitical relationships with neighboring areas. This is especially true for Palestine, a small and relatively poor country, which derives its main importance from it unique centralized location at a juncture of continents and a crossroads for the nations.[257]

—Yohanan Aharoni, archaeologist

The "Fifth Gospel"

Geography of the land of the Bible is the fifth gospel. I first became familiar with this concept when I attended a lecture in Jerusalem given by Bargil Pixner, an archaeologist who wrote *With Jesus through Galilee According to the Fifth Gospel.* The book sounds as if Pixner is reconstructing Jesus' ministry based upon a lost or apocryphal gospel, but actually he believes that the geography of the land—the places themselves—is a fifth gospel that illuminates the other four gospels. Pixner writes:

The soil of the Holy Land as the scene of the events centering around the person of Jesus can be understood as a Fifth Gospel. . . . Whoever has learned to read and peruse this *book* of biblical landscape will experience the message of the four Gospels with a new and greater clarity.[258]

An example of the land becoming the fifth gospel occurred for me when I visited Caesarea Philippi in Northern Galilee. Phillip the son of

Herod built the great city of Caesarea Philippi in the first century, dedicating the city to Caesar Augustus—thus the name Caesarea Philippi. He made it his capital city in the northern region of Galilee.

The city was built on one of the three tributaries that fed the Jordan River. It backed up to a huge cliff that served as a backdrop to the city. Just in front of the cliff was the sacred section of the city with a temple dedicated to Augustus and a temple dedicated to the god Pan. It looked as if these temples were built right out of the rock that made up the cliff behind the city. Perhaps this is why Jesus chose Caesarea Philippi to make the statement, "On this rock I will build my church and the gates of Hades will not overcome it (Matthew 16:18)." The pagan temples were built on rock—the rock foundation of Caesarea Philippi. The church of Jesus would be built on a more substantial rock, so substantial that even the gates of Hades could not prevail against it. The church was built on the confession that Jesus is the Christ, the Son of the living God. When you visit Caesarea Philippi, it makes this scene from the life of Jesus come alive.

Geography and Jesus

Israel is not a large country, being 350 miles long and 50 miles wide. From the ancient biblical borders of Israel—from Dan to Beer-sheva—it measures only 220 miles. You can drive it north to south in just a matter of hours. You can drive from the Mediterranean Sea in the west to the Jordan River in the east in just over an hour. Why did this little strip of land get so much attention throughout history? The same reason real estate is valued today—location, location, and location.

Israel lies in the Fertile Crescent—also known as the cradle of civilization—between the two most powerful geographical areas of ancient civilization: ancient Mesopotamia in the north and ancient Egypt in the south. In order for Egypt to travel to Mesopotamia, it had to go through Israel. Therefore both areas wanted to control Israel to serve as a buffer zone between the two great powers of the ancient world. Because Palestine lay between Egypt and Mesopotamia, dozens of battles throughout history were fought over this tiny piece of real estate. Of course, in Jesus' day, the Romans controlled the Fertile Crescent. During the life of Jesus, Israel was known as Judea, and the Romans occupied it.

Israel: Palestine/Philistia, or the Holy Land—A Rose by Any Other Name?

William Shakespeare wrote, "That which we call a rose by any other name would smell as sweet." The land west of the country of Jordan, south of Lebanon and Syria, and north of Egypt goes by several names. In the Bible it is referred to as Canaan, the Promised Land, or Israel. It acquired the name Palestine/Philistia by the ancient Greek and Romans because the ancient Philistines lived in the coastal plain of the land. (Philistia means "land of the Philistines"). It is known in archaeological circles as the Levant and studies there are considered studies of the Ancient Near East. Since Israel and Palestine carry political significance within their names today, many people refer to this territory as the Holy Land.

The Geographical Areas of Judea

The geographical layout of the Holy Land can be divided into four sections from west to east: the Coastal Plain, the Central Highland, the Rift Valley, and the Highlands of the Transjordan.

1. The Coastal Plain

The Coastal Plain runs seventy miles north to south and twenty-four miles east to west. This is the flat, fertile land that extends from the Mediterranean Sea to the foothills of the Central Highland. Rainfall is plentiful in this land. The clouds coming east from the Mediterranean often get stopped by the hills of the Central Highland and dump their water on the plains below. In the north of the Coastal Plain is located the Plain of Acco, named after the ancient city of Acco that served as a port during Old Testament times. The Phoenicians who were skilled at shipbuilding controlled this land. Today Haifa is a modern city that lies in the Carmel Mountain range overlooking the Plains of Acco. The Old Testament prophet Elijah challenged the prophets of Baal on a mountain in this area.

As one journeys south along the coast, next is the Plain of Sharon. This area is located between land once controlled by the Phoenicians in the north and the mighty Philistines in the south. The coast of the Plain of Sharon was not suited for a harbor. In the first century BC, Herod the Great built a harbor by using a new technology developed by his engineers—underwater cement. This harbor was named Caesarea. Today the modern city of Tel Aviv lies in the Plain of Sharon.

In the southern coastal plain is the Philistine Plain. The Philistines built five major cities in this area—Gaza, Ashdod, Ashkelon, Gath, and Ekron. The Philistines used the fertile land in the south to raise crops and took advantage of the coastal area to build ports for maritime trade. They flourished in this plain. Today the Palestinian territory of the Gaza strip lies in the Philistine plain.

2. The Central Highland

The Central Highland is a mixture of mountains and hills that run north and south through the middle of Israel. In the north is Galilee. Upper Galilee is a beautifully wooded area that hosts the tributaries of the Jordan River and the highest peak in Israel: Mount Hermon (rising to over 9,000 feet in the Lebanon Range). The ancient city of Dan was built in this area. Jereboam I set up a golden bull in Dan. This area hosted the Israelite tribes of Naphtali and Dan (Deuteronomy 3, Joshua 21). The northern neighbors of ancient Israel were Phoenicia along the coast in the west (modern Lebanon) and Syria in the east. Lower Galilee includes the area surrounding the Sea of Galilee. The Sea of Galilee is actually a lake thirteen miles long and seven miles wide. It lies 680 feet below sea level (and the sea sinks another 200 feet into the depths of the Rift Valley). Many of the villages around the Sea of Galilee supplied fish for the rest of the country. Out of the forty-three species of fish that live in the lake, fourteen species can be found only in the Sea of Galilee. A popular fish from the Sea today is named the "Saint Peter's fish." The bulk of Jesus' ministry occurred in a three-city triangle on the northwestern corner of the Sea of Galilee—Capernaum, Corazin, and Bethsaida. Bargil Pixner has given this three-city area the name "The Evangelical Triangle" because Jesus performed the bulk of his ministry there. The Sea of Galilee was also known as the Sea of Tiberias, the Lake of Chinnereth, and the Lake of Gennesaret. In the first century, Herod the Great built the city of Tiberias along sulfur springs on the western edge of the lake.

South of Galilee runs the Jezreel Valley. The valley cuts across the Central Highland from west to east. It served as an ancient highway connecting points east to the Mediterranean Sea. The ancient city of Meggido was located in the Jezreel Valley. Meggido was an important strategic city because whoever controlled the Jezreel Valley controlled the trade route from east to west. Many battles throughout history were fought in the Jezreel Valley, so much so that Meggido and the Jezreel Valley became synonymous with warfare.

Below the Jezreel Valley is ancient Samaria. Today Samaria lies in the Palestinian territories. The hills of Samaria are perfect for olive farming. Olive production in the first century and today was and is a major industry for Samaria. The ancient city of Shechem is located in this area. Joshua spoke to the tribes of Israel in this area. It was also in this area where Jesus had the conversation with the Samaritan woman at Jacob's well (John 4).

Below Samaria lies Judea or Judah. This was the home of the southern kingdom of Reheboam in the Old Testament. Judah was difficult to farm. Shepherds raised sheep along the hills of Judea. Thus a shepherd that was born in Bethlehem, King David, made a city in Judea his capital—Jerusalem. Jerusalem rises over 2,600 feet above sea level at the Mount of Olives. This makes the mount a perfect spot to gaze at the ancient city of Jerusalem.

Just to the west of Jerusalem is a group of hills that separate the plains from the Central Highlands. These hills are called the *shephelah,* meaning lowlands. These hills served as a natural border between the ancient Israelites and the Philistines. It is in this area the shepherd boy David challenged the Philistine giant Goliath to a duel.

South of Judah lies the Negev. This is a desert land. It receives only 6–8 inches of rainfall annually. Beer-sheva, the southern border of ancient Israel, is located here.

3. The Rift Valley

The Rift Valley is a natural depression in the earth that runs from Palestine in the north to Kenya in the south. The valley is so distinct that it can be seen from the moon. It is the deepest fault line on the earth. The Northern part of the Rift Valley contains the Huleh Valley and the Huleh Lake. This lake lies to the north of the Sea of Galilee. In Old Testament times tributaries of the Jordan River fed the Huleh Lake, and it was a small lake. Today the water has been drained from the lake, and it is used for farmland and as a nature preserve.

South of the Huleh Valley is the Jordan Valley, in which lies the Jordan River. The Jordan flows from the Sea of Galilee south to the Dead Sea. It covers some seventy miles in distance, but because it twists and turns at the bottom of the Jordan Valley, the river is 200 miles long. The Jordan River serves today as the border between Israel and Jordan.

The Jordan River empties into the Dead Sea. As the Jordan courses its way through the Jordan Valley it picks up mineral and salt deposits from the soil. These are dumped into the Dead Sea, which has no outlet. The Dead Sea is both the lowest point on the earth (1,300 feet below sea level) and the saltiest water on the earth (seventeen to nineteen percent saline; the Hebrew name is "the Salt Sea"). Fish are unable to live in this high concentration of salt—thus the name Dead Sea. The Essences built their ascetic community of Qumran along the western edge of the Dead Sea. South of Qumran, Herod the Great built the ancient fortress called Masada.

As you travel from Jerusalem to the Dead Sea, you pass the ancient city of Jericho. Jericho has the distinction of being the oldest continually occupied city in the world (some 10,000 years) as well as being, in terms of altitude, the lowest occupied city in the world (some 840 feet below sea level).

South of the Dead Sea is Arabah. This is a desert area that extends to the Red Sea. South of Arabah and the Negev is the Sinai Peninsula. Almost no rain falls in this area. Travel through this region depends upon an occasional oasis. It was on a mountain in the Sinai Peninsula that Moses received the Ten Commandments. Traditionally, this location is identified as the Byzantine Monastery of St. Catherine's on Mount Sinai.

4. The Highlands of the Transjordan

The Transjordan refers to the area east of the Jordan River. Today Syria and Jordan occupy this area. In the Old Testament, this region was occupied by tribes from Israel, as well as the Arameans, the Edomites, and the Moabites. Mount Nebo, the burial site of Moses, rises some 4,580 feet overlooking the Arabah Valley and the Negev. The Transjordan is the location of the ancient city of Petra, many of the cities of the Decapolis, and an area to which the early Christians fled when the Romans destroyed Jerusalem in AD 70.

The People of Jesus' Day

The land of Judea was densely populated. Villages were located two or three miles apart. Towns of thousands of people were located ten miles apart. There were one million to five million people living in close proximity to one another in Palestine.

Almost one half of the people who populated the land of Palestine were non-Jewish. Most of these people were there because of the Roman occupation. When you think of Judea in the first century, you have to remember that it was an occupied land. A foreign nation, the powerful Roman Empire, controlled the land. The Roman army kept the peace. Almost everyone could speak Greek (the official language of the Empire at this point in time).

The average Jewish man or woman was interested in religion, but not devoted. This is not much different from Israel today. People were worried about making a living and taking care of their children. That is what preoccupied their minds.

Scholars estimate that up to ninety percent of the people of Judea during Jesus' life were the poor of the land. They were called the *Am-ha-Eretz*, which means "the people of the land." They lived day to day and truly looked for "daily bread" to feed their family. The other ten percent were the landed gentry, the military officials, the politicians, and the upper-level priests. In Jerusalem, archaeologists have discovered the house of the high priest, and it sits in one of the nicest, most expensive sections of ancient Jerusalem.

The high priests were the religious rulers. The Romans used them to control the people. They were rich and powerful. For the most part, they were more political leaders than spiritual leaders.

The Rabbis were like judges. People came to the rabbis to have their disputes settled. They also taught the Torah. The scribes were writers and teachers. We would look on them as lawyers today. If anyone wanted an official document written, they would go to a scribe.

The Pharisees

The largest and most influential group among the sects of first-century Judaism was the Pharisees (around six thousand members in Judea). Their origin dates back to the time of Hyrcanus I (reigned 134–104 BC). The word "Pharisee" means "separate or separated one"—they felt they were to be separate from the common people.

The Pharisees placed great emphasis on oral traditions, laws that had been established outside the written code of the Old Testament. The goal of their sect was to build a hedge around the law so that the law would never be broken. They believed that on Sinai God gave Moses a body of rules orally, and Moses passed them on to Joshua and then to the elders, prophets, and the men of the Great Synagogue. In their minds, they were the "Keepers of the Traditions."

The Pharisees believed in a bodily resurrection after death. They also believed in angels and spirits and a punishment after death for the unrighteous. They relied upon the divine providence of God, but they put an undue importance on the oral law.

In summary, the Pharisees believed in:

1. God's control of the lives of men

2. The resurrection of the body and a reward for piety

3. A world of angels and demons (a real spirit world)

4. A two-part Scripture system: (1) the written Scripture and (2) the oral traditions of the rabbis

The Pharisees also had their own ideas of how to live a life faithful to the Judaism to which they were devoted. Their internal rules were sectarian with an emphasis on ritual purity, food tithes, and Sabbath observances. They were admired by the people and functioned at least some of the time as a social and political force against foreign and Hellenized Jewish leaders (those Jewish leaders who were sympathetic to the Greek language and culture). Many were very educated in the law and some were politically powerful.

During Jesus' day, two leading schools among the Pharisees existed. Hillel led the moderate school, and Shammai the conservatives. These groups basically agreed with each other in many areas, but small disagreements regularly occurred. One area of disagreement centered on divorce. Hillel approved of divorce, saying a man could divorce his wife for any reason, great or small, including if he met someone he liked better or if his wife had burned breakfast. Shammai said that the only reason for divorce was adultery.

The Sadducees

The Sadducees considered themselves the "Sons of Zadok," priests of God (1 Kings 2:35). The origin of the Sadducees goes back to John Hyrcanus I. The Sadducees wanted to follow the Greek culture and side with Roman rulers in the land. Because of their tolerance of the Romans, the Romans favored the Sadducees in their dealings with the Jews. They were the wealthy social elite. Only a thousand lived in Judea in the first century.

Theologically, the Sadducees accepted only the Pentateuch, the first five books of the Bible, as their Scripture. They rejected the bodily resurrection, angels, and spirits. They went strictly by the written law and rejected the oral traditions. They approached the Pentateuch literally. While the stronghold of the Pharisees was the synagogue, the stronghold of the Sadducees was the temple.

The beliefs of the Sadducees can be summarized as follows:

1. Individual freedom (God is distant.)

2. No resurrection

3. A rejection of the spirit world

4. Scripture consisting only of the written law (the Pentateuch)

The Essenes

The Essenes (100 BC–AD 100) are not mentioned in the New Testament. They were an extreme sect of the Jews who abandoned the changing rabbinic Judaism of Jerusalem and opted to move near the northwestern corner of the Dead Sea to form a separate community of holy people. This sect became known as Qumran.

The Essenes lived a simple, ascetic life of hard work. They practiced celibacy, communistic communalism, baptism for ritual cleansing, and vows of secrecy. Sources reveal that approximately four thousand people joined this movement. Scholars often associate John the Baptist with the Essenes. For example, Albright and Mann write, "There seems no question that John took over the practice of baptism, including the emphasis on repentance, from the Essenes, but gave it a far more profound meaning." But we need not insist that John adopted the practice of baptism from the Essenes. All the Jewish sects of that day practiced cleansing by ritual immersion in water. Hundreds of mikvaot (pools for ritual cleansing, singular *mikveh*) have been discovered in the Holy Land by archaeologists. Also, the Essenes were baptized over and over again as a purity rite. John's baptism was a one-time immersion.

The Romans

Palestine under Herod the Great

After Octavian defeated Pompey for control of the Roman Empire, he gave himself a new name: Caesar Augustus (27 BC). At about the same time in Palestine, Herod was purging the land of all his opponents. He married Mariamne who was of the lineage of the Hasmoneans, which gave him the appearance of continuing the Hasmonean dynasty. Later he killed his wife Mariamne and their two sons, Alexander and Aristobulus, for fear of their Hasmonean blood. The NT account, which describes the murder of infant boys two years and younger for fear that one was a future king, fits the historical depiction of Herod the Great (Matthew 2:16).

Herod ruled both Judea and Galilee. He was over both Jews and Gentiles. He wanted to be accepted as a Jew by the Jews and as a Gentile by the Gentiles. For the Gentiles he rebuilt their cities, adding gymnasiums, theaters, and pagan temples. For the Jews he rebuilt their temple and enlarged it, keeping the form it had in Solomon's day. It became known as Herod's temple. In spite of rebuilding the temple, many Jews hated Herod because he was a ruthless tyrant and a friend of Romans and pagans.

Herod accomplished much during his reign. He built Sebaste on the site of the destroyed city of Samaria. He built Caesarea on the coast. He constructed Antonia, a strong citadel in Jerusalem, which looked down upon the temple courts. He built Masada on the top of a mountain in the Dead Sea. Masada was a great fortress, which later became the spot of a tremendous battle between the Romans and the Jews. It became a symbol of Jewish perseverance and determination.

During Herod's reign, both Jesus and John the Baptist were born. When Herod died, he passed his kingdom on to three sons whom he had not killed:

- Archelaus who ruled over Judea, Samaria, and Idumea
- Herod Antipas who ruled over Galilee and Perea
- Philip who ruled over the territory northeast of the Jordan

Herod's Progeny

Of the three sons of Herod the Great, the most hated was Archelaus. In AD 6 a petition was sent to Augustus in Rome asking for the removal of Archelaus. The Romans agreed with the populous and exiled him on Gaul. A Roman governor replaced him, thus in the time of Jesus you have Roman princes ruling over Judea, Samaria, and Idumea (Luke 3:1). The governor adopted a lenient policy toward the Jews, allowing them to keep their religious ceremonies without interference from Rome. He allowed the Sanhedrin to rule over the Jewish populace, but they could not inflict the death penalty.

In Jesus' day Pontius Pilate was the Roman governor over Judea. Philo of Alexandria noted that his office was known for corruption, violence, depredations, ill treatment, offenses, numerous illegal executions, and incessant, unbearable cruelty. Pilate cared little for the religious sensitivities of the Jews. He openly displayed pictures of the emperor in Jerusalem. He took money from the temple treasury to build an aqueduct into Jerusalem. The New Testament testimony confirms this harsh picture of Pilate. He would have easily complied with the Jewish leaders to execute an innocent man on the charges of sedition. Thus Jesus of Nazareth died outside the gates of Jerusalem suffering the most intense, shameful punishment devised by man.

In the north in Galilee, Herod Antipas ruled from 4 BC to AD 39. He built a palace on a cemetery and named it Tiberius after the reigning emperor. None of the Jews would live there because they considered it unclean. His first wife was a daughter of the Nabataean king. Later he took Herodias the wife of his half brother Herod as his wife. He sent his first wife back to her father. His marriage to Herodias would haunt him throughout his reign. Not only did he run into conflict with John the Baptist over it, but also the Nabataean king was highly offended by the return of his daughter. He attacked Galilee and handed Herod Antipas a sound defeat. Some saw this defeat as retribution from God for the way Antipas had killed John the Baptist.

Since Herod Antipas was in control of Galilee and most of Jesus' ministry was in Galilee, Herod ruled over Jesus' homeland. Herod's first exposure to Jesus was startling in that he thought that Jesus was John the Baptist returned from the dead (Mark 6:16). Herod Antipas met Jesus just before the crucifixion. Pilate sent Jesus to Herod so that Antipas might pass judgment upon him (Luke 23:6–16). Antipas declined to pass sentence and returned Jesus to Pilate.

Josephus identifies the place where Herod Antipas imprisoned John as the fortress of Machaerus. It was located on the eastern side of the Dead Sea. He imprisoned John because John had the effrontery to challenge Herod's marriage to the wife of his half brother, Philip. According to the Pentateuch it was illegal to marry your brother's wife while your brother was still alive.

When Herod Antipas had his birthday celebration, his stepdaughter performed a dance for him. He enjoyed her dance so much that he promised to grant any request that she made. Josephus mentions that her name was Salome. She was the daughter of Herod Philip and Herodias. She requested the head of John the Baptist on a platter. Although it was unlawful to execute a man without a trial, Herod had John executed and his head delivered to Salome.

In the end Herodias was Antipas' undoing. She persuaded him to press Caligula for the title of King of Galilee. Caligula rejected his petition for the title and chose instead to exile Herod Antipas on Gaul in AD 39.

In the Northern Transjordan, Philip was the ruler. He built a new city, which he named Caesarea Philippi. Philip was the first Jewish ruler to mint a coin bearing his image. He died in AD 34 leaving no heir.

End Notes

257. Yohanan Aharoni, *The Land of the Bible: A Historical Geography* (Philadelphia: Westminster Press, 1979).

258. Bargil Pixner, *With Jesus through Galilee According to the Fifth Gospel* (Rosh Pina, Israel: Corazin Publishing, 1992), 7.

Helpful Books

A Harmony of the Gospels places the four gospels side by side so that the student can compare the similarities and the differences between the four gospels. This is an indispensible tool for a study of the gospels. A.T. Robertson's version is standard. His book has been updated many times over the years. It is also available in several translations including the KJV, RSV, NRSV, and NIV. You can also find a harmony of the gospels for the Greek New Testament. The United Bible Society publishes it. I first used this when I was studying the synoptic gospels with Dr. Cook at Southeastern Baptist Theological Seminary in Wake Forest, North Carolina. It is a valuable tool for those with a knowledge of the Greek.

Orville E. Daniel's *A Harmony of the Four Gospels,* The New International Version, Second Edition (Grand Rapids: Baker Academics, 1996). I used this harmony of the gospels as I wrote this book. You will see it listed in the Selected Bibliography. You can follow along in this harmony of the gospels as you read this text.

A Simplified Harmony of the Gospels Using the Text of the HCSB with notes by George W. Knight. Knight follows A.T. Robertson's lead but he provides a central tract to follow as you read through the harmony. Unfortunately, the Holman Christian Standard Bible isn't the most readable text and Mr. Knight's notes aren't very helpful, but the idea of providing a central tract of the storyline throughout the Gospels is very beneficial.

The Renovaré Spiritual Formation Bible. The NRSV with notes focusing on spiritual formation and the spiritual disciplines.

Marcus Borg's *Jesus: Uncovering the Life, Teachings, and Relevance of a Religious Revolutionary.* Although Dr. Borg is a liberal scholar who rejects the idea of a bodily resurrection of Jesus and many other evangelical beliefs, his comments on the teaching ministry of Jesus are golden. Plus,

Dr. Borg writes in an easy-to-read, engaging manner, which always makes reading fun.

Robert H. Stein's *Jesus the Messiah: A Survey of the Life of Christ.* Stein's book is informational Bible study at its best. If you want one book that attempts to answer all the tough questions about the Gospels from chronology to apparent contradictions, then Stein's is one to get. Unfortunately, for me at least, reading Stein wasn't fun. Helpful, but no fun.

Scot McKnight's *The King Jesus Gospel: The Original Good News Revisited.* This book separates the gospel of Jesus from the salvation gospel preached by so many evangelical preachers today. McKnight begins by using 1 Corinthians 15 to define "gospel." Then he shows what the Gospels say about "gospel." This is a great little book. It's also fun. It helps see how the biblical writers defined "gospel."

N. T. Wright's *Simply Jesus: A New Vision of Who He Was, What He Did, and Why He Matters.* A nice introduction to the life of Jesus. Wright is an excellent scholar who focuses most of his work on Jesus in the synoptic gospels.

Selected Bibliography

Aharoni, Yohanan. *The Land of the Bible: A Historical Geography.* Philadelphia: Westminster Press, 1979.

_____ and Avi-Yonah, Michael. *The Macmillan Bible Atlas.* New York: Macmillan, 1977.

Allen, Charles Livingston. *The Life of Christ.* Westwood, NJ: Revell, 1962.

Allen, Willoughby C. *A Critical and Exegetical Commentary on the Gospel According to St. Matthew.* Edinburgh: T. & T. Clark, 1912.

Anderson, L. *Jesus: An Intimate Portrait of the Man, His Land, and His People.* Minneapolis, MI: Bethany House, 2004.

Archer, Gleason L. *The Encyclopedia of Bible Difficulties.* Grand Rapids: Zondervan, 1982.

Aune, David E. *Jesus and the Synoptic Gospels.* Madison, WI: InterVarsity, 1980.

Augsburger, M. S., and Ogilvie, L. J. *Matthew.* Vol. 24 of *The Preacher's Commentary Series.* Nashville, Tennessee: Thomas Nelson Inc., 1982.

Bacon, Benjamin W. *Studies in Matthew.* London: Constable, 1930.

Bailey, Kenneth. *Jesus Through Middle Eastern Eyes.* Downers Grove, IL: IVP Academic, 2008.

Bammel, E., ed. *The Trail of Jesus.* London: SCM, 1970.

_____ and Moule, C.F.D., eds. *Jesus and the Politics of His Day.* Cambridge University Press, 1984.

Barton, Stephen A. *The Spirituality of the Gospels.* London: SPCK/Peabody: Hendrickson, 1992.

Barclay, William. *Jesus as They Saw Him.* New York: Harper & Row, 1962.

_____. *New Testament Words.* London: SCM Press, 1964.

Barnett, Paul. *Is the New Testament History?* Ann Arbor, MI: Vine, 1986.

Barker, Margaret. *The Risen Lord: The Jesus of History as the Christ of Faith.* Harrisburg, PA: Trinity Press International, 1996.

Bauckham, Richard, ed. *The Gospels for All Christians.* Grand Rapids: Eerdmans, 1998.

Bauer, W. *A Greek-English Lexicon of the New Testament and Other Early Christian Literature.* Translated and adapted by W. F. Arndt and F. W. Gingrich; second edition revised and augmented by F. W. Gingrich and F. W. Danker. University of Chicago Press, 1979.

Baughman, Ray E. *The Life of Christ Visualized.* Chicago: Moody, 1968.

Baxter, Margret. *Jesus Christ: His Life and His Church.* Philadelphia: Westminster, 1987.

Beare, F. W. *The Gospel According to Matthew: A Commentary.* Oxford: Blackwell, 1981.

Beasley-Murray, G.R. *Baptism in the New Testament.* London: Macmillan, 1954.

_____. "Baptism, Wash." In *New International Dictionary of New Testament Theology.* Edited by Colin Brown, 1:143–54. Grand Rapids, MI: Zondervan, 1975.

Beasley, James R., et al. *An Introduction to the Bible.* Nashville: Abingdon Press, 1991.

Beausay, W. *The Leadership Genius of Jesus.* Nashville, TN: Nelson, 1994.

Bettenson, Henry, ed. and trans. *The Early Church Fathers.* Oxford University Press, 1956.

Betz. Otto. *What Do We Know about Jesus?* Translated by M. Kohl. London: SCM Press/Philadelphia: Westminster, 1968 [1965].

Black, Matthew. *An Aramaic Approach to the Gospels and Acts.* Oxford University Press, 1967.

Blair, Edward P. *Jesus in the Gospel of Matthew.* New York: Abingdon, 1960.

Blanchard, Ken and Phil Hodges. *Lead Like Jesus.* Nashville: Thomas Nelson, 2008.

Blomberg, Craig L. *The Historical Reliability of the Gospels.* Downers Grove, IL: InterVarsity, 1987.

_____. *Jesus and the Gospels: An Introduction and Survey.* Nashville: Broadman & Holman, 1997.

Bockmuehl, Markus. *This Jesus: Martyr, Lord, Messiah.* Downers Grove, IL: InterVarsity, 1994.

Bonhoeffer, Dietrich. *The Cost of Discipleship.* 6th ed. London: SCM, 1959.

Borg, Marcus. *Conflict, Holiness and Politics in the Teachings of Jesus.* Vol. 5 of *Studies in Bible and Early Christianity.* New York/Toronto: Edwin Mellen Press, 1984.

_____. *Jesus: A New Vision.* San Francisco: Harper and Row, 1987.

_____. *Jesus: Uncovering the Life, Teachings, and Relevance of a Religious Revolutionary.* San Francisco: HarperSanFrancisco, 2006.

_____. *Meeting Jesus Again for the First Time.* San Francisco: Harper, 1997.

_____ and Wright, N. T. *The Meaning of Jesus.* San Francisco: Harper, 1995.

Bornkamm, Gunther. *Jesus of Nazareth.* London: Hodder and Stoughton, 1960.

Boyd, Gregory A. *Cynic, Sage or Son of God? Recovering the Real Jesus in an Age of Revisionist Replies.* Wheaton, Ill.: BridgePoint, 1995.

Brandon, S. G. F. *Jesus and the Zealots: A Study of the Political Factor in Primitive Christianity.* New York: Scribner, 1967.

Brouwer, S. *Can the Real Jesus Still Be Found?* Eugene, OR: Harvest House, 2000.

Bromiley, G. W. *The International Standard Bible Encyclopedia,* revised ed. Grand Rapids: Eerdmans, 1979.

Brown, Colin, ed. *Jesus in European Protestant Thought 1778–1860.* Grand Rapids: Baker, 1988 [1985].

_____. *Miracles and the Critical Mind.* Grand Rapids, Michigan: Eerdmans, 1984.

_____. *The New International Dictionary of New Testament Theology.* Grand Rapids: Zondervan, 1967/Exeter: Paternoster Press, 1975–1978.

Brown, Raymond E. *The Birth of the Messiah.* New York: Doubleday, 1979.

_____. *The Death of the Messiah: From Gethsemane to the Grave. A Commentary on the Passion Narratives in the Four Gospels.* New York: Doubleday, 1994.

Bruce, F.F. *Jesus and Christian Origins Outside the New Testament.* Grand Rapids, Mich.: Eerdmans, 1974.

_____. *"The Kingdom of God: A Biblical Survey"* in *Evangelical Quarterly* 15, 1943: 263–68.

_____. *The New Century Bible Commentary: Corinthians I and II.* Grand Rapids: Wm. B. Eerdmans Publishing Co., 1971.

_____. *New Testament History.* London: Pickering and Inglis, 1982.

Bryan, William Jennings. *The Prince of Peace.* Chicago: Reily and Briton Company, 1909.

Buchanan, D. *The Counseling of Jesus.* Downers Grove, IL: InterVarsity, 1985.

Bultmann, Rudolph Karl. *Form Criticism.* Translated by Frederick C. Grant. New York: Harper and Row, 1963.

_____. *History of the Synoptic Tradition.* Translated by J. Marsh. Oxford; Blackwells, 1963.

_____. *Jesus Christ and Mythology.* New York: Scribner, 1958.

_____. *Theology of the New Testament.* 2 vols. Translated by K. Grobel. London: SCM, 1952–1955.

Burgess, A. *Man of Nazareth.* New York: Bantam, 1979.

Burkhart, R. *To Be Like Jesus.* Springfield, MI: Gospel, 1988.

Burridge, Richard A. *Four Gospels, One Jesus? A Symbolic Reading.* Grand Rapids: Eerdmans, 1994.

_____. *What Are the Gospels? A Comparison with Graeco-Roman Biography.* Cambridge University Press, 1992.

Caird, G. B. *The Gospel of St. Luke.* Philadelphia: Westminster, 1963.

_____. *Jesus and the Jewish Nation.* London: Athlone Press, 1965.

_____. *The Language and Imagery of the Bible.* Grand Rapids: Eerdmans, 1996.

Cameron, Ron, ed. *The Other Gospels: Non-Canonical Gospel Texts.* Philadelphia: Westminster Press, 1982.

Camp, Lee. *Mere Discipleship: Radical Christianity in a Rebellious World.* Grand Rapids, MI: Brazos Press, 2003: 23.

Carroll, John T., and James R. Carroll. *Preaching the Hard Sayings of Jesus.* Peabody, MA: Hendrickson, 1996.

Carson, D.A. *The Expositor's Bible Commentary with the New International Version.* Grand Rapids, Michigan: Zondervan Publishing House, 1995.

_____. *The Gospel according to John* in *The Pillar New Testament Commentary.* Leicester, England: Inter-Varsity Press/Grand Rapids: Eerdmans, 1991: 377.

_____. *The Sermon on the Mount.* Grand Rapids: Baker, 1978.

Cassels, L. *This Fellow Jesus.* New York: Family Library, 1975.

Charlesworth, J. H. *Jesus and the Dead Sea Scrolls.* New York: Doubleday, 1992.

Chilton, Bruce D. *The Temple of Jesus: His Sacrificial Program Within a Cultural History of Sacrifice.* University Park, PA: Pennsylvania State University Press, 1992.

Colquhoun, F. *Four Portraits of Jesus.* Downers Grove, IL: InterVarsity, 1984.

Cooper, R. L. *Mark.* Vol. 2 of *Holman New Testament Commentary.* Nashville, TN: Broadman & Holman Publishers, 2000.

Covey, Stephen R. *The 8th Habit: From Effectiveness to Greatness.* New York: Free Press, 2004.

Cranfield, C.E.B. *The Gospel According to St. Mark.* Cambridge University Press, 1972.

Crossan, J. Dominic. *The Historical Jesus: The Life of a Mediterranean Jewish Peasant.* San Francisco: Harper, 1991.

_____. *Jesus: A Revolutionary Biography.* San Francisco: HarperSanFrancisco, 1994.

_____. *Jesus Parallels: A Workbook for the Jesus Tradition.* 2nd ed. Philadelphia: Fortress, 1991.

_____. *Who Killed Jesus? Exposing the Roots of Anti-Semitism in the Gospel Story of the Death of Jesus.* San Francisco: HarperSanFrancisco, 1995.

Crossan, J. Dominic and Jonathan L. Reed. *Excavating Jesus.* San Francisco: Harper, 2001.

Cullman, Oscar. *The Christology of the New Testament.* Translated by Shirley C. Guthrie and Charles A.M. Hall. 2nd ed. Philadelphia: Westminster, 1963.

Culver, Robert Duncan. *The Life of Christ.* Grand Rapids: Baker, 1988.

Daniel, Orville E. *A Harmony of the Four Gospels, The New International Version,* 2nd ed. Grand Rapids: Baker Academics, 1996.

Danielou, Jean. *The Work of John the Baptist.* Baltimore: Helicon, 1966.

Davies, W. D. *The Setting of the Sermon on the Mount.* Cambridge University Press, 1963.

Davis, Stephen T. *Risen Indeed: Making Sense of the Resurrection.* Grand Rapids: Eerdmans, 1993.

Dibelius, Martin. *From Tradition to Gospel.* Translated by Bertram Lee Woolf. London: Redwood Press Limited, 1919.

Dodd, C. H. *The Parables of the Kingdom.* New York: Charles Scribner's Sons, 1961.

Douglas, J. D. and Norman Hillyer, eds. *New Bible Dictionary.* Leicester: InterVarsity Press, 1982.

Drane, John. *Introducing the New Testament.* San Francisco: Harper & Row, 1986.

Dunn, James D. G. *Jesus and the Spirit: A Study of the Religious and Charismatic Experience of Jesus and the First Christians as Reflected in the New Testament.* Grand Rapids: Eerdmans, 1997.

Edersheim, Alfred. *The Life and Times of Jesus the Messiah.* Grand Rapids: Eerdmans, 1956.

Edwards, J. R. *The Gospel According to Mark* in *The Pillar New Testament Commentary.* Grand Rapids: Eerdmans/Leicester, England: Apollos, 2002.

Elliot, J. K. *The Apocryphal New Testament.* Oxford: Clarendon, 1993.

Evans, C. Stephen. *The Historical Christ and the Jesus of Faith: The Incarnational Narrative as History.* Oxford: Clarendon, 1996.

Evans, Craig A. *Life of Jesus Research: An Annotated Bibliography.* Leiden: Brill, 1989.

Farmer, William R. *The Gospel of Jesus: The Pastoral Relevance of the Synoptic Problem.* Philadelphia: Westminster/John Knox, 1994.

_____. *Jesus and the Gospel.* Philadelphia: Fortress, 1982.

_____. *Maccabees, Zealots and Josephus: An Enquiry into Jewish Nationalism in the Greco-Roman Period.* New York: Columbia University Press, 1956.

_____. *The Synoptic Problem: A Critical Analysis.* New York: Macmillan, 1964.

Fee, Gordon D. "A Text-Critical Look at the Synoptic Problem." *Novum Testamentum* 22, January 1980: 12–28.

Fenelon, Francis. *Christian Perfection: Devotional Reflections on the Christian Life.* Bethany House, 1976.

Finegan, Jack. *The Archaeology of the New Testament.* Princeton University Press, 1992.

_____. *Handbook of Biblical Chronology.* Princeton University Press, 1964.

France, R. T. *Matthew. Tyndale New Testament Commentaries.* Grand Rapids: Eerdmans, 1985.

_____. "Matthew, Mark, and Luke." In G. E. Ladd, *A Theology of the New Testament,* rev. ed. Grand Rapids: Eerdmans, 1993: 212–245.

Freyne, Sean. *Galilee, Jesus and the Gospels: Literary Approaches and Historical Investigations.* Philadelphia: Fortress Press, 1988.

Fuller, Daniel P. *Easter Faith and History.* Grand Rapids: Eerdmans, 1965.

Funk, Robert W., and Roy W. Hoover. *The Five Gospels: The Search for the Authentic Words of Jesus.* New York: Macmillan, 1993.

Gaebelein, Arno C. *The Gospel According to Matthew: An Exposition.* 2 vols. New York: Our Hope Publications, 1910.

Galloway, Dale E. *20/20 Vision.* [n.pl.]: Scott Publishing, 1986.

Geisler, Norman L. and Thomas Howe. *When Critics Ask.* Wheaton, IL: Victor, 1992.

Goleman, Daniel. *Emotional Intelligence.* New York: Bantam Books, 2005.

Grant, Robert M. *A Historical Introduction to the New Testament.* New York: Harper and Row, 1963.

Grasser, Erich. "Jesus in Nazareth." *New Testament Studies* 16, 1969–1970: 1–23.

Green, H. Benedict. "The Gospel According to Matthew." *The New Clarendon Bible.* Oxford University Press, 1975.

Green, Joel B., Scot McKnight, and I. Howard Marshall, eds. *Dictionary of Jesus and the Gospels.* Downers Grove, IL: InterVarsity, 1992.

Grundmann, Walter. "dunamai/dunamis," in *Theological Dictionary of New Testament Theology,* vol. 2. Edited by Gerhard Kittel, translated by Geoffrey W. Bromiley. Grand Rapids: Eerdmans, 1964.

Guelich, R. A. *The Sermon on the Mount: A Foundation for Understanding.* Waco, TX: Word Books, 1975.

Gundry, R. H. *Matthew: A Commentary on His Literary and Theological Art.* Grand Rapids: Eerdmans, 1982.

_____. *The Use of the Old Testament in St. Matthew's Gospel. A Survey of the New Testament,* 18. Leiden: E. J. Brill, 1967.

Guthrie, Donald. *New Testament Introduction.* Downers Grove, IL: InterVarsity Press, 1970.

_____. *New Testament Theology.* Downers Grove, IL: InterVarsity Press, 1981.

_____. *A Shorter Life of Christ.* Grand Rapids: Zondervan, 1970.

Hagner, D. A. "Matthew 14–28" in *Word Biblical Commentary,* vol. 33B. Dallas: Word, Incorporated, 1998.

Harvey, Anthony E. *Jesus and the Constraints of History: The Bampton Lectures.* London: Duckworth, 1982.

Head, David. *Shout for Joy.* New York: Macmillan, 1962.

Hendriksen, William. *The Gospel of Matthew.* Grand Rapids: Eerdmans, 1972.

_____ and Simon J. Kistemaker. "John 12:47" in *Exposition of the Gospel According to John.* Vols. 1–2 of *New Testament Commentary,* Grand Rapids: Baker Book House, 1953–2001.

Hengel, Martin. *The Charismatic Leader and His Followers.* Translated by James Grieg. New York: Crossroad Publishing, 1981.

_____. *Crucifixion.* Philadelphia: Fortress Press, 1977.

_____. *Studies in Early Christology.* Edinburg: T & T Clark, 1995.

Hill, David. "The Gospel of Matthew" in *New Century Bible.* London: Marshall, Morgan, and Scott, 1972.

Hoehner, Harold W. *Chronological Aspects of the Life of Christ.* Grand Rapids: Zondervan, 1977.

Hooker, Morna D. *Beginnings: Keys that Open the Gospels.* Harrisburg, PA: Trinity Press International, 1997.

Horsley, Richard A. *Jesus and the Spiral of Violence: Popular Jewish Resistance in Roman Palestine.* San Francisco: Harper and Row, 1987.

Jefferson, Charles. *Jesus the Same.* Edited and Revised Edition. Woburn, MA: Discipleship Publications International, 1997.

Jeremias, Joachim. *Jerusalem in the Time of Jesus: An Investigation into Economic and Social Conditions during the New Testament.* Translated by F.H. and C.H. Cave. London: SCM Press 1962.

_____. *The Parables of Jesus.* Translated by S. H. Hooke. New York: Charles Scribner's Sons, 1954

_____. *New Testament Theology: The Proclamation of Jesus.* Translated by John Bowden. London: SCM Press, 1971.

_____. *Unknown Sayings of Jesus.* London: SPCK Publishing, 1958.

Johnson, Luke Timothy. *The Real Jesus: The Misguided Quest for the Historical Jesus and the Truth of the Traditional Gospels.* San Francisco: HarperSanFrancisco, 1996.

Kee, Howard Clark. *Miracle in the Early Christian World: A Study in Sociohistorical Method.* New Haven, CT: Yale University Press 1983.

King, Martin Luther, Jr. *Strength to Love.* Glasgow: William Collins Sons,1964.

Kingsbury, Jack Dean. *Matthew.* Philadelphia: Fortress Press, 1977.

_____. *Structure, Christology, Kingdom.* Philadelphia: Fortress Press, 1975.

Kittel, Gehard and Gerhard Friedrich, eds. Geoffrey W. Bromiley, trans. *Theological Dictionary of the New Testament.* Grand Rapids: Eerdmans, 1964–1974.

Klappert, Bertold. "King" in Vol. 2 of *The New International Dictionary of New Testament Theology.* Edited by Colin Brown. Grand Rapids: Zondervan Publishing House, 1967.

Kummel, W.G. *Introduction to the New Testament.* Translated by S.H. Hooke. London: SCM Press, 1958.

_____. *The Theology of the New Testament.* Translated by John E. Steel. Nashville: Abingdon Press, 1973.

Ladd, G.E. *I Believe in the Resurrection of Jesus.* Grand Rapids: Eerdmans, 1975.

_____. *A Theology of the New Testament.* Grand Rapids: Eerdmans, 1974.

Lane, William L. *The Gospel According to Mark.* Grand Rapids: Eerdmans, 1974.

Latourelle, Rene. *The Miracles of Jesus and the Theology of Miracles.* New York: Paulist, 1988.

Leon-Dufour, Xavier, Editor. *Dictionary of Biblical Theology.* Translated by Joseph Cahill. New York: Desclee Company, 1962.

Lightfoot, Neil. *Lessons from the Parables.* Grand Rapids: Baker, 1976.

Linnemann, Eta. *Is There a Synoptic Problem? Rethinking the Literary Dependence of the First Three Gospels.* Grand Rapids: Baker, 1992.

Lohse, Eduard. *The New Testament Environment.* Translated by John Steely. Nashville: Abingdon Press, 1971.

Longenecker, R. E. and M.C. Tenney, eds. *New Dimensions in New Testament Studies.* Grand Rapids: Eerdmans, 1974.

MacDonald, William. "Luke 9:24" in *Believer's Bible Commentary: Old and New Testaments.* Edited by Arthur L. Farstad. Nashville: Thomas Nelson, 1997.

Machen, J. Gresham. *The Virgin Birth of Christ.* New York: Harper, 1930.

Maier, Paul L. *First Christmas.* New York: Harper, 1971.

Marshall, I. Howard. *Commentary on Luke. New International Greek Testament Commentary.* Grand Rapids: Eerdmans, 1978.

____. "The Kingdom of God in the Teaching of Jesus" in *The Bible in Transmission,* Winter 2008, Bible Society UK.

McGarvey, J.W. *Commentary on Mark.* Delight, Arkansas: Gospel Light Publishing, 1875.

McKenzie, John L. "The Gospel According to Matthew" in *The Jerome Biblical Commentary.* Edited by R.E. Brown, J.A. Fitzmyer, and R.E. Murphy. Englewood Cliffs: Prentice-Hall, 1968.

McKnight, Scot. *The King Jesus Gospel.* Grand Rapids: Zondervan, 2011.

Meadors, Edward P. *Jesus the Messianic Herald of Salvation.* Peabody, MA: Hendrickson, 1997.

Meier, John P. *A Marginal Jew: Rethinking the Historical Jesus.* Vol. 1, *The Roots of the Problem and the Person.* Vol. 2, *Mentor, Message, and Miracles.* New York: Doubleday, 1991.

Meyer, Ben F. *The Aims of Jesus.* London: SCM Press, 1979.

Miguens, Manuel. *The Virgin Birth.* Westminster, MD: Christian Classics, 1975.

Mims, Gene. *The Kingdom-Focused Church.* Nashville: B&H Books, 2003.

Mitchell, Stephen. *The Gospel According to Jesus: A New Translation and Guide to His Essential Teachings for Believers and Unbelievers.* New York: Harper Perennial, 1993.

Moltmann, Jurgen. *The Way of Jesus Christ.* Philadelphia: Fortress Press, 1995.

Morison, Frank. *Who Moved the Stone?* London: Faber and Faber, 1958.

Moule, C.F.D. *The Phenomenon of the New Testament: An Inquiry into the Implications of Certain Features of the New Testament.* SBT second series, vol. 1. Naperville, IL: Allenson, 1967.

Moulton, J. H. and Milligan, G. *The Vocabulary of the Greek Testament, Illustrated from the Papyri and other Non-Literary Sources.* 1930, reprinted Grand Rapids: Eerdmans, 1974.

Mulholland, Jr., M. Robert. *Shaped by the Word.* Revised ed. Nashville: Upper Room Books, 2000.

Nouwen, Henri J.M. *In the Name of the Father: Reflections on Christian Leadership.* New York: The Crossroad Publishing Company, 1992.

Oden, Thomas C. *The Word of Life.* Vol. 2 of *Systematic Theology.* San Francisco: Harper Collins, 1989.

Ogg, George. *The Chronology of the Public Ministry of Jesus.* Cambridge University Press, 1940.

Patterson, Stephen J. *The God of Jesus: The Historical Jesus and the Search for Meaning.* Harrisburg, PA: Trinity Press International, 1998.

Piper, J. *Seeing and Savoring Jesus Christ.* Wheaton, IL: Crossway, 2005.

Pollack, J. *The Master: A Life of Jesus.* Edison, NJ: Inspirational, 1997.

Potter, C. F. *The Lost Years of Jesus Revealed.* New York: CBS Publications, 1962.

Pritchard, James B. *The Harper Atlas of the Bible.* New York: Harper and Row, 1987.

The Renovaré Spiritual Formation Bible. San Francisco: HarperSanFrancisco, 2005.

Richardson, Alan D., ed. *A Theological Word Book of the Bible.* London: SCM Press, 1957/ New York: Macmillan, 1976.

Riches, John K. *Jesus and the Transformation of Judaism.* New York: Seabury, 1980.

Rienecker, Fritz. Translated by Cleon L. Rogers, Jr. *A Linguistic Key to the Greek New Testament.* Grand Rapids: Zondervan, 1976.

Robinson, John A.T. *Redating the New Testament.* London: SCM Press, 1976.

Russell, D.S. *Between the Testaments.* Philadelphia: Fortress Press, 1960.

Sanders, E. P. *The Historical Figure of Jesus.* London: Penguin Books, 1993.

_____. *Jesus and Judaism.* Philadelphia: Fortress Press, 1985.

Schneemelcher, Wilhelm, ed. *New Testament Apocrypha.* Louisville, KY: Westminser Press, 1991.

Scobie, Charles H. H. *John the Baptist.* Philadelphia: Fortress Press, 1964.

Schweitzer, Albert. *The Quest of the Historical Jesus.* New York: Macmillan, 1948.

Schweizer, Eduard. *The Good News According to Luke.* Translated by David E. Green. Atlanta: John Knox Press, 1984.

_____. *The Good News According to Mark.* Translated by Donald H. Madvig. Richmond, Va.: John Knox Press, 1970.

_____. *The Good News According to Matthew.* Translated by David E. Green. Atlanta: John Knox Press, 1975.

Stanton, Graham N. *Gospel Truth? New Light on Jesus and the Gospels.* Harrisburg, PA: Trinity Press International, 1995.

_____. *The Gospels and Jesus.* Oxford University Press, 1989.

Stein, Robert H. *Jesus the Messiah: A Survey of the Life of Christ.* Downers Grove, IL: InterVarsity, 1996.

_____. *The Synoptic Problem.* Grand Rapids: Baker, 1987.

Stroker, William D. *Extracanonical Sayings of Jesus.* Atlanta: Scholars, 1989.

Tasker, R.V.G. *The Gospel According to St. Matthew: An Introduction and Commentary.* London: Inter-Varsity Press, 1961.

Taylor, Vincent. *The Gospel According to St. Mark.* London: Macmillan, 1953.

_____. *The Life and Ministry of Jesus.* New York: Abingdon Press, 1955.

Tenney, Merrill C. *New Testament Survey,* revised. Grand Rapids: Eerdmans, 1985.

Theissen, Gerd. *The Gospels in Context: Social and Political History in the Synoptic Tradition.* Translated by Linda M. Maloney. Minneapolis: Augsburg Fortress, 1991.

_____. *The Miracle Stories of the Early Christian Tradition.* Philadelphia: Fortress, 1983.

_____. *The Shadow of the Galilean: The Quest of the Historical Jesus in Narrative Form.* Translated by John Bowden. Philadelphia: Fortress, 1987.

_____. *Sociology of Early Palestinian Christianity.* Translated by J. Bowden. Philadelphia: Fortress Press, 1978.

Thiede, Carsten. *Rekindling the Word: In Search of Gospel Truth.* Valley Forge, PA: Trinity Press International, 1996.

_____ and Matthew D'Ancona. *The Jesus Papyrus.* London: Weidenfeld & Nicolson, 1996.

Tolbert, Malcolm O. *Good News from Matthew.* Nashville: Broadman Press, 1975.

Vermes, Geza. *Jesus the Jew: A Historian's Reading of the Gospels.* Philadelphia: Fortress Press, 1973.

_____. *The Religion of Jesus the Jew.* Philadelphia: Fortress Press, 1993.

Wall, Robert W. "Divorce" in *The Anchor Bible Dictionary,* vol. 2. New York: Doubleday, 1992.

Walvoord, John F. Matthew: *Thy Kingdom Come.* Chicago: Moody, 1974.

_____. Zuck, R. B., and Dallas Theological Seminary. "Mt 12:30–37" in *The Bible Knowledge Commentary: An Exposition of the Scriptures*. Wheaton, IL: Victor Books, 1983.

Weber, S. K. *Matthew*. Vol. 1 *of Holman New Testament Commentary*. Nashville, TN: Broadman & Holman Publishers, 2000: 171.

Wenham, David. *The Parables of Jesus: Pictures of Revolution*. Downers Grove, IL: InterVarsity, 1989.

Wenham, J.W. *"When Were the Saints Raised?"* in *Journal of Theological Studies* 32, 1981: 150–152

Willard, Dallas. *Renovation of the Heart*. San Francisco: Harper and Row, 1988.

Wilkinson, J. *Jerusalem as Jesus Knew It: Archaeology as Evidence*. London: Thames and Hudson, 1978.

Witherington, Ben. *The Christology of Jesus*. Minneapolis: Fortress Press, 1990.

_____. *Jesus the Quest: The Third Search for the Jew of Nazareth*. Downer's Grove, IL: InterVarsity Press, 1995.

_____. *Jesus the Sage: The Pilgrimage of Wisdom*. Minneapolis: Fortress Press, 1994.

Wood, Clyde. *Leviticus-Numbers-Deuteronomy*. Vol. 2 of *The Living Way Commentary on the Old Testament*. Shreveport, Louisiana: Lambert Book House, 1974.

Wright, N.T. *Jesus and the Victory of God*. Vol. 2 *of Christian Origins and the Question of God*. Minneapolis: Fortress Press, 1996.

_____. *The New Testament and the People of God*. Vol. 1 of *Christian Origins and the Question of God*. Minneapolis: Fortress Press, 1992.

_____. *The Original Jesus*. Grand Rapids: Eerdmans, 1996.

_____. *Who Was Jesus?* Grand Rapids: Eerdmans, 1992.

Yancey, Philip. *The Jesus I Never Knew*. Grand Rapids: Zondervan, 1995.

Yoder, John H. *The Politics of Jesus: Vicit Agnus Noster*. Grand Rapids: Eerdmans, 1972.

Young, Brad H. *Jesus the Jewish Theologian*. Peabody, Massachusetts: Hendrickson Publishers, 1995.

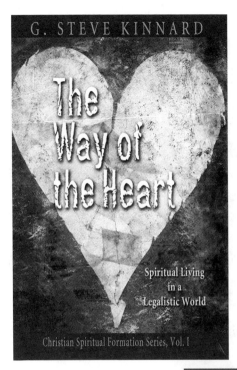

G. STEVE KINNARD

The
Way of
the Heart

Spiritual Living
in a
Legalistic World

Christian Spiritual Formation Series, Vol. I

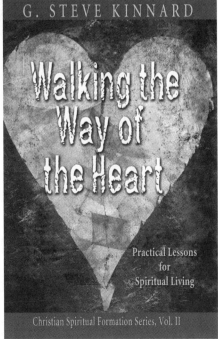

G. STEVE KINNARD

Walking the
Way of
the Heart

Practical Lessons
for
Spiritual Living

Christian Spiritual Formation Series, Vol. II

A Practical Exposition

THE GOSPEL OF
MATTHEW

A Fresh Look at Jesus
the Messiah & King

G. Steve Kinnard

SPIRITUAL PERSONAL DEVELOPMENT
FOR THE EVERYDAY CHRISTIAN

Like A Tree
planted by
Streams of Water

DR. G. STEVE KINNARD

The Prophets of the Assyrian Period
Dr. G. Steve Kinnard

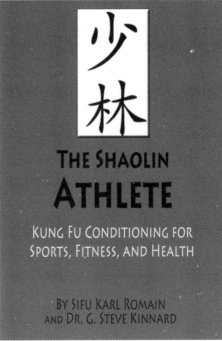

少林

THE SHAOLIN
ATHLETE

KUNG FU CONDITIONING FOR
SPORTS, FITNESS, AND HEALTH

BY SIFU KARL ROMAIN
AND DR. G. STEVE KINNARD